Hieronymus Bosch

Visions of Genius

Jheronimus Bosch 500

Published on the occasion of the exhibition of the same name
in Het Noordbrabants Museum, 's-Hertogenbosch,
13 February to 8 May 2016

Exhibition curated by
Matthijs Ilsink, Jos Koldeweij and Charles de Mooij

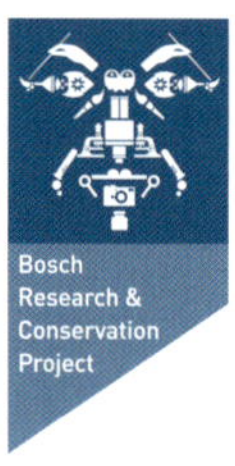

This publication and the exhibition are based by and large on the results of the Bosch
Research and Conservation Project (BRCP), with team members Matthijs Ilsink
(coordinator), Jos Koldeweij (chairman), Ron Spronk, Luuk Hoogstede, Robert G.
Erdmann, Rik Klein Gotink, Hanneke Nap, Daan Veldhuizen. This international
research project was initiated by Het Noordbrabants Museum, the Radboud University
Nijmegen and the Jheronimus Bosch 500 Foundation.

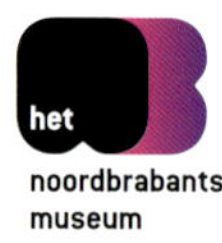 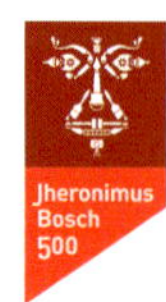 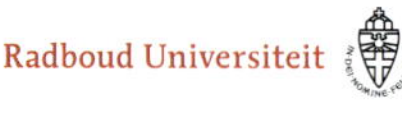

Left flap
Hieronymus Bosch, *Model sheet with 'witches'*
(detail), Paris, Musée du Louvre

Right flap
Hieronymus Bosch, *Infernal Landscape*
(detail), private collection

Cover
Hieronymus Bosch, *The Haywain* (detail),
Madrid, Museo Nacional del Prado.
With the special collaboration of
the Museo Nacional del Prado.

Hieronymus Bosch

Visions of Genius

Matthijs Ilsink and Jos Koldeweij

MERCATORFONDS

DISTRIBUTED BY YALE UNIVERSITY PRESS, NEW HAVEN AND LONDON

Contents

V
Saints

VI
The End of Days

Foreword

Half a century ago, in 1967, the former Noordbrabants Museum in 's-Hertogenbosch played host to a large retrospective exhibition dedicated to the work of Hieronymus Bosch, the most important late-medieval artist to have emerged in the Netherlands. The occasion was the 450th anniversary of the death of the famous painter and draughtsman, who died in 1516 in his native city of 's-Hertogenbosch. The exhibition was an unqualified success and attracted as many as 267,000 visitors. Against all the odds, the organizers had succeeded in bringing a large number of panels and drawings by the master back to the city in which they had been produced. Thus, the exhibition gained a special place in the collective memory of art-lovers and the people of 's-Hertogenbosch.

Many years later, in 2001, the Hieronymus Bosch exhibition at the Museum Boijmans Van Beuningen provided a fresh opportunity to think about organizing a Bosch exhibition in the artist's hometown. It was the mayor of 's-Hertogenbosch in particular, Ton Rombouts, who passionately advocated a major retrospective in 2016 to mark the 500th anniversary of the master's death. At the invitation of the city council, Het Noordbrabants Museum, together with the Nijmegen professor and Bosch expert Jos Koldeweij, developed a plan for just such an exhibition. This proposal, which was presented in October 2007 with the working title 'Bosch Visions', paved the way for a research programme that could serve as a foundation for this type of venture: the Bosch Research and Conservation Project.

This intensive, large-scale research programme, now completed, involved a scientific investigation of the approximately fifty paintings and drawings attributed to Hieronymus Bosch, works that are held in twenty-five different collections across ten countries. The study was conducted by a team of specialists using advanced techniques, and all this in close cooperation with the curators of the relevant museums. In addition, the programme supported the restoration of works that, for the conservation reasons stipulated by their owners, could not be lent to the exhibition at Het Noordbrabants Museum. The Bosch Research and Conservation Project eventually resulted in an unprecedented expansion of knowledge about Bosch, his work and his studio practice. At the same time, it also led to special collegial contacts, many of which contributed to the willingness of collection-owners to make their valuable works available for the 's-Hertogenbosch exhibition. The undertaking has crystallized into numerous publications and media, including the website boschproject.org and a two-volume scholarly publication, published by Mercatorfonds.

The culmination of the research, however, is the exhibition 'Hieronymus Bosch – Visions of Genius'. In the book before you, and within the exhibition, we learn about Hieronymus Bosch as a child of his age and as a citizen of his affluent hometown, 's-Hertogenbosch, one of the four capitals of the Duchy of Brabant. But above all, we are acquainted with the artist as a genius, one who had the capacity to develop a unique visual language. In his magisterial paintings and his equally astonishing drawings and sketches, Bosch proves himself a keen observer, an artist who could depict the world around him with exceptional realism. And also a thoroughly Christian moralist, who warns against life's temptations, and holds Christ and his saints up as an example to his audience. But Bosch excels not only in his realism: he also appears to be able to visualize the invisible, from that which is feared to that which is coveted, from paradise to hell, from the temptations of evil to the promise of heavenly salvation.

Hieronymus Bosch reveals himself, in equal measure, to be both an ordinary resident of 's-Hertogenbosch and a singular intellectual. A craftsman who, thanks to his humanistic education, his profitable marriage and his association with prominent fellow citizens, could develop a visual language that was appreciated by the princes, nobility and intellectuals of his time. An artist who worked with assistants and members of his own family, some of whom were also painters, in a certain artistic isolation – seemingly untouched by the artistic trends in cities such as Antwerp, Bruges, Venice, Rome or Paris. This might explain why he was able to develop an imagery that was as individual as it was unprecedented, and thus worth imitating. An ingenious portrayer of the natural and the supernatural, whose work has lost none of its eloquence after five hundred years, and who, for this reason alone, is commemorated with exhibitions in Het Noordbrabants Museum and the Museo Nacional del Prado in 2016.

The exhibitions in 's-Hertogenbosch and Madrid are the highlights of 2016, a year that is dedicated to the commemoration of Hieronymus Bosch, which, in the Netherlands, has been accorded the status of a national event. For the organization of this calendar of activities and the multi-year international manifestation entitled 'Jheronimus Bosch 500', the similarly titled foundation counted upon the leadership of Ad 's-Gravesande, Paul van der Eerden and Lian Duif. It was also the Jheronimus Bosch 500 Foundation (established in 2009) that the city of 's-Hertogenbosch commissioned to oversee the financing and fundraising for the Bosch Research and Conservation Project, a joint initiative with Het Noordbrabants Museum and Radboud University Nijmegen, which is inextricably intertwined with the exhibition 'Hieronymus Bosch – Visions of Genius'.

A nine-year research and exhibition project is only possible if it can count upon broad support. And the support was there. I would like to thank the many partners who, over the years, have assisted us in the realization of this special endeavour. First and foremost to be mentioned is Jos Koldeweij, with whom I began this project in 2007, and who has led the Bosch Research and Conservation Project, together with Matthijs Ilsink, since 2010. The three of us were responsible for developing the project and the structure of the exhibition, which naturally involved the cooperation of the research team and the scientific committee, the boards, management, trustees and employees of the participating institutions, and colleagues from Het Noordbrabants Museum and the many other museums that are recorded elsewhere.

It is with gratitude that I also mention the public bodies, funders and sponsors who have made this very costly project possible, either through their support of the research programme and exhibition via the Jheronimus Bosch 500 Foundation, or by contributing to the realization of the renewed Noordbrabants Museum. Besides the moral and financial support on the part of governments, funders and sponsors, it gives me the utmost pleasure to acknowledge the unstinting cooperation of the more than fifty lenders in Europe and the United States. Sometimes it was easy to get that cooperation, but often it proved to be a lengthy and complicated process. It is hardly surprising, since the loans we were requesting for the exhibition are, without exception, extremely valuable; the works are often vulnerable because of their age; and they also take pride of place in the permanent displays within the lending institutions. I am therefore immensely grateful for the generosity of spirit shown by their respective owners, and for their willingness to part with these masterpieces for the duration of the exhibition. Over the many years of preparation, I must also acknowledge the helpfulness of the Dutch embassies in the countries where the works by Bosch are held, as well as that shown by their international counterparts in The Hague. This diplomatic support proved to be of immense value.

In 2016, five hundred years after the death of Hieronymus Bosch, most of his surviving paintings and drawings have returned to the city in which they were created – a memorable event that does justice to the greatness of the artist. I would like to thank all those who made this special project possible.

Charles de Mooij
Director Het Noordbrabants Museum

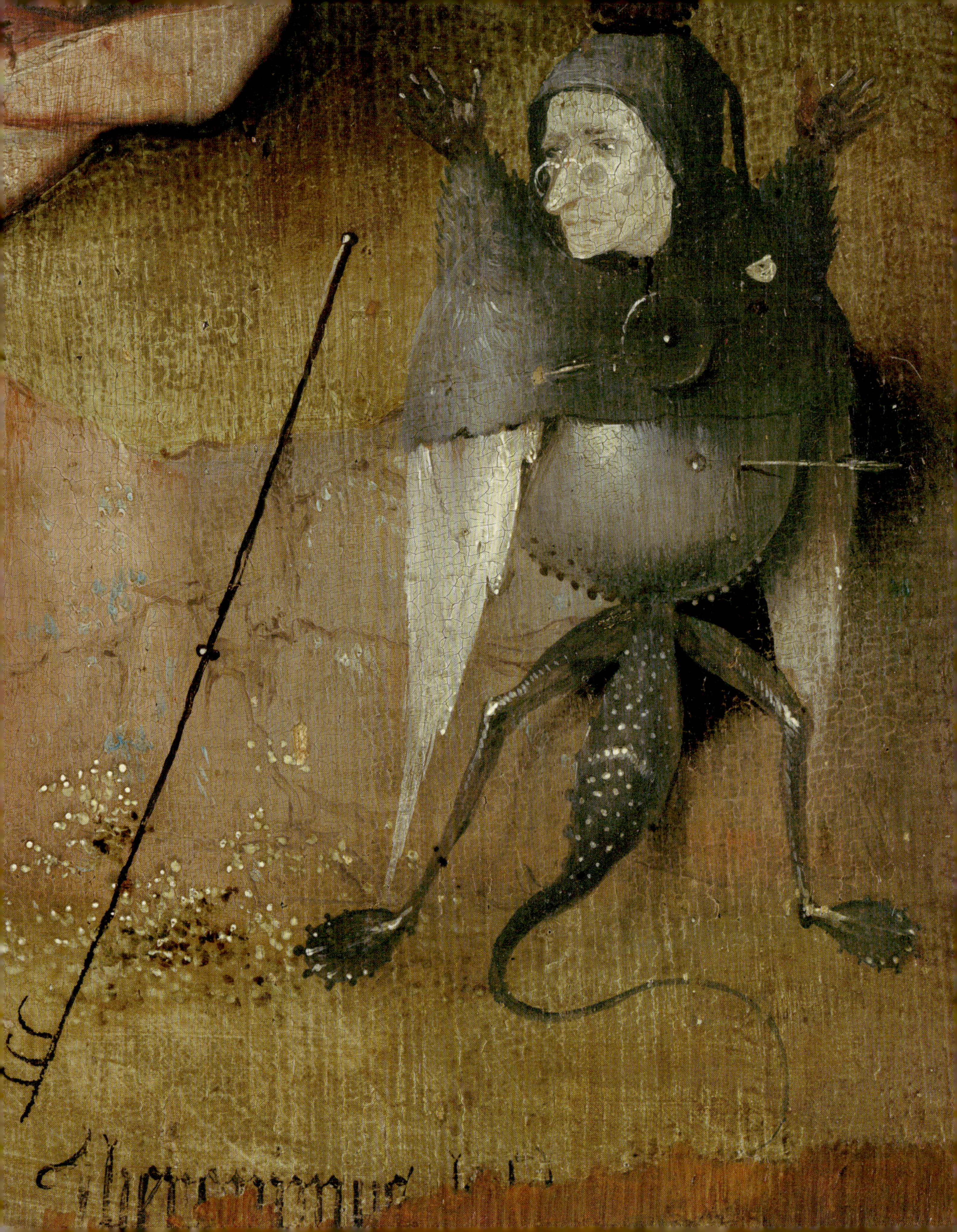
Jheronimus bos

Visions of Genius

Hieronymus Bosch must have lived in two different worlds: the real one around him, and the universe of his imagination. The real world had been created and was governed by the Christian God. No matter how bad, violent or threatening it could be, as far as Bosch and his contemporaries were concerned, everything that happened in it was decided by God and watched over by angels, saints and demons. It was a world in which God had set humanity to toil: human beings created in his image, whose intelligence set them apart from the animals; human beings with a responsibility to choose for themselves between good and evil. Bosch – who was born a craftsman and who developed into a great artist – grew up in this world and made his own way in it. His talent as a painter and draughtsman allowed him to climb the social ladder and to join the elite of his city and region. He observed reality and created his own world alongside it: a universe in which non-existent creatures existed; tree-people and human trees; chimeras and monsters. It fuelled the visions of a genius, for he was able as an artist to visualize that reality drawn on paper or painted on wooden panels. There had been no one like him before; and although his imitators copied him, they were going through the motions, lacking his naturalness, originality and creativity. Bosch was simultaneously a craftsman in the late-medieval tradition and an artist who broke with established conventions of technique, form and imagery.

's-Hertogenbosch was a flourishing commercial town and a regional centre – the Duchy of Brabant's fourth capital. In artistic terms, however, it was very much a backwater. Hieronymus Bosch worked there in splendid isolation on altarpieces, memorial panels and other commissions, in which he combined tradition and reality with the world of his own imagination. The results did not go unnoticed. By drawing on these two distinct worlds, Bosch was able to convey the messages he was called on to visualize both intensely and persuasively. The evidence is there to see in his small surviving body of work. In each of the paintings known to be by his own hand, we can trace his creative process in the way he pursued the right form and the right balance between visible reality and the unknown and the never seen, which are part of that reality too.

In the six chapters of this book, we follow Hieronymus Bosch as an artist born and raised in 's-Hertogenbosch. We do not know whether he travelled, and if he did, where to, how far or for how long. We do have a certain amount of information concerning his family, his possessions, his wife, his homes and his social career. We also know more about Bosch's works and about several others from his immediate sphere of influence thanks to the recent work of the Bosch Research and Conservation Project (BRCP), which focused primarily on the painstaking examination of the paintings and drawings, but also on archive and literature research (BoschDoc, the written documents). This research has revealed more about his patrons too, about the early reception of his work and – most important, perhaps – about the creative process through which his paintings came into being. The group of paintings that has grown slowly but surely since the nineteenth century to form what we now think of as Hieronymus Bosch's oeuvre has been analysed as precisely as possible using the most up-to-date optical techniques available. A team combining a range of art-historical disciplines studied and documented the paintings in situ according to a strict protocol. The resulting documentation therefore highlights affinities and differences pertaining to the works of art themselves rather than those that might ensue from the very methods and means of investigation. It was obtained using high-resolution photography in both visible and infrared light, alongside infrared reflectography (which can partially reveal layers hidden beneath the painted surface), microscopic examination and on-site sampling. The material provided the foundations on which the BRCP was able to reconstruct the autograph oeuvre of 'J(er)oen van Aken, who styles himself Bosch'. The key questions addressed by the BRCP were these: which paintings and drawings really are the work of the enigmatic 's-Hertogenbosch master, and to what extent did he collaborate with relatives, apprentices, assistants and others? We set out as a team to answer that question as rationally as possible. Which is not to say that all this is the final word on the matter: other arguments will no doubt be advanced and other works drawn into the discussion, and so it is always possible that the picture will have to be adjusted again. What truly counts at the end of the day is the artistic and substantive meaning of the work produced by Hieronymus Bosch – two aspects that are inseparably linked in great art and which have been our focus throughout in *Hieronymus Bosch – Visions of Genius*.

Hieronymus Bosch

(c. 1450–1516)

A funeral ceremony for the painter Hieronymus Bosch was held at St John's Church in 's-Hertogenbosch on 9 August 1516. The service took place in the recently completed chapel of the Brotherhood of Our Lady (Lieve Vrouwe Broederschap). Bosch was a 'sworn member' of this Marian religious association, which meant that he belonged to its elite inner core. His Requiem Mass was arranged by the brotherhood and the costs were borne by his fellow brethren in the customary way. We can tell from those costs – of which precise accounts were kept – that this was a final and highly respectful tribute to an important man. It is not known where the painter was buried, but his tomb is likely to have been just outside the brotherhood's chapel on the north side of the choir.

We assume that Hieronymus was about sixty-five years old at the time of his death, possibly a little younger, and that he most likely succumbed to an infectious disease that cost many lives in 's-Hertogenbosch in 1516–17. Joen or Jeroen van Aken, as he was actually called, was born around 1450. His grandfather, the painter Jan van Aken, had moved to 's-Hertogenbosch from Nijmegen around 1426; four of his five sons, including Antonius, Hieronymus's father, became painters. From 1462, the latter lived with his family in a house with a workshop on the east side of the city's main square, the Markt. Hieronymus too followed the family tradition and became a painter, just like his two brothers and – a generation later – two nephews, one of whom was also a sculptor. Although there are no surviving works of art that can be securely attributed to any of his relatives, it is safe to assume that Hieronymus was trained by his father and uncles in the family workshop and that his career began there on the Markt. He must have

married Aleid van de Meervenne, a daughter of a fairly well-to-do family, around 1480. Hieronymus and Aleid moved to the slightly more prestigious north side of the Markt in a house called Inden Salvatoer ('The Saviour') and later Het root Cruijs ('The Red Cross'), which Aleid had inherited from her grandfather. It can be seen in *The Cloth Market*, an anonymous painting from around 1530 (fig. p. 12). The couple remained childless and Aleid outlived her husband by over six years. Following her death in 1522–23, the house reverted to her family. There is no evidence that Hieronymus set up his own painter's workshop there, although it is possible. It is more likely, however, that he continued to work with his relatives at the workshop set up by his father. We know from tax returns and other sources that Hieronymus was reasonably well off, but by no means rich.

As we find with all other late-medieval painters, Bosch's activities were not limited to paintings on panel or canvas; he also polychromed all sorts of objects, produced designs for items as varied as stained-glass windows, embroidery and brasswork, and even advised on commissions to other artists. The first known activity in which Hieronymus seems to have been involved occurred in 1475, when 'thonys den maelder ende syn soenen' (Bosch's father 'Antonius the painter and his sons') were consulted about a new carved altarpiece for the Brotherhood of Our Lady. Years later, Bosch would paint a set of shutters for the same altarpiece. Between 1480 and 1482, he and his brother Goessen painted a large triptych for the high altar of St John's Church, which fell out of favour in the early seventeenth century and was removed. Hieronymus painted another large altarpiece – which has not survived

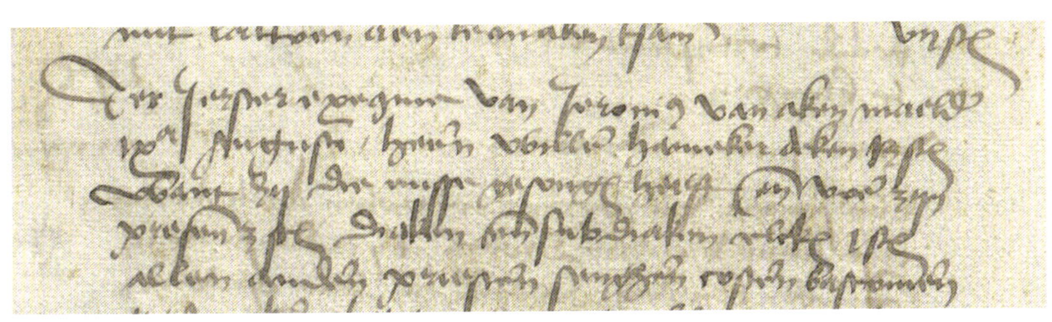

Extract from the accounts of the Brotherhood of Our Lady in 's-Hertogenbosch, 9 August 1516: expenses for the Requiem Mass of Jheronimus van Aken 's-Hertogenbosch, Museum Het Zwanenbroedershuis, BHIC, AILVB, 126, fol. 166v

either – for the main altar in the church of the Dominican abbey in Brussels. The monks probably did not pay the artist for his work, but celebrated an annual mass for his soul for many years in return. We can conclude from this prestigious commission that Bosch was also highly appreciated during his lifetime outside 's-Hertogenbosch. This is evident too from the fact that in 1505 Philip the Fair, Duke of Burgundy, presented a triptych of the *Temptation of Saint Anthony* painted by Bosch to his powerful father, Maximilian of Austria. A year earlier, a payment was recorded by the ducal chamber of accounts in Lille for a large painting of the *Last Judgement*, which Philip the Fair had commissioned during a visit to 's-Hertogenbosch from 'Jheronimus van Aken called Bosch'. This far from home, therefore, the painter was explicitly identified by the name with which he signed himself: 'Jheronimus bosch'. He was based, after all, not in Aachen ('Aken' in Dutch) but in 's-Hertogenbosch. Yet the surname 'Bosch' was more than merely a geographical identifier; his paintings and drawings show that Joen van Aken was an ingenious artist who constantly played with double and multiple meanings, and the same applies to his assumed name. He was christened for Saint Jerome, whose Latinized, originally Greek name 'Hieronymus' was believed at the time to mean 'sacred grove' or 'holy wood' ('heilig bos' in Dutch). This must have inspired Bosch when painting *Saint Jerome at Prayer* (cat. 42). In one of his most famous and intriguing drawings, *The Wood Has Ears, The Field Has Eyes* (cat. 17) – where he uses a learned proverb to appeal for originality over imitation – Bosch plays a game with himself and with the viewer. The drawing is simultaneously an allusion to the city where he lived and worked ('s-Hertogenbosch, 'the Duke's Forest'), and a kind of drawn self-portrait, in that the proverb it visualizes is a statement that anything can be observed or overheard anywhere and that we should act accordingly. It is also an apt description of an unfailingly original artist who always looked and listened carefully before creating his drawings and paintings.

No more than twenty-five panels and triptychs, and a similar number of drawings, can be viewed nowadays as authentic works by Bosch, all of them produced between around 1480 and his death in the summer of 1516. As a member of a family of artists, he must, however, have started drawing and painting at a very early age. His true career is therefore likely to have stretched over a good sixty years, indicating that the bulk of his work has been lost. What remains, however, is intriguing enough.

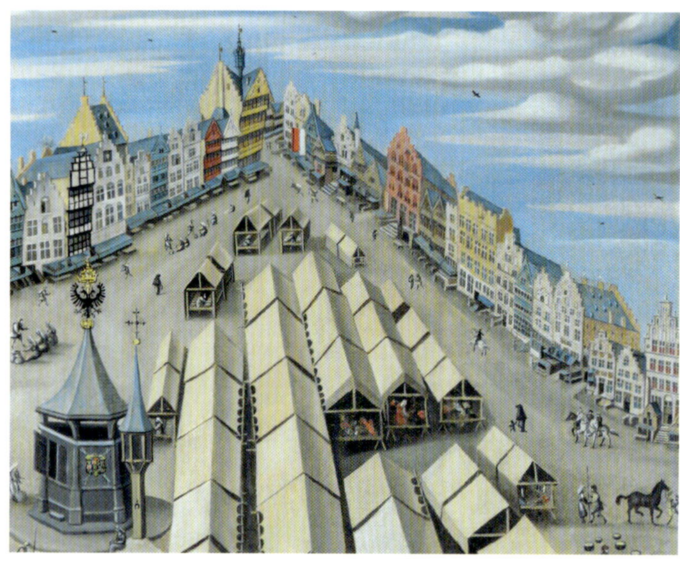

Anonymous, *The Cloth Market, 's-Hertogenbosch*, c. 1530 (detail)
Oil on panel, 134 × 76.5 cm
's-Hertogenbosch, Het Noordbrabants Museum, 01596
Bosch's house is seventh from the right

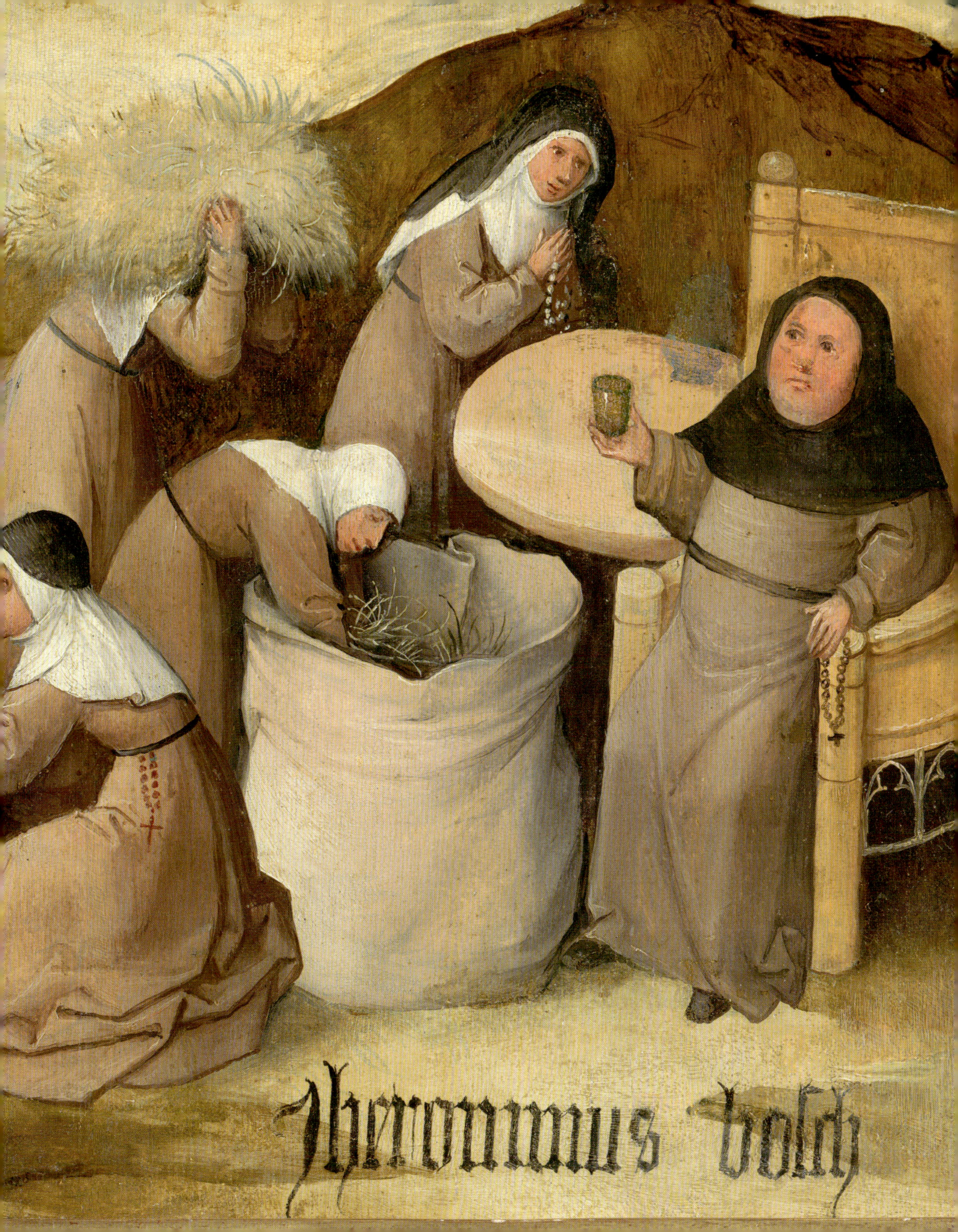

Iheronimus boſch

I

Life's Pilgrimage

They used to teach us in school that the Middle Ages lasted from ad 500 to around 1500. Then came the Renaissance, when the individual increasingly took centre stage in the Western worldview, diminishing the importance of God and paving the way for our modern individualistic culture. It is a simplistic analysis that is hard to sustain intellectually and to which any number of objections and qualifications can be made.

And yet, when we look at the work of Hieronymus Bosch, his paintings and his drawings, we are constantly reminded of that same oversimplified model of historical development. Bosch was active in the period around 1500 – the years the history books tell us formed the transition between the old era and the new. And it was in these same years that Bosch produced a number of paintings that were highly unusual, both then and now. The *Wayfarer* and the *Haywain* are two good examples of this. Each triptych has a similar figure on its closed wings of an elderly man carrying all his worldly goods in a wickerwork backpack. He is not the saint we would normally expect to find on the exterior of a triptych in that period. Men like this were no doubt a common sight in and around 's-Hertogenbosch in the year 1500. He is a traveller, making his way through life. Worn down by that life, he is constantly being tempted to make the wrong choices. This is what Bosch chose to show the viewer, and it is both unusual and innovative.

Bosch makes art personal, on different levels, and that makes him modern. He was one of the first artists in the Low Countries to sign his paintings: 'Jheronimus bosch'. It was plainly important to him that the works he left behind should be traceable to him. The *Haywain* (cat. 5) too was signed with his standard signature, affixed like a stamp to the bottom right of the central panel. Bosch also made his art personal, however, for those who look at it. The *Haywain* is so famous nowadays that it is hard to imagine that when he created it no other painting existed with this subject matter or anything remotely resembling it. We do not know of a single visual precursor for either the *Haywain* or the *Wayfarer*. Bosch created an image here that is entirely contemporary – hypermodern art from around 1510–15. Despite their moralizing content, the *Haywain* and the *Wayfarer* are not dogmatic paintings; they hold up a mirror to their viewers, to teach them to see themselves better. It was important to Bosch to make his viewers aware of how they bumble their way through life, longing for earthly things. He offered them a personal, exploratory way to realize that if they were to avoid hell and damnation they needed to turn to the good. It is also an important shift in emphasis in the approach to the question of what it means to be a good Christian. Bosch's work is closely related in this respect to the message of the Devotio Moderna.

According to this spiritual movement, which was particularly strong at the time in the Low Countries, human beings themselves are responsible for their actions: they have to reflect and to make choices, and will be held to account for them personally. 'Modern Devotion' also believed that everyone should read the Bible in their own language so they could truly understand the Christian message. Bosch painted in such a way that his paintings likewise have to be 'read'. We are invited to look, reflect, relate the image to ourselves, and to take its moral to heart.

Alongside the familiar positive examples, Bosch introduced *exempla contraria* – ones to be avoided. In these cases, turning to the good was a question of turning away from evil: a long and arduous road, and a lifelong pilgrimage.

A lone traveller has come from somewhere and plods his way somewhere else in a scene that contains all sorts of elusive elements. Hieronymus Bosch did not create this as an autonomous painting: the round image was originally located on two wings which, when closed, formed a vertical, rectangular surface. The join divided the scene in two, running straight through the traveller and the precise point where the wickerwork pack on his back is fastened shut. The interior of the two wings featured the *Ship of Fools* (cat. 2–3) on the left and *Death and the Miser* (cat. 4) on the right. The subject of the now lost central panel is not known. Death is the lone figure's ultimate destination, as he travels onwards without knowing his future. The road ahead is closed by a gate, while an aggressive dog growls at his heels. The traveller has just passed a house of ill repute, and the landscape in the distance looks barren and desolate. The man's identity has been left deliberately vague: we cannot see what he has in his pack. There is nothing to specify that he is a pedlar (as the painting is frequently titled), nor does he wear a pilgrim's badge. With what few possessions he has, he trudges cautiously, perhaps even hesitantly, through life, looking back over his shoulder and moving ever forwards. Like all of us, he can do nothing else. He is 'Everyman' – the literary figure in whom everyone should recognize themselves. The tondo is like a mirror on a wall; the viewer sees life's pilgrim on his road and like him must choose which course to take without deviating from the true path. Will the traveller open the gate and continue on his way, despite the ox who blocks his path? Or will he wander off into sin and vice? He will ultimately be held to account for the choices he has made, for how he has led his life. Whatever the precise subject of the triptych's central panel, the message must have been the one Bosch depicts here.

The pig's trough on the left behind the traveller will immediately have reminded Bosch's contemporaries of the Parable of the Prodigal Son. Christ told the story of a man who was such a wastrel that he ended up having to tend pigs and envying them their swill. He eventually returned to his father, full of remorse, and was received with great rejoicing (Luke 15:11–32). Yet that is not the story depicted here, either.

The scene Bosch has painted is at once realistic and elusive; it makes the viewer think. All sorts of details contribute to this effect: why is the man wearing a pig's trotter as an amulet and why is there a cat skin hanging from the spoon on the outside of his pack? Why is there an awl with a loop of thick yarn stuck

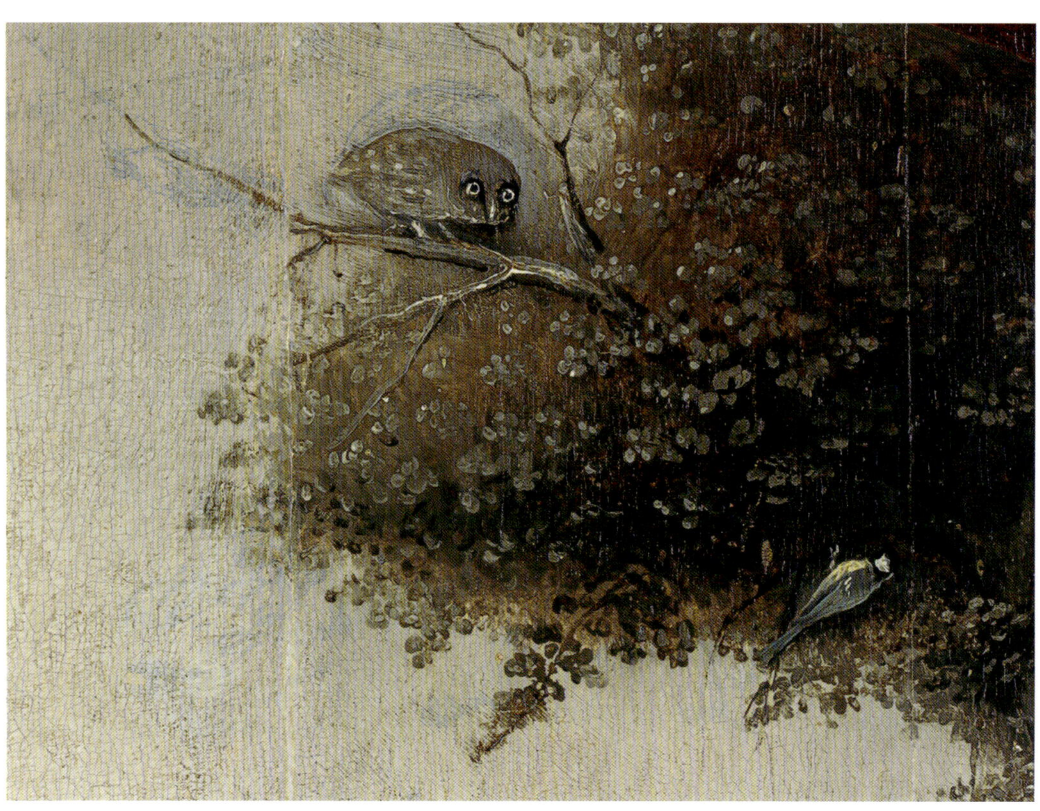

Hieronymus Bosch
The Wayfarer, c. 1500–10
Oil on oak panel, 71.3 × 70.7 cm
Rotterdam, Museum Boijmans
Van Beuningen, 1079

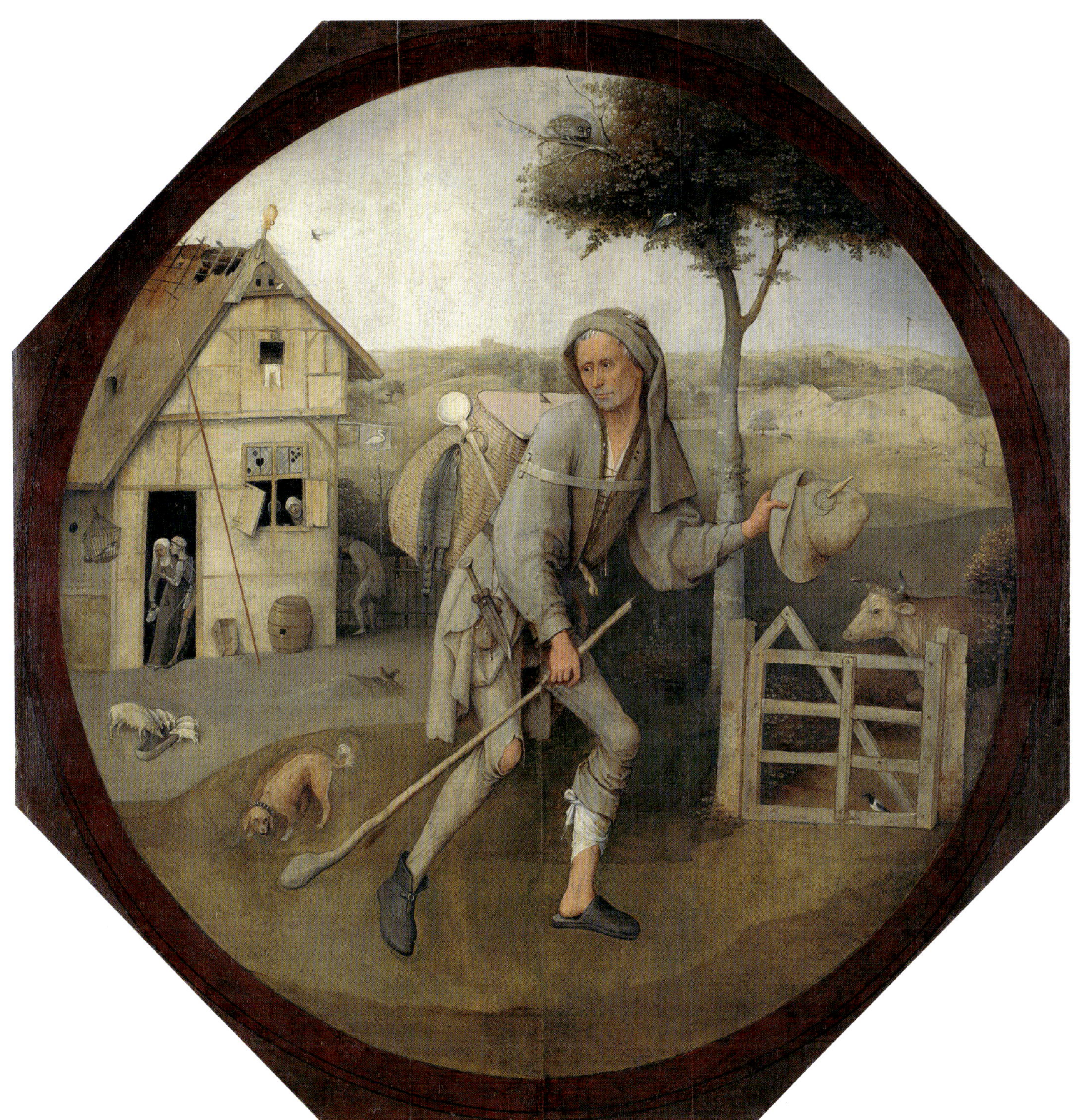

in the hat he clutches while wearing a chaperon on his head? There are all sorts of dubious goings-on at the tavern he has just passed: the inverted jug that sticks up from the apex of the gable, the underwear hanging from the window, the little swan on the inn sign, the man urinating round the corner, and the couple canoodling in the doorway are all ominous signs.

An owl high up in the tree has its eye on a titmouse perched a few branches lower, in a visual echo of our own observation of the painting (fig. p. 16). It is not clear whether the kneeling ox is aware of the magpie at the bottom of the closed gate in front of him, but he probably is. This is all about watching and being watched; human beings too are constantly observed on their life's path.

The same idea is expressed more explicitly and with detailed commentary in a contemporary German woodcut, in which the principal character is likewise a traveller. While the devil seeks to waylay him, the human being has to travel onwards as a pilgrim until death tears him away from life. He is surrounded by angels offering good advice, while God – shown high in the middle as the Holy Trinity – looks on and will judge. The image as a whole is presented as a mirror, as emphasized by the title and the text in the banderole: 'Look, see your reflection and take the message to heart.' Bosch too has painted a mirror showing the hazardous road through life and the choices that humans must make between good and evil.

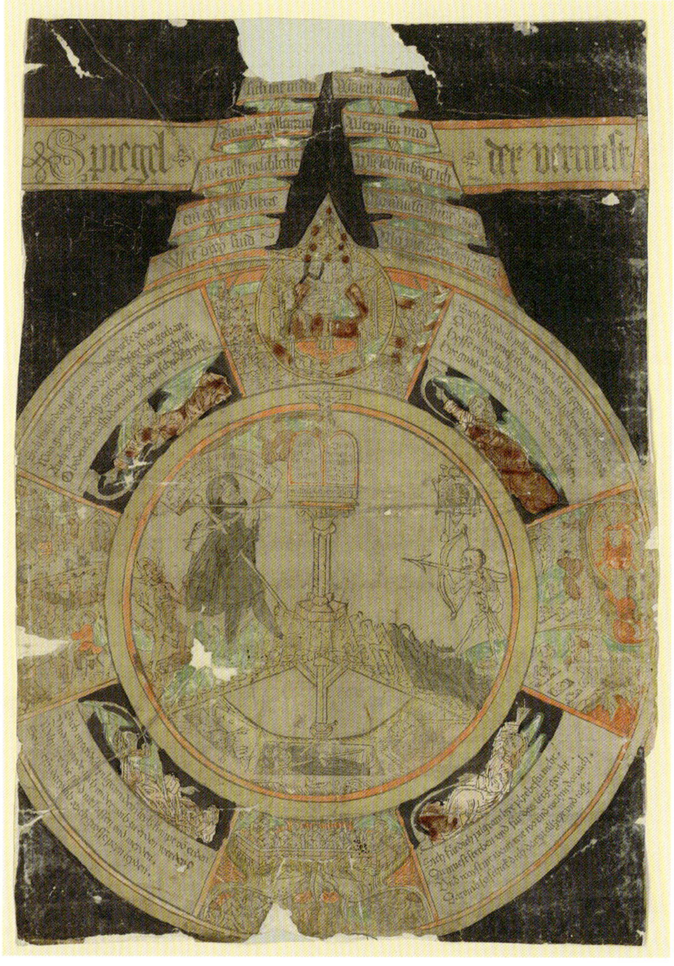

Der Spiegel der Vernunft
Germany, c. 1488
Woodcut, 40.4 × 29.1 cm
Munich, Staatliche Graphische
Sammlung, 118319 D, Schr. 1861

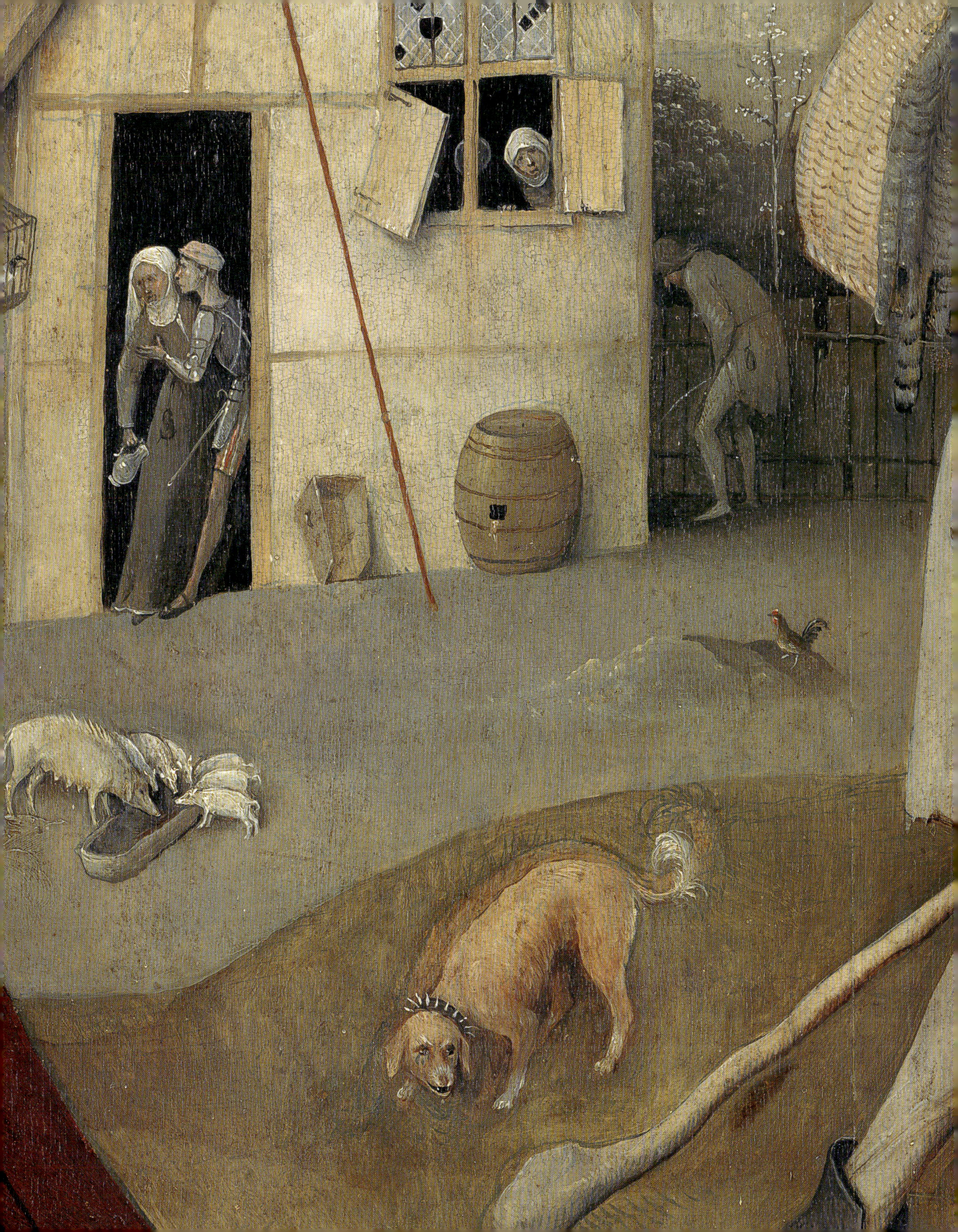

20 The panel with the *Ship of Fools* as Bosch painted it was split into two separate paintings following the dismantling of the *Wayfarer Triptych* in the eighteenth or early nineteenth century. The main part of the scene ended up in the Louvre (cat. 2), and the much smaller fragment, known by the title 'Gluttony and Lust', in Yale University Art Gallery (cat. 3). The fragments have been treated totally differently in the course of at least two hundred years, and so no longer resemble one another. However, scientific analysis of the wood and the way the images match prove beyond doubt that they originally belonged together. Study of the wood also indicates, moreover, that the left half of the *Wayfarer* (cat. 1) is a fragment from the back of the *Ship of Fools*. The latter scene ought to be interpreted, therefore, as a continuation of the *Wayfarer*, with the opposite open wing showing life's ultimate destination in the shape of *Death and the Miser* (cat. 4).

The *Ship of Fools* is crewed by a colourful band of revellers who take their pleasure from food and drink, flirting and music. An owl gazes down on the carefree company from the green branches lashed to the top of the boat's mast. The men and women are unaware, however, that their sinful behaviour is being observed as they devote their time to idleness and earthly amusement.

It is a precarious way to pass the time; the table-top that juts over the side of the little boat, for instance, is likely to fall into the water at any moment. The ship is virtually rudderless; the man holding the gigantic spoon used to steer the vessel from the bow seems more interested in the game of 'bite-the-cake'. The already sagging mast is fastened to the stern with a rope and is tied on the other side to the loose bough of a tree, in which the fool sits. The little boat seems to be drifting to the right, into the wind. The ultimate destination of this happy-go-lucky company is described in Sebastian Brant's *Ship of Fools*. The Middle Dutch version of the book, which Bosch must have used as his source, was published in 1497. 'Who takes his place on the ship of fools', Brant tells us, 'sails laughing and singing to hell.'

The boat, richly decorated with foliage, must immediately have reminded Bosch's contemporaries of spring and early summer – that pleasant time of year when they could relax and enjoy nature's return to life, and when love was very much in the air. This association was expressed in images of 'May boats' or 'love boats' in the calendars of late-medieval prayerbooks. There is an appealing parallel for Bosch's ship of fools, for instance, in the illumination for May in the *Hours of Joanna of Castile*, wife of Duke Philip the Fair. It shows a couple of young sweethearts in a boat decorated with budding branches, and with a fool playing the bagpipes at the helm to provide an ironic touch. Bosch's *Ship of Fools* could not be further removed from a peaceful and optimistic 'Maying' scene like this. The friar and the nun playing music together are fairly advanced in age, and the leafy branches are well past the budding stage; one of the revellers pukes over the bow, while the ones in the stern are quarrelling. The fool has turned his back on the rest of the company and drinks alone. The nun plays a coursed (double-strung) lute – a difficult instrument, which had two contrary symbolic meanings at the time: it could refer to the ideal of courteous harmonizing as we find in the illuminated May boat, or to the less elegant sexual behaviour we see in the ship of fools. The mood of the May boat is as positive as that in Bosch's scene is negative. He shows how easily human beings can fall into unthinking and foolish pleasures. The moral of the *Ship of Fools* must have been obvious before the triptych was dismantled. As Brant put it in the foreword to his *Stultifera Navis* – the Latin version of the *Ship of Fools* – 'In the ship, we are separated but three fingers' breadth from death.'

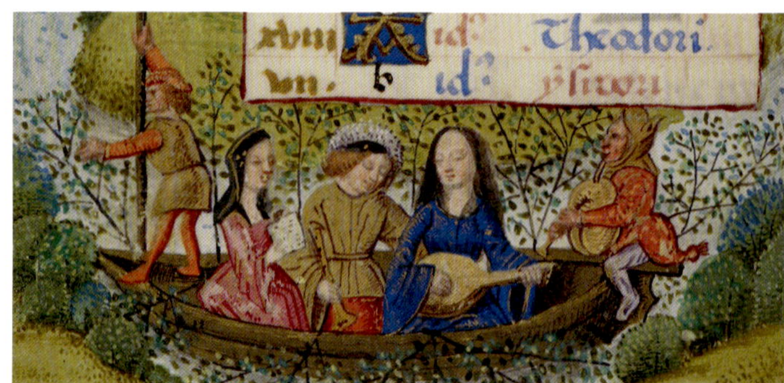

Hours of Joanna of Castile
Bruges, between 1496 and 1506
Parchment, 11 × 8 cm
London, The British Library,
Add Ms 18852, fol. 5v (detail)

Hieronymus Bosch
The Ship of Fools, c. 1500–10
Oil on oak panel, 58.1 × 32.8 cm
Paris, Musée du Louvre, Département
des Peintures, RF 2218

Hieronymus Bosch
Gluttony and Lust, c. 1500–10
Oil on oak panel, 34.9 × 30.6 cm
New Haven, Yale University Art Gallery, 1959.15.22,
Gift of Hannah D. and Louis M. Rabinowitz

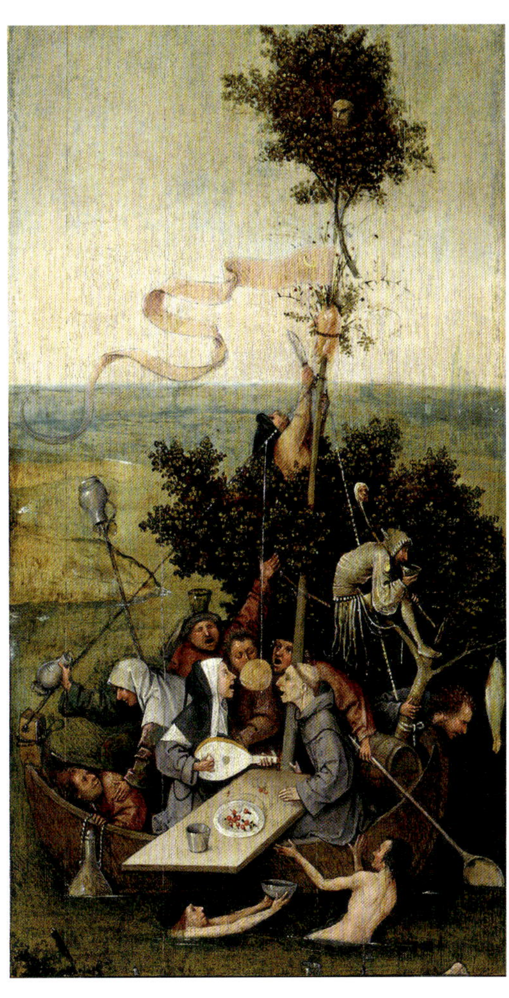

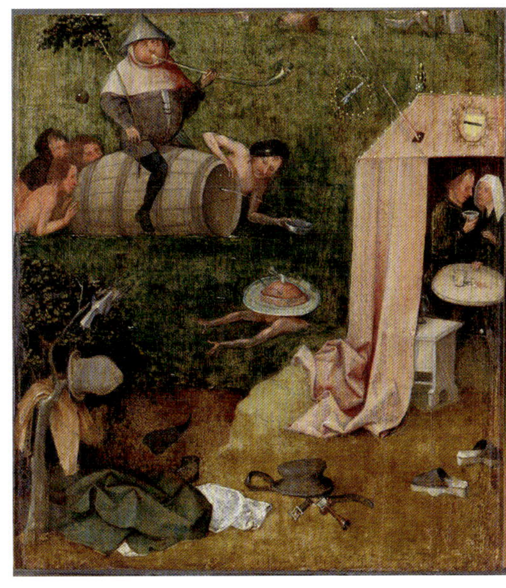

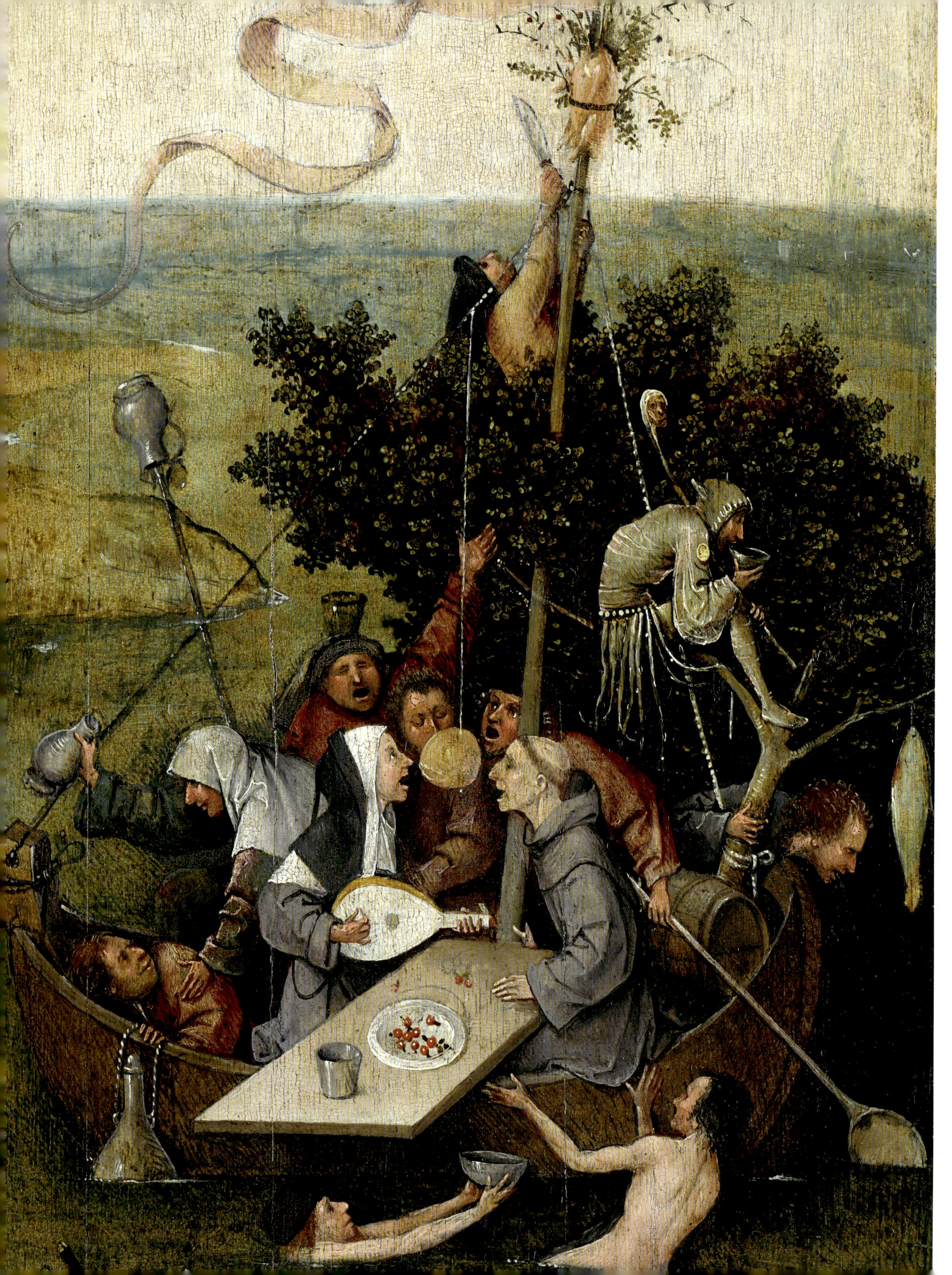

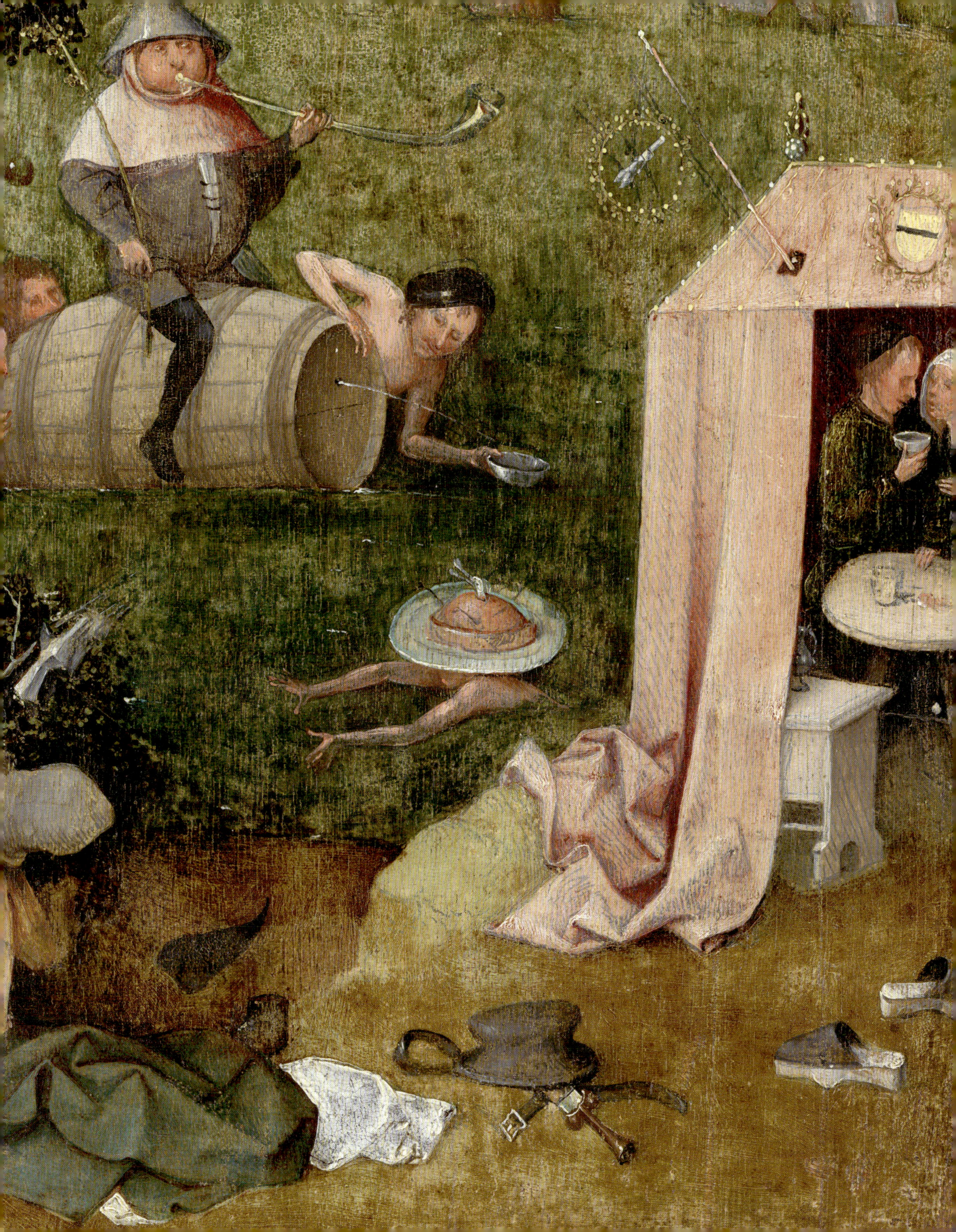

24 The last word in the *Wayfarer Triptych* is given to the emaciated old man sitting in his deathbed, where an angel clasps his shoulder and points to the crucified Christ in the window. Death is close at hand: he enters the scene wrapped in a shroud and aiming his arrow at the dying man, who stares at him. A demon appears from beneath the curtain around the bed to offer him a bag stuffed with coins. It is up to the mortal to choose between earthly goods on the one hand and salvation and forgiveness of his sins through Christ on the other. A second demon peers over the edge of the canopy above the bed, awaiting the outcome of that choice: will evil triumph, or will these devils be left empty-handed and frustrated? Responsibility for the decision lies with the man himself; it is he, after all, who will have to bear the consequences: will it be heaven or hell? This is the key to what Bosch wished to convey as effectively as possible in the painting. He initially drew the scene differently, only arriving at the final version as he was actually painting. In the underdrawing, it is not the demon that takes the initiative but the man, with the final choice left to Death: here the man holds an expensive jar in his left hand and a bag of money in his right, which the demon seems to

have offered him. Armed with these treasures he addresses Death, who, it seems, is willing to be induced to allow the man to continue his earthly, and no doubt sinful, existence for a while longer.

Bosch has painted a treasure-chest at the foot of the deathbed, which another man is busy filling, assisted by demons. This miser is probably the same person as the bed-ridden figure threatened by Death, although he might also be a personification of avarice. A set of tournament armour lies a little further in the foreground, either as an expensive possession or – more likely – as a reference to the earlier life of the dying man who, in better times, indulged in the expensive, risky and senseless pleasure of the joust.

Just as the *Ship of Fools* was inspired by the successful illustrated book of the same name by Sebastian Brant, the starting point for *Death and the Miser* will have been the popular publication known as the *Ars Moriendi* ('The Art of Dying'). This book, which helped people prepare for a 'good death', includes eleven full-page woodcut illustrations, each showing a man on his deathbed. In five of them, he is tempted by the devil, while an angel helps him to resist. The third

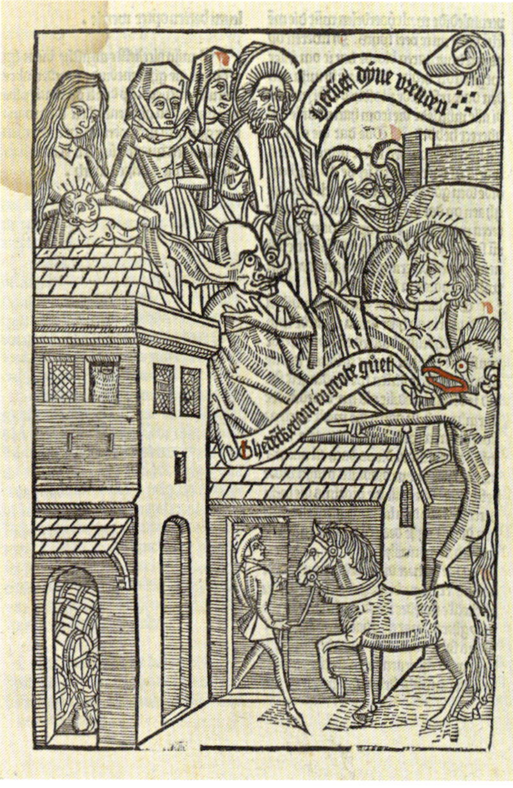

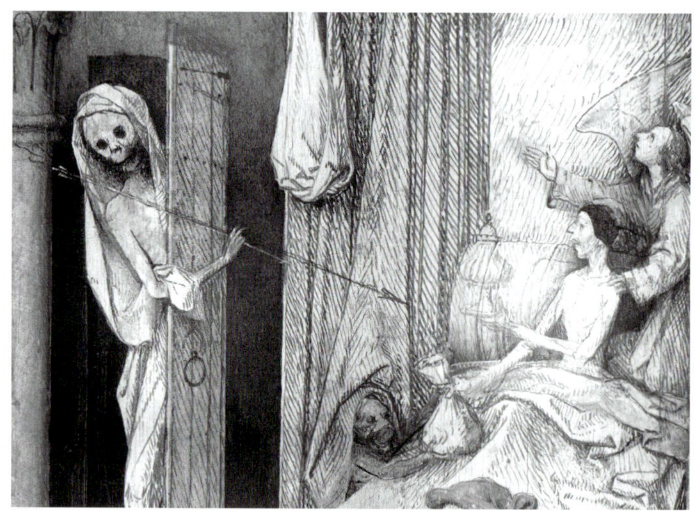

Ars Moriendi, 'The Art of Dying'
Delft (Christiaen Snellaert), 1488,
fol. 37
Woodcut, 4to
The Hague, Koninklijke Bibliotheek,
KW 169 G 84

Infrared photograph

Hieronymus Bosch
Death and the Miser, c. 1500–10
Oil on oak panel, 94.3 × 32.4 cm
Washington, National Gallery of Art,
Samuel H. Kress Collection, 1952.5.33

temptation is that of avarice, in which the devil tries to persuade the dying man to cling to his worldly possessions and to give them to his family and friends rather than the Church. The illustration accompanying this enticement shows his family and friends at the bedside, while representing his earthly goods in the shape of a well-stocked house and a fine horse (fig. p. 24). Bosch's challenge was to capture the dying man's dilemma in a single image in such a way as to make it clear that he himself is responsible for choosing between good and evil.

Death and the Miser was prepared at length and in surprising detail in the sketches done on the ground layer of the painting. This underdrawing is in keeping with the other panels of the *Wayfarer Triptych*, but differs from those of all other known works by Hieronymus Bosch and his workshop. The actual painting of the *Wayfarer*, the *Ship of Fools* and *Death and the Miser*, by contrast, fits perfectly with what are considered to be Bosch's autograph works. The conclusion, therefore, is that an assistant was responsible for the underdrawing, while Bosch himself did the painting. The underdrawings are executed in such detail that they almost resemble an engraving, possibly reflecting the fact that they were directly inspired by printed examples of the theme.

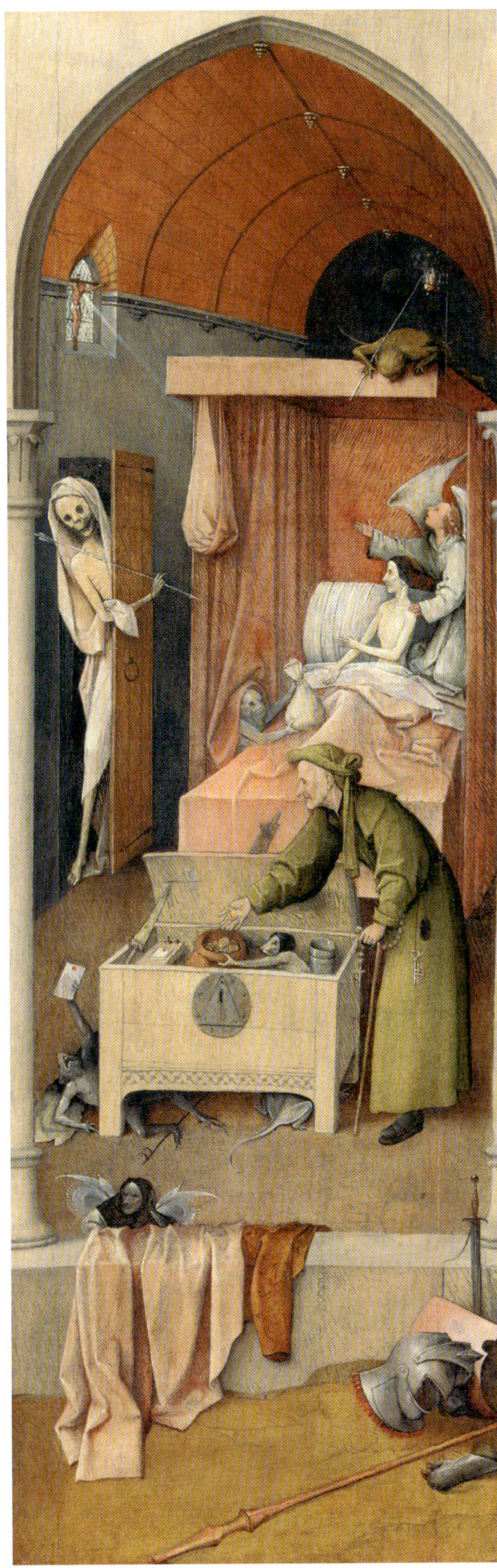

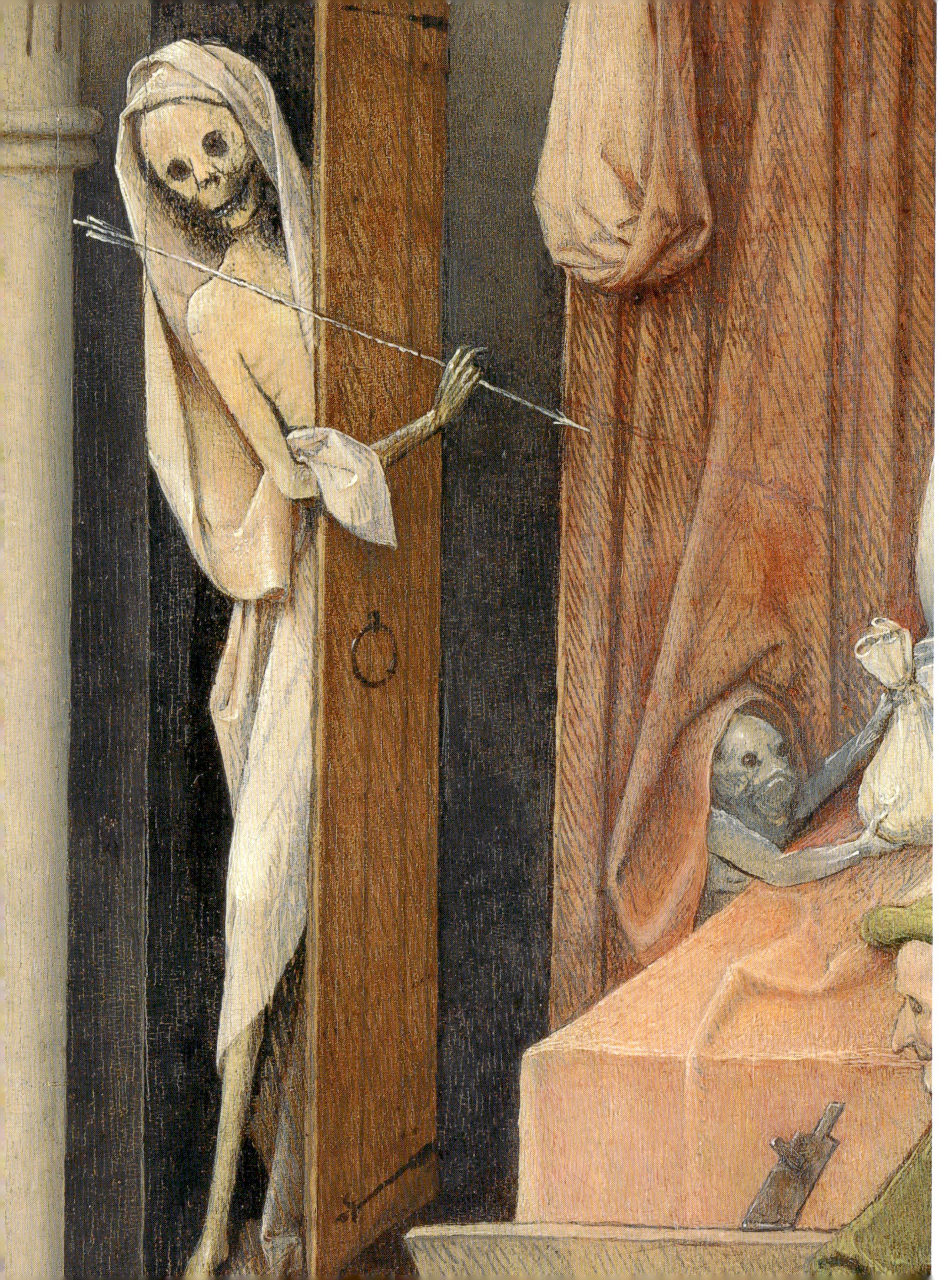

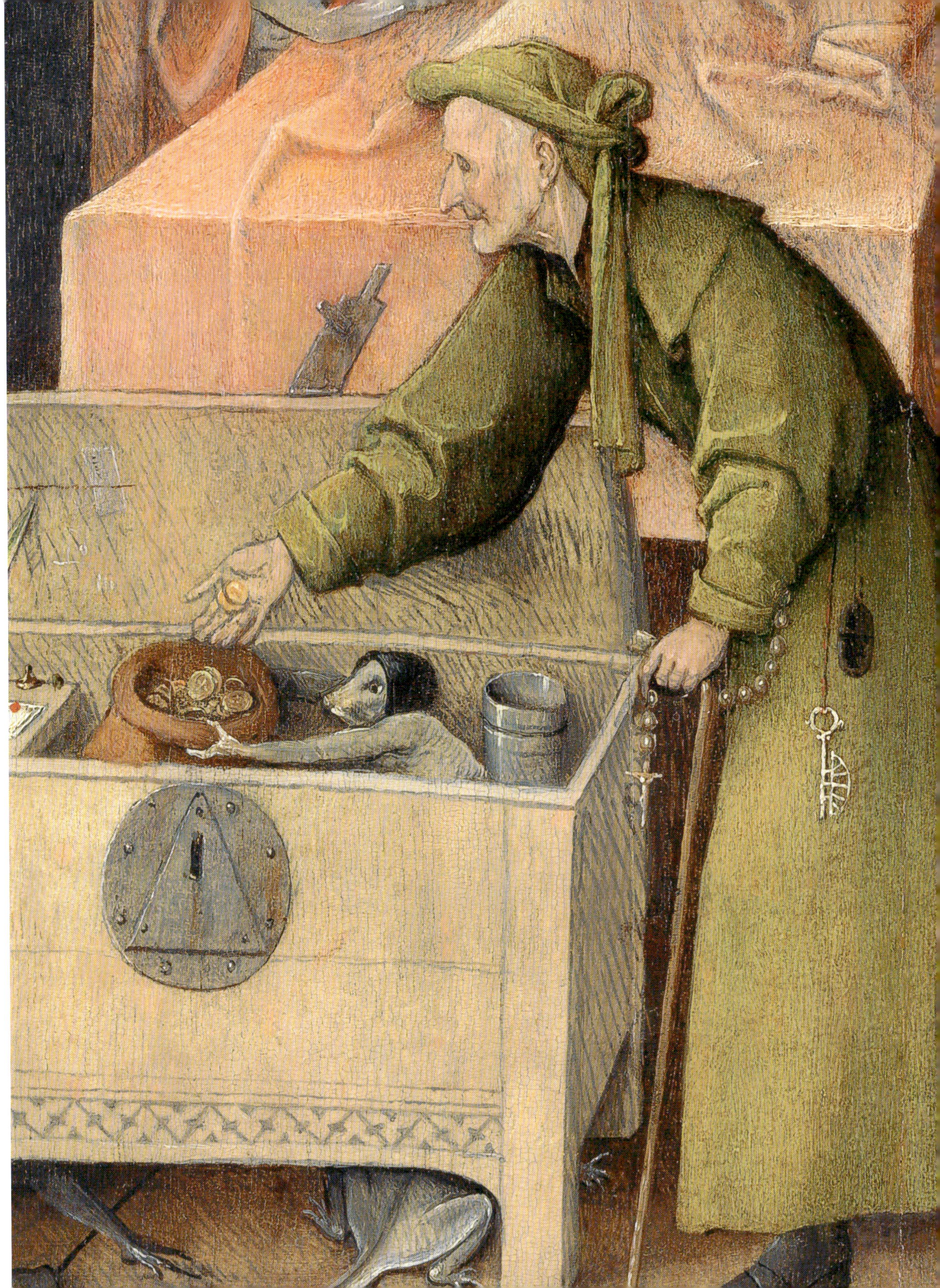

We do not know how unexpectedly death came for Hieronymus Bosch in early August 1516. He was probably about sixty or sixty-five years old at the time, and still very much active as a painter. Dendrochronological analysis of the panels making up the *Haywain* suggests that the work was painted some time after 1510 and more likely after 1512. In other words, the triptych was produced at a time when Bosch's name was already firmly established and it was painted in the style of the artist's final years. Examination of the preparatory sketches beneath the paint layer under infrared light shows that they were done in different materials and phases. It seems likely that several different artists worked on the underdrawings, that is to say Bosch and one or more assistants.

The closed triptych features a single multicoloured scene which is fitted in a black frame across its full width. Indeed, the artist entirely ignored the join between the two exterior wings running right up the middle of the painting. The figure depicted here is that of the wayfarer – the human being journeying through life. The subject matter is essentially the same as that painted by Bosch on the closed wings of the *Wayfarer* triptych (cat. 1). The man with the pack on his back walks along a sandy path that leads him from a hilly landscape to the little bridge he is about to cross. It is not clear where or how far his journey will take him, as is the case with everyone's life. He has just passed a couple of shepherds dancing to the bagpipe music, and another traveller being attacked by three robbers. An interesting adjustment was made in the paint layer compared to the underdrawing; the road the man has walked was initially drawn closer by, and there was a large wayside crucifix just behind the little bridge. This was omitted during the painting process, while a little shrine, in which a Calvary group can just be made out, was added over the already finished tree against which the bagpipe-player is leaning. On further reflection, the artist decided that the traveller's road would be determined less by his faith; it is now left entirely open what direction his life's journey will take on the other side of the water.

Opening the triptych doubles its visual area, in which the moral story about the course of human life is continued. A cart stacked high with hay is shown in the middle of the central panel. The hubbub of earthly life goes on around and on top of it, observed pityingly from on high by the resurrected Christ. Bosch characteristically repeats this observation of human behaviour in the figure of the large owl placed as a decoy on the bare branch protruding from the mass of foliage on the haywain. The scene set at the top of the lurching haystack seems to convey precisely the same moral as the *Ship of Fools* (cat. 2). The haywain is drawn by a band of demonic creatures in the direction of hell, depicted in the right wing. It is followed by a procession of people on foot and on horseback, in which literally every class and rank is represented, from the emperor, pope, king and duke to the simplest peasants and townsfolk. Others jostle around the haywain, trying to grab handfuls of hay for themselves, which leads to blood and mayhem. Although the hay is worth little or nothing, they all pursue it as if it were gold. Hay is also a symbol of transience: the grass dries up and withers to nothing. The message is that a humanity fixated on earthly possessions is heading straight to hell.

The left wing shows the Garden of Eden. We see God creating the first human couple, reprimanding them and then expelling them from paradise after the Fall, and also casting down from heaven to earth the rebel angels who, as they fall, metamorphose into demons. In other words, the threat of evil is present from the very earliest days of creation. Human beings, unlike the animals, have been given intelligence and free will; Bosch stresses that everyone must make the right choice themselves, just like the traveller on the closed triptych, who must not stray from the narrow path of virtue.

Hieronymus Bosch
The Haywain Triptych, 1510–16
Oil on oak panel, left wing 136.1 × 47.7 cm,
central panel 133 × 100 cm, right wing 136.1 × 47.6 cm
Madrid, Museo Nacional del Prado, P2052

Closed triptych

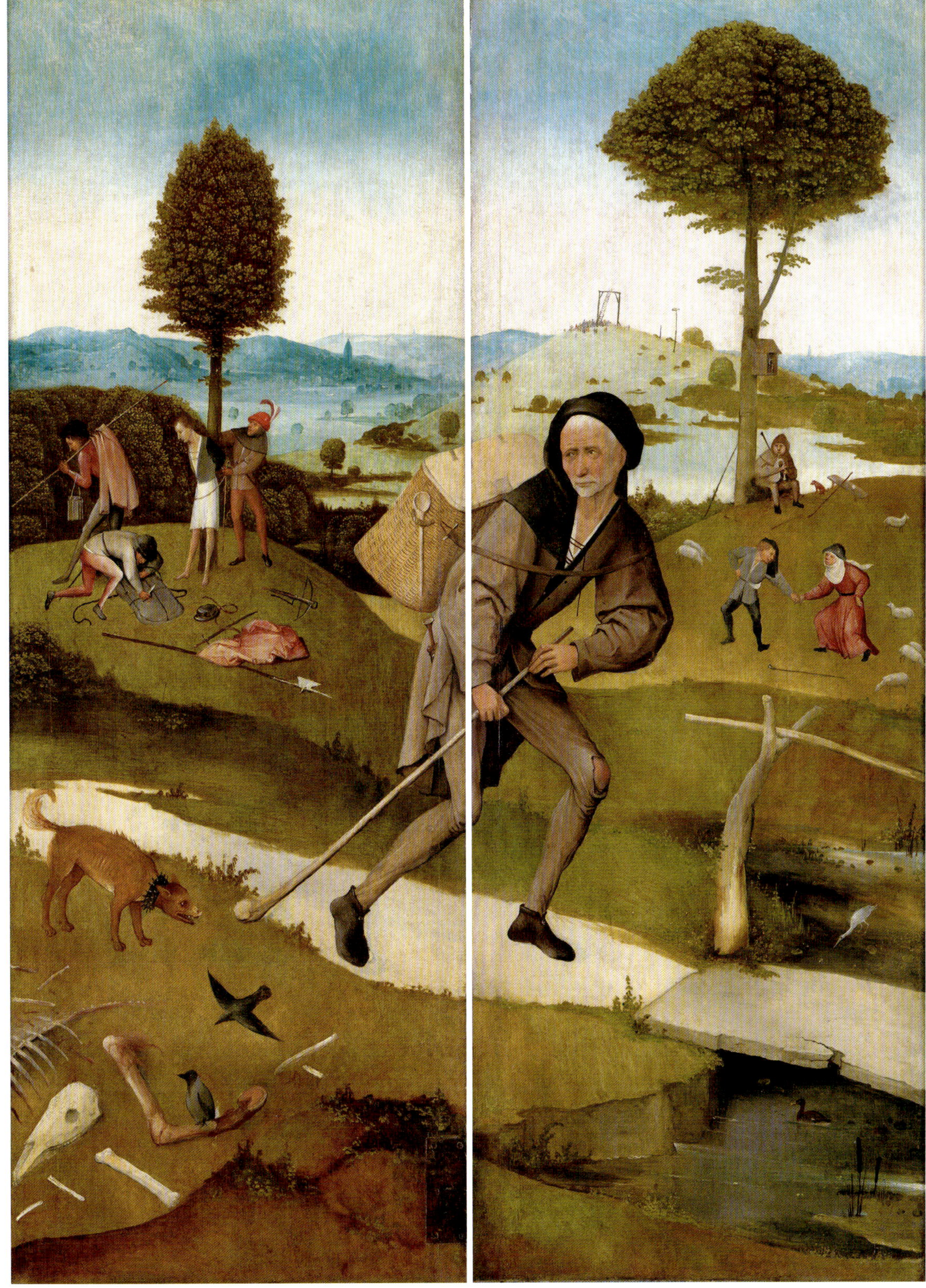

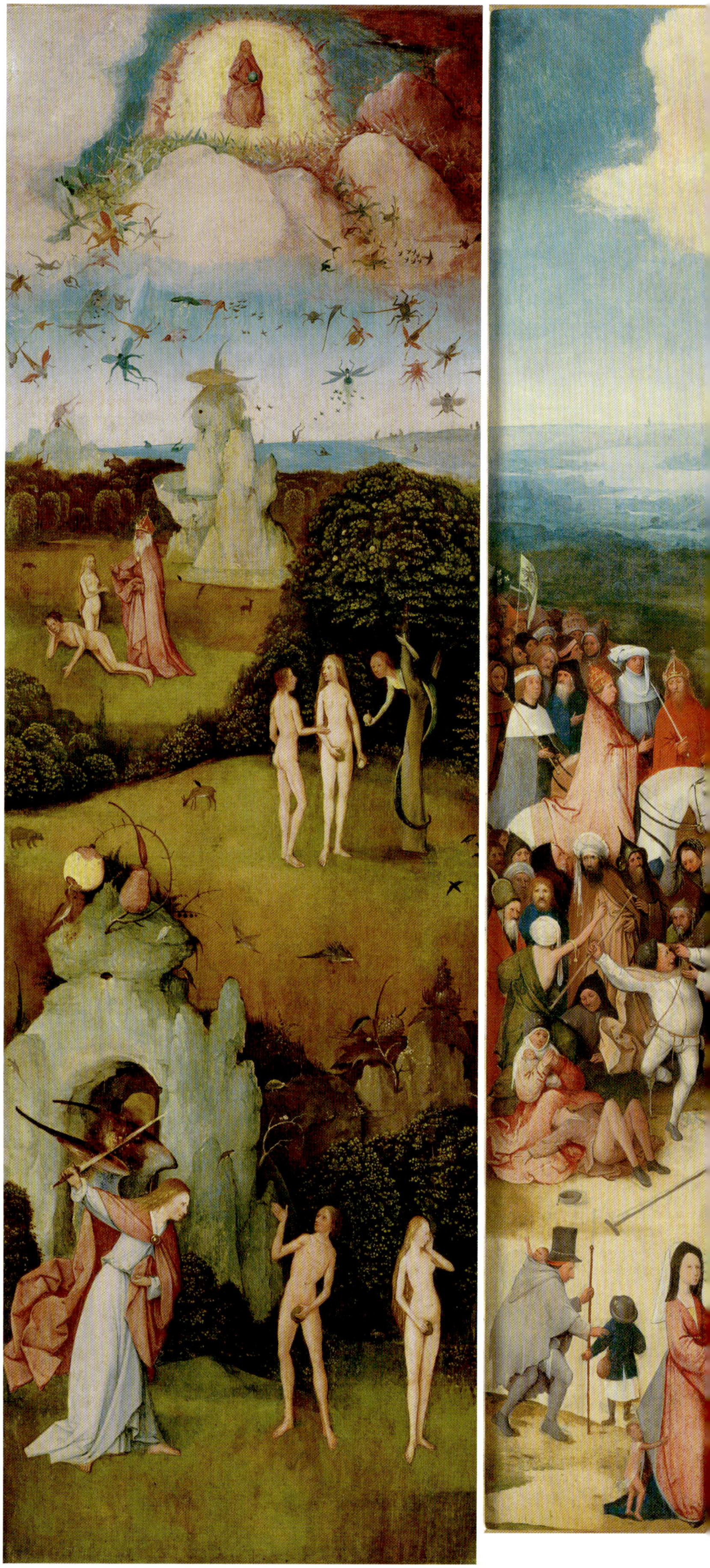

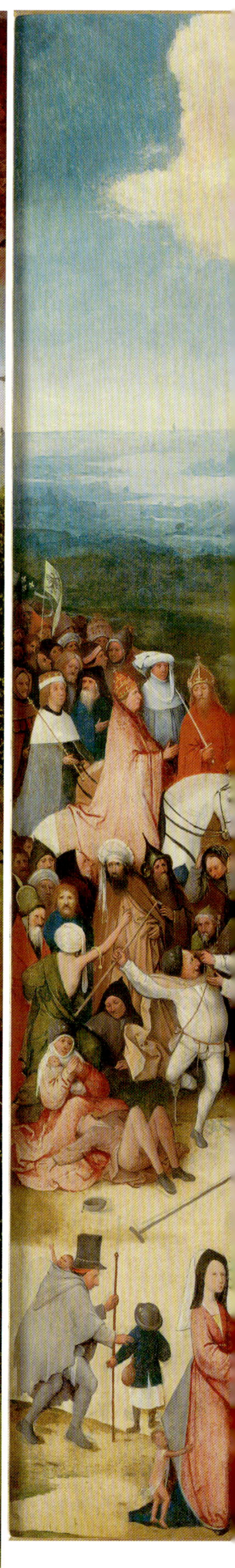

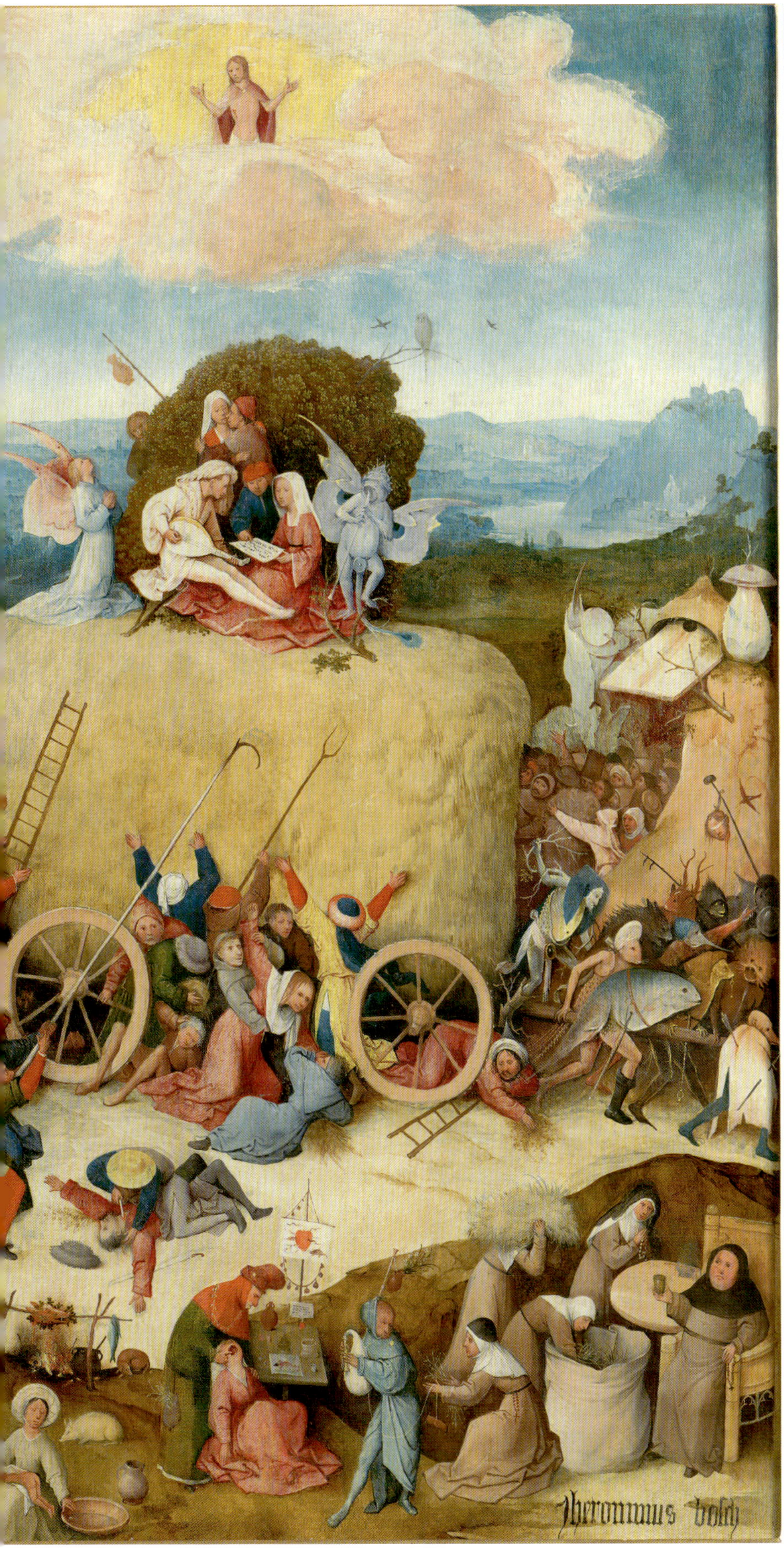

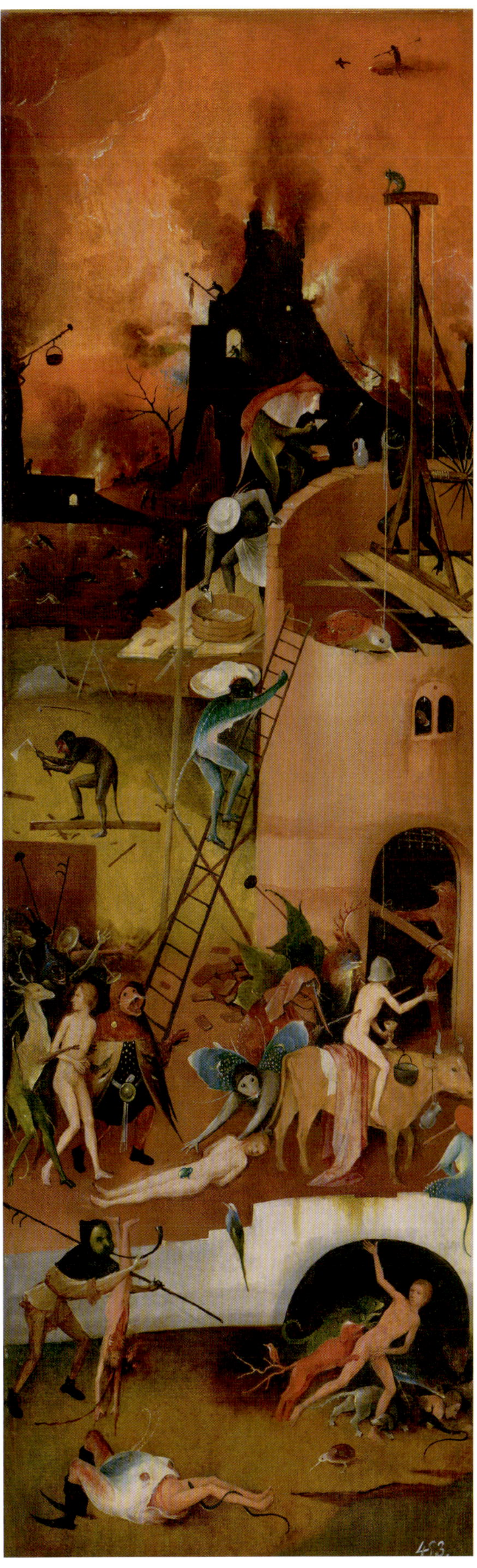

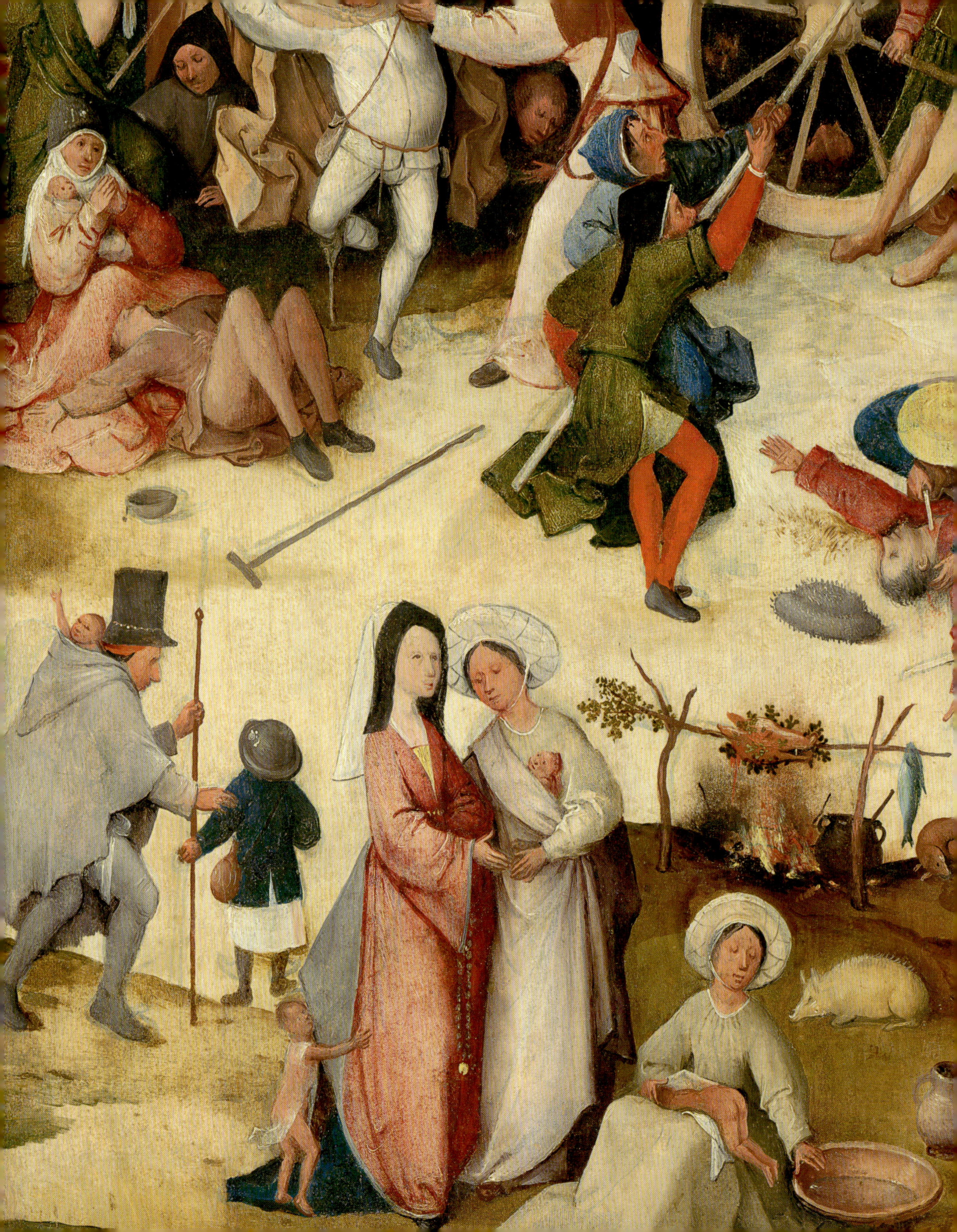

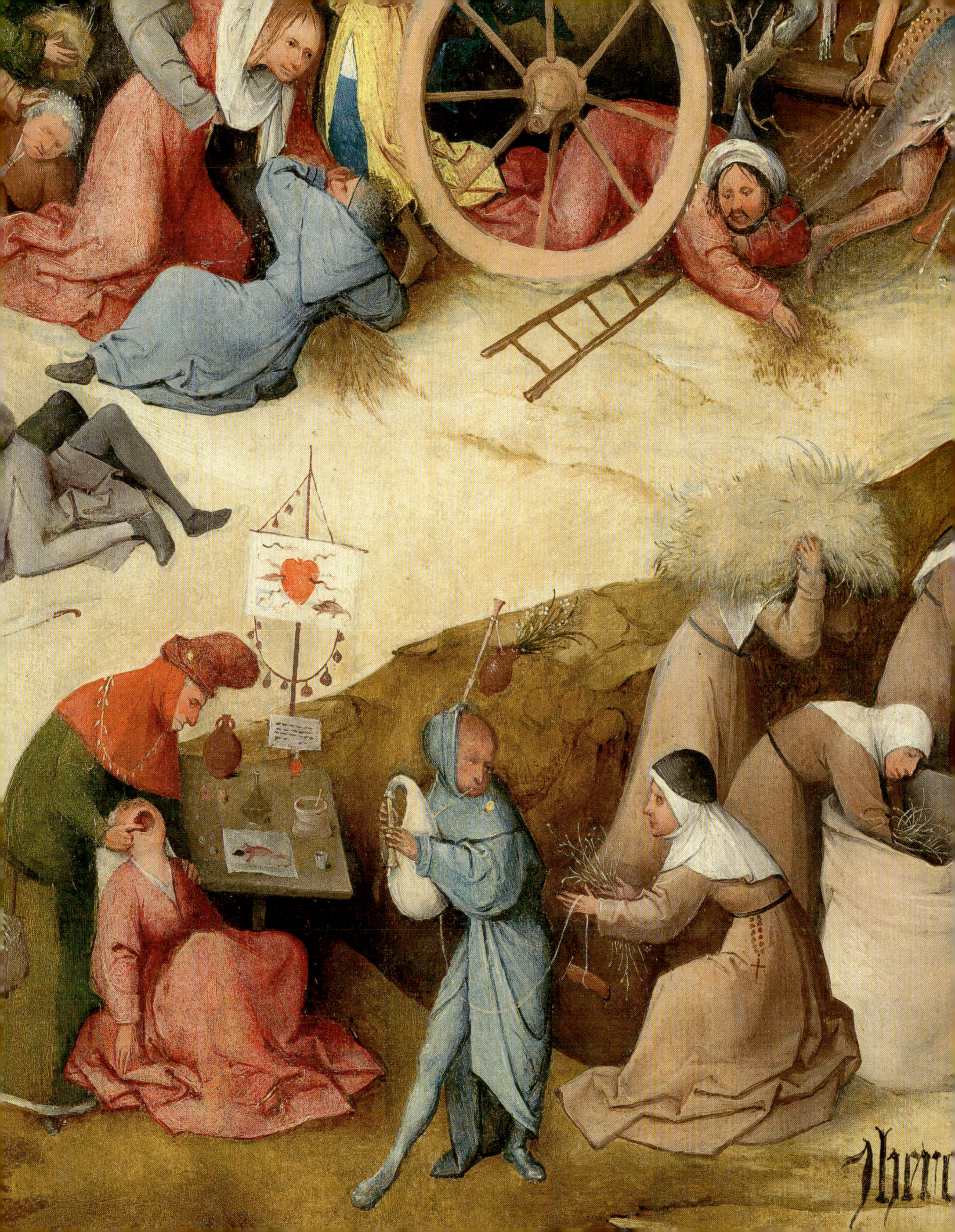
Jheroni

II

Hieronymus Bosch in 's-Hertogenbosch

's-Hertogenbosch grew significantly during Hieronymus Bosch's lifetime. Between eleven and twelve thousand people lived there in 1464, a year after the city suffered a major fire, rising to over eighteen thousand in 1496 and to more than twenty thousand by 1526, ten years after the artist's death. The second half of the fifteenth century was marked by economic stagnation and social upheaval, caused by wars and extremely high taxes. Things began to improve once more in the 1490s, bringing increased levels of trade and prosperity. 's-Hertogenbosch became the third most important city in Brabant after Brussels and Antwerp, while in the Northern Netherlands, only Utrecht and Amsterdam were larger. The town centred on the Markt, where Hieronymus lived from 1462 onwards, and the Romanesque St John's Church, which was transformed into a late-Gothic collegiate church with the allure of a French cathedral. There was no scope, however, for the kind of flourishing cultural life or artistic production found at the time in Southern Netherlandish cities like Bruges, Ghent, Brussels or Antwerp. This would change towards the end of the fifteenth century, when high-quality artistic products began to be imported to 's-Hertogenbosch and also produced there on behalf of churches and monasteries, public authorities and private customers. This was the environment in which Jeroen van Aken, the talented son of a family of painters and craftsmen, was able to develop into the original and brilliant artist we know as Hieronymus Bosch. In a sense, it was precisely the 'splendid isolation' resulting from the lack of local tradition and of strict conventions that allowed him to arrive at his distinctive and original work. On the one hand, he inevitably continued the early Netherlandish painting tradition of Jan van Eyck, Rogier van der Weyden and Dirk Bouts, while on the other, he firmly broke with his predecessors in terms of style, iconography and technique.

Religion, politics and trade were the factors that shaped life in 's-Hertogenbosch and Hieronymus Bosch's artistic career. His primarily religious oeuvre was strongly influenced by the Devotio Moderna movement, and was intended to communicate the message of Christian salvation to worshippers in as intense a manner as possible. Bosch's patrons from the Burgundian-Habsburg elite were drawn to 's-Hertogenbosch for strategic reasons. His more local customers, meanwhile, found themselves in a position to invest in his art – for reasons of prestige, artistic interest and above all their personal salvation – thanks to the success of regional and international trade. St John's Church was an ambitious architectural project entailing a great deal of activity, and so played an essential part in all this, as did the Brotherhood of Our Lady, which numbered thousands of members from all over the region and beyond, in fact,

the city's entire economic hinterland. The brotherhood also had a small administrative and devotional core group of 'sworn brothers' (fig. p. 36), most of whom sprang from the local elite. Hieronymus Bosch himself was enrolled as a 'sworn brother' in 1487–88. It must have been an immense step for him up the social ladder, given that he was a craftsman and neither a nobleman nor especially rich. It was no doubt his acclaimed artistry that led to his membership of this select company, which celebrated its annual banquet in the summer of 1488, at Bosch's home. The artist showed his gratitude by painting two large and two small altarpiece wings, which were added to the brotherhood's precious altarpiece in the chapel at St John's (cat. 6, 7). The chapel – funded like the altarpiece by numerous pious gifts from all the ordinary brethren – had recently been completed under the architect, sculptor and engraver Alart Duhameel (c. 1450–1506). In addition to architectural sculpture and his contribution to construction projects in towns including 's-Hertogenbosch, Leuven and Antwerp, we know of a dozen engravings by him, several of which are directly related to the work of Hieronymus Bosch.

Bosch also painted another work for St John's – an *Adoration of the Magi*, which as far as we know has not survived – and a triptych for the main altar, done in collaboration with his brother Goessen, and which has likewise disappeared without trace. The design of the *Cure of Folly* (cat. 9) was most likely prompted by a chapter meeting of the Order of the Golden Fleece, which brought a small group of senior noblemen from the Burgundian empire to the choir of St John's in 1481. As noted already, the Brotherhood of Our Lady regularly called on Bosch's services in connection with all sorts of painting assignments and designs, for which he generally accepted no payment. The brotherhood did pay on one occasion, though, for heraldic painting work performed by one or more of his journeymen, and also for designs that Hieronymus and one of his nephews produced for the embroidery of liturgical vestments. The Holy Ghost Table (Tafel van de Heilige Geest) – a local poor-relief charity – was another of Bosch's customers, along with several other individuals and monasteries, which managed to acquire work by their fellow townsman (cat. 8, 14).

36 The panels showing *Saint John on Patmos* and *Saint John the Baptist* (cat. 7) can almost certainly be identified as the two upper wings that Bosch painted for the Marian altarpiece in the chapel of the Brotherhood of Our Lady at St John's Church in 's-Hertogenbosch. The polyptych was carved in 1475–77 by Adriaen van Wesel of Utrecht, and was added to in the years that followed. The carved upper wings showed the *Vision of Emperor Augustus* and the apocalyptic vision of *Saint John on Patmos* (fig. p. 39). The upper wings, painted on both sides, were fastened to these. When the altarpiece was fully closed, the now lost image on the back of *Saint John the Baptist* (cat. 7) and the semi-grisaille painting on the reverse of *Saint John on Patmos* were visible. When the wings were opened, unidentified paintings on the back of the cases containing the carvings were displayed, flanked by John the Baptist on one side and Saint John on Patmos on the other.

Saint John's vision of the Apocalypse was a key piece of imagery for the Brotherhood of Our Lady, as it featured both the Virgin Mary, its own patron saint, and John, the Apostle and Evangelist, the patron saint of the church and hence also of 's-Hertogenbosch. The scene with Saint John on Patmos appeared in the altarpiece twice, therefore, although not in such a way that both were visible at once. The brotherhood had a woodcut showing Saint John on Patmos looking up at the 'Woman in the Sun' – whom we again recognize as the Virgin Mary with the Christ Child – inserted as the only illustration in an indulgence booklet dating from 1518/19.

Hieronymus was admitted to the brotherhood's elite inner core in 1487–88 and accepted as a sworn brother. Perhaps he painted the altarpiece wings as a token of his gratitude and as a tribute to the Virgin Mary. He signed the Patmos panel bottom right in Gothic letters using the Latinized version of his name (detail p. 8). As far as we can tell, this was the first time that he used the signature 'Jheronimus Bosch', firmly presenting himself as a learned and self-assured artist. It is not impossible that he also incorporated a self-portrait in the little monster beneath which he signed his name.

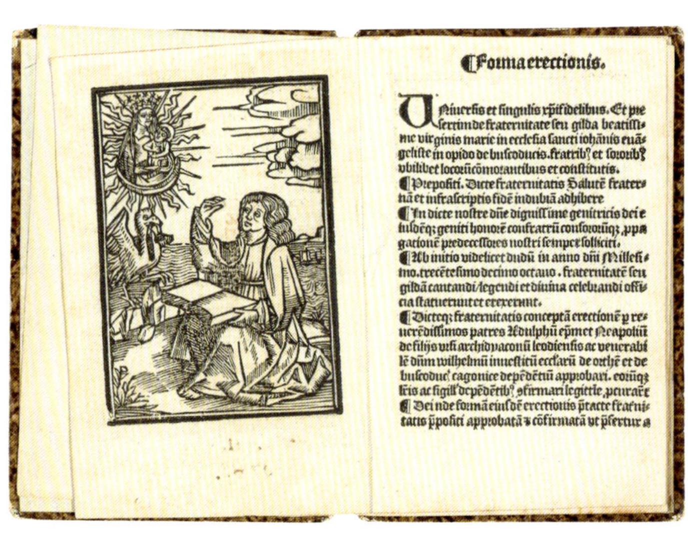

Saint John on Patmos
In the indulgence booklet of the Brotherhood of Our Lady, 1518–19
Woodcut and letterpress, 13 × 10 cm
Brussels, Bibliothèque royale de Belgique / Koninklijke Bibliotheek van België, II 29.403A

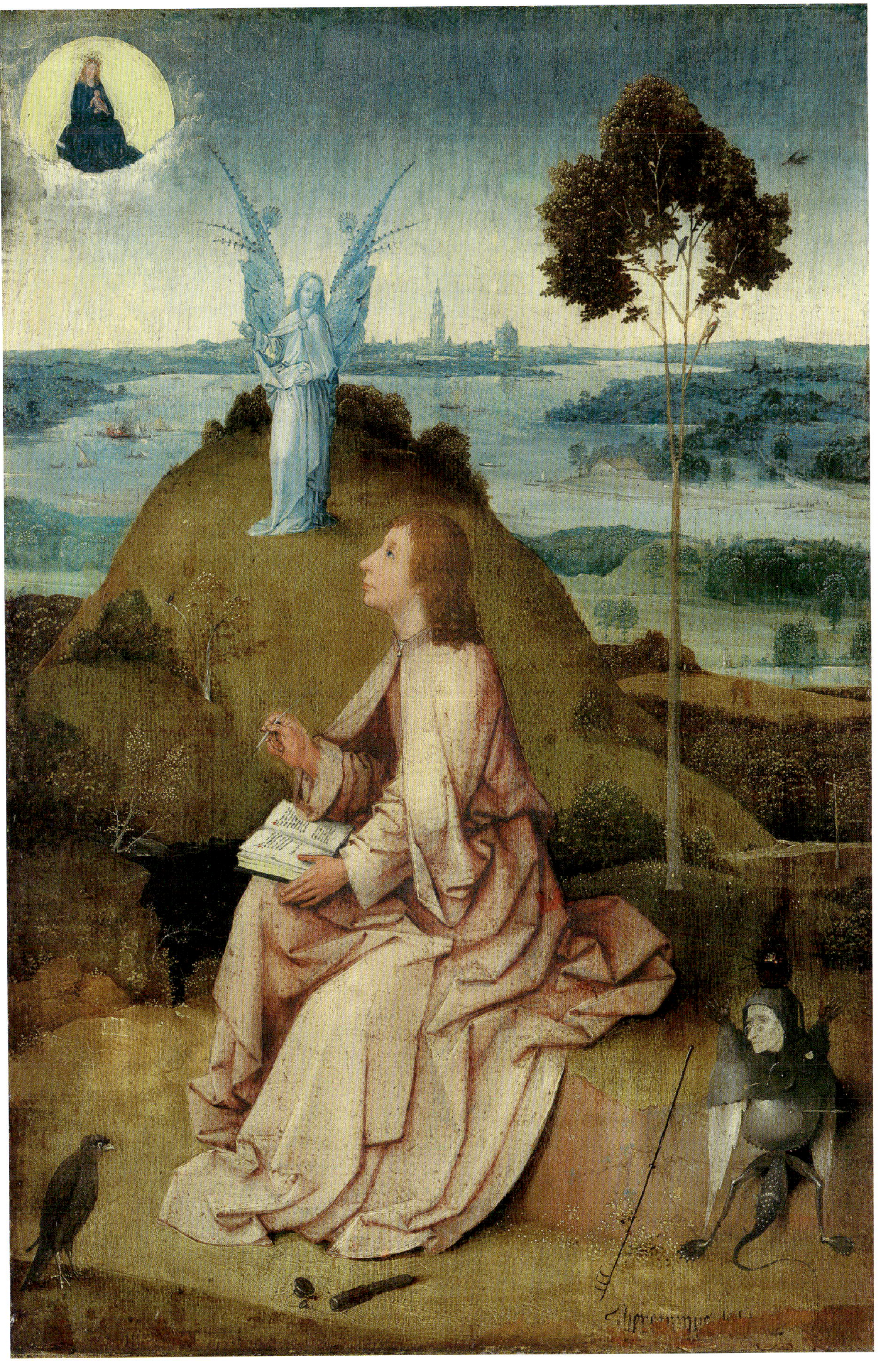

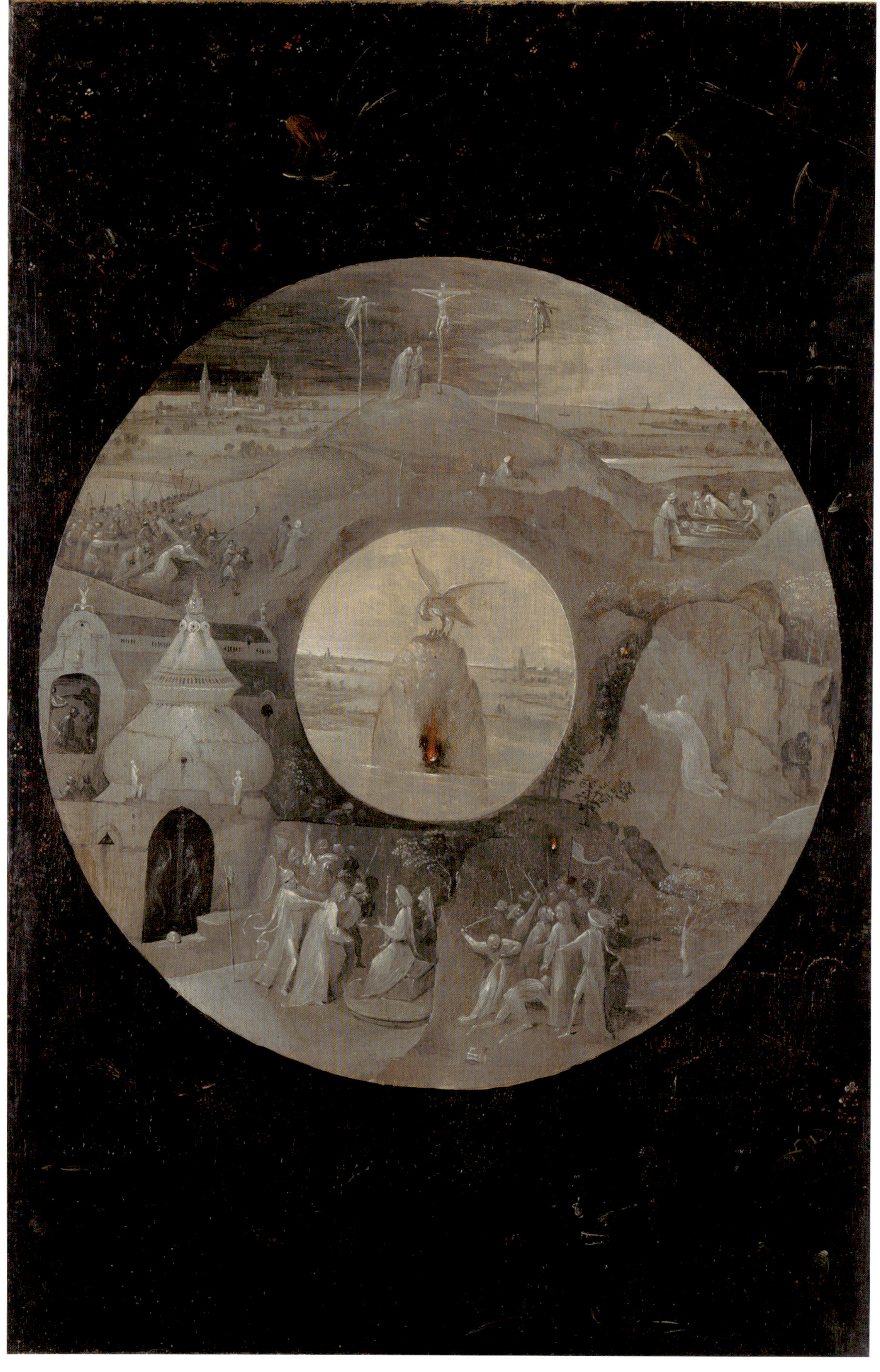

Hieronymus Bosch
Saint John on Patmos – Passion Scenes, 1490–95
Oil on oak panel, 63 × 43.2 cm
Berlin, Staatliche Museen zu Berlin,
Gemäldegalerie, 1647

The small eagle painted at Saint John's feet is the gospel-writer's customary attribute. The world in the distance already seems Christianized, as a wooden cross has been raised next to the road winding between the hills. The angel who has appeared to John points to the apparition of the Apocalyptic Woman in the sky, who simultaneously represents the Holy Virgin. The calamities associated with the End of Days have already begun in the sea, deep below her and behind the hill.

The back of the panel is painted in semi-grisaille, with Christ's Passion presented in an illuminated circle surrounded by hellish darkness. The pelican at the centre of the circle, which feeds its young with its own blood, refers to the Son of God, who gave his life for humanity. The Passion cycle is set out in eight scenes: Agony in the Garden, Betrayal of Christ, Christ before Pilate, Flagellation, Crowning with Thorns, Christ Carrying the Cross, Crucifixion and Entombment.

The Passion scenes around the allegory of Christ's self-sacrifice are surrounded by deep darkness, in which Bosch has painted all sorts of barely visible figures in dark tones.

Some of them are recognizable from other paintings. A bell, for instance, hangs directly above the crucified Christ, and a flying fish moves towards the left, on his head a naked little figure bent in the other direction. The same figure appears again in reverse in the right wing of the *Last Judgement* in Bruges (cat. 49); in that case, it has a jousting lance inserted in its backside, whereas here the remains of a long white pole are still visible. A giant dog in the lower left corner growls menacingly at three deer loitering peacefully on a riverbank. While not identical, the aggressive dog is directly comparable with the ones in the *Wayfarer* panel in Rotterdam and the *Haywain* triptych in the Prado (cat. 1, 5). A winged knight riding a fish hurries up on the right of the dog, armed with a jousting lance from which a tankard is suspended. A similar knight can be seen high in the air in the *Saint Anthony Triptych* in Lisbon (fig. p. 150). The overall effect is that of a chaotic mass in deep darkness, in the midst of which Christ brings salvation.

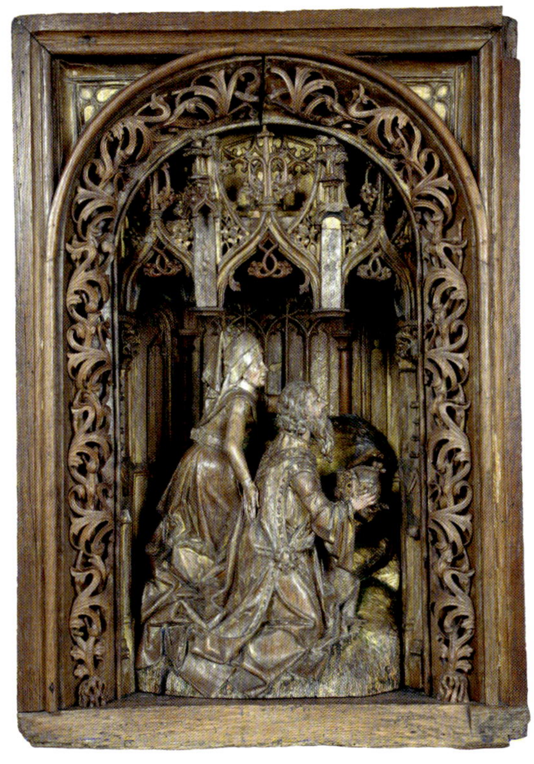
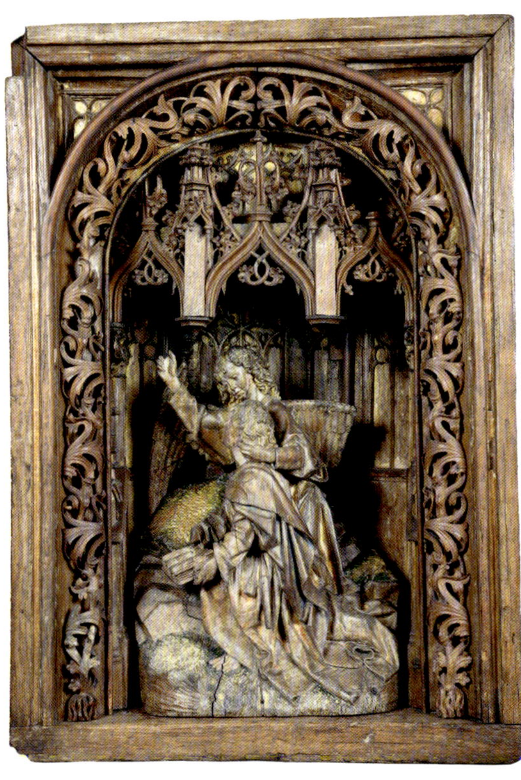

Adriaen van Wesel, *The Vision of Emperor Augustus and Saint John on Patmos*, 1475–77
Oak with traces of the original polychromy, 86.7 × 61.5 × 32 cm and 86.5 × 61.6 × 32 cm
's-Hertogenbosch, Museum Het Zwanenbroedershuis, B8 and B7

40   John the Baptist lies pensively in an expansive landscape that represents the wilderness or natural solitude into which he temporarily withdrew. The scene seems peaceful enough, yet in the background we see a bear devouring a deer and another shaking a tree. John points with his right hand to the object of his meditation: the lamb, or rather the Lamb of God. Shortly afterwards, this last of the Old Testament prophets would come forward to baptize Jesus in the River Jordan, marking the beginning of Christ's public ministry.

The entire composition is firmly oriented to the right, just as that of *Saint John on Patmos* is oriented entirely to the left (cat. 6). They are pendants that once flanked two (unidentified) images high up in the altarpiece of the Brotherhood of Our Lady in 's-Hertogenbosch. John the Baptist is an excellent pendant for Saint John on Patmos. The feasts of the two Saint Johns were celebrated with similar pomp at St John's Church, which was dedicated to the Evangelist. The image of John the Baptist, who announced the advent of Christ as Redeemer during the baptism in the Jordan, is also directly relevant as part of the original Marian altarpiece.

The John the Baptist panel is slightly smaller than the one with Saint John on Patmos, as it has been cropped on all sides. It has also been severely thinned and retains no trace of its original back. This is because the front and the back of the panel were sawn apart at some point to separate them, as also occurred with *Death and the Miser*, the *Ship of Fools* and the *Wayfarer* (cat. 1–4).

The alterations in the panel with Saint John the Baptist are substantial. The painting follows the underdrawing fairly closely – at least where the latter can be detected. However, the large fanciful plant and the green bush behind which John stretches out conceal the figure of a male donor, kneeling in prayer (fig. p. 42). He was hidden behind the vegetation relatively soon after being painted, presumably because he was no longer wanted. The high quality of the overpainting, which is perfectly in keeping with Bosch's imagery, suggests that it was done by the master himself.

The identity of the overpainted donor is not known. It is hard to estimate his age, but he might have been the local dignitary Jan van Vladeracken (c. 1450–1532), who paid for the large lower wings of the altarpiece in 1488/89. He was an alderman in 's-Hertogenbosch for many years, a sworn member of the brotherhood from 1475, dean in 1503/04, and also previously in 1487/88, when Hieronymus Bosch was admitted as a sworn member. The donor, kneeling before his probable namesake Saint John, is directly comparable with Peter van Os on the left inside wing of the *Ecce Homo Triptych* in Boston (cat. 8). They wear similar brimless hats and tabards trimmed with fur. Bosch and Jan van Vladeracken must have known each other well; they both had houses on the north side of the Markt, and Van Vladeracken was one of the hosts of the 'Swan Banquet' in 1488, when Bosch was accepted as a sworn brother. Whatever the identity of the donor who originally featured next to John the Baptist, his conspicuous presence must have been deemed surplus to requirements shortly afterwards and he was painted out. It is possible that he died, and that his heirs did not assume responsibility for the commission. It is also plausible that the presence of a single donor's portrait in the brotherhood's precious altarpiece was felt to be inappropriate. The ensemble was, after all, the collective possession and focus of devotion of the Brotherhood of Our Lady as a whole.

The back of the John the Baptist panel must have been similar to the tondo floating in the darkness on the exterior of the Saint John on Patmos wing. It is not possible, of course, to reconstruct its subject matter with any certainty, but the Passion cycle and the theme of self-sacrifice in the right wing mean that it is likely to have focused on the childhood and ministry of Christ, lighting up once again out of the unearthly darkness. When the wings were closed, the two images alongside one another would have seemed like a pair of eyes regarding the viewer. In this way, beholders were both exhorted to pay extra attention to these scenes and reminded that they too were constantly seen by God.

Hieronymus Bosch
Saint John the Baptist, c. 1490–95
Oil on oak panel, 48.5 × 40.5 cm
Madrid, Museo Fundación Lázaro Galdiano, 8155

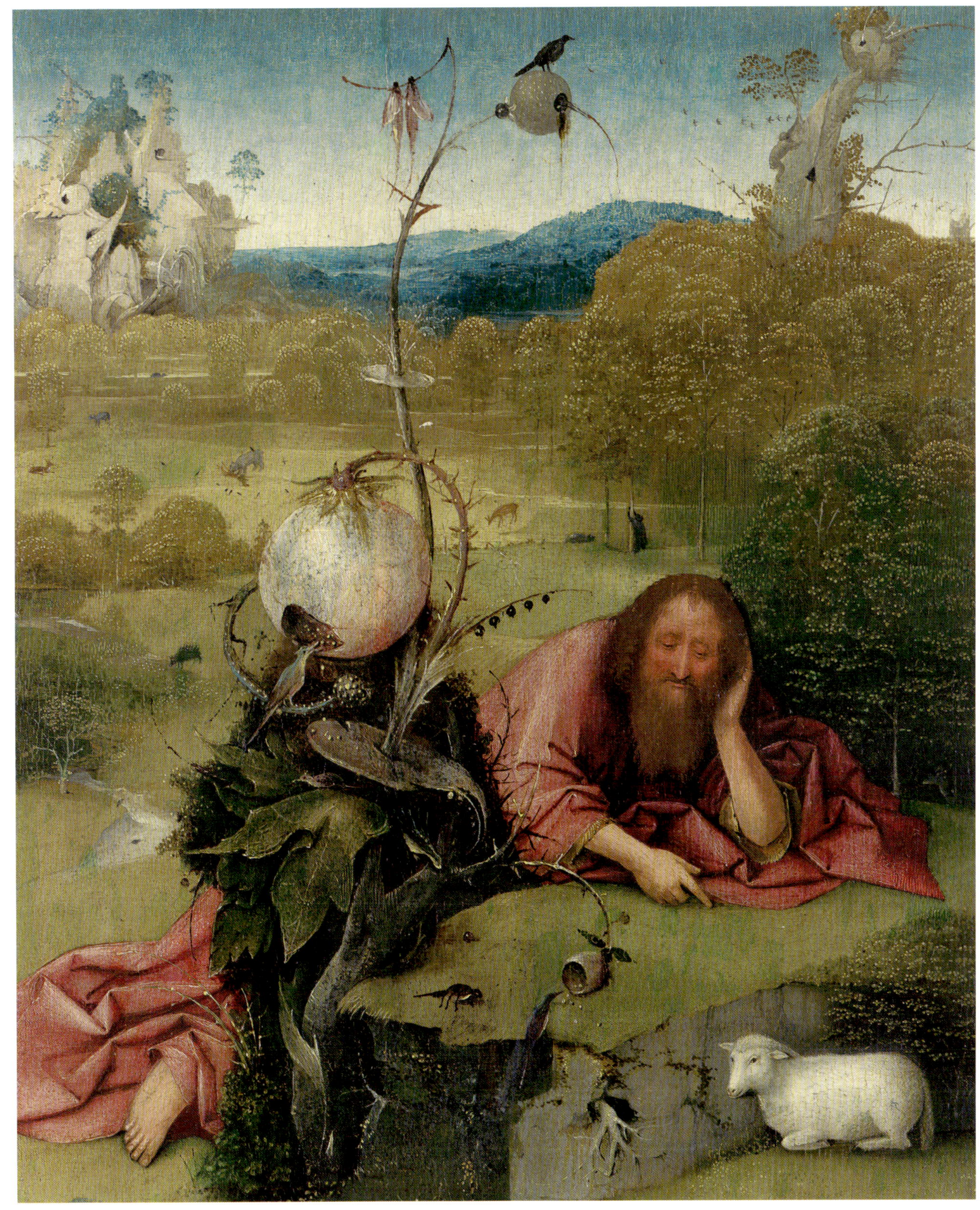

The hidden donor
(detail of *Saint John the Baptist*)
Photograph in visible light (left) and
infrared photograph (right)

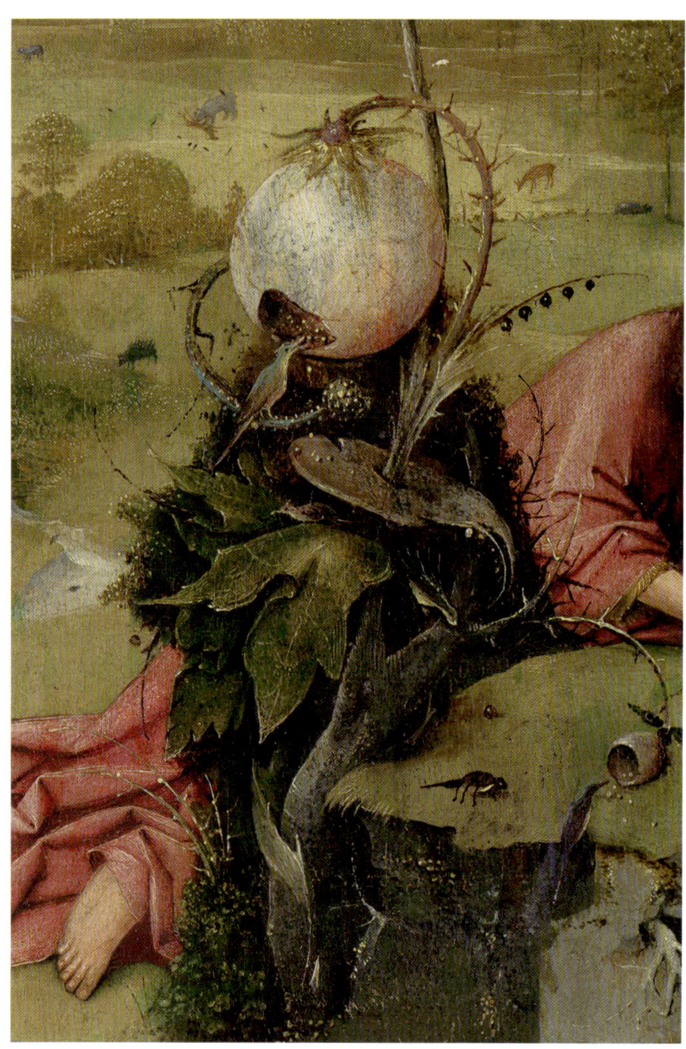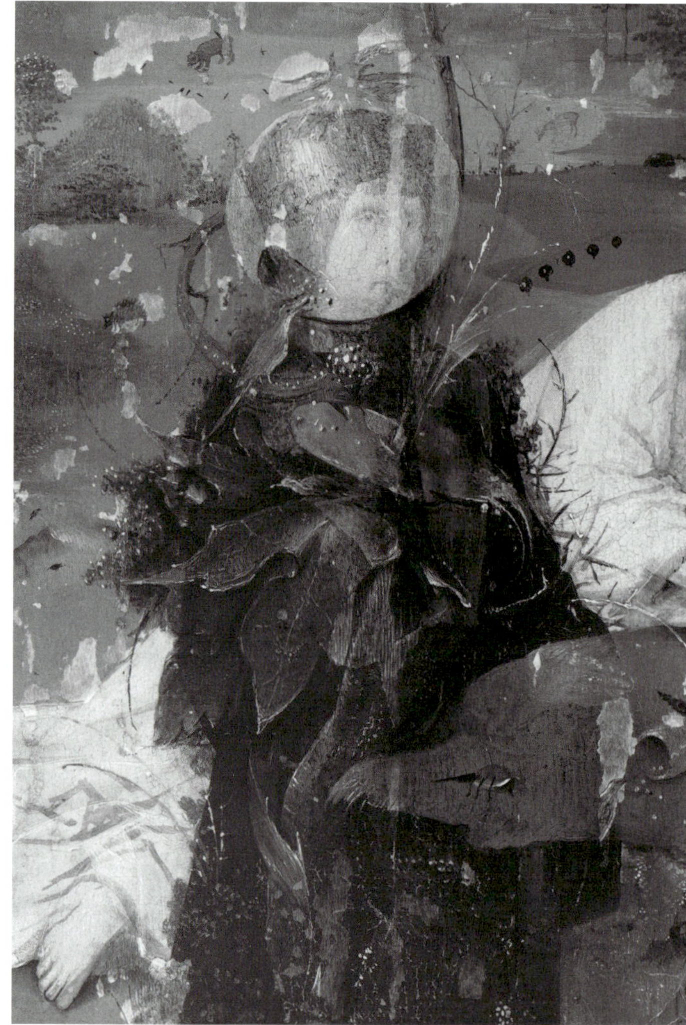

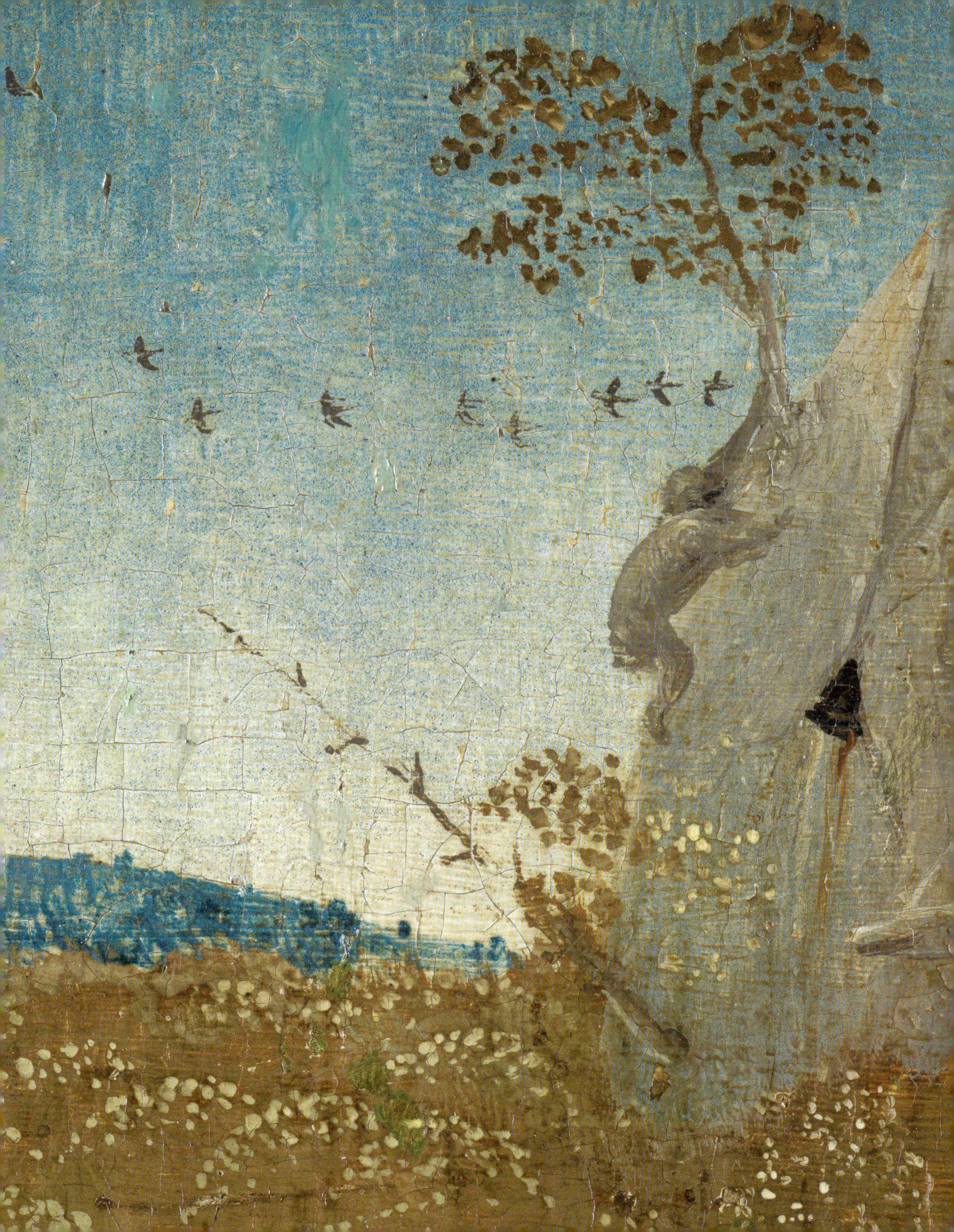

Hieronymus Bosch's triptychs systematically present a continuous narrative that begins with the image displayed on the outside of the closed wings. When the triptych is opened, the central panel is the main focal point, with the overall composition almost always read from left to right. This is not the case, however, with the *Ecce Homo Triptych* painted in Hieronymus Bosch's workshop for Peter van Os, the 's-Hertogenbosch municipal secretary. This is a memorial painting rather than an altarpiece or a triptych intended for meditation or prayer. The central panel features a variation on Bosch's *Ecce Homo* in Frankfurt – Pontius Pilate showing the tortured Christ to the people just before sentencing him to death by crucifixion (John 19:5). That panel too is a memorial painting (cat. 14). What comes next is shown to the right on the square in the background, where we see Christ carrying his cross towards Golgotha – an image similar to the corresponding scene on the back of the *Saint John on Patmos* panel in Berlin (cat. 6). Two families are depicted in full colour in the wings of the triptych – one on the inside, one on the outside. The respective couples have been identified from the inserted coats of arms and the distinctive costume worn by several of the family members. It has been established on technical and stylistic grounds, moreover, that the overall triptych was produced in four distinct phases and that at least four different painters worked on it.

The central panel with the *Ecce Homo* was the first element to be painted. Peter van Os must then have commissioned two wings around 1500 to turn it into a triptych as a memorial to his late wife, Henrickxen van Langel. Peter and Henrickxen, with a deceased infant before her, are painted in the open wings, accompanied by their respective patron saints. The triptych was completed by the incorporation in the frame beneath the central panel of a somewhat more primitively painted predella, which refers to the Crucifixion of Christ through the 'Instruments of the Passion'. The final phase in the painting's genesis occurred several years later, when Peter van Os's in-laws were added to the closed shutters: the notary Franco van Langel and his wife Heylwich van der Rullen, with their five sons, six daughters and the couple's patron saints. Henrickxen appears here again, now as the second daughter.

Unusually, three of the four saints included in the closed wings are not the donors' namesakes, but have a different devotional connection with the two families. Mary Magdalene was the most important patron saint of Bethany Priory, where one of Van Langel's daughters was a canoness; Saint Catherine was the patroness of a fraternity devoted to her in 's-Hertogenbosch, with which Heylwich van Langel was probably associated. Saint John the Evangelist was the patron saint of Franco's son Jan, who became a monk. And as the saint to whom the principal church in 's-Hertogenbosch was dedicated, he can also be viewed as the protector of the city as a whole. The Evangelist was likewise held in high esteem by the Brotherhood of Our Lady. Peter van Os and Franco van Langel were both sworn members of the brotherhood, as indicated by the silver insignia on their coloured chaperons (hoods). Saint Peter, lastly, was the namesake of Peter van Os and the patron saint of the Dominican church, where the Van Os and Van Langel families were buried. It is in this church, therefore, that the memorial painting will have been installed.

Two small but noteworthy alterations were made during the painting of the exterior wings: Friar Jan van Langel's head was significantly increased in size, while Lysbeth the nun was given a more pious expression, with her eyelids lowered. The adjustments seem to have been instigated by Jan and Lysbeth themselves, which might indicate their direct involvement with the commission for this family portrait. The order is likely to have been placed, therefore, to mark Jan's profession as a monk at the Cistercian monastery of Mariëndonk in Heusden on 24 June 1503. He was probably twenty-one at the time, and taking his vows meant withdrawing into monastic life and definitively renouncing his worldly possessions. It would have been the perfect moment to add the portraits of his late parents and their offspring to the as yet unpainted exterior of the memorial painting.

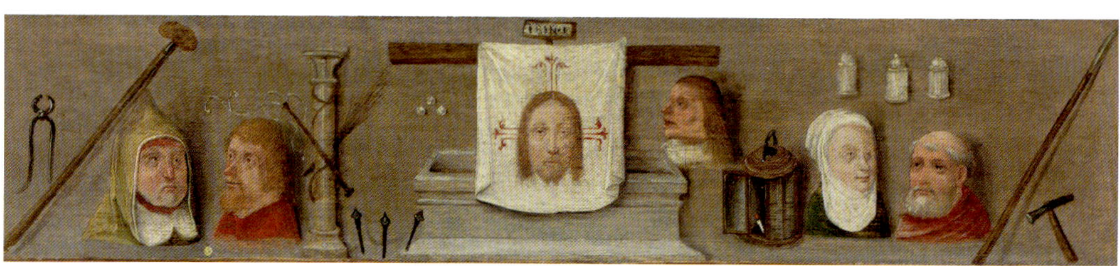

Closed triptych

Workshop of Hieronymus Bosch
Ecce Homo Triptych, c. 1495–1503
Oil on oak panel, left wing 69.3 × 26 cm,
central panel 73.4 × 58.4 cm, right wing
69.2 × 26 cm, predella 15.5 × 68.4 cm

Boston, Museum of Fine Arts, William
K. Richardson Fund; William Francis
Warden Fund; Juliana Cheney Edwards
Collection, 53.2027; and Gift of Arthur
Kauffmann, 56.171

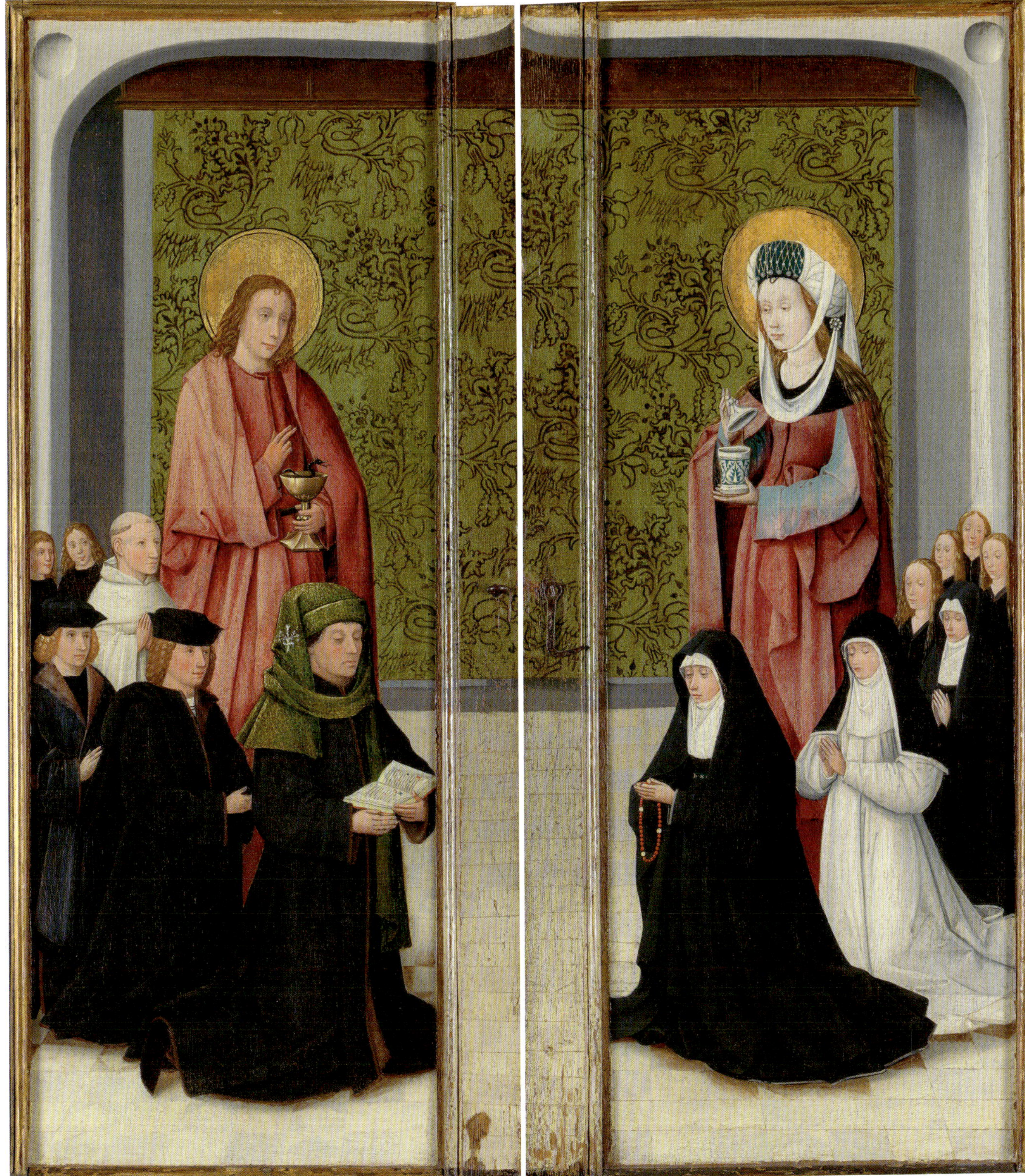

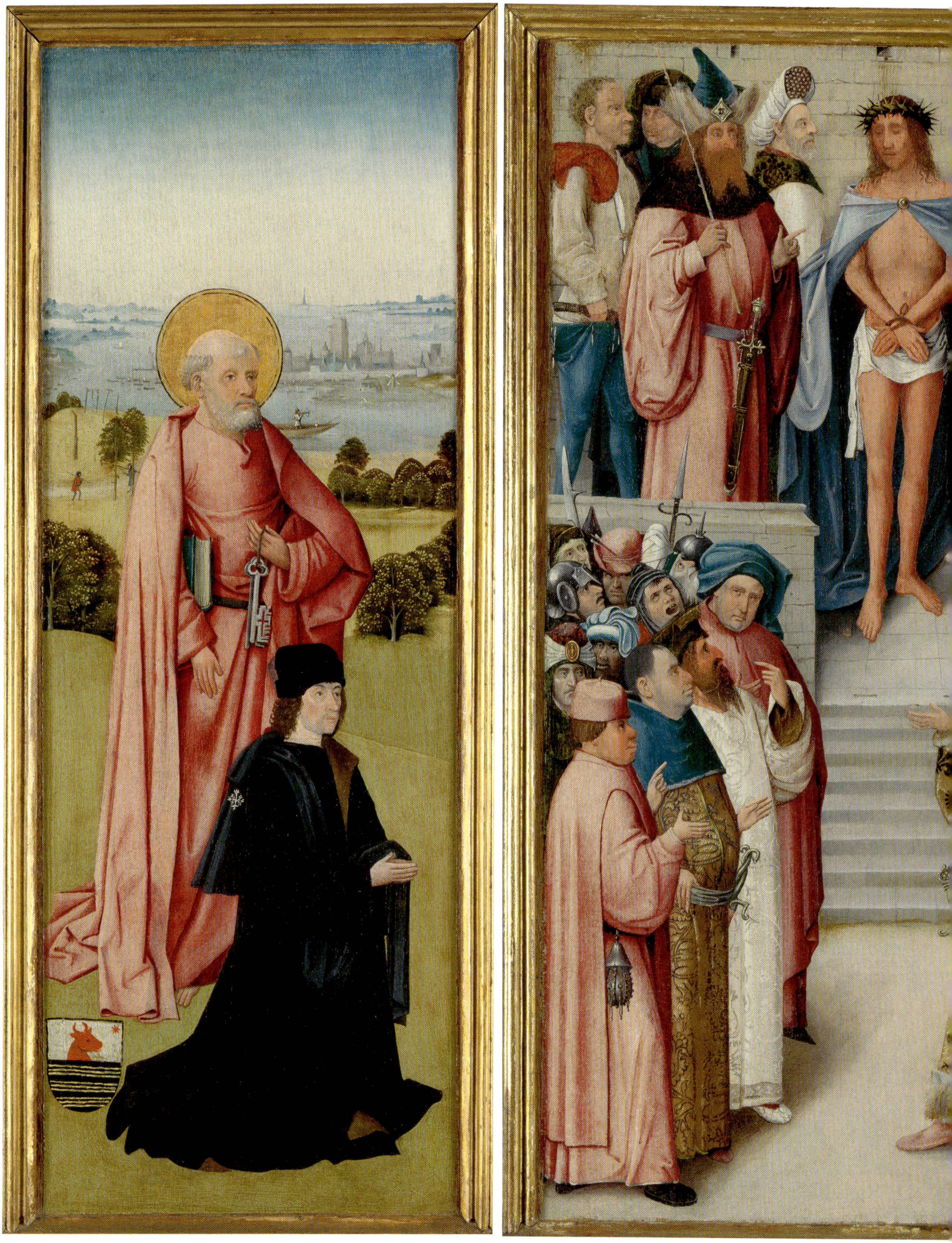

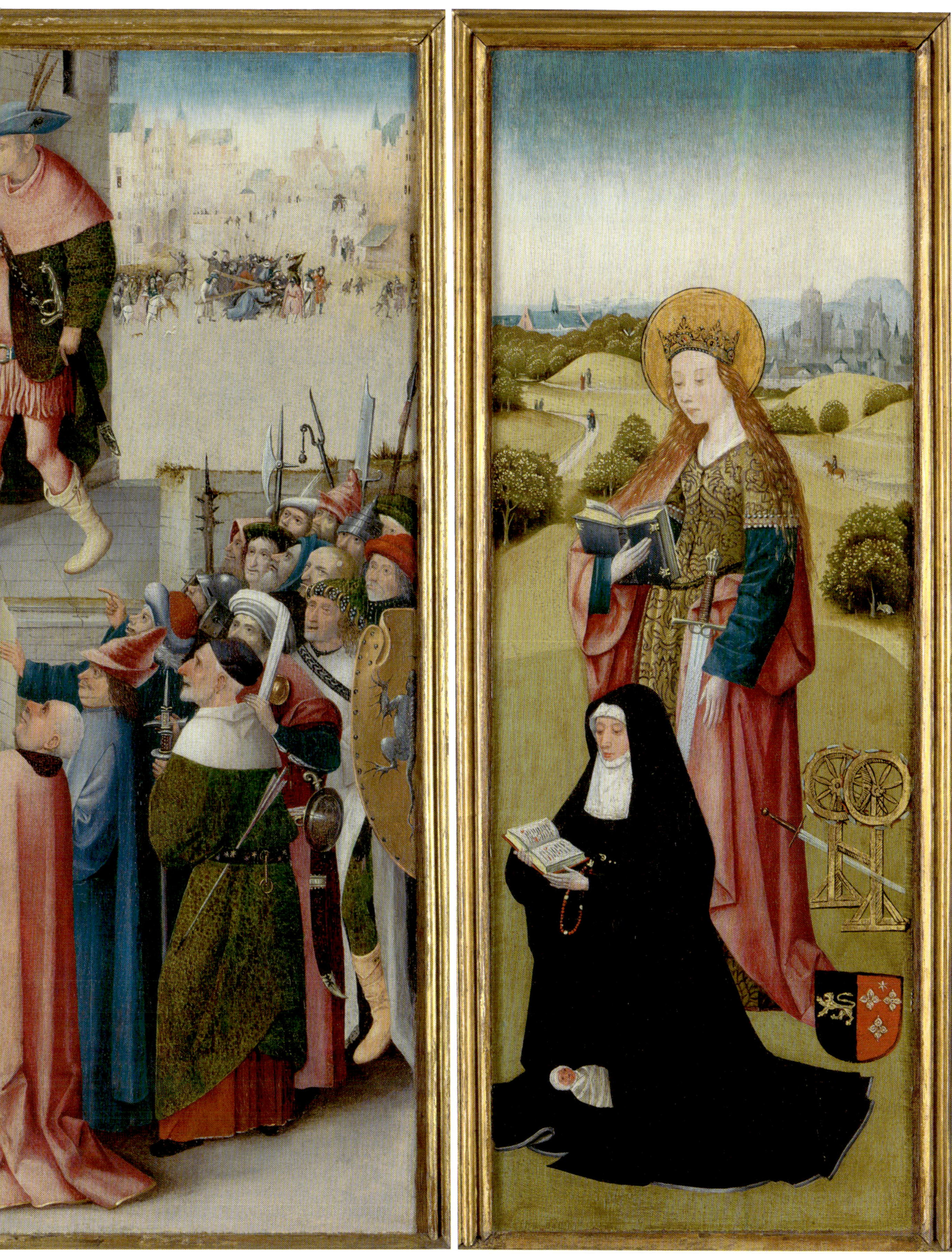

Workshop or follower of
Hieronymus Bosch
The Cure of Folly, c. 1510–20
Oil on oak panel, 48.8 × 34.6 cm
Madrid, Museo Nacional del Prado,
P2056

48

The scene set in a tondo against an otherwise uniformly black background is accompanied by a text above and below: '*Meester snijt die keye ras/ Myne name Is lubbert das*' (Master, cut the stone out quickly, my name is Lubbert Das). The gold, calligraphic letters contrast sharply with the shabbily dressed protagonist who evidently utters them: an idiot who hopes to be cured when the surgeon extracts the stone of folly from his head. To have a stone or rock in your head was a common expression denoting a mental handicap or extreme stupidity. The painting has a double meaning and employs wordplay and visual puns to set the viewer thinking. Because there is more going on here than may be apparent at first sight: a fat, simple man leans back in a chair while surgery is performed on his head. It is not immediately obvious whether the man and the elderly woman watching the procedure are accomplices of the 'surgeon' or are there to provide the patient with moral support. If we look more closely, however, we realize that Lubbert Das is the victim of this far from trustworthy trio. The man holds a beer or wine-jug in his hand, while the woman has a well-stuffed purse hanging from her belt and a closed book on her head. The quack doctor has a similar jug on his belt, and wears a funnel as a hat, from which knowledge escapes instead of entering. Looking more closely still, we notice that rather than the stone of folly, it is a flower that is extracted from Lubbert's head. The Middle Dutch word *keye* meant not only 'stone' but also 'flower', or more specifically 'carnation'. What we see here, therefore, is something that was common knowledge: that there was no such thing as a 'stone of folly' and that no such operation could be performed. The 'surgeon' is a fraud, and what we witness is an illusion. The inscription too has a double meaning; the expression 'to cut

the stone' from someone also meant to rob or deceive them. The name 'Lubbert Das' is plainly invented too, and emphasizes the victim's stupidity. Although the first name 'Lubbert' does exist, it has a secondary meaning, since the verb *lubben* also means to emasculate or castrate. The badger (*das*) was considered a lazy animal since, being a nocturnal hunter, it always seems to be asleep in daylight.

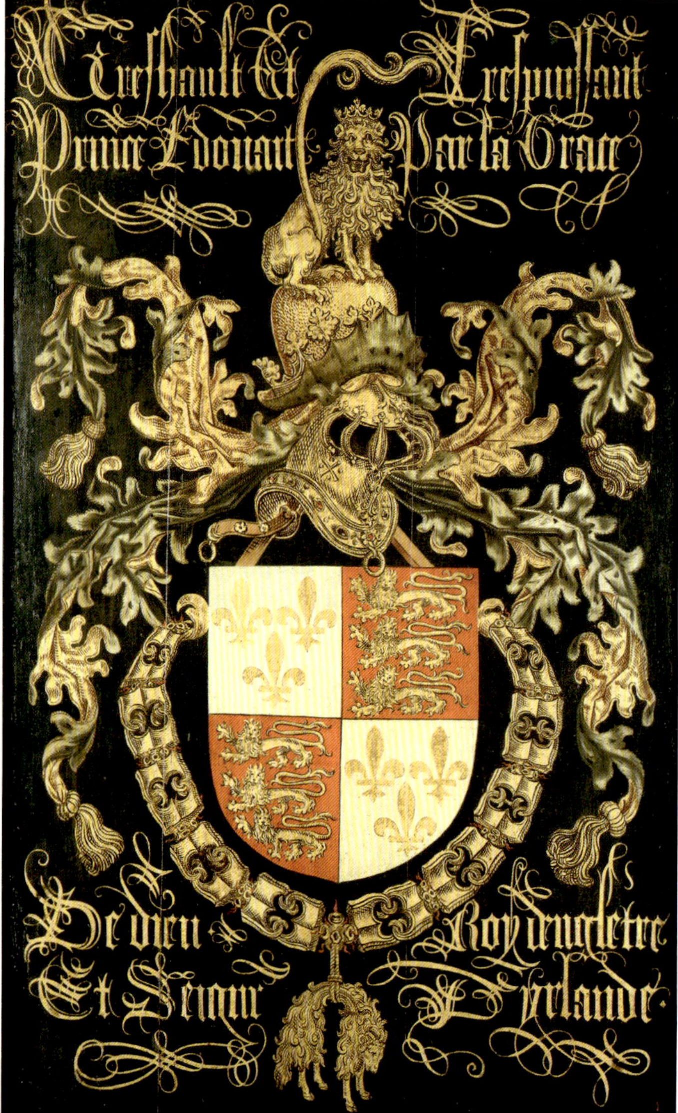

Pierre Coustain, *Blazon of Edward IV of England (1443–1483), painted for the Chapter of the Golden Fleece in St John's Church, 's-Hertogenbosch*, 1481
Oil on panel, 120.5 × 72 cm
's-Hertogenbosch, Het Noordbrabants Museum, 12064 (on loan from the Rijksmuseum Amsterdam, inv. SK-A-4641)

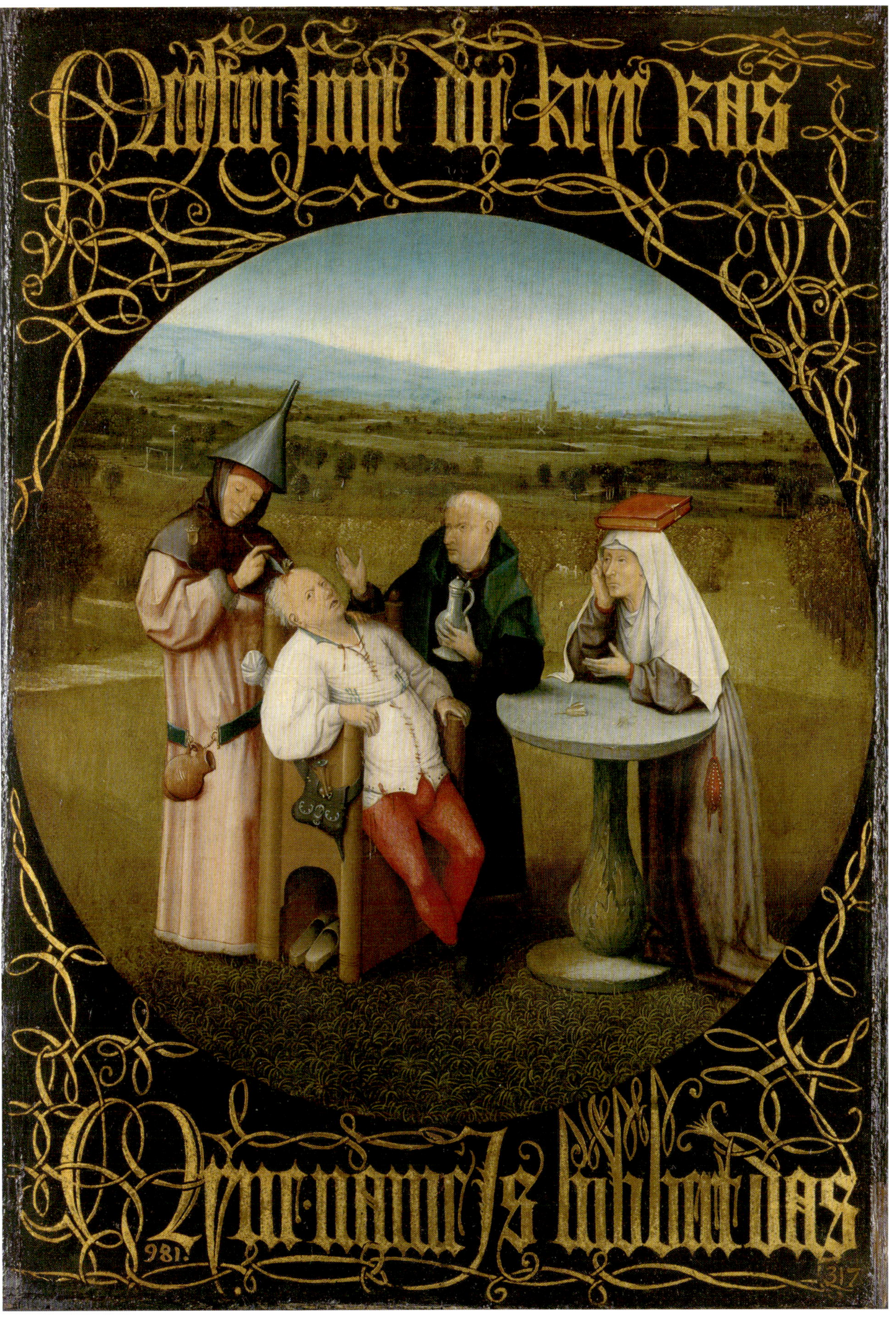
Meester snijt die keye ras
981.
Mijne name is lubbert das
317

Word and image complement one another, therefore, in this painting, making it an early example of an emblem – a mostly moralizing message in the form of an illustration with an accompanying text. Each is incomplete without the other. The emblem genre became immensely popular, culminating for Dutch readers a century later in the work of the poet Jacob Cats (1577–1660).

The scene with the stone operation is set in a tondo against a black background on which the explanatory text is laid out in gold letters with elaborate decorative 'doodling'. The visual association with the blazons of the Order of the Golden Fleece is unmistakable; these heraldic paintings were installed from 1430 onwards in every church where the Burgundian chivalric order held a chapter meeting. The venue in 1481 was 's-Hertogenbosch. Only four of the thirty-six blazons installed in St John's Church at that time have survived (fig. p. 48). Hieronymus Bosch will certainly have known them, especially since one was hung upside-down in a porch outside the church as a humiliating punishment for a knight who was condemned during the meeting. The *Cure of Folly* appears therefore to be a kind of parody of chivalric blazons of this kind. This panel, or a similar one, which hung in the dining room of Bishop Philip of Burgundy's castle at Wijk-bij-Duurstede must have had a similar effect. The portrait of Philip himself as a knight of the Order of the Golden Fleece hung not far from a painting with the same inscription – possibly even this one.

The *Cure of Folly* was recorded in a Spanish aristocratic collection just before the middle of the eighteenth century. It was in the Prado by the mid-nineteenth century as part of the royal collection, at which point it was attributed to the Netherlandish school under the title 'Operacion quirurgica burlesca' ('comical surgical operation'). The *Cure of Folly* was first published as a work of Hieronymus Bosch in 1889, since when the panel has generally been attributed to him, and mostly as an early painting. Doubt as to Bosch's authorship has also been expressed, however, since the end of the nineteenth century. Based on the painting style and the underdrawing of the *Cure of Folly*, it has to be concluded that the panel is not the work of Hieronymus Bosch himself, but was most likely produced in his 's-Hertogenbosch workshop.

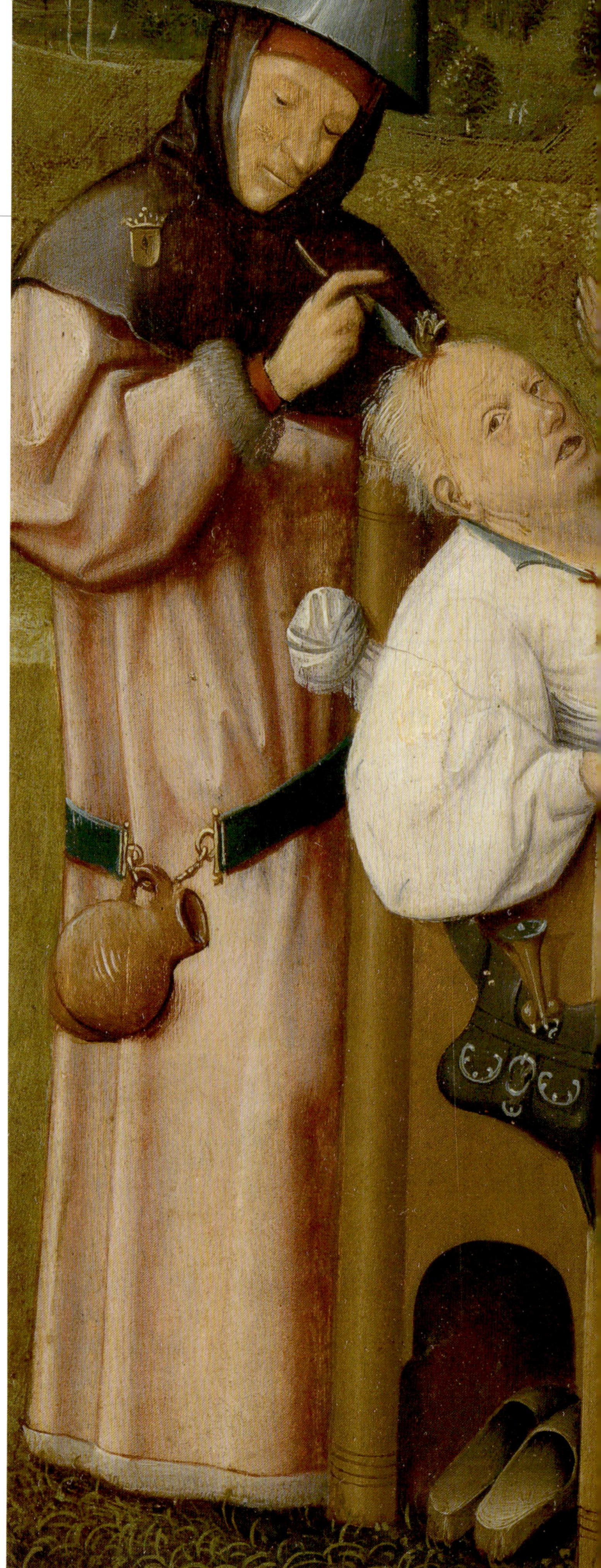

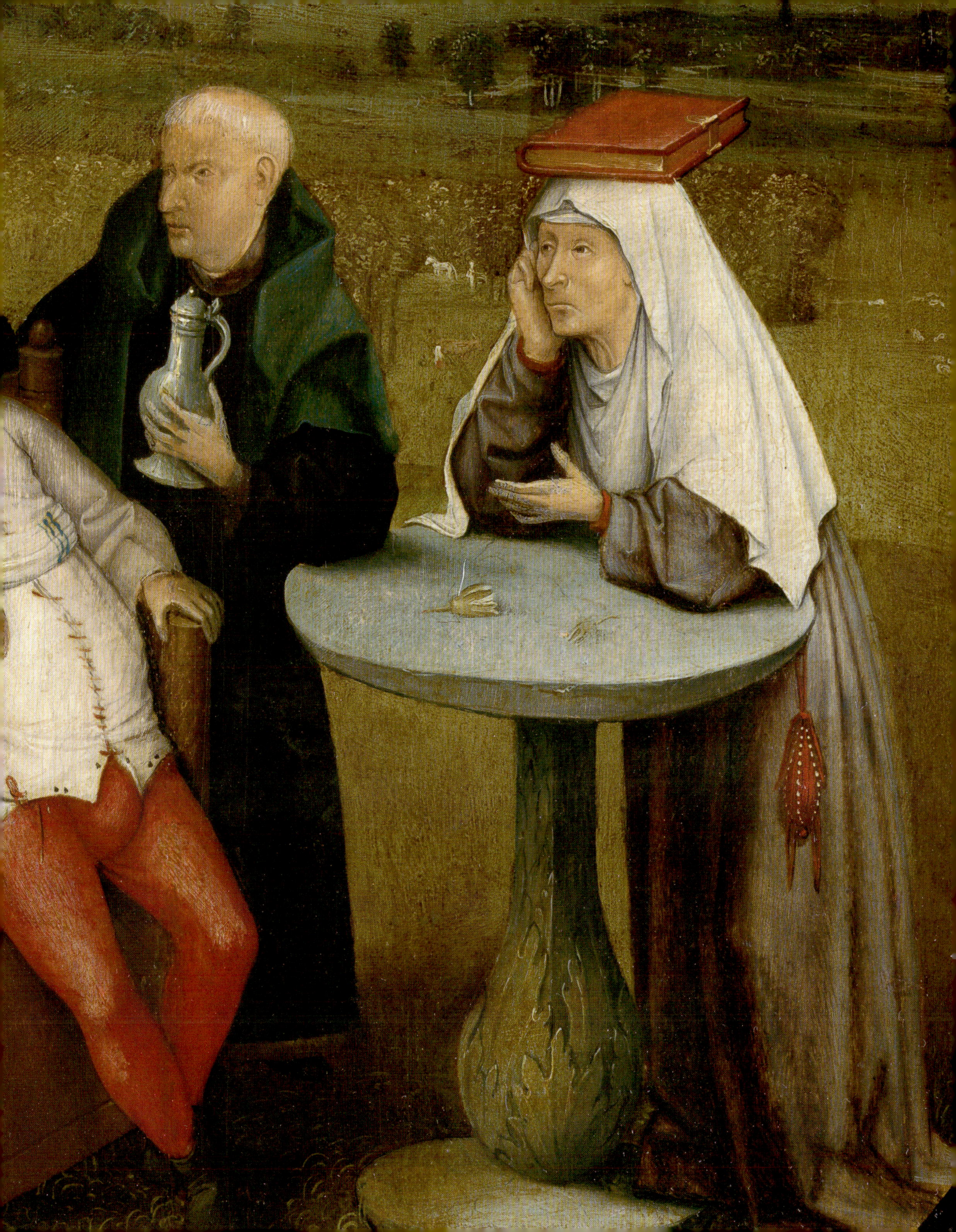

III

The Life of Christ

The sinfulness of humanity plays a dominant role in the work of Hieronymus Bosch, who alludes over and over to the immense seductiveness of evil. Good and evil have existed side by side since God created the world (cat. 10). High above the Garden of Eden in the paradise wing of the *Haywain* (cat. 5) we see a group of rebel angels fluttering down to earth as a horde of demonic monsters. The first human couple had to make choices of their own and fell into sin. They themselves chose to disobey, but could they have done otherwise? Bosch wrong-foots us in the paradise of the *Garden of Earthly Delights* (cat. 10): the Fall has yet to occur as the Creator presents Eve to her husband, Adam. Everything should be peaceful, yet menace and evil are already firmly present in the animal world around them.

Two panels from Bosch's workshop focus on the world after the Flood and after the Last Judgement (cat. 48a–b). Having observed humanity wrestling with good and evil for a long time and watching as sin took the upper hand, God decided to put an end to it all, while simultaneously protecting the good in his creation. That creation would be destroyed once and for all on Judgement Day, but there would be salvation even then for people of good will. There are no surviving Old Testament scenes by Hieronymus Bosch other than the *Flood panels* and the paradise wings of the *Garden of Earthly Delights*, the *Last Judgement* and the *Haywain triptychs*. There is plenty of attention, by contrast, for episodes from the New Testament: the advent of God's Son on earth, the Adoration of the Christ Child by the Magi (or the Kings) and above all the Passion of Christ (cat. 11–15). The Magi and the shepherds chose to come and honour the new-born king. The destiny of the Christ Child is made plain immediately in the most elaborate Adoration scene, as the closed triptych shows a visionary image which already depicts his Passion and Resurrection. The open triptych, meanwhile, also includes the menacing presence of the Antichrist, who must be defeated.

Bosch presents the story of the Passion very movingly. The Son of God allows himself to be humiliated, tortured and ultimately killed by humanity, in order to redeem that same humanity from original sin. The evil that entered the world under God's watchful eye is negated by the self-sacrifice of his son, who is at once God but also a man. Hieronymus Bosch manages to paint all this in such a way that the viewer understands his message. To do so, he deploys all the resources available to him: form, technique and choice of subject matter. Viewers have to recognize themselves both in the suffering Christ and in the sinners who are responsible for his suffering. This is about the individual's relationship with God. Not humanity in general, but each person individually. Seeing Bosch's paintings was supposed to inspire viewers to make the right choices: to follow Christ's example, to bear their own cross and to adopt Christian charity as their basic principle.

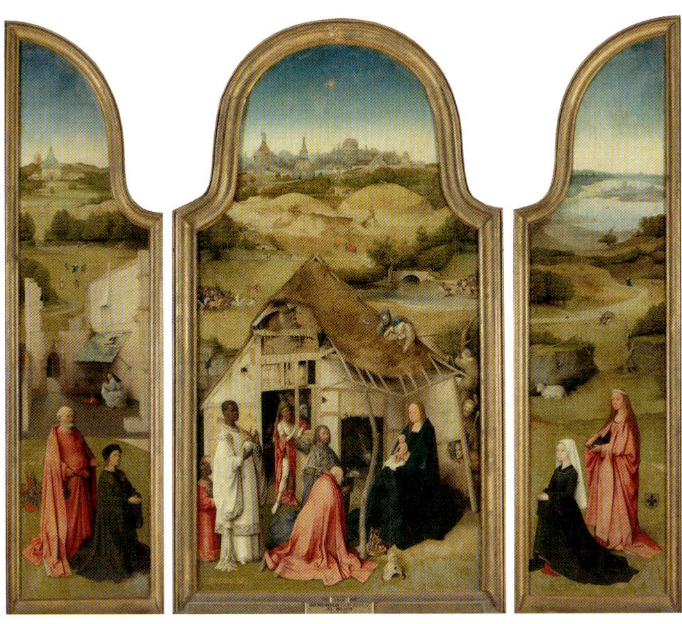

Hieronymus Bosch,
The Adoration of the Magi, 1490–1500
Oil on oak panel,
central panel 138 × 72 cm, wings 138 × 32 cm
Madrid, Museo Nacional del Prado, P02048

54　Hieronymus Bosch's *Garden of Earthly Delights* is the largest of his surviving works and probably the biggest triptych he painted (fig. p. 57). A traveller who saw the painting at the palace of the Counts of Nassau in Brussels as early as 1517 called it highly remarkable and extraordinary. It was most likely Henry III of Nassau, or his nephew Engelbert II, who commissioned the triptych, which came into Spanish ownership in the course of the sixteenth century. King Philip II had it transferred in 1593 to the monastery, mausoleum and palace he had founded at San Lorenzo de El Escorial. The painting did not enter a museum until 1939, when it was moved to the Prado.

There has been a great deal of writing and speculation as to the triptych's precise meaning. It was listed in the Escorial's records in 1593 as 'la bariedad del mundo', which is generally translated as 'the variety of the world'; it could be interpreted equally well, however, as the 'world's variety show' – the theatre or spectacle of human life. The visual account runs from the creation of the world to Judgement Day and hell. The closed shutters of the triptych contain a grisaille view of the beginning of world history. God the Father sits high in the upper left corner, above a transparent sphere containing the earth, of which living creatures have yet to take possession.

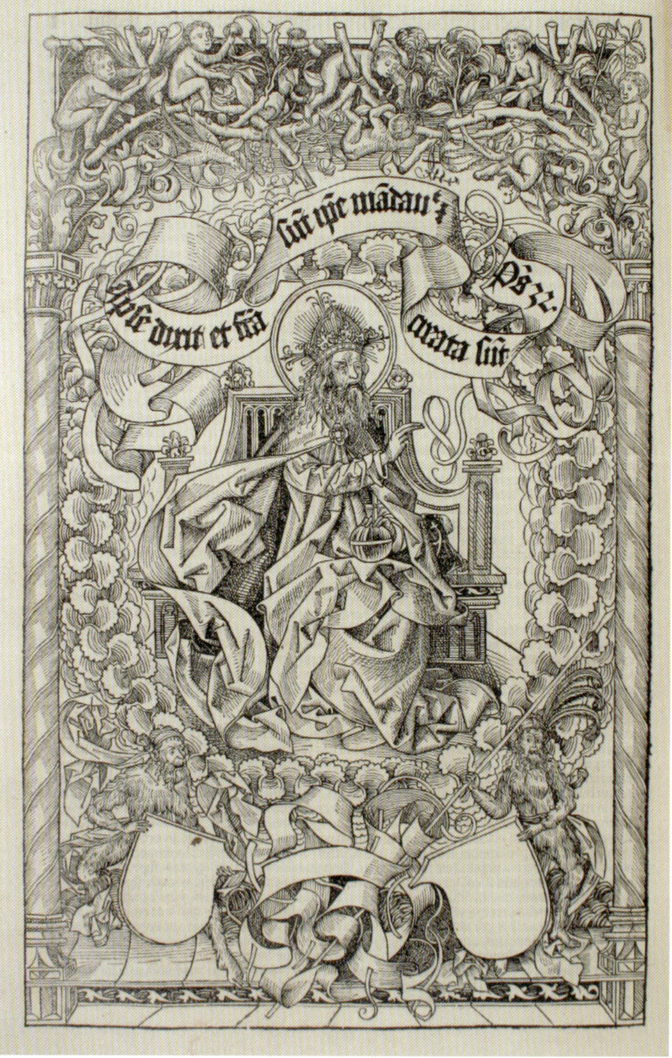

Hartmann Schedel, *Weltchronik*, Nuremberg, 1493, fol. 1: God the Father Sint Agatha, Erfgoedcentrum Nederlands Kloosterleven, Inc. 1

Follower of Hieronymus Bosch
Left wing of the *Garden of Earthly Delights*, c. 1520–30
The Creation of the World (exterior) and *The Garden of Eden* (interior)
Oil on oak panel, 186 × 77 cm
El Escorial, Patrimonio Nacional, Real Monasterio de San Lorenzo de
El Escorial. Depósito del Museo Nacional del Prado, P2053

When the triptych is opened, the desolate grey tones of the
very first days give way to a colourful expanse, twice as large,
devoted to the spectacle of human behaviour. The left wing,
set in the Garden of Eden, shows God introducing Eve to
Adam. At the same time, we see from the conduct of several of
the animals that evil has already entered this world too: a cat
has caught a mouse in the foreground, while a hybrid creature
spears a frog with its beak; a lion feasts on a deer in the
background. The central panel teems with naked people
engaged with one another and with the nature around them
in a manner that seems very harmonious and affectionate.
The right wing forms a powerful contrast, with demonic
monsters using countless human-made instruments to
torture the souls of the damned in every possible manner.

The dating of the *Garden of Earthly Delights* has also been
the subject of intense debate. The triptych is hard to place
stylistically, and in so far as the wood could be analysed
dendrochronologically, the date obtained was little help
either, as the triptych could have been painted from 1479
onwards. It seems clear, however, that Bosch based several
of his details on the *Weltchronik* ('World Chronicle') by
Hartmann Schedel – a book, illustrated with woodcuts, that
was published in Nuremberg in December 1493. Both the
figure of God the Father and the words he speaks can be
linked directly with the very first, full-page woodcut in that
book (fig. p. 54). The same goes for the Garden of Eden, with
the palm tree, the *dracaena* ('dragon tree') and the tree with
red fruit, around which the serpent has coiled itself, which
also feature in the *Weltchronik* (fig. p. 56). The implication
of this is that the triptych cannot have been painted before
1494 at the earliest. It was probably commissioned from
Hieronymus Bosch – along with several other prestigious
triptychs – by senior members of the Burgundian court in
the early sixteenth century.

The copy of the left wing is very close to the original, but not
in style and execution. It must have been painted in the 1520s,
when the original triptych was in Brussels.

Unusually, God the Father is depicted in the left wing of
the triptych in two very different ways. On the outside, which
shows the origin of the world, he is enthroned high in the sky
as a wise old man crowned with a tiara. He looks down on his
creation, which takes shape far below him. On the paradise
side, God the Father appears in the foreground with Adam
and Eve as a considerably younger man. He has the familiar
features of Christ, with wavy shoulder-length hair and a short
forked beard. It is entirely natural to a pious Christian that
God the Father, the Son and the Holy Spirit form a mystical
whole – the Holy Trinity. In Bosch's time too, therefore, the
difference in God's appearance on the inside and the outside

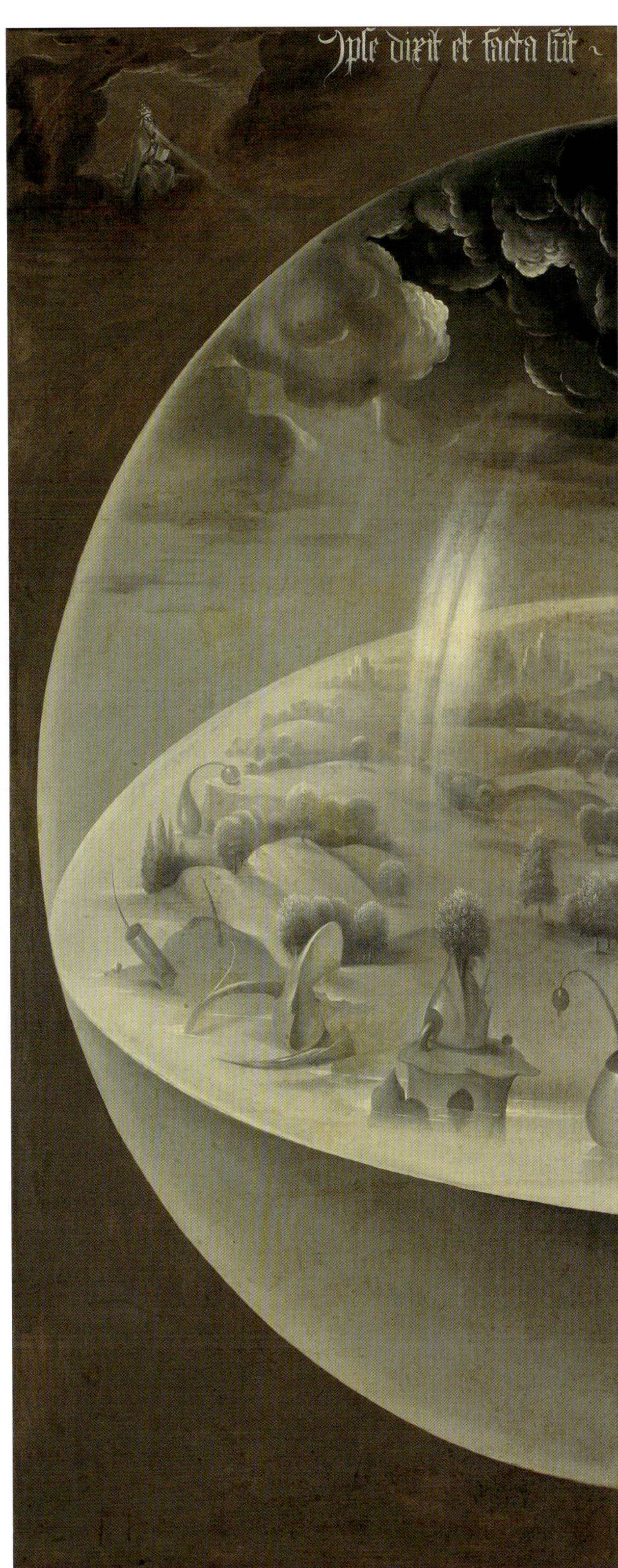

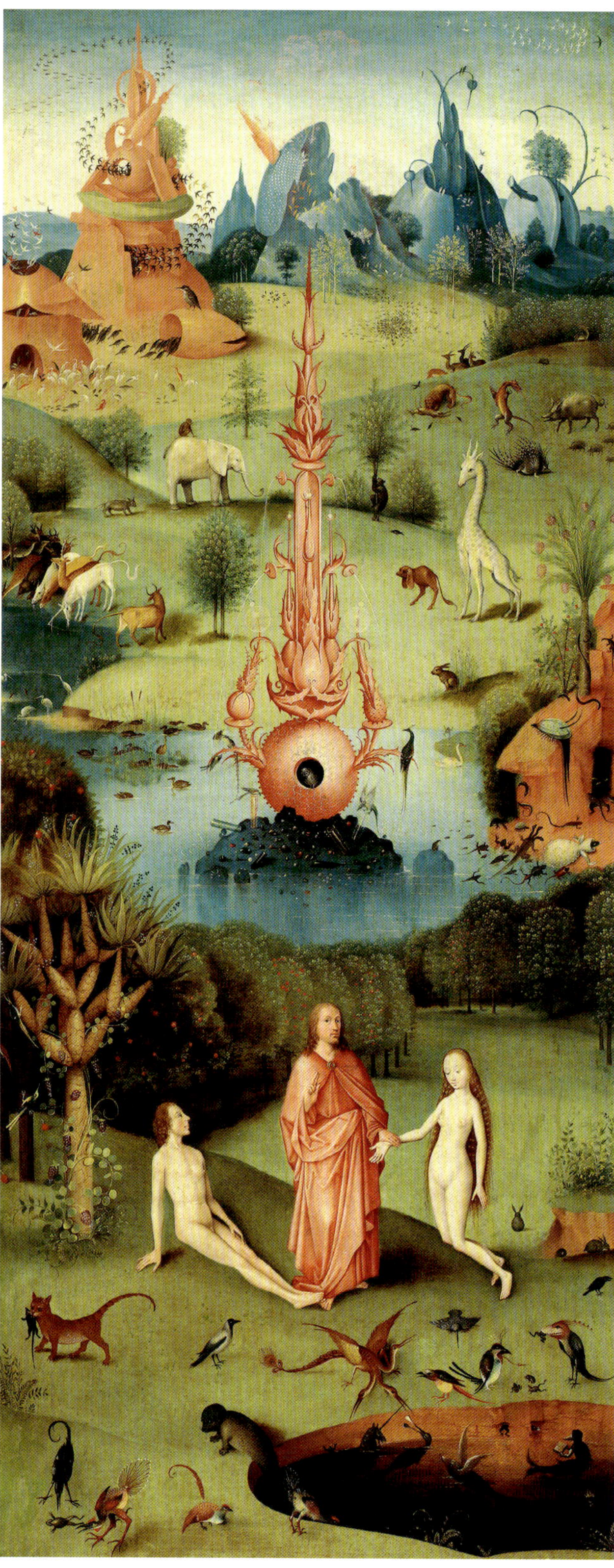

of the triptych wing will not have been confusing or unclear. The artist actually emphasizes Christ's words here from the Bible: 'The one who looks at me is seeing the one who sent me' (John 12:45). The depiction of the Father as Christ in a scene with Adam and Eve also looks forward in history, in the sense that Christ is the 'New Adam' through whom the death and the sin that entered the world with the first Adam will be vanquished. Jesus Christ, the Son, is God *and* Man, and came to the world to redeem humanity from original sin through his death. It is for that reason that Hieronymus Bosch depicted God in the Garden of Eden – before the Fall of Man and the advent of original sin – in a shape we associate first and foremost with Christ. The contrast between the two figures of God is even more direct in the paradise wing of Bosch's *Last Judgement* in Vienna (fig. p. 159), in which the Father is enthroned high in the firmament as an elderly sovereign, surrounded by the angelic host and the Fall of the Rebel Angels. We see him again in a different guise, far below in the foreground of the Garden of Eden, where he is a man in the prime of his life: an image that is familiar to us as his son, Jesus Christ, come to earth.

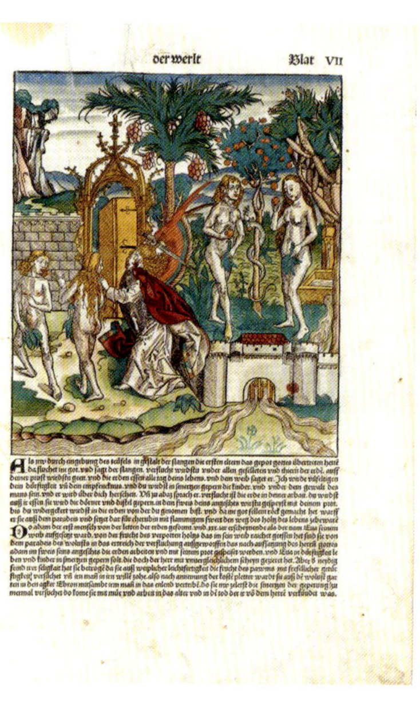

Hartmann Schedel, *Weltchronik*, Nuremberg, 1493, fol. 1: The Fall of Man

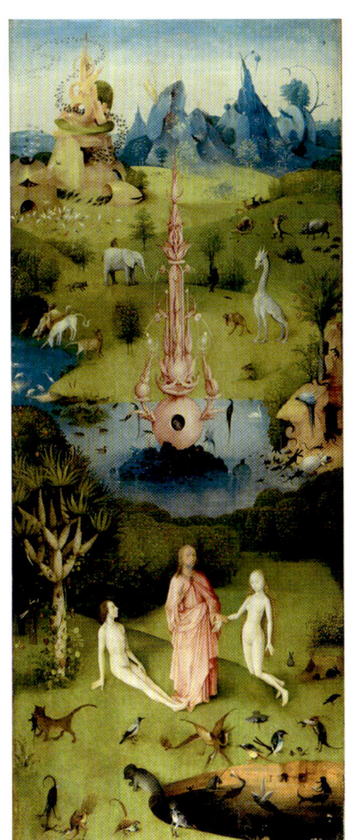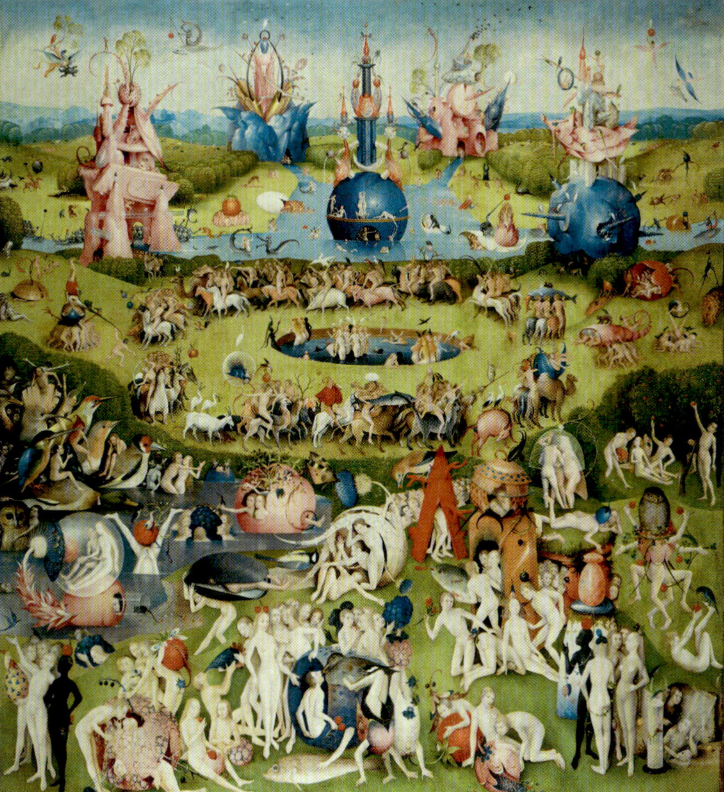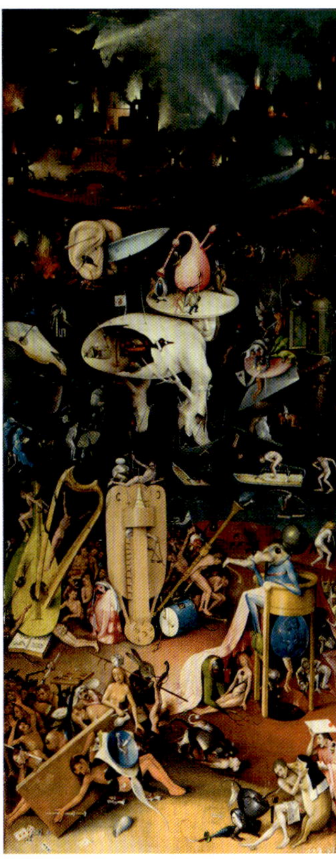

Hieronymus Bosch,
The Garden of Earthly Delights, c. 1495–1505
Oil on oak panel, central panel 190 × 175 cm,
wings 187.5 × 76.5 cm
Madrid, Museo Nacional del Prado, P2823
(on loan from the Patrimonio Nacional)

Hieronymus Bosch
The Adoration of the Magi, c. 1470–80
Oil on oak panel, 71.1 × 56.7 cm
New York, The Metropolitan Museum of Art,
John Stewart Kennedy Fund, 1913, 13.26

The painting of the Magi paying tribute to the Christ Child on his mother's lap is likely to have been done relatively early in Bosch's career. Dendrochronological dating of the panel shows it could have been painted from 1470 onwards, slightly earlier than the Frankfurt *Ecce Homo* (cat. 14), which could have been done from 1472. The panel is not signed but is attributed to Bosch on stylistic grounds. Several details are typical of the artist, including the finely painted view in the distance, with the outline of a city on the horizon to the left, bands of horsemen advancing between the hills, the shepherds with their flocks, and the couple followed by a little dog crossing a bridge on the right. Mary's head, for instance, with its wavy hair, rendered glossy by lead-tin yellow applied with a fine brush, and her subtly lowered eyelids also match perfectly the way Eve and other women are represented in the *Garden of Earthly Delights*. If we look closely at the head of the Christ Child, we can only conclude that it was painted by the same hand as the slightly older child with a toy windmill that appears on the back of *Christ Carrying the Cross* in Vienna (cat. 15). It was precisely for reasons like this that the Metropolitan Museum of Art in New York bought the painting in 1904 as an autograph work by Hieronymus Bosch. Doubt was cast on this attribution in 1930, but since the 2001 Bosch exhibition in Rotterdam, it has once more been generally accepted that the *Adoration of the Magi* was painted by Bosch himself.

As far as we can tell from his surviving paintings, the generous use of gold leaf here is unusual for Bosch. It is found in the cloth over the elevation on which Mary is sitting, the clothes and attributes of the Magi, and the wings of the angels high up above them. The gold was applied over a red base layer and then painted with a fine brush to add relief and detail. The small but brilliant star shining upper centre over the scene is painted, by contrast, in bright yellow.

The viewer is struck by the strong perspective effect, with orthogonals running more or less to a single vanishing point, which turns the building into a huge space. The angels holding up a cloth of honour for the Virgin and Child are positioned quite a long way behind them. Two angels originally held the green cloth on the left too, but the rearmost figure was subsequently painted out. There was also an angel in the large window-frame high in the tower, now concealed beneath dark overpainting and the little dove. The way the ox and the ass are rendered at the bottom of the fortified tower is a striking detail: the ox is shown kneeling and looking sideways at Mary with her baby and the Three Kings. All we see of the donkey, by contrast, which has turned away from the central event, is its hindquarters. The New Testament does not actually mention either animal, but they do feature in the

Old Testament. The Prophet Isaiah describes how God, incensed by a rebellion on the part of his people, declared that 'The ox knows its master, the donkey its owner's manger, but Israel does not know, my people do not understand' (Isaiah 1:3). The passage was first linked with the story of the Nativity as early as the beginning of the third century, with the ox – considered a clean animal – representing those who follow God's word, and the unclean donkey those who turn their faces against him. It will, therefore, have been a deliberate choice on Bosch's part to represent the ox and the ass this way.

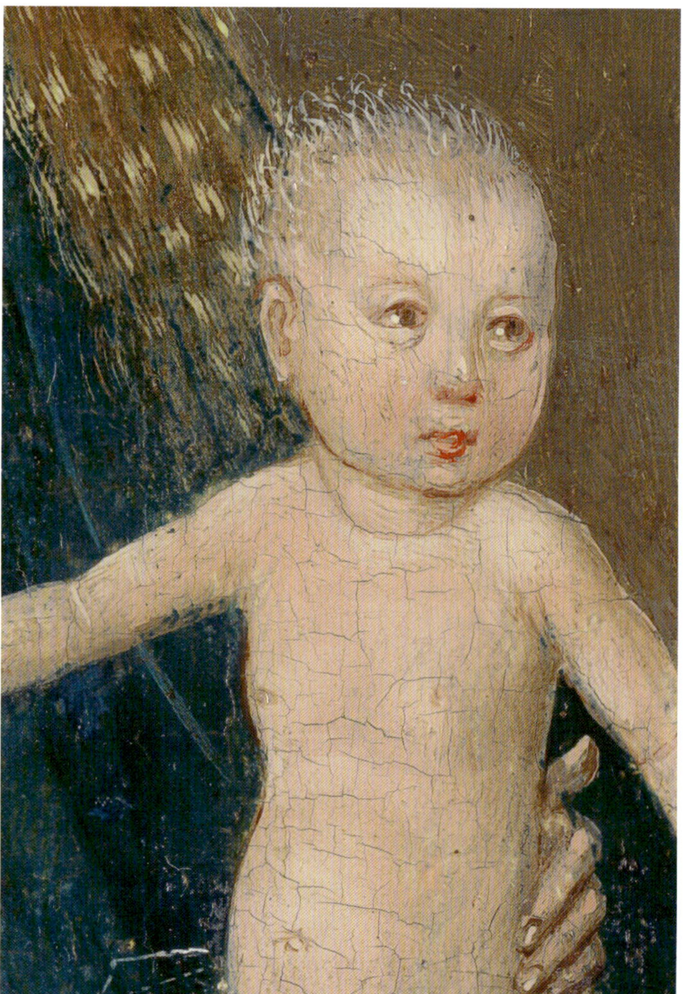

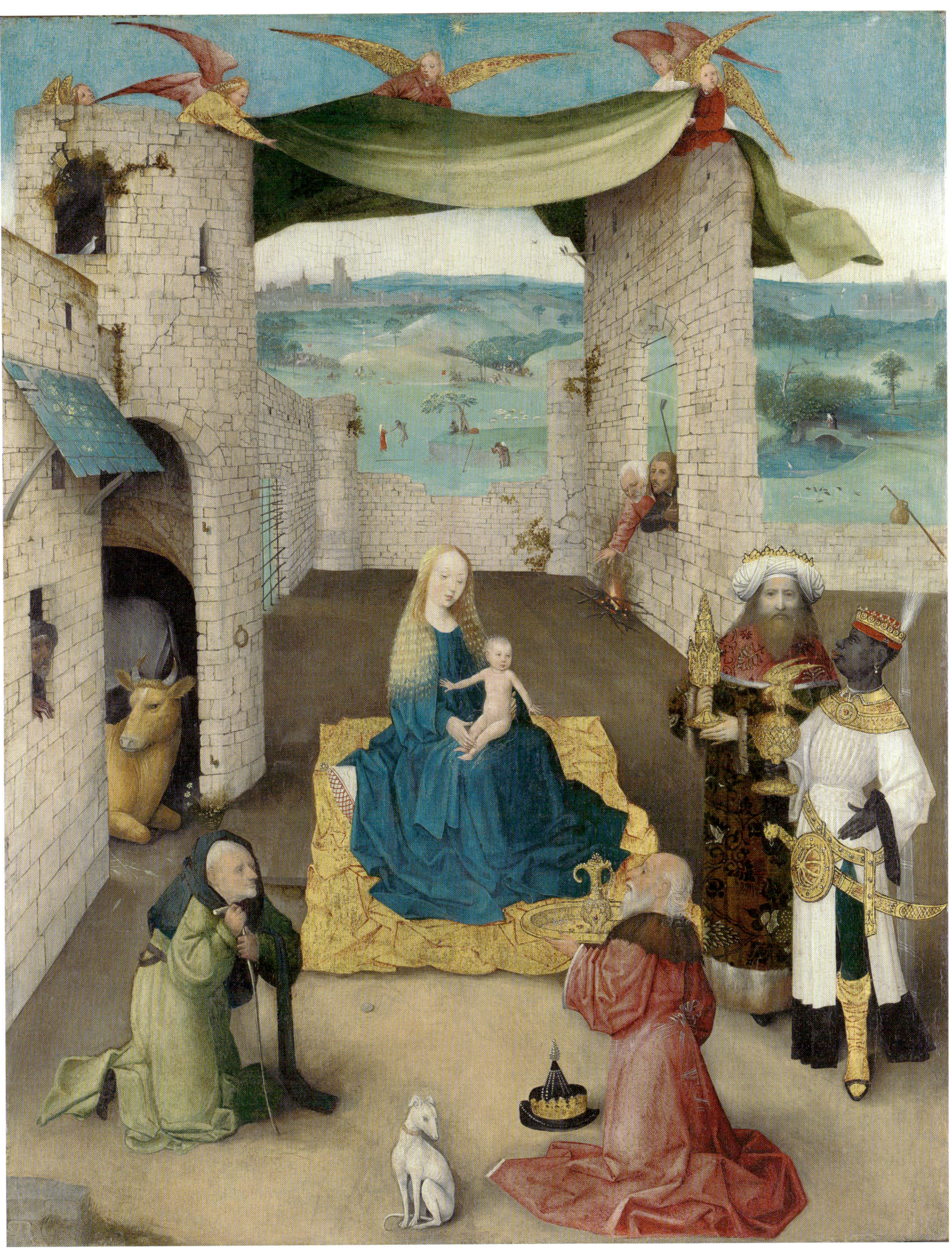

The Magi have brought their gifts to the new-born king.
Melchior, the oldest king, kneels and has placed his crown
on the ground respectfully. He offers a gold dish and jug.
The jar held by the black king is decorated with a phoenix,
a bird associated with fire, indicating that the contents will
be frankincense. The pot offered by the third king must
then contain fragrant myrrh. Christ's elderly adoptive father,
Joseph, is positioned at something of a distance from the
Adoration; a shepherd peers through a window behind him.
A little higher up, in a niche beneath the awning, we make
out an owl – the bird that crops up time and again in Bosch's
paintings.

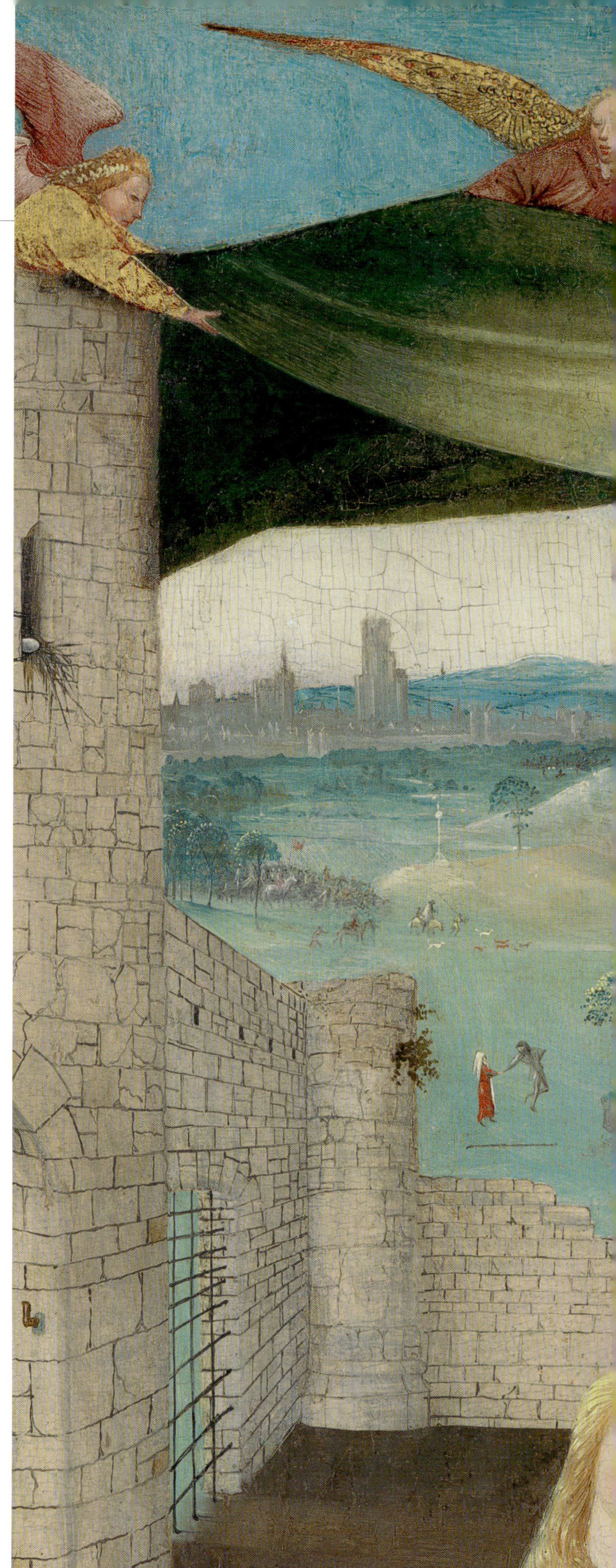

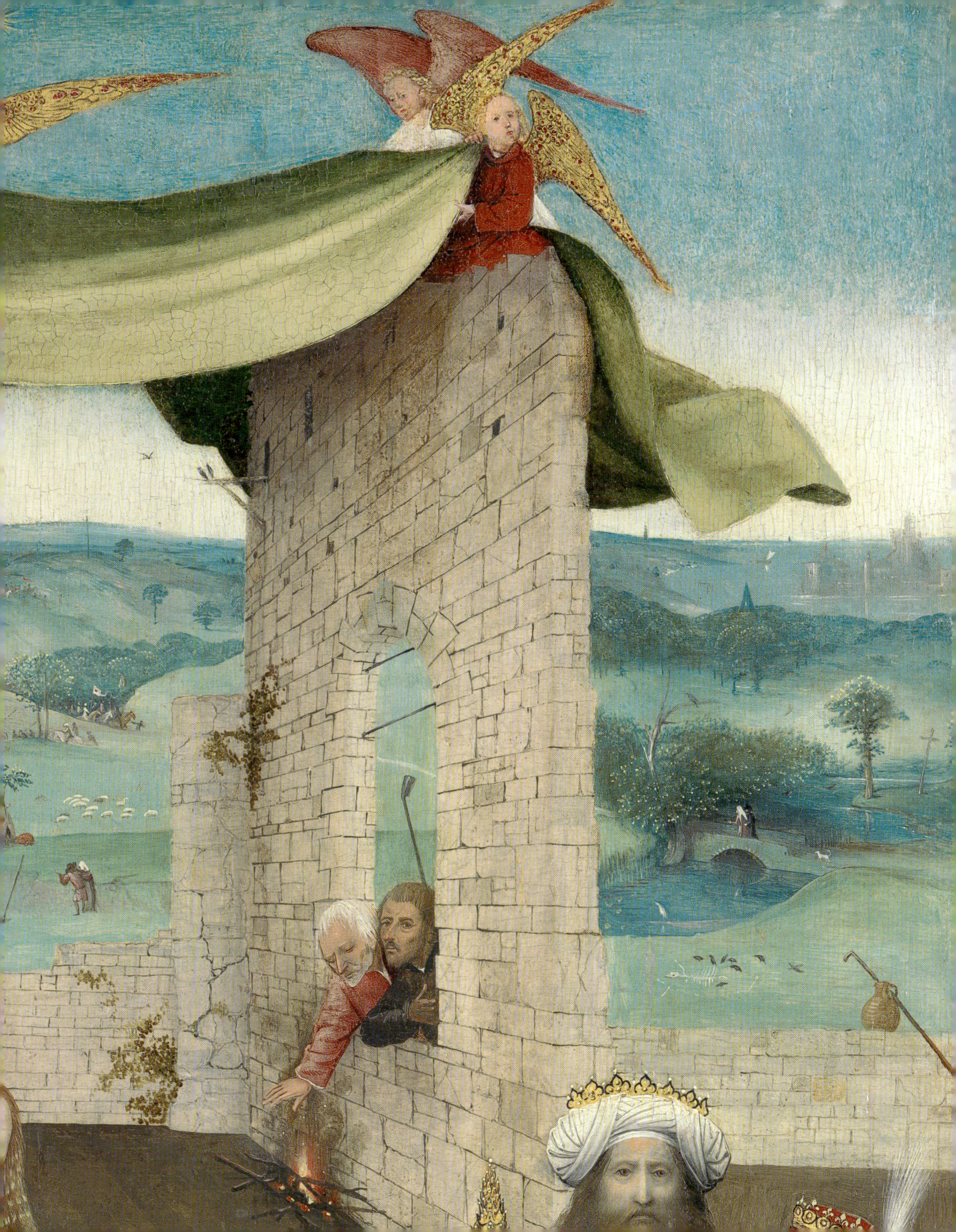

Workshop of Hieronymus Bosch
The Adoration of the Magi, c. 1495–1520
Oil on oak panel, 77.5 × 55.9 cm
Philadelphia Museum of Art, John G. Johnson
Collection, 1917, 1321

62

Together with the paintings in Madrid (fig. p. 53) and New York (cat. 11), this is the third *Adoration of the Magi* to be linked to Bosch. There are substantial differences between the three paintings, not only in terms of presentation, but stylistically and compositionally too. What strikes the viewer immediately on seeing the painting in Philadelphia is the strange spatial effect of the architecture. Mary sits at an angle behind the wall on the left, which runs up to the thatched roof of the stable. This ought to mean that the figures are located largely beneath the thatch; in the painting, however, it seems as though the roof – which is, moreover, disproportionately small – is positioned much further back. The interior of the stable is also impossible to read in perspective terms. All this differs sharply from the *Adorations* we know from Madrid and New York, in which the painter might also have wrestled with the spatial effect, but where the perspective is nevertheless substantially more accurate.

When this panel was first presented in 1914, it was viewed fairly generally as an early work, if not Bosch's earliest. Because of its somewhat inferior quality, however, it has rarely been linked with the painter in recent decades. All the same, various elements in the painting correspond with details that are generally ascribed to Bosch. The ox, which is shown here standing in the stable, is very similar, for instance, to the ox in the *Wayfarer* (cat. 1). The gift held by the black king is painted in loose and sketchy but confident strokes reminiscent of Bosch's painting style.

The six most important figures in the painting are placed around the table in the middle of the scene. The Virgin Mary, with the Christ Child on her lap, sits on the longest side, nearest to the viewer. The oldest king presents his gift to the infant. Jesus reaches out enthusiastically for the gilded object, full of grains of frankincense or myrrh. The two other Wise Men wait their turn further to the right. The black king has a gold object with Gothic decoration similar to the ciborium held by the king in the middle of the New York panel. As in that painting, the king in the middle makes eye contact with the viewer, as if he or she were really present on the historic occasion and could be seen by the figures in the painting.

We can see clearly from the black king's white sleeve that the surface of the paint has suffered severe localized damage. The wide hanging sleeve is embroidered with the shower of manna, which flutters down from a cloud and is caught and gathered by the starving Israelites. Christians viewed this Old Testament story as a prefiguration of the advent of Christ, whose body and blood in the form of the Eucharist would offer help and spiritual sustenance to worshippers. The table in the middle of the scene might also be a reference to the Last Supper and the Eucharist. Just as the manna came to the Israelites, Christ came to all humanity, and it is his advent that is celebrated in the painting. The gold leaf has worn off the mordant of the embroidered sleeve almost entirely, as it has from the Kings' gifts, as a result of which the scene is now hard to read.

The restoration of the panel in 2014–15 has given the painting back something of its original condition, which ought to assist in its attribution. The work was dendrochronologically analysed in 1987; the annual growth rings in the wood of the panels were counted to arrive at the most recent possible date. This analysis shows that the painting could have been done from 1493 onwards, which means that the Philadelphia *Adoration* cannot have been an early work by Bosch, who was born around 1450 and would have been aged about forty-five in 1495. In so far as the work was still considered to be that of Bosch after the dendrochronological study, it was dated to late in his career. Most authors view it, however, as a product of the master's workshop. Stylistic and qualitative differences compared to the Madrid and New York *Adorations*, for example, virtually rule out the possibility that this is an entirely autograph work by Bosch. Given the painting's affinities with other works that are believed to be by the master himself, it seems most plausible that it was produced in his workshop.

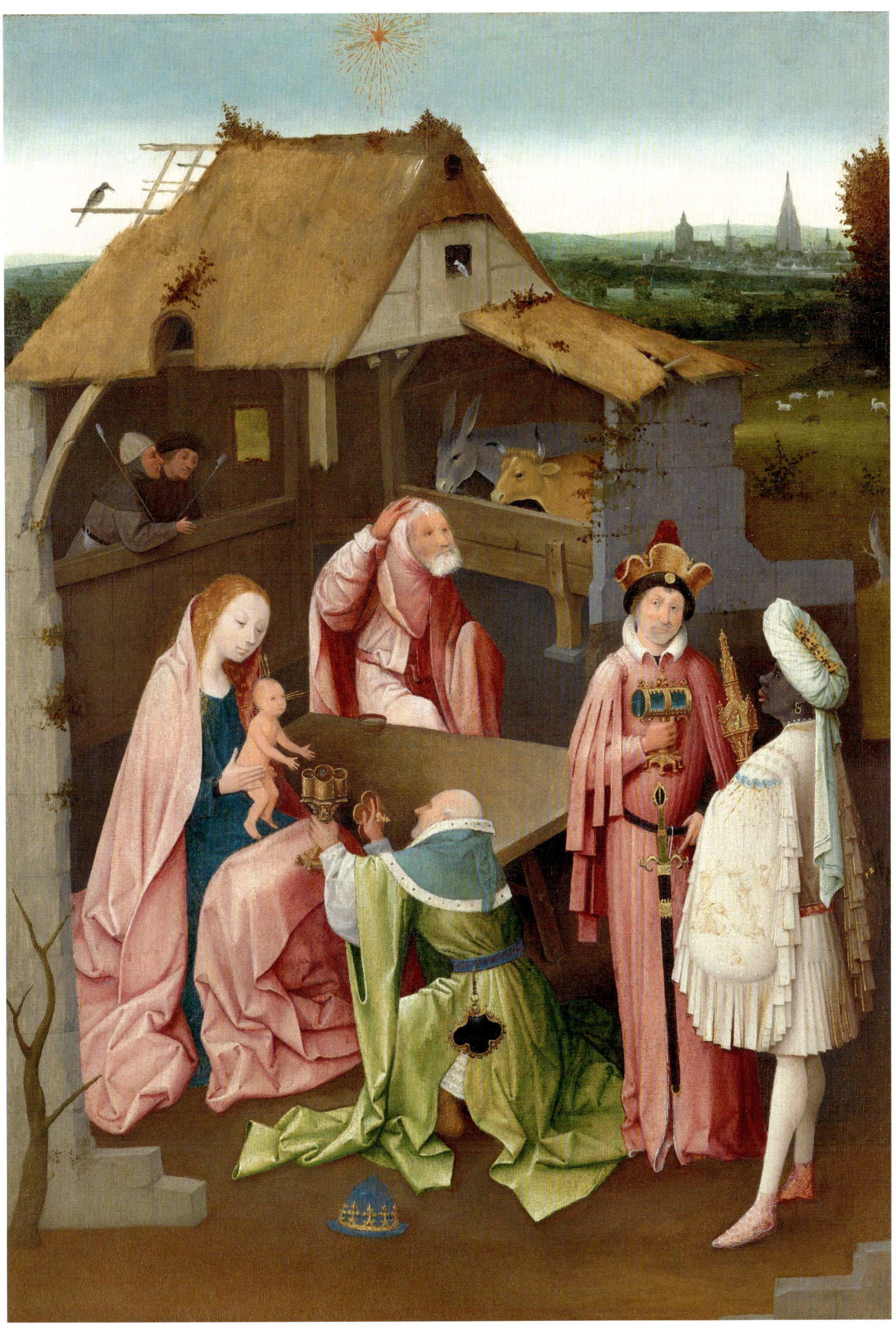

64 Until the late nineteenth century the large and dramatic
Passion Triptych in Valencia was still considered an original
work by Hieronymus Bosch, as suggested by the clear
signature lower left in the central panel. But around 1900 the
attribution was being questioned, and ever since, the triptych
has generally been regarded as a work in the style of Bosch.
The principal scene of the *Crowning with Thorns* is flanked
by the *Arrest of Christ* and the *Flagellation*. The three scenes
are placed against a gold ground, surrounded in turn by
deep darkness. Angels painted in grisaille do battle with
fire-breathing demons in the corners around them. The
composition of the three Passion episodes is strongly
interrelated, with six, five and four men respectively grouped
around the Christ figure at the centre. Four guards take Christ
prisoner in the left wing. Peter is shown in the foreground,
on the point of cutting off the ear of one of the officers,
while James towers above the group at the back. In the scene
in the middle, the crown of thorns is placed on Christ's head,
while the Roman governor Pontius Pilate and the high priest,
Caiaphas, look on. Christ is flogged on the right. The exterior
wings are painted with imitation stone.

The central panel differs stylistically in its painting and
preparatory underdrawing from the *Arrest* and the *Flagellation*,
which are closely related to one another. It is thought,
therefore, that these images were inspired by the *Crowning
with Thorns* and were added to it to form a monumental
triptych. This was probably done in Antwerp in the years
1530/33–39 and in the years 1540 on the order of the Spanish
princess Mencía de Mendoza – the third wife of Count
Henry III of Nassau (1483–1538). She definitively returned to
Spain as a widow in 1538 and had her possessions shipped
there from the Low Countries. Following her death in 1554,
the triptych was placed in her memorial chapel, the Capilla
de los Reyes in the Dominican monastery in Valencia, where
the central panel was installed as one altarpiece, and the
two wings as another. The frames of the respective panels
were probably fitted in the years 1540–50 in Antwerp. Since
the confiscation of Church property in the second quarter of

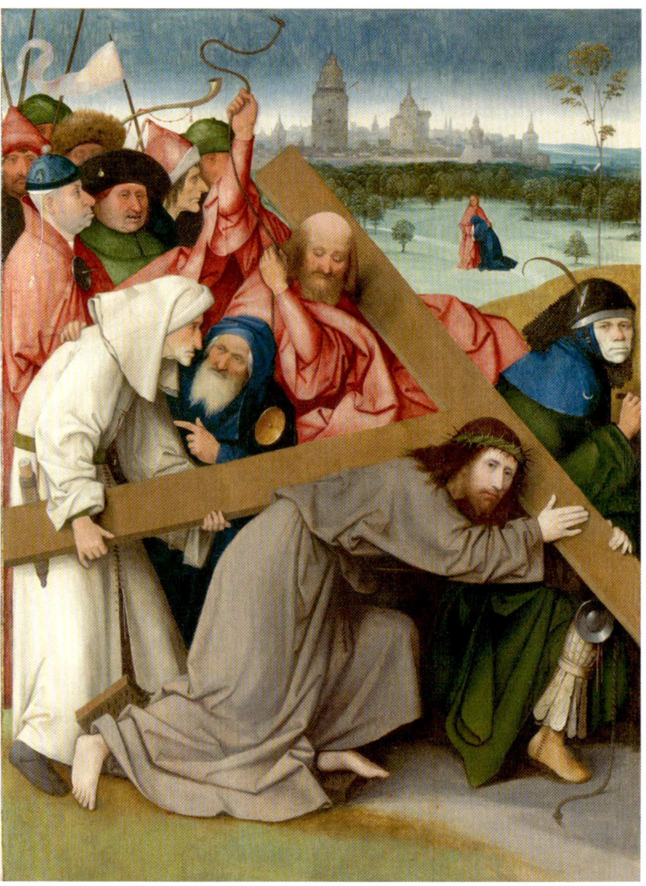

Hieronymus Bosch
Christ Carrying the Cross, c. 1495–1505
Oil on oak panel, 142.8 × 104.3 cm
El Escorial, Patrimonio Nacional,
Real Monasterio de San Lorenzo de
El Escorial, 10014739

Follower of Hieronymus Bosch
The Arrest, Crowning with Thorns and Flagellation of Christ,
c. 1530–40 (central panel) and 1540–50 (wings)
Oil on oak panel, left wing 152.2 × 85.6 cm,
central panel 139.7 × 170.2 cm, right wing 152.4 × 84.5 cm
Valencia, Museo de Bellas Artes de Valencia, 264–266

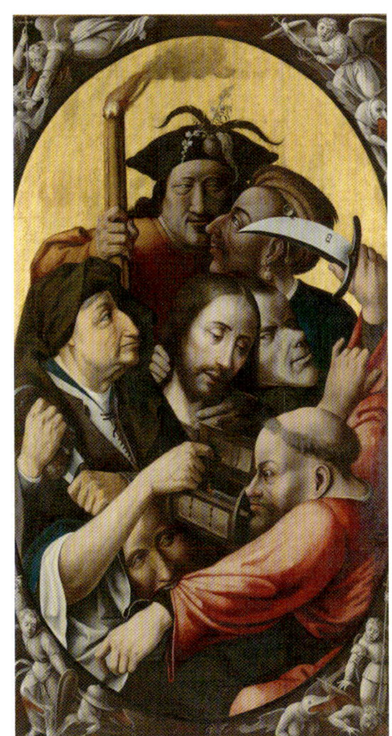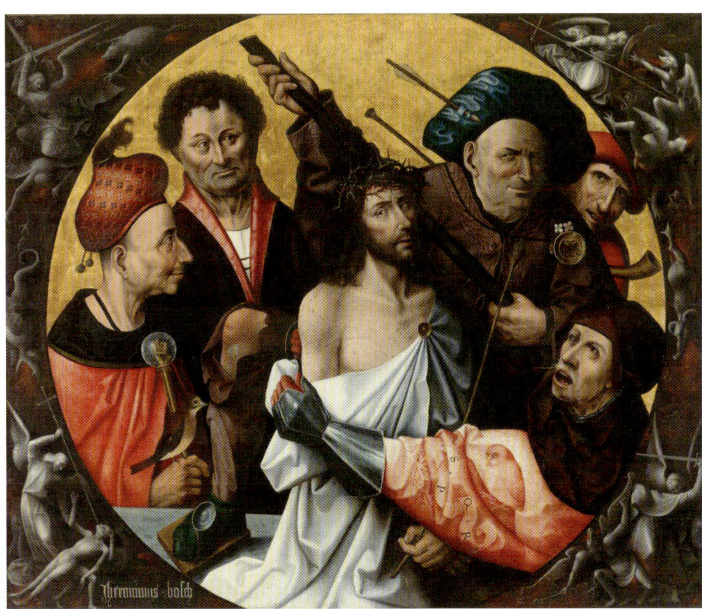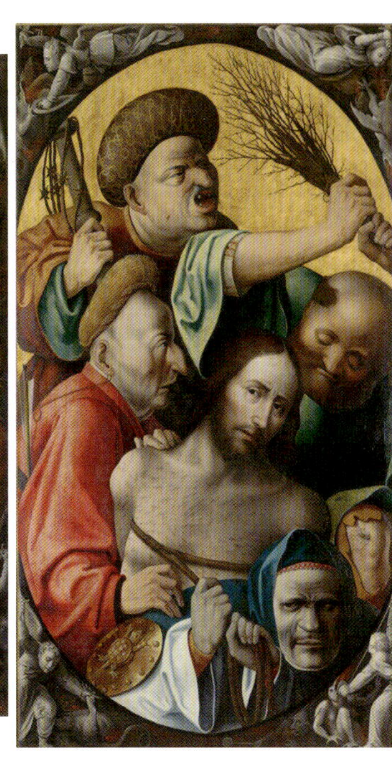

the nineteenth century, the triptych has been kept at the museum of art in Valencia.

Mencía de Mendoza was familiar with and admired the work of Hieronymus Bosch. The *Garden of Earthly Delights* hung in the palace of the Counts of Nassau in Brussels, where she regularly stayed during her time in the Low Countries. After she returned to Spain, she instructed her agent in Antwerp to acquire a version of the *Haywain* (cat. 5) for her, and the inventory of her estate listed three paintings by Bosch on canvas. There is no way of telling at this remove whether they really were by him. Like the *Passion Triptych*, they are more likely to have been paintings in his style. That work belongs to a group of paintings with large figures by imitators of Bosch, probably working in Antwerp, all of which are notable for their exaggerated, caricature-like heads. The celebrated *Christ Carrying the Cross* in Ghent also belongs to this group. The artists who produced these paintings were familiar with Hieronymus Bosch's original work, as suggested, for instance,

by the fairly accurately imitated signature on the *Passion Triptych*. Further evidence is provided by a number of details, including the letter 'M' on Peter's sword, which also features on the knife-blade in the *Garden of Earthly Delights* and in the *Last Judgements* in Vienna and Bruges (cat. 49). Several of the heads in the *Arrest of Christ* and the *Flagellation* seem to have been inspired by figures in the Escorial *Christ Carrying the Cross*. The owl, the banderole, the thorn branches and the pearls on the officer's red sleeve in the central panel are directly comparable with the embroidered hose of the man in the foreground of the *Saint Wilgefortis Triptych* (cat. 41).

On account of its style and painting technique the *Passion Triptych* cannot have been painted during Bosch's lifetime. This is also apparent from the physiognomy of the angels and demons surrounding the three Passion scenes, the decoration of the sword of the man on the far left in the *Arrest of Christ* and the *trompe-l'oeil* bee on the bared knee of the torturer on the far right of the *Flagellation* (fig. p. 66).

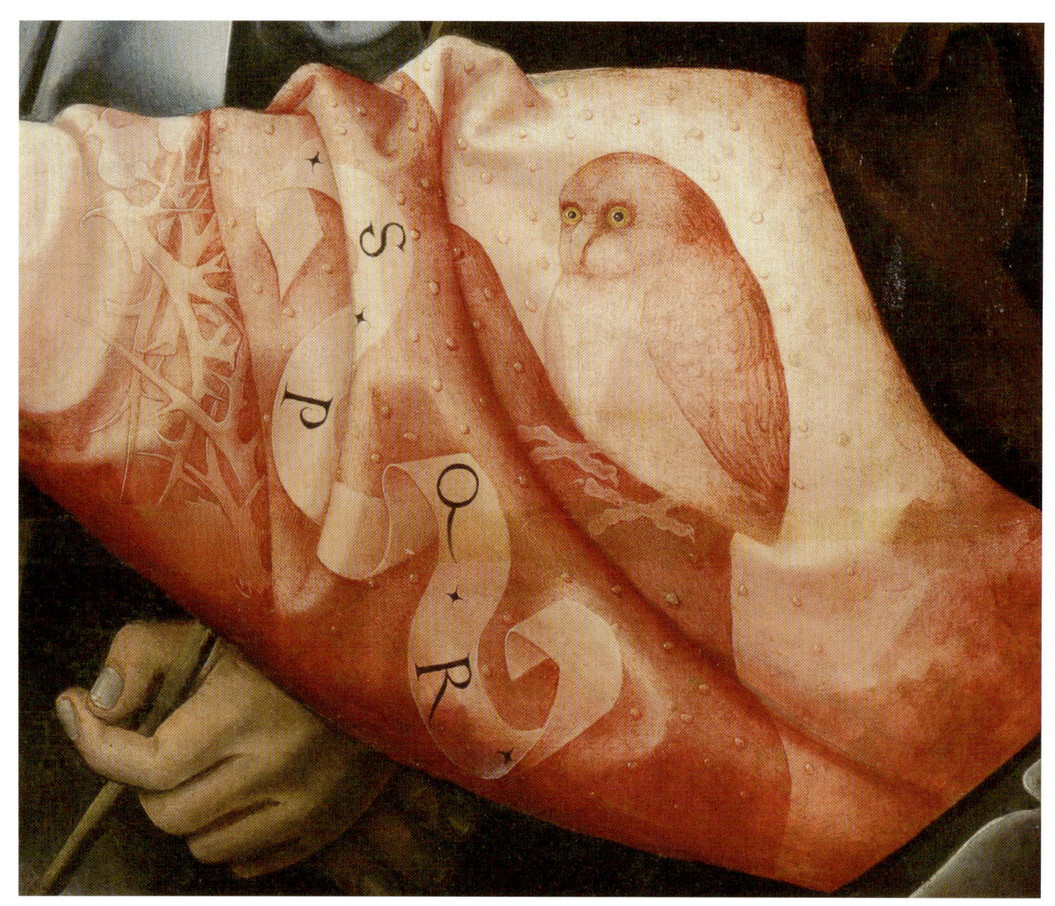

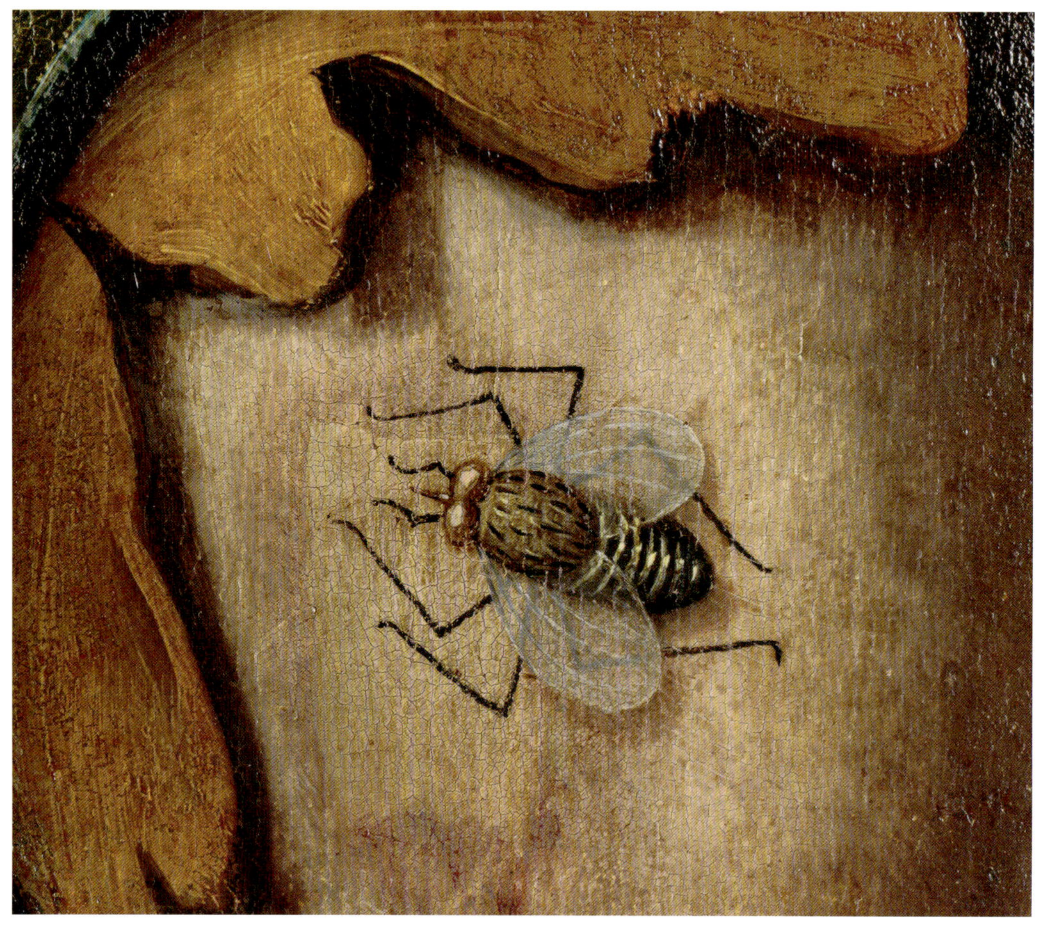

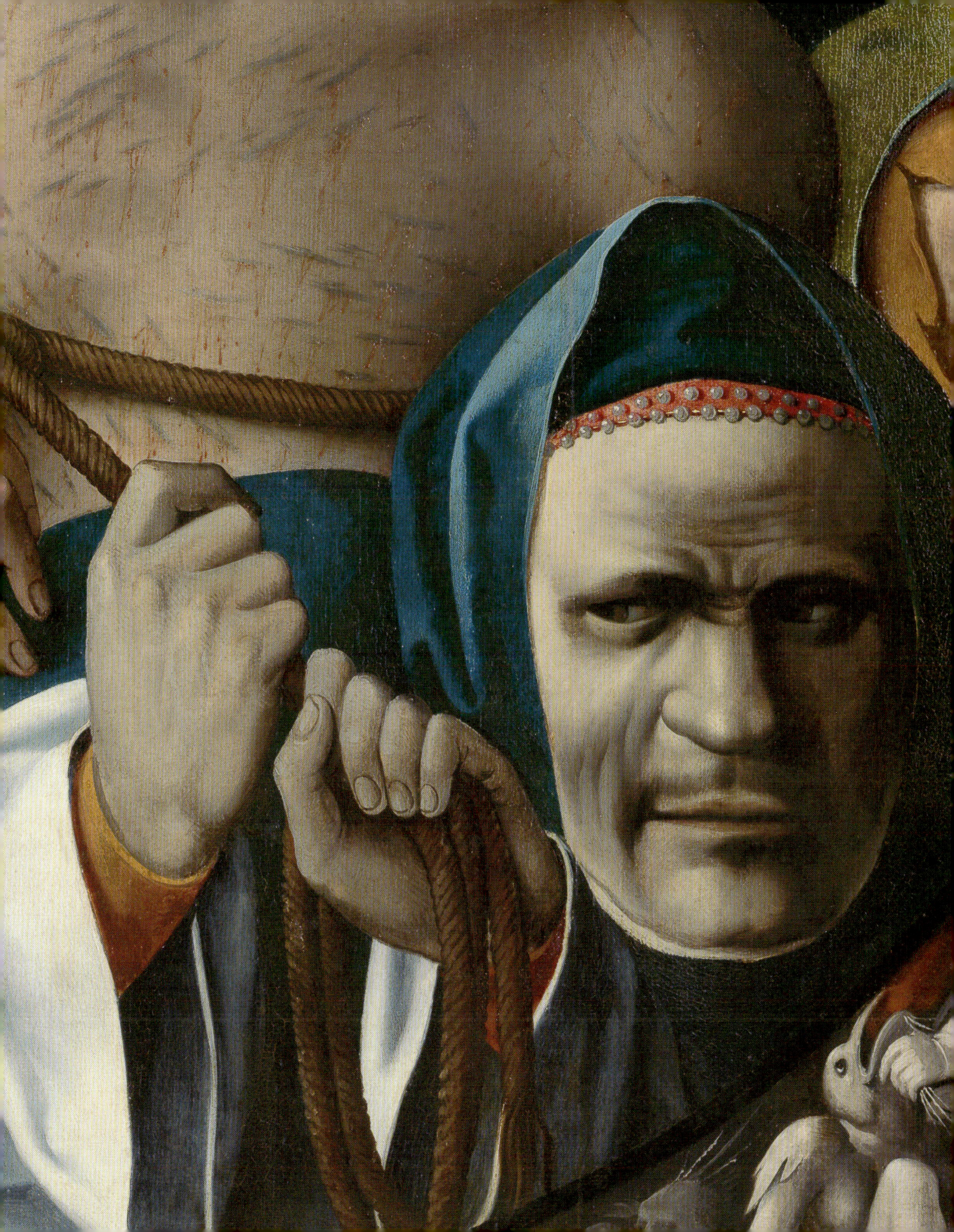

It is clear at first glance that something odd is going on with this painting. The panel shows a traditional scene from the Passion cycle, in which the tortured Christ is displayed to an angry crowd. In the foreground, however, we also vaguely make out a large donor family: a kneeling man can be seen on the left, followed immediately by the relatively large figure of a monk and by the heads of six boys. Six girls' heads appear on the right. Infrared and X-ray photographs reveal that there was originally a kneeling woman opposite the man, no doubt his wife and the mother of the various girls and boys. The family group was planned from the outset and therefore formed part of the original purpose of the panel as a memorial painting. Ironically, that memorial function lapsed at some point and the panel was fundamentally altered by painting out the whole fifteen-headed donor family. The overpainting faded over time, however, and when an X-ray photograph was taken in the 1930s, the concealed donor family was rediscovered beneath the unsightly dark patches. During the panel's thorough restoration in 1983, it was decided to remove the old overpainting and to restore the original composition as far as possible. This resulted in the current state, with the ghostly family in the foreground. We do not know the identity of the painting's donors or in which church or chapel it was to be installed as a memorial.

The *Ecce Homo* is the only autograph painting by Hieronymus Bosch to contain an inscription with words spoken by the depicted characters. Pontius Pilate, the Roman prefect, points to Jesus and declares 'ecce homo' ('behold the man'). The crowd of people looking up at him call out 'crucifige eum' ('crucify him'). The monk in the foreground, now visible again, prays for his family: 'Salva nos christe redemptor' – 'Christ, Redeemer, save us.' The lettering was done using oil gilding – gold leaf laid onto mordant – as were the rays of the cross nimbus behind Christ's head and the slender judge's staff held by Pilate. Gold leaf, which we also find in the *Adoration of the Magi* in New York (cat. 11), generally appears only rarely in Bosch.

Hieronymus Bosch does something new in this painting compared to the visual tradition of *Ecce Homo* scenes by opening up the composition and adding a view of a city. The little figures – laid down with a few strokes of a fine paintbrush – who are already out and about in Jerusalem at this early hour seem oblivious to the summary justice being meted out so dramatically. Bosch's hand can be recognized in this distant view, which is 'drawn in paint' rather than painted as such; we also find it in details like the familiar little owl, shown here high up in a niche in the wall, and in the flames of the torch carried by one of the bystanders. The torch, which was painted wet-in-wet, is a striking detail, given that the scene is set in daylight and with a clear sky; it emphasizes the haste with which Christ was arrested, just before daybreak, and then tried and sentenced. The subtle detail enables Bosch to heighten the sense of injustice at this kangaroo court.

Bosch referred for his composition to *Ecce Homo* engravings by Martin Schongauer and Israhel van Meckenem, although he certainly did not follow these slavishly; this is evident, for instance, from the view of the quiet town square in the distance. The two groups of men (there is not a single woman here) are positioned in a balanced but dynamic way to form an interlocking sequence of malicious faces. Christ, presented as the 'King of the Jews', is the victim; his bloody footprint and the wounds that cover his body highlight the sacrifice he is about to make on humanity's behalf. Bosch wants the viewer of the painting to notice this and to digest the full implications.

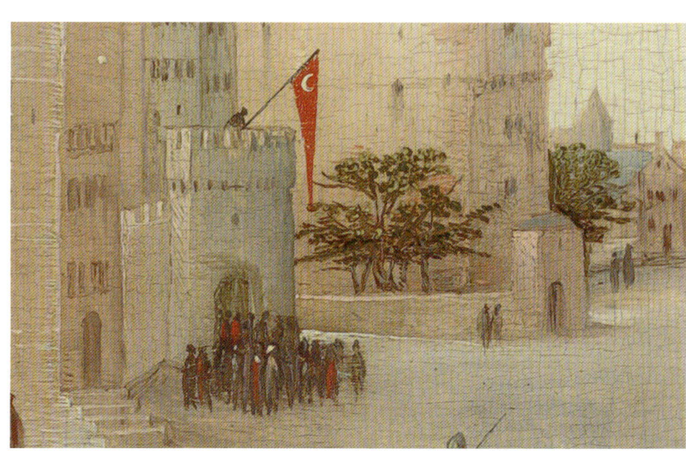

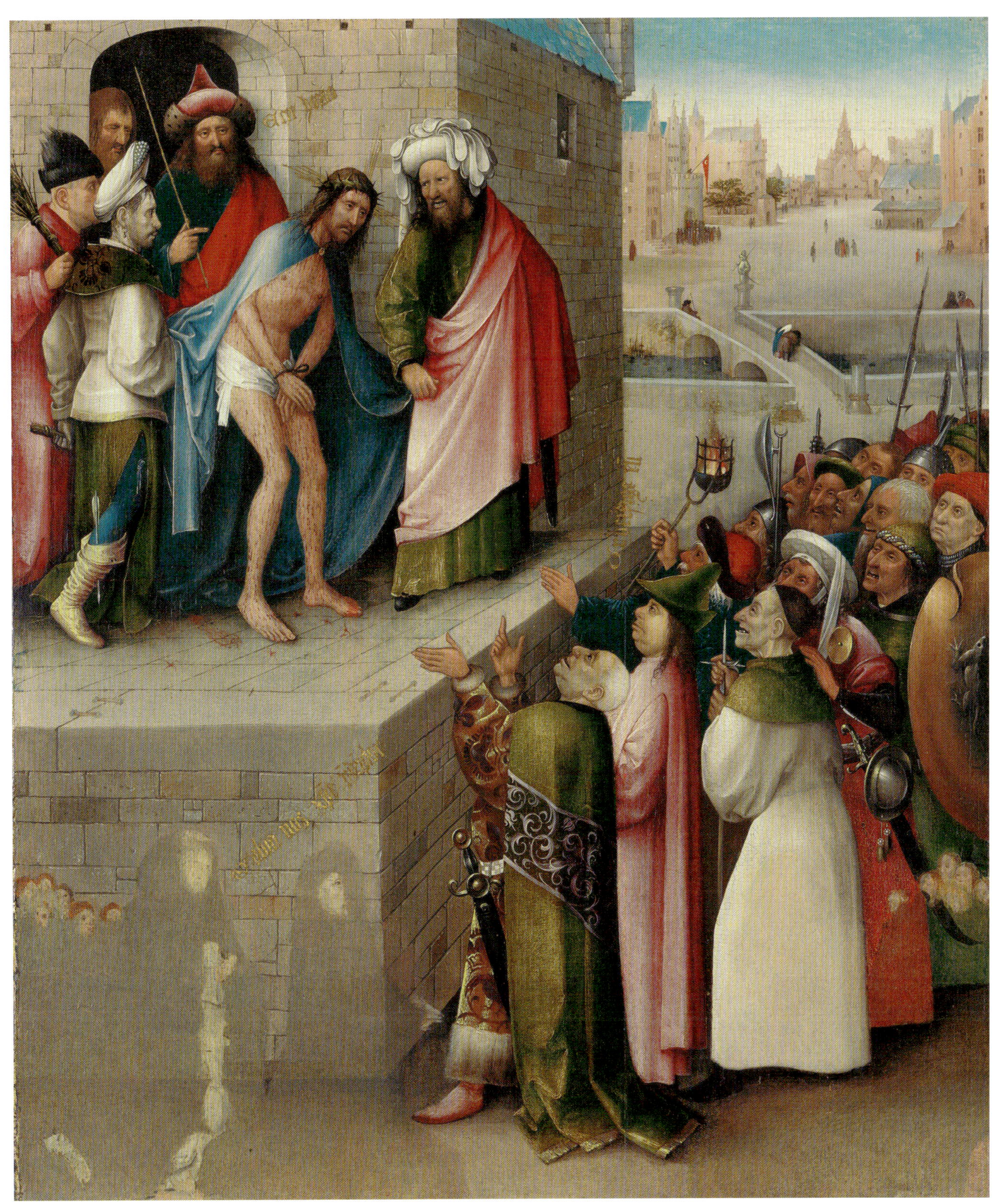

Hieronymus Bosch
Ecce Homo, c. 1475–85
Oil on oak panel, 71.4 × 61 cm
Frankfurt am Main, Städel Museum, Eigentum
des Städelschen Museums-Vereins e.V., 1577

70 Hieronymus Bosch painted this double-sided panel as the left wing of a triptych. It shows a naked child with a toy windmill on one side and *Christ Carrying the Cross* on the other. The beginning of a rounded corner can be seen in the upper right of the panel, above the struggling figure of Christ. The wing was originally about 23–25 cm taller at the top and a strip of the painted surface is missing from the bottom too. Nothing is known about the corresponding right wing or the central panel, which will have had a semi-circular top, although the open triptych as a whole is likely to have been devoted to the Passion of Christ.

The closed triptych will also have had a tondo on the right shutter. The two tondi together formed a coherent whole, and must have served as an introduction to the scenes displayed when the triptych was opened. The little boy trying to stay on his feet behind the little walking frame is located in the exact spot where Christ is shown on the other side of the panel hauling the heavy cross on his back. It is logical, therefore, to identify him as the Christ Child. The opposite tondo probably showed John the Baptist as a child, also clutching a windmill, and coming to meet the young Jesus. Various fifteenth-century examples have survived in book illuminations and prints of Jesus and John as toddlers. Stories – obviously apocryphal – about Christ's childhood were popular in the late Middle Ages and often featured content that could be interpreted as a prefiguration of events later in his life. Popular devotion found it entirely natural that John and Jesus would have grown up together; the Bible describes, after all, how their respective mothers – Mary and her cousin Elizabeth – met during their pregnancies (Luke 1:39–56), an event that was celebrated every year on the Feast of the Visitation (31 May). The adult John later marked the beginning of Christ's public ministry when he baptized him in the River Jordan (see also cat. 7).

Christ's childhood and public ministry were followed by a third phase, that of the Passion, which Bosch painted several times, including on the reverse of the panel with *Saint John on Patmos* (cat. 6). Christ Carrying the Cross is the sixth scene of the cycle in that picture, with Christ led alone to his place of execution by soldiers and an angry mob. He has almost reached that destination in the panel discussed here, as the two criminals who will be crucified with him are visible in the foreground freed of their shackles. The 'Bad Thief' – the one who refuses to repent – is on the left. Bosch shows the 'Good Thief' on the right, turning with folded hands to a monk who hears his confession. This anachronistic detail will have made it immediately plain to the artist's contemporaries that this was the penitent criminal – the one who showed remorse and was forgiven his sins just before his death. The two thieves are to be executed on rough-hewn crosses, whereas the one on which Christ will be crucified is the careful work of a carpenter. There is a similar difference between the faces of the three condemned men: the resigned expression of Jesus, who takes the final steps on the road to Calvary, contrasts with the coarse faces of the other two. Bosch includes the sadistic detail of spiked wooden blocks hung from the rope around Christ's waist, which make every step he takes almost impossible. We detect Bosch's hand in numerous picturesque details, including the stippled shield of the oddly dressed soldier in the middle foreground, the many striking headdresses, and above all the wide variety of malevolent and stupid faces.

The overall composition of this *Christ Carrying the Cross* is oriented strongly towards the right. Its underlying visual strategy guides the viewer's gaze swiftly from the impenitent thief lower left to the other thief in the right foreground, and then via the already raised upright of his cross to the crowd above. The mob drives Christ onwards, while simultaneously directing our attention to the missing central panel of the triptych.

Hieronymus Bosch
Christ Carrying the Cross (interior), c. 1490–1510
Oil on oak panel, 59.7 × 32 cm
Vienna, Kunsthistorisches Museum,
Gemäldegalerie, GG-6429

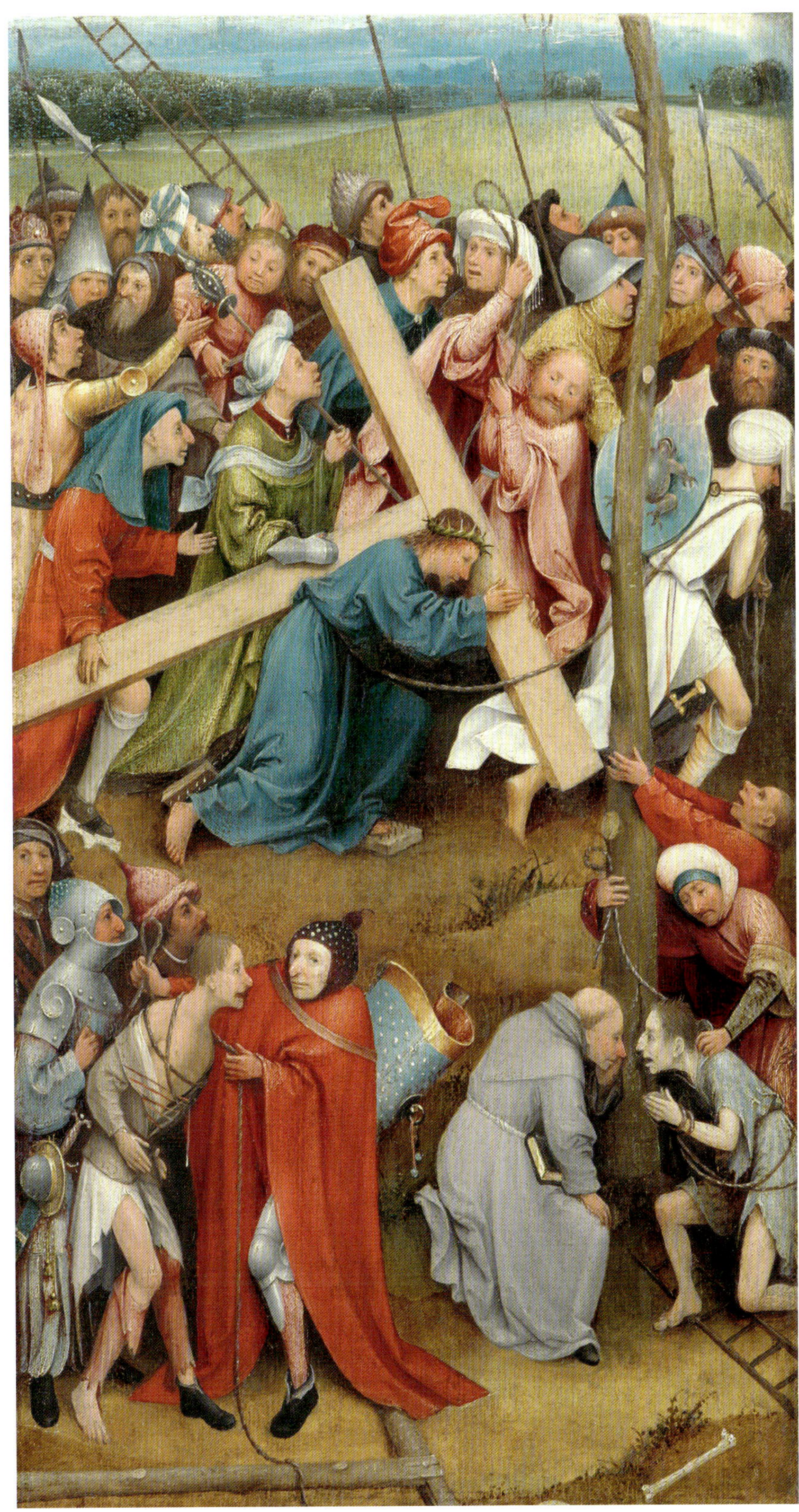

72

Hieronymus Bosch
Christ Child with walking frame (exterior),
c. 1490–1510
Oil on oak panel, 59.7 × 32 cm
Vienna, Kunsthistorisches Museum,
Gemäldegalerie, GG-6429

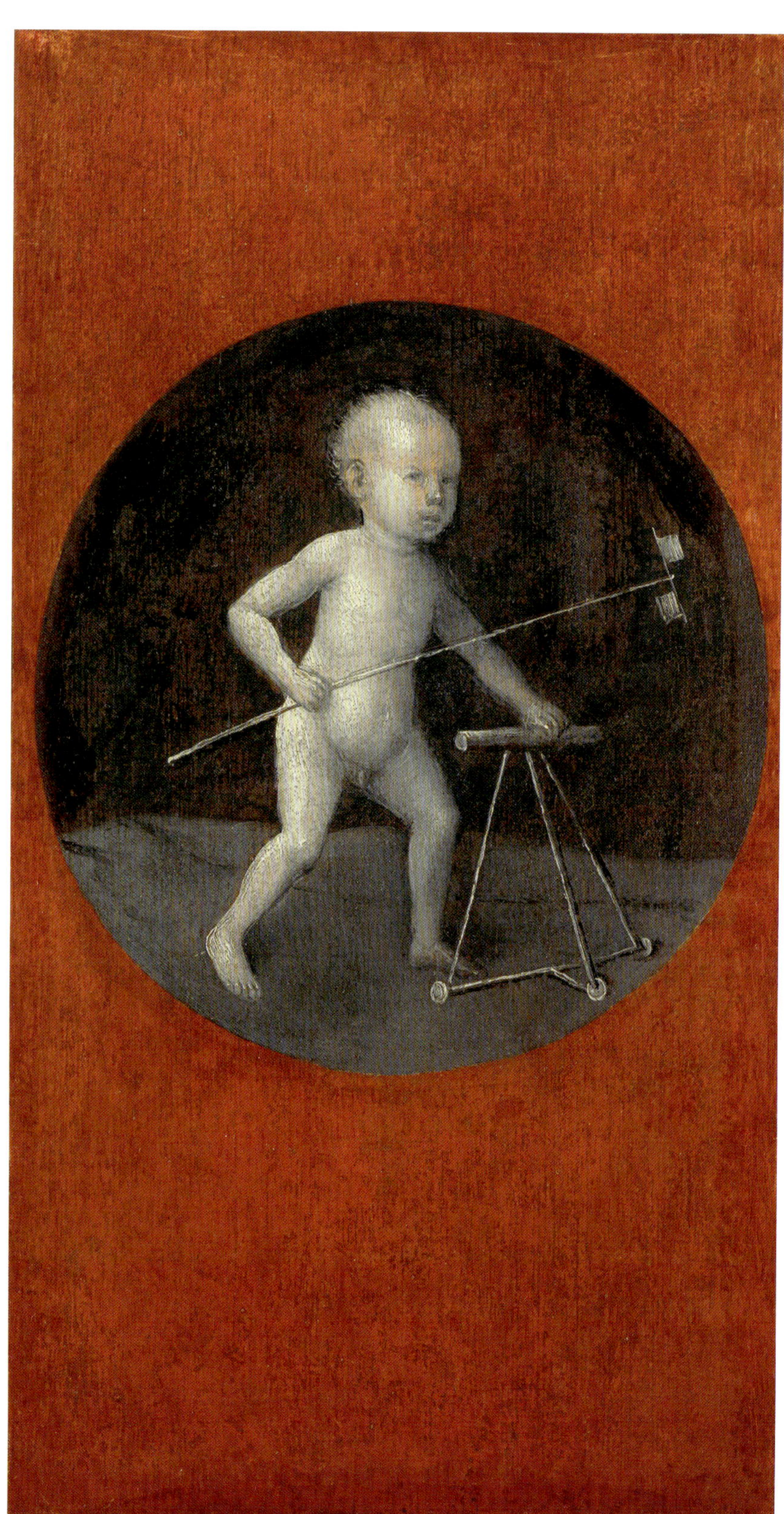

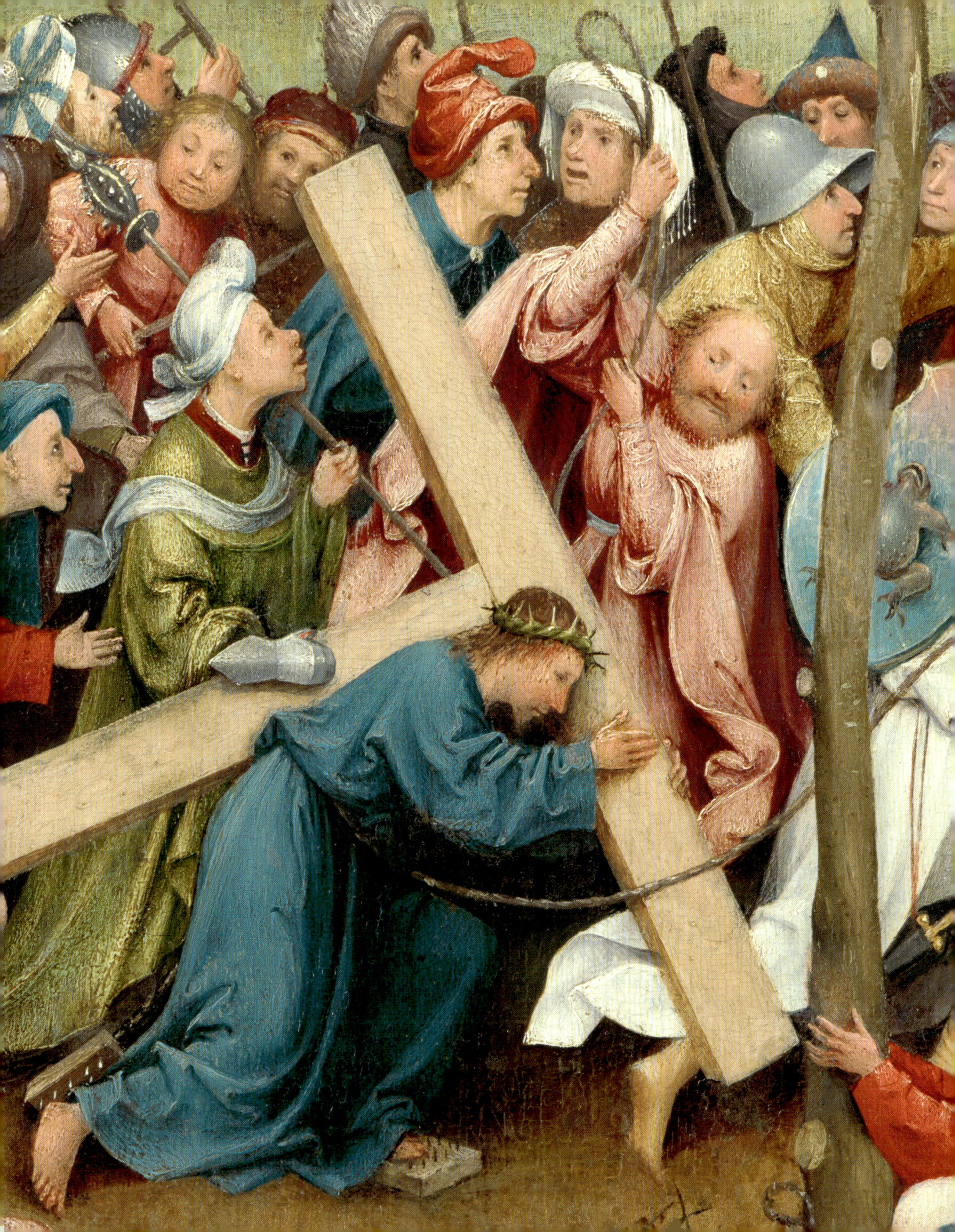

IV

Bosch as Draughtsman

Hieronymus Bosch's drawings form a world all of their own. Where his paintings often take on themes of cosmic proportions, it is the world of small things that is foregrounded in his drawings. Not that small things do not play a part in Bosch's paintings: on the contrary, they are full of details that, taken individually, are often just like drawings in paint. Drawings as such, however, are simpler and more direct, and often more spontaneous too. We feel they somehow bring us close to the artist. It is easy for us to imagine the draughtsman bent over the paper with his pen; drawings are the most direct result of an artist's desire to create.

The fact that we are able to talk about Hieronymus Bosch as a draughtsman at all is very unusual, as few if any drawings are known by his contemporaries. He is the first Netherlandish artist by whom a drawn 'oeuvre' has survived. 'Oeuvre' might seem like a big word for the body of twenty or so drawings we consider to be autograph, yet that is almost twice the dozen or so that were attributed to Bosch until recently.

Whatever the case, Hieronymus Bosch and his drawings stand at the beginning of a tradition in which paper was used as a vehicle for sketching. He is also one of the first artists in the North by whom several sheets have survived that were not made simply as sketches, preliminary studies or records of completed paintings, but which appear to be works of art in their own right. The figures in Bosch's drawings are almost never repeated exactly in his paintings. He seems instead to have used his drawings to give free rein to his ideas; to come up with images and to capture and preserve ideas. Drawing for Bosch was mostly a question of inventing or creating forms.

This is wonderfully illustrated by a drawing of an infernal landscape, full of impossible creatures – a spectacular sheet from a private collection, which is presented here for the first time as an autograph drawing by Bosch. New photographic documentation of this and other drawings enables us to follow in great detail how Bosch went about inventing his wondrous creatures.

Hieronymus Bosch was more, however, than simply the inventor of monsters and demons; he drew people too, albeit with an obvious penchant for marginal types, fraudsters, cripples and beggars. Bosch is not known historically as a great visualizer of classical beauty, which makes it all the more surprising among this shady company to find drawings of children, playing happily with birds.

On closer consideration, we find that Bosch – the master of the unnatural – was an attentive student of nature, who accurately observed and depicted long-eared, little and barn owls. These skills are, admittedly, more apparent in his animals than his plants; but he clearly knew the difference between a duck and a drake – the male has a curl in his tail – and how to express it in pen and ink, without resorting to colour. He was likewise familiar with horses' skulls, foxes, cockerels, swans, spoonbills and deer, and drew them all convincingly.

Nature for Bosch was full of life, spirit and magic; forests have ears and fields, eyes. Birds wage war against mammals as if they were people. He was truly at home when it came to crossing humans, animals and things. This is when walking wine-barrels start to appear, and bells with human clappers. And if you ignore differences of scale, or even reverse them, it is perfectly possible to fit five sinners on the blade of a knife.

The Greeks had their Chimaera (the lion with a goat's head on its back and a serpent for a tail), Cerberus (the three-headed dog that guarded the entrance to Hades) and Hydra (the monster with many heads). Bosch's monsters do not illustrate stories or existing types; they are creatures he invented himself, which grew out of his careful observation of nature and his conviction that God's creation and order were disrupted and corrupted by evil.

The sombre view of humanity we often find in Bosch's paintings is less acute in his drawings; his sketches in pen and ink are more expressive of his urge to create, of the joy of finding new forms. Bosch took creativity and originality very seriously, going so far as to write above one of his drawings: 'Poor is the mind that always uses the inventions of others and invents nothing itself.'

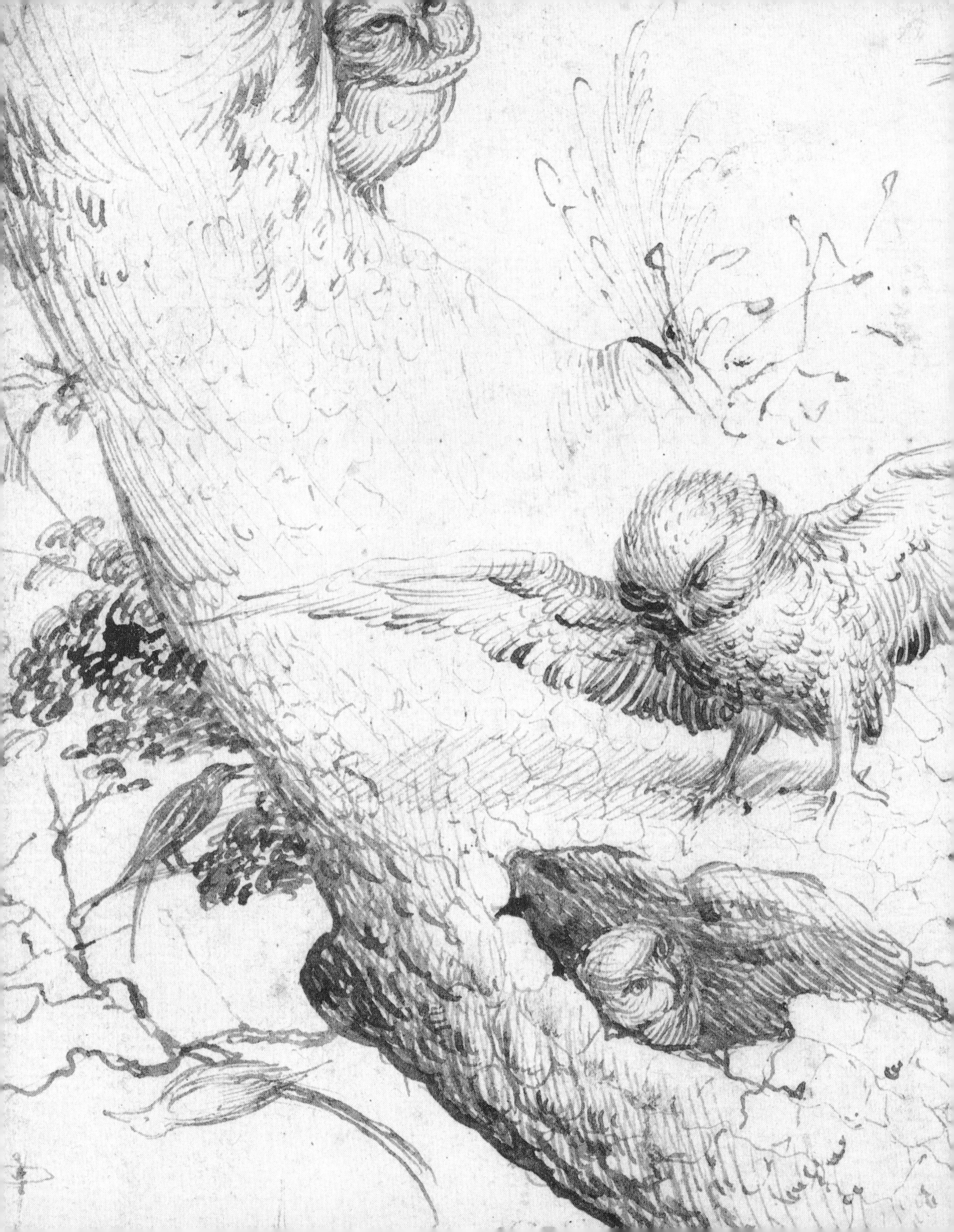

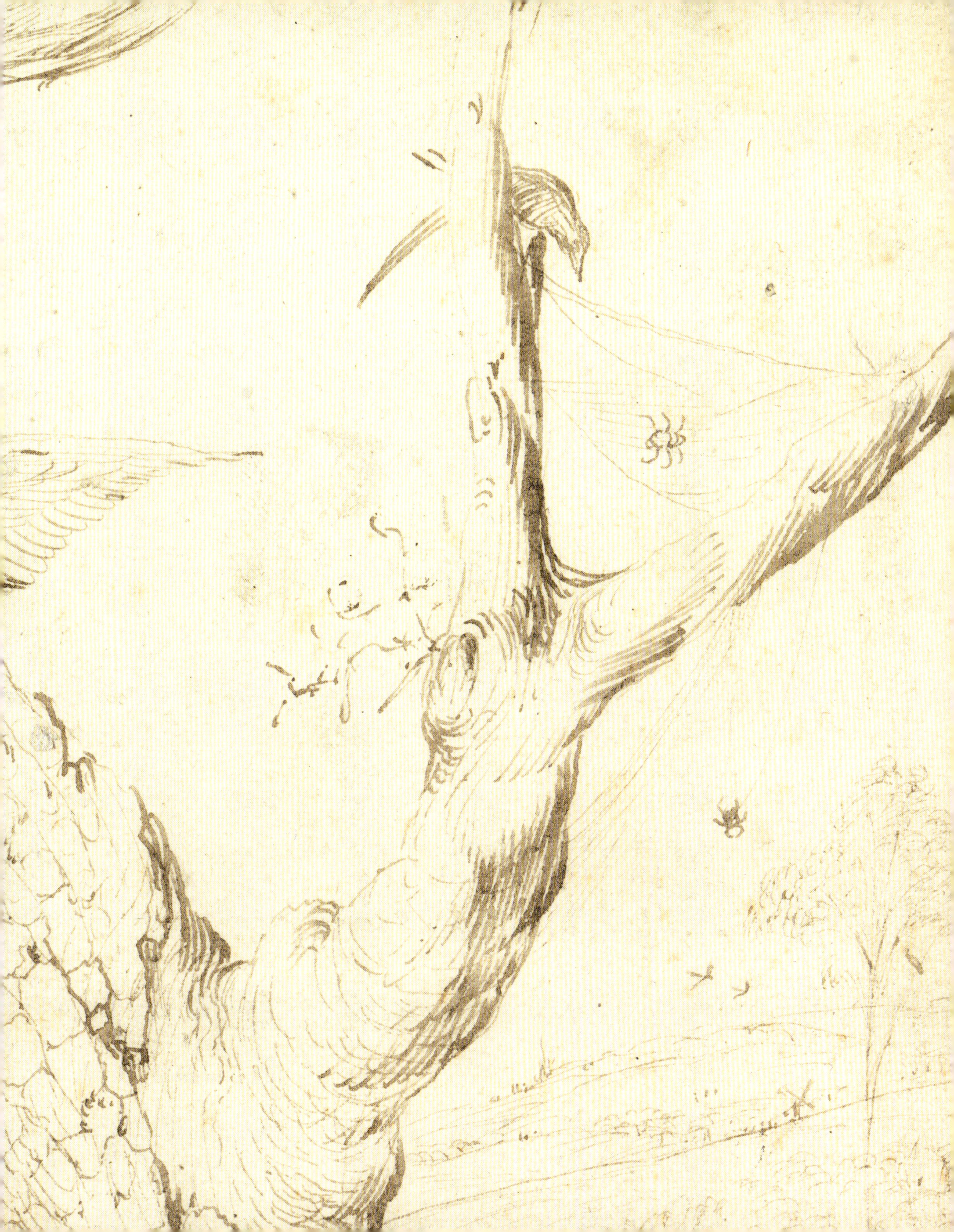

Pen and brown ink on paper,
140 × 196 mm
Rotterdam, Museum Boijmans
Van Beuningen, N 175

78 Bosch must have been really fascinated by owls, which are a recurring element in both his paintings and his drawings. The artist mostly employs them as a negative factor within a larger whole. The *Owl's Nest* – one of the finest drawings by Bosch we know of – includes a trio of owls as its main subject. The artist has lovingly and attentively drawn a little owl with its wings spread, approaching another, smaller owl (its young?) in the hollow of the tree. As usual, they are surrounded by a group of agitated birds, one of which swoops in to attack the third owl at the top of the tree. The close-up rendition of the tree, very unusual for a drawing of that time, is further emphasized by the expansive landscape with a view of a village in the background. The *Owl's Nest* is not a sketch but a highly finished drawing. It is a carefully balanced composition featuring the birds of which Bosch, for whatever reason, was so fond.

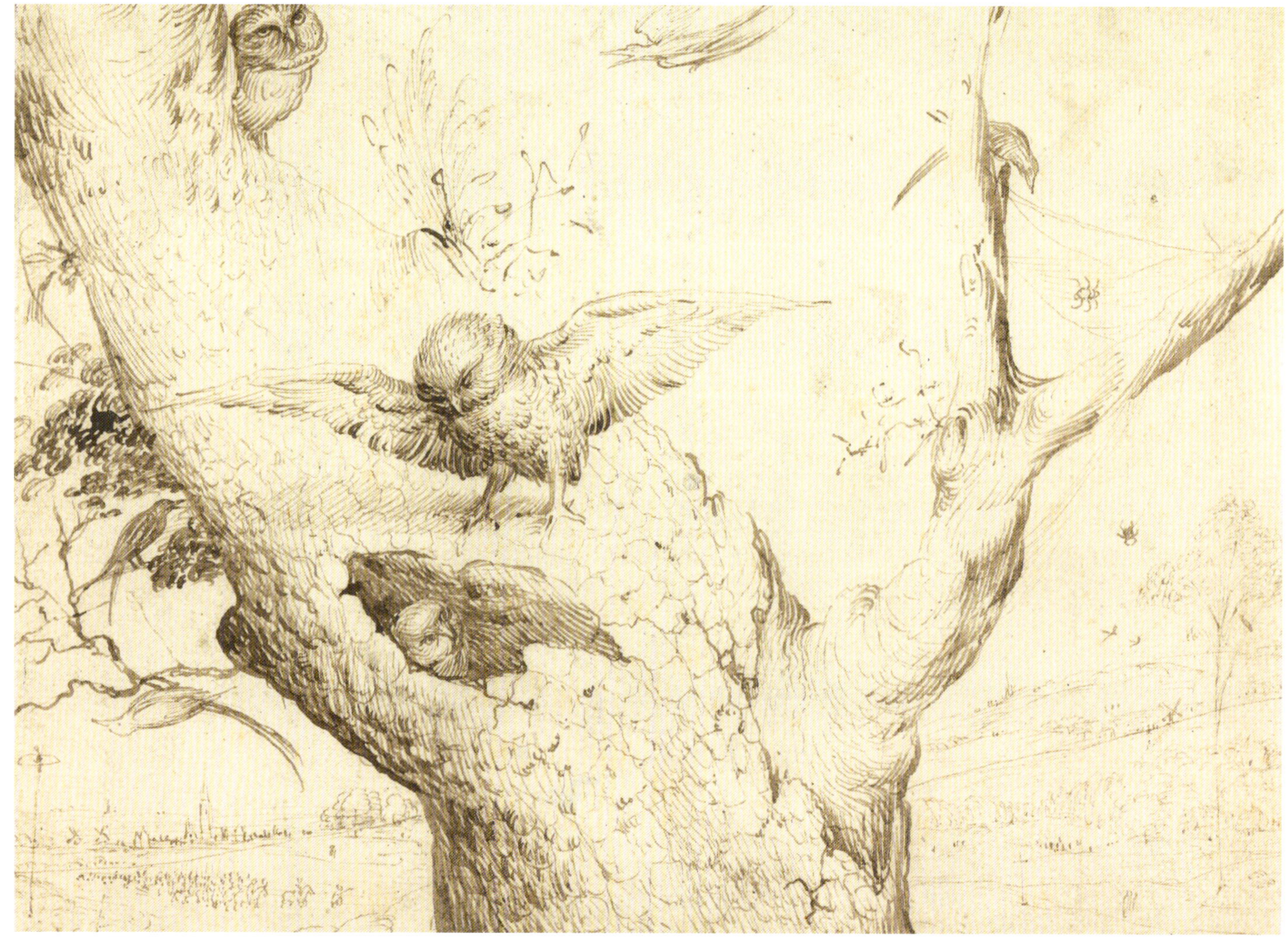

17. The Wood Has Ears, The Field Has Eyes
– Study of a beggar and workshop sketches

Hieronymus Bosch

Pen and brown ink on paper,
205 × 130/127 mm
Berlin, Staatliche Museen zu Berlin,
Kupferstichkabinett, KdZ 549

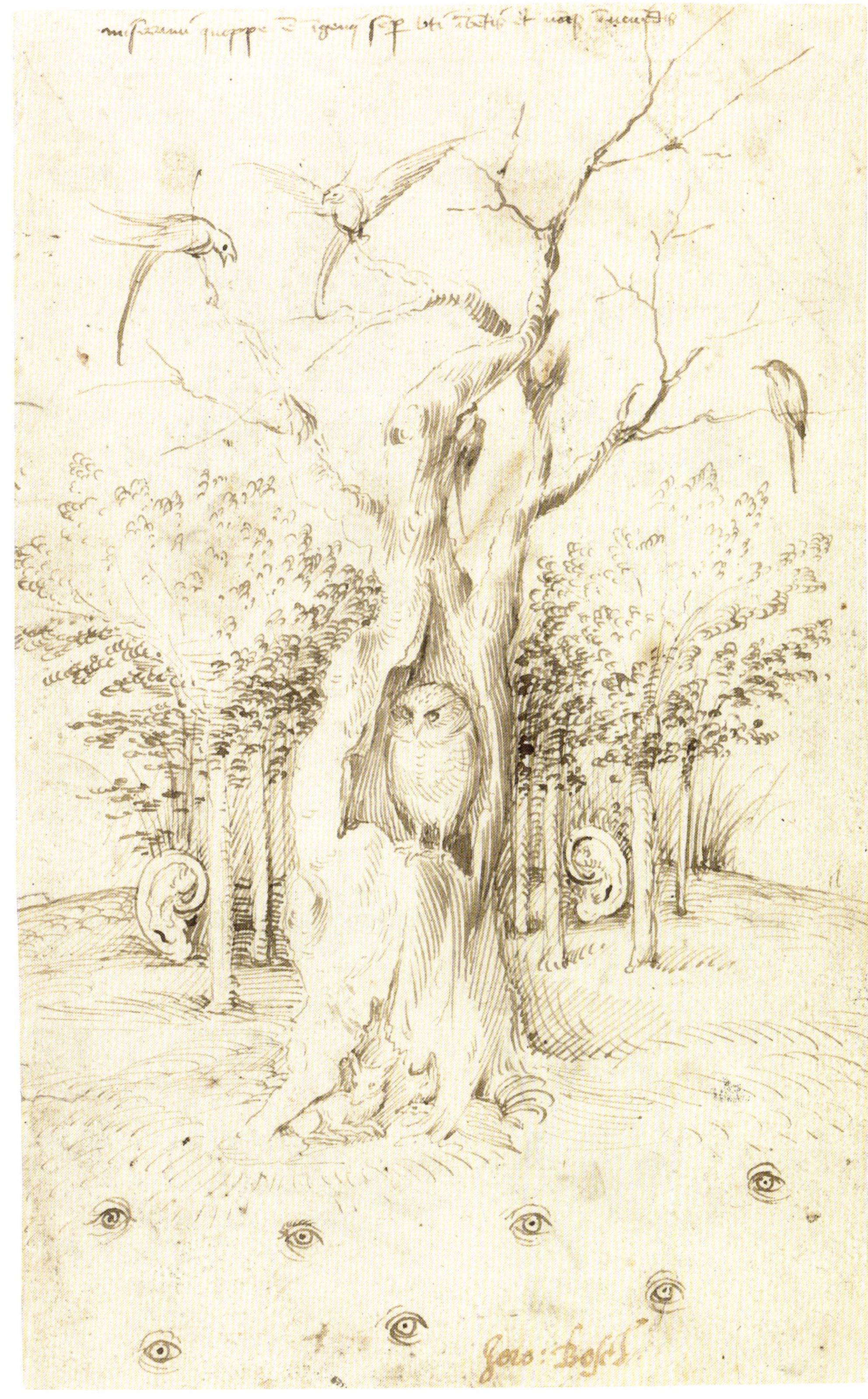

The owl plays an important part once again in *The Wood Has Ears, The Field Has Eyes*. The drawing features an oversized little owl in the hollow of a dead tree, from where it peers out of the picture at the viewer. It is plain from the large human ears in the wood and the eyes scattered over the field that this is a very different kind of image from the *Owl's Nest*. Rather than representing a scene from nature, this is an allegorical image – a composition depicting an abstract concept.

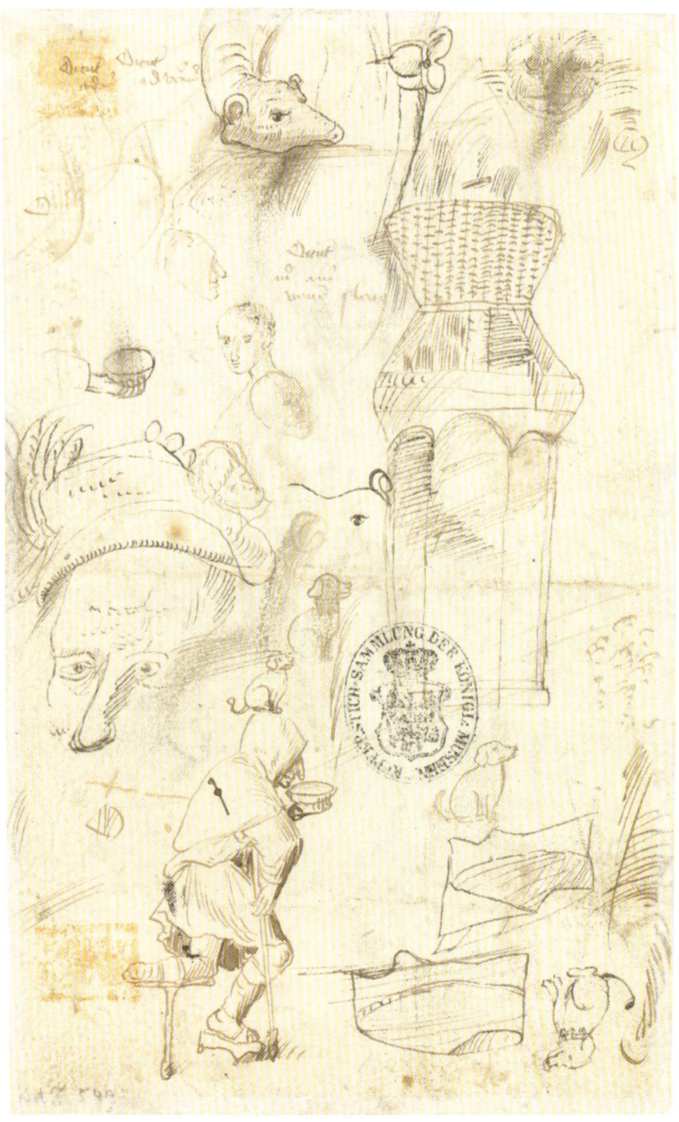

It is a visual expression in the first instance of the Middle Dutch saying that the wood has ears and the field has eyes. According to a dictionary of proverbs published in 1500, this means that we are always observed and should not indulge in behaviour we would rather keep to ourselves. A Dutch print of 1545 repeats the proverb and expands on it: 'The field has eyes, the wood has ears. I want to see, keep silent and hear.' A treatise titled 'The Art of Silence' was published in 's-Hertogenbosch during Bosch's own lifetime. The proverb illustrated by the drawing is therefore an appeal to the viewer to be vigilant. The unsuspecting cockerel who steps into the fox's earth in the hollow at the foot of the tree would have done well to follow that advice.

The humour lies in the fact that the drawing is a unique and original depiction of a cliché. Bosch has added a Latin quotation above the drawing from a medieval treatise on the training of apprentices: 'Poor is the mind that always uses the inventions of others and invents nothing itself.' The drawing also serves, therefore, as an emblem of Bosch's artistry and – like the *Owl's Nest* but in a different way – is closely related to the Jeroen van Aken who adopted the professional name of 'Bosch' (the 'wood' in the title of the work).

The way Bosch constructed the image suggests he was playing a game that weaves together the individual, the artist, the name of the city and his personal philosophy. The composition of the drawing is structured in the same way as the 's-Hertogenbosch municipal seal, in which the city is represented by a large tree at the centre, flanked by two smaller ones. The symbol must have been well known to Bosch and his circle. By using that image, combined with the owl – also referred to as a 'forest bird' (*bosvogel*) – Bosch created as it were the coat of arms of his artistry, making this drawing something of a 'self-portrait'.

Bosch drew a beggar on the other side of the sheet, where his apprentices also tried their hand at a number of sketches. The contrast with the assurance of the master's drawing is plain.

Pen and brown ink over black chalk on
paper, 204 × 264 mm
Paris, Musée du Louvre, Département
des Arts graphiques, 19721

Several elements from *The Wood Has Ears, The Field Has Eyes*
crop up again in the Louvre *Model sheet with 'witches'*. First
of all, we see the owl once again, perched this time on the back
of the baking paddle on which a woman is riding. The owl is
used in this instance as the attribute of a lunatic, and hence
as a pejorative symbol. Next to the woman we see a figure with
a pot on her head, who is strongly reminiscent of the beggar
on the verso of *The Wood Has Ears*; the Louvre drawing is
undoubtedly by the same hand.

All the figures here – a collection of madwomen, possibly
witches – are juxtaposed without overlaps. The drawing is
a model sheet containing a group of examples that the artist
and his workshop could consult at a later date for use in
a painted composition. If any such painting by Bosch ever
existed, we no longer know of it.

A later owner of the drawing, probably in the sixteenth
century, thought it was the work of Pieter Bruegel, and
inscribed it 'Bruegel, manu propria' ('Bruegel, in his
own hand').

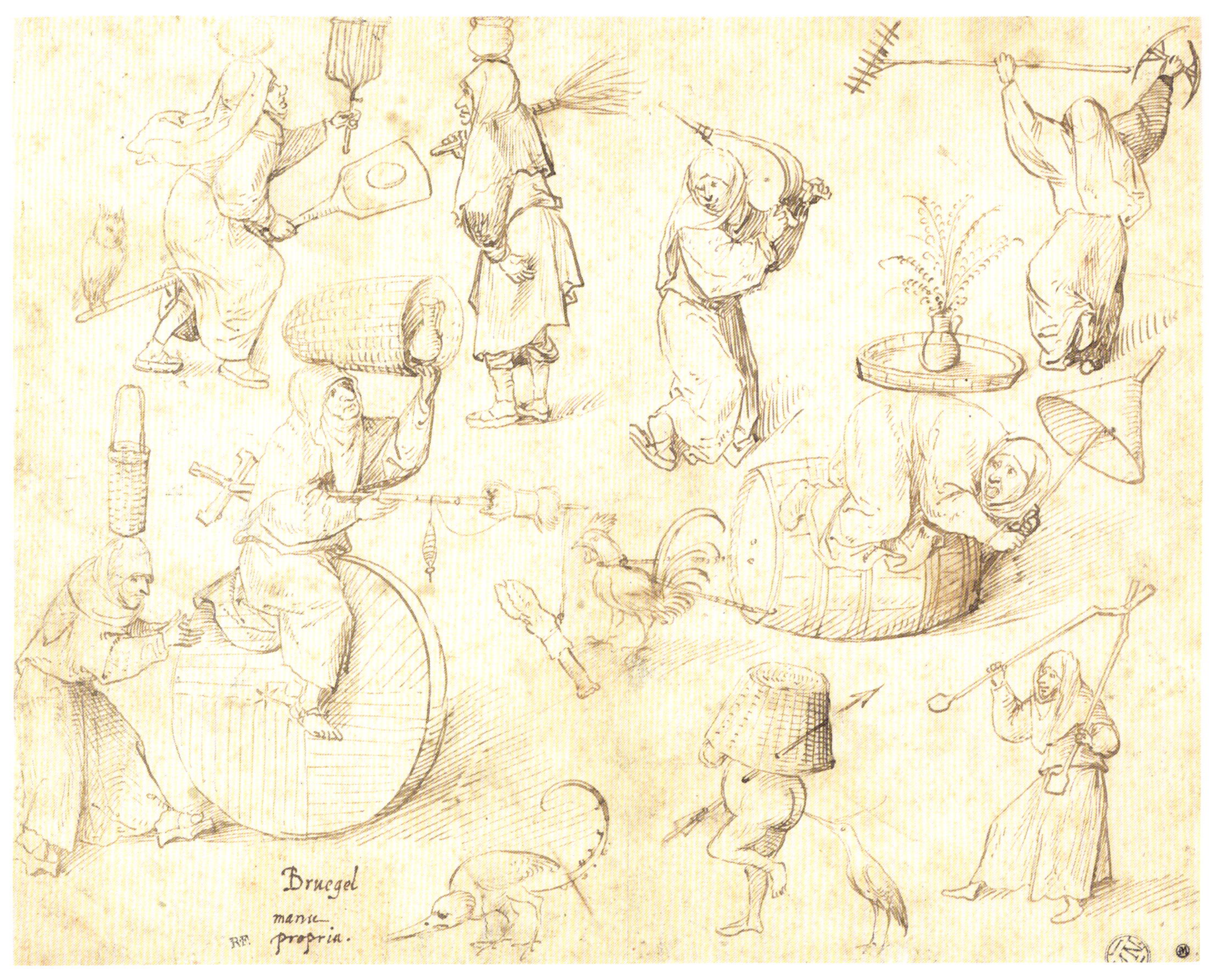

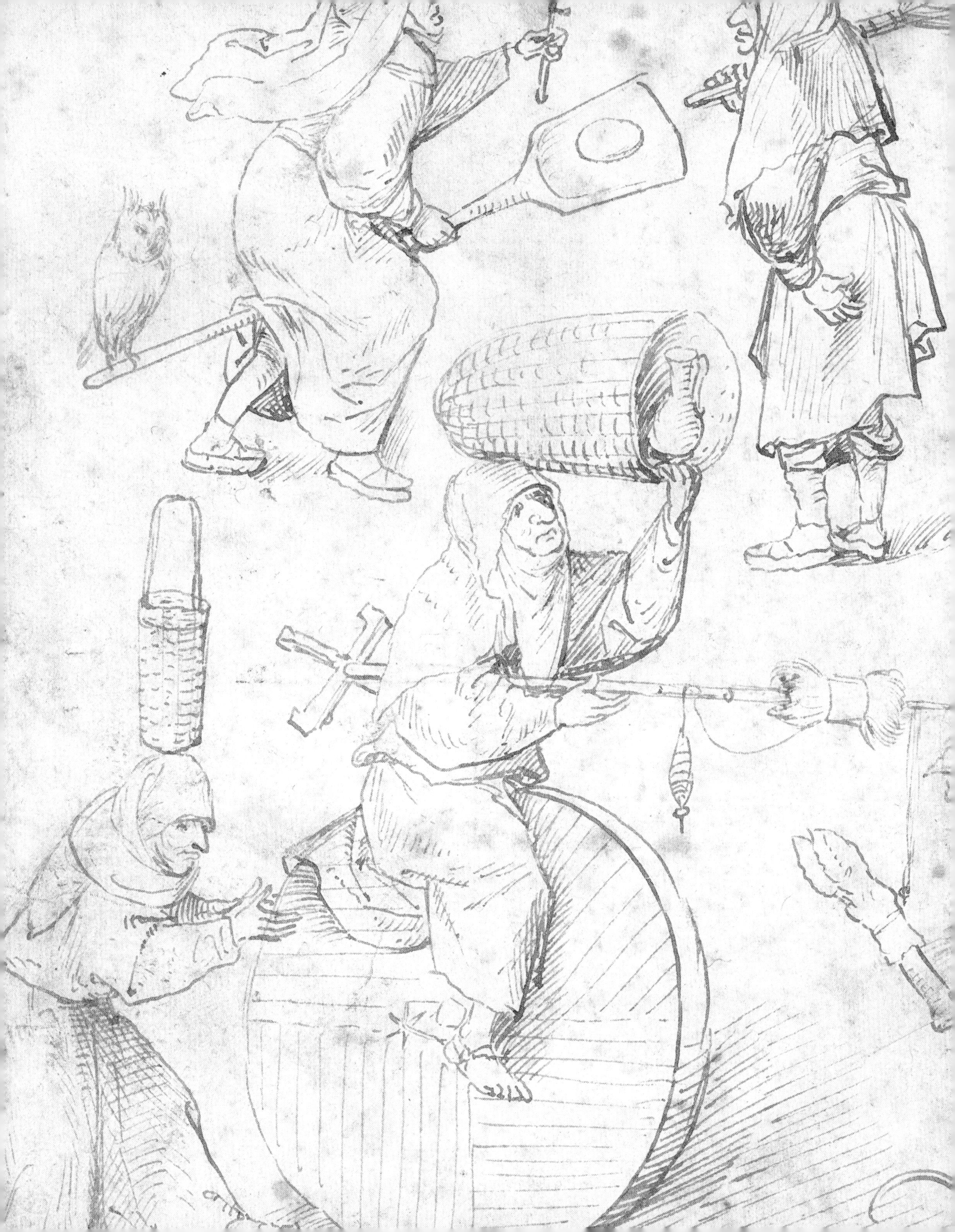

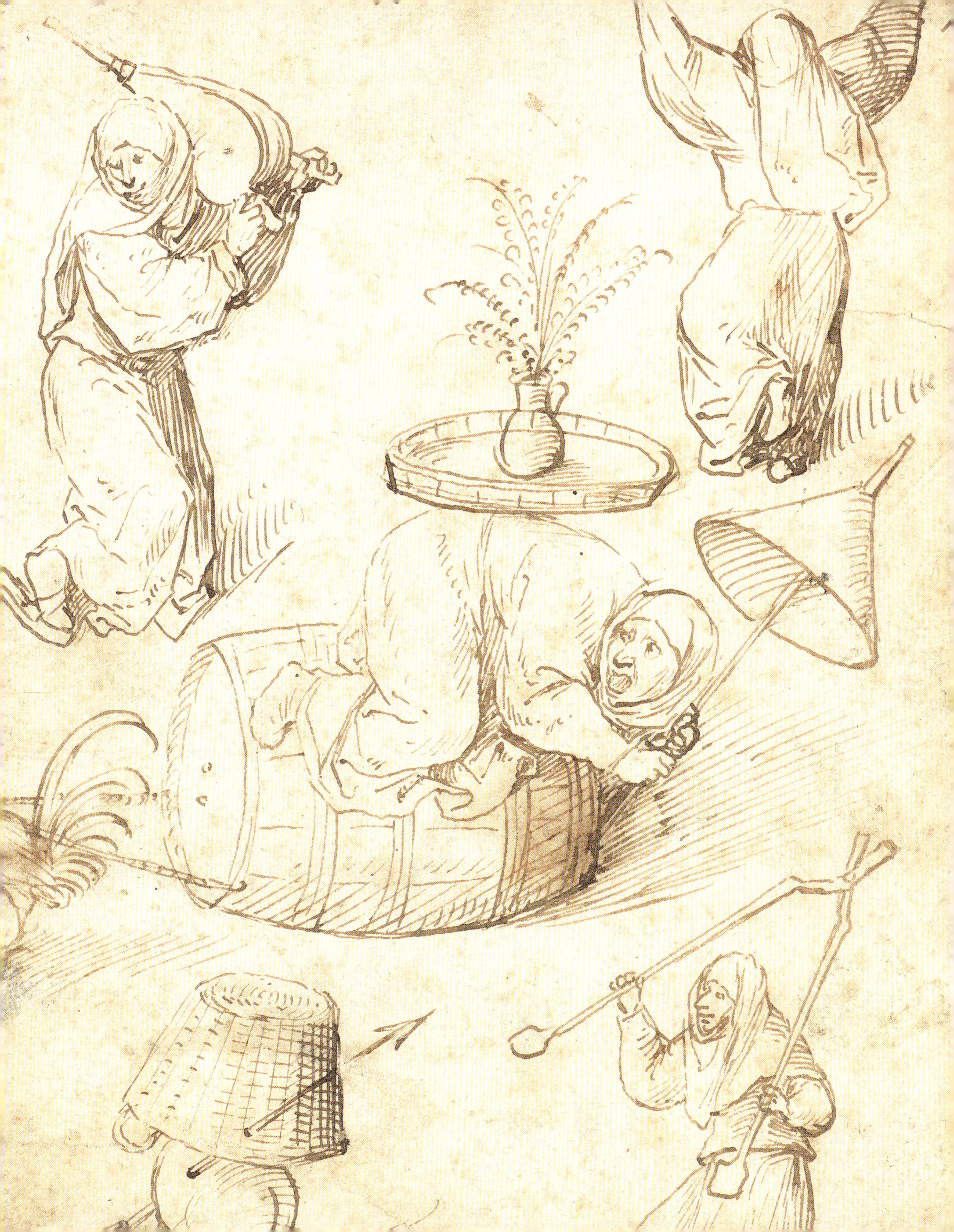

Pen and brown ink on paper,
195 × 284 mm
Berlin, Staatliche Museen zu Berlin,
Kupferstichkabinett, KdZ 13136

84 There are owls here too: a whole group of them this time, in the left foreground of the drawing of an army of birds preparing to do battle with the mammals. The latter are assembled in the background under the command of a stag, which stands out against the sky alongside a cross.

Bosch's image is packed with energy: the excitement of the birds in the moments before they engage their enemy is palpable and is literally drummed up by the bird on the right. A large bird shown from the rear stands prominently in the foreground looking at the generals in the middle of the scene, where we see a griffin as standard-bearer facing two other large and menacing birds. Like a gang of hooligans, they are itching to get at their opponents.

The battle is shown in another drawing, which has to be considered a pendant. We make out an owl once again, its wings outspread, on the far left of the chaos of the battlefield, which is littered with severed wings, legs and heads. The birds are evidently the aggressors in this fable, as they advance into the picture from behind a hill in the upper left. Although the outcome of the conflict is far from settled at this point, things are not looking good for the birds: the griffin, their standard-bearer, is shown to the left of centre, where a lion tears at his throat.

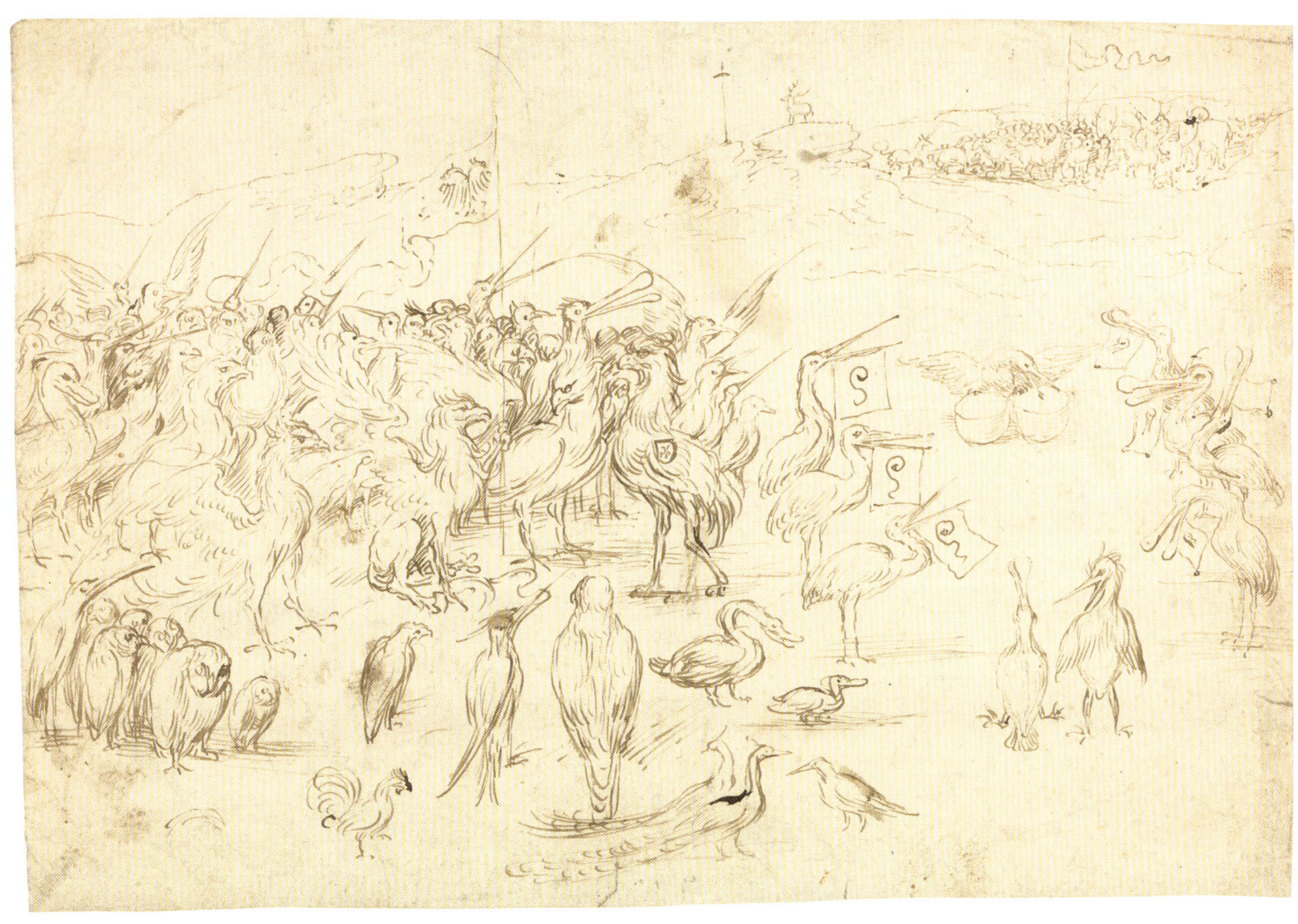

Pen and brown ink on paper,
203 × 290 mm
Berlin, Staatliche Museen zu Berlin,
Kupferstichkabinett, KdZ 14715

The two drawings probably lack any specific philosophical or political meaning: they are not sufficiently explicit for that and are more likely to be dynamic studies, exploring the interaction between the figures. They nevertheless recall the moral fables that were popular around 1500. One of Aesop's tales, for instance, is about a battle between the birds and the beasts. The principal figure in the story is the bat, who tries to make sure he ends up on the winning side by telling the birds he is a bird, and the beasts that he is a beast. Once the battle has been fought, both sides shun the bat and punish him. The moral of the tale is that you cannot serve two masters. Bosch's drawings are certainly not an illustration of Aesop's fable, as there is no bat to be seen; they are studies in which the artist explores the kind of dynamism that can be created with pen and ink.

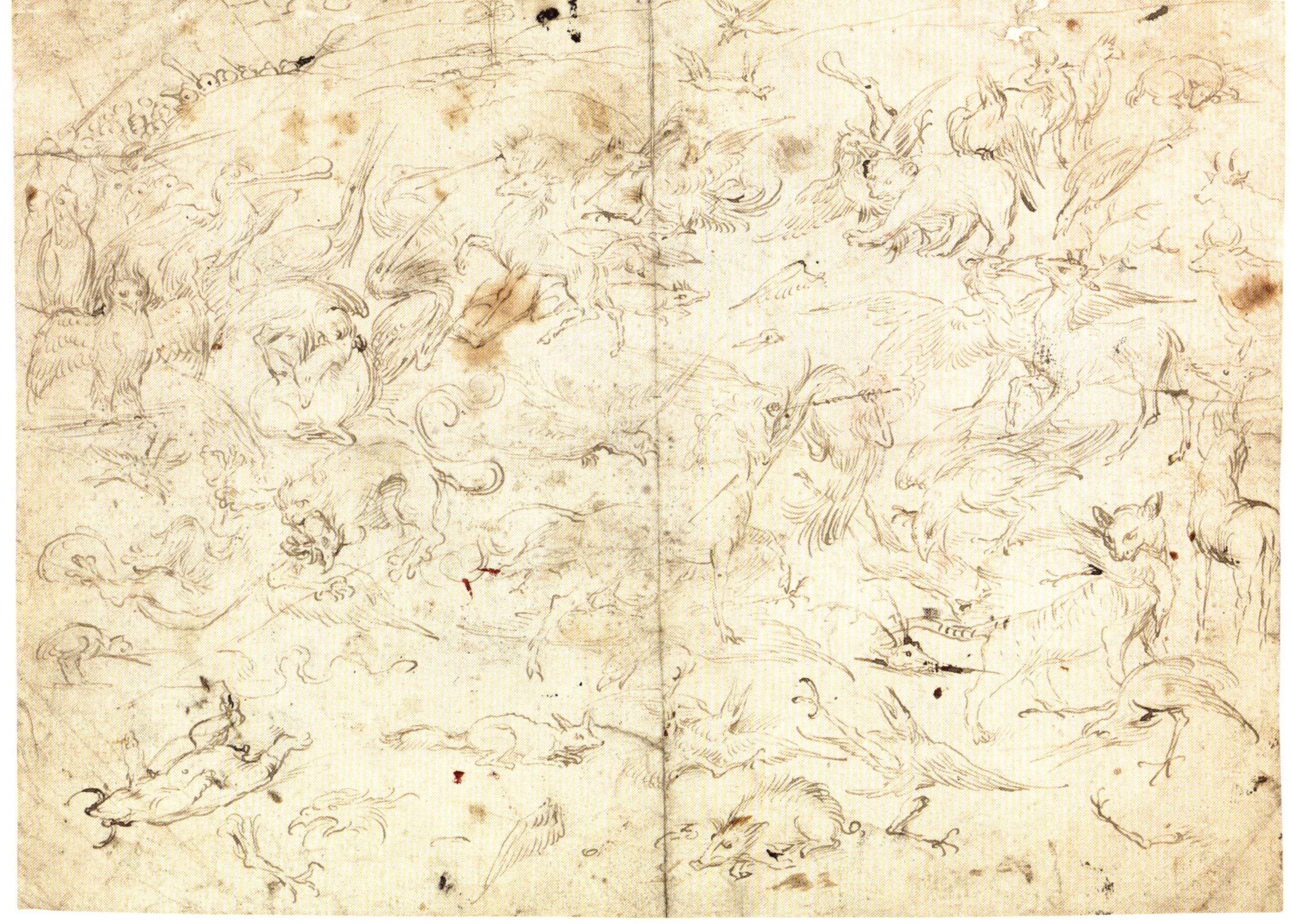

This becomes clearer if we compare Bosch's drawings with contemporary book illustrations. A popular reference book called *Van den proprieteyten der dinghen* ('Of the Properties of Things') included a woodcut with a gathering of birds (fig. p. 86). It seems very likely that Bosch knew this print, as the griffin and the strapping bird facing it are very similar to the two birds at the centre of his first drawing. The woodcut is, however, less convincing than Bosch's version: the print is charming but – almost by definition – a little wooden; the birds are distributed across the surface as if in a model sheet, whereas Bosch focuses on the interaction between the figures and on movement. This is shown most clearly in the leg of the large bird with the shield on its plumage. It initially stood stiffly with its two legs planted parallel on the ground. Bosch then scratched out the left leg and replaced it with one that is bent, giving the bird a classical *contrapposto* pose.

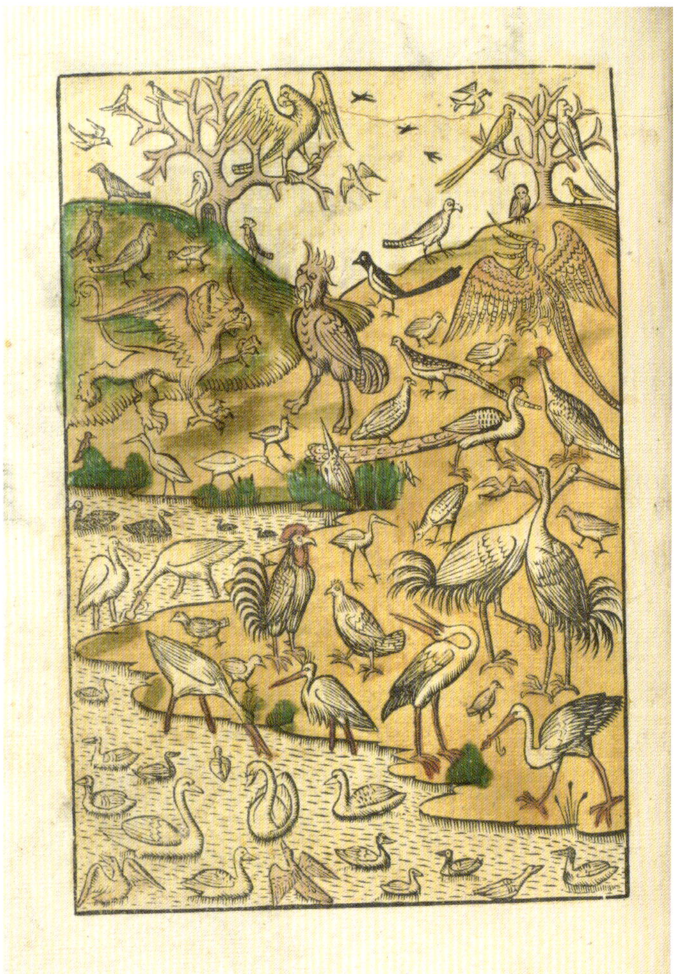

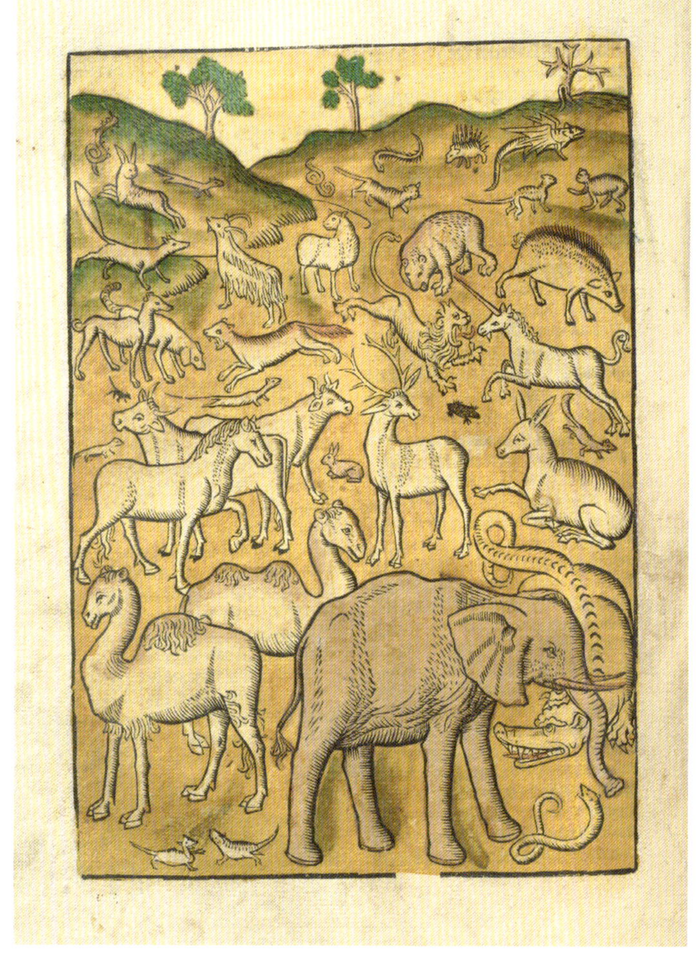

Bartholomeus Anglicus
De proprietatibus rerum, 'Van den proprieteyten der dinghen'
Haarlem (Jacob Bellaert van Ziericzee), 1485
Woodcuts, fol. 216v and 366v
The Hague, Koninklijke Bibliotheek, KW 168 E 8

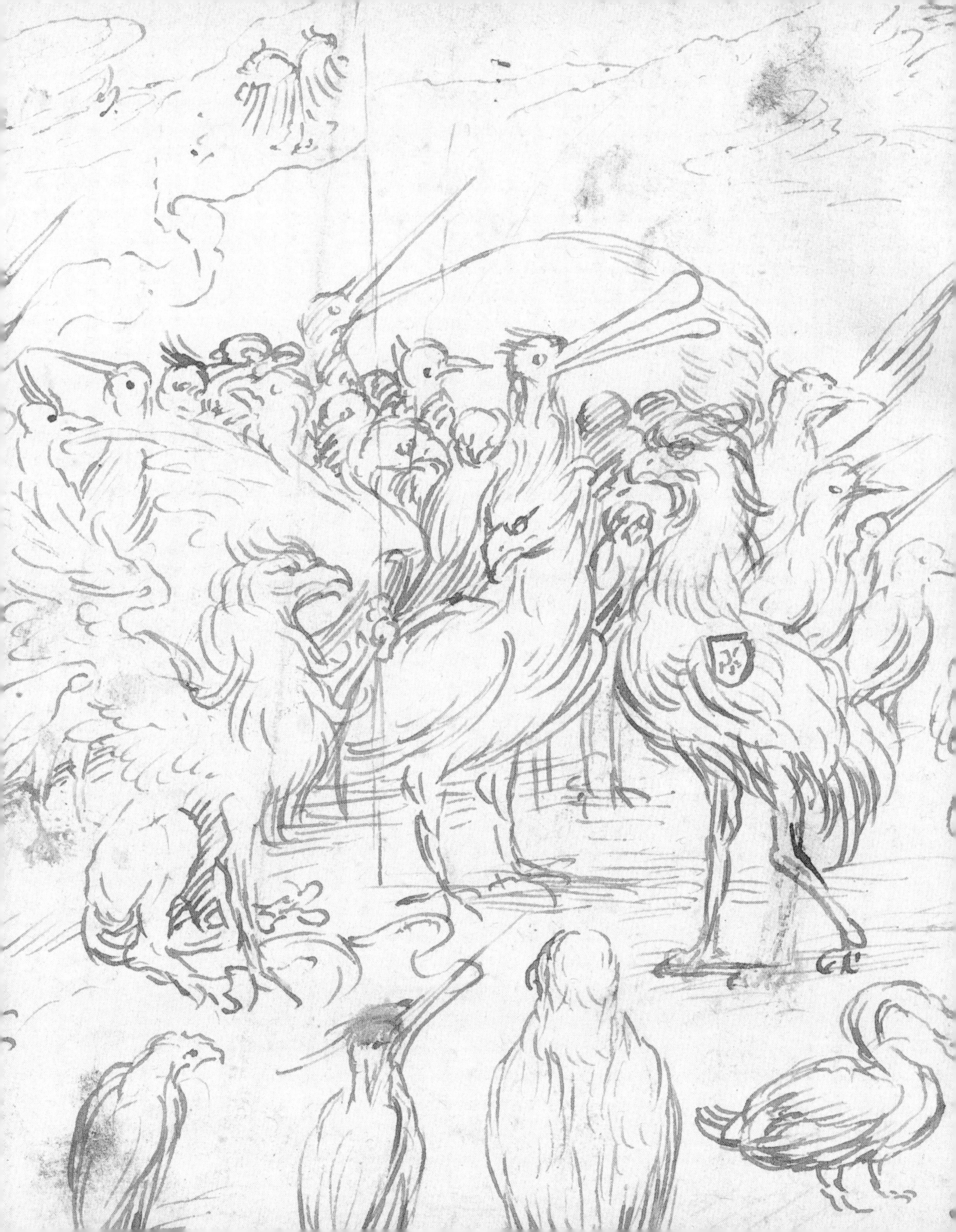

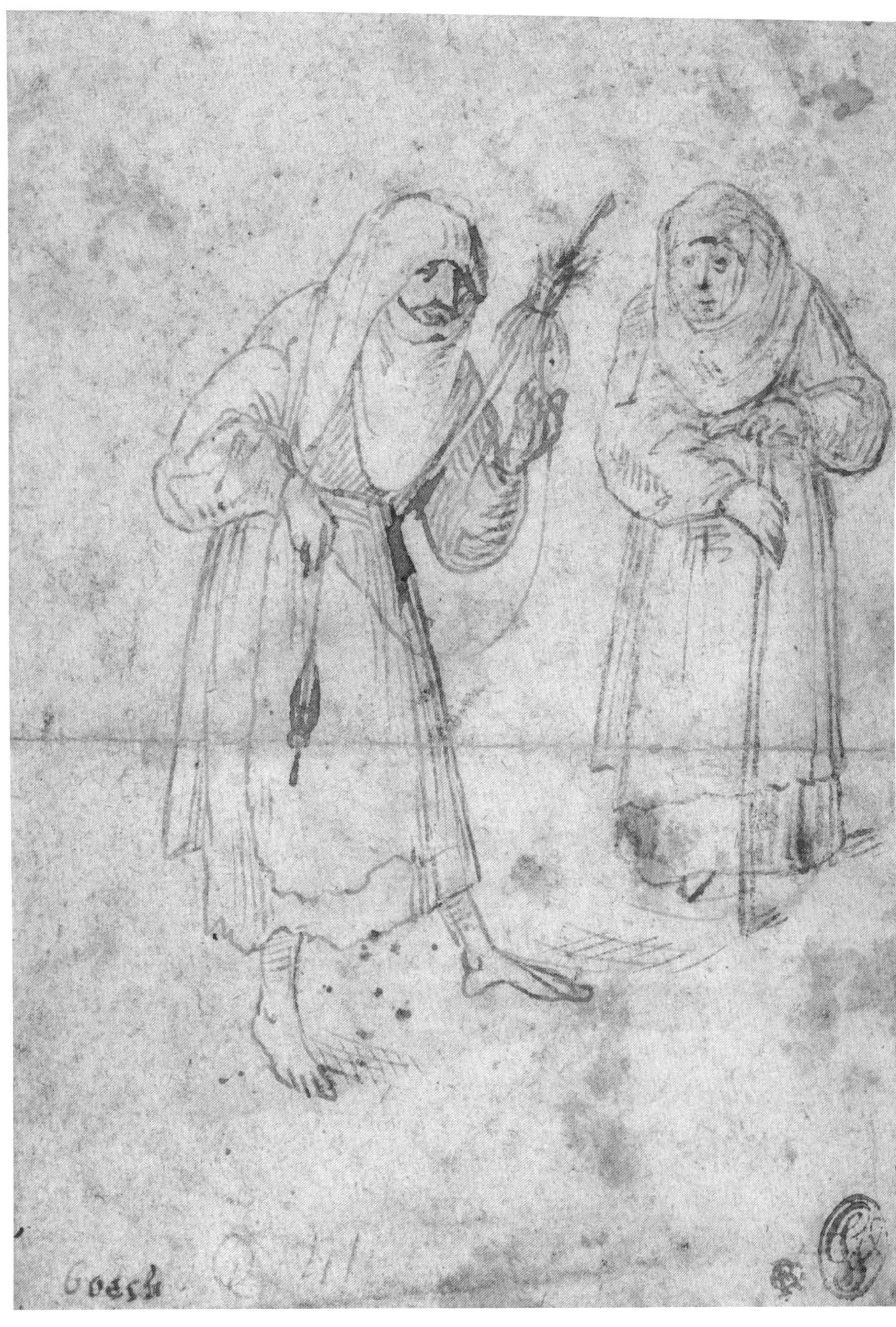

Bosch

**Pen and brown and brown-grey ink
on paper, 120 × 85 mm
Rotterdam, Museum Boijmans
Van Beuningen, N 190**

The two elderly women in this drawing – undoubtedly a fragment of a larger sheet – stand somewhat stiffly facing each other. One leans on a stick while the other is bent over a little and clutches a distaff. Her clothes seem frayed and she is barefoot. The lack of context makes it hard to say anything further about the pair. They are less caricatured than the madwomen in the *Model sheet with 'witches'* (cat. 18), but these women too must have lived on the margins of society around 1500.

Bosch drew the sketch in two different inks: brown for the outlines and a greyer ink for a little additional hatching – a drawing technique we find quite often in his work. It tells us that he sometimes executed his drawings in phases. This is not the case with the sketch on the back of this sheet, which was done in a single type of ink. It is a quick but amusing little sketch of an unwary cockerel approaching a fox's lair – a small but fine example of Bosch's sense of suspense. The viewer sees the whole thing and knows from the duck's head and leg scattered on the ground in front of the earth where this scene is heading. The fox patiently awaits its opportunity, as it does in the drawing of *The Wood Has Ears, The Field Has Eyes* (cat. 17).

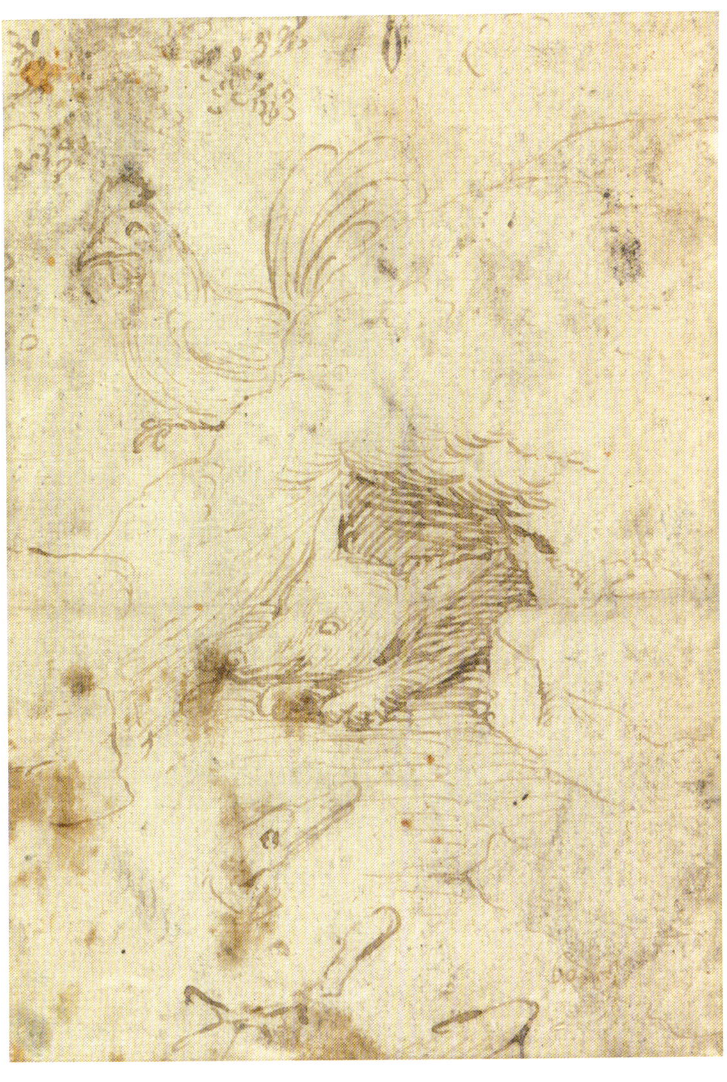

22. Man in a basket, old woman with tongs and children
– Sketch of a man in a basket and a head-and-feet figure

Bosch was a skilled image-maker who knew how effective it could be to incorporate a spectator in the depicted scene. Figures like this draw us into the action: looking through someone else's eyes automatically makes us part of the scene. Bosch uses the technique in this drawing of a figure in a large basket, with a flock of birds flying out of his behind. It is an entirely absurd piece of theatre, especially when we see that someone else has climbed on top of the basket and is about to smash a lute to pieces on the bare buttocks below.

The woman on the left reacts appropriately, raising her arms in astonishment and showing her palms. Her mouth has dropped open with surprise. Even this was evidently not enough for Bosch, who has also placed a huge pair of tongs in her hands; he leaves it to the viewer to decide what she is doing with them.

The children in the margin of the scene do not care either way; they are having great fun trying to catch the birds. Drawn with immense skill, they recall the *putti* of Raphael and Leonardo, which were drawn in the same period.

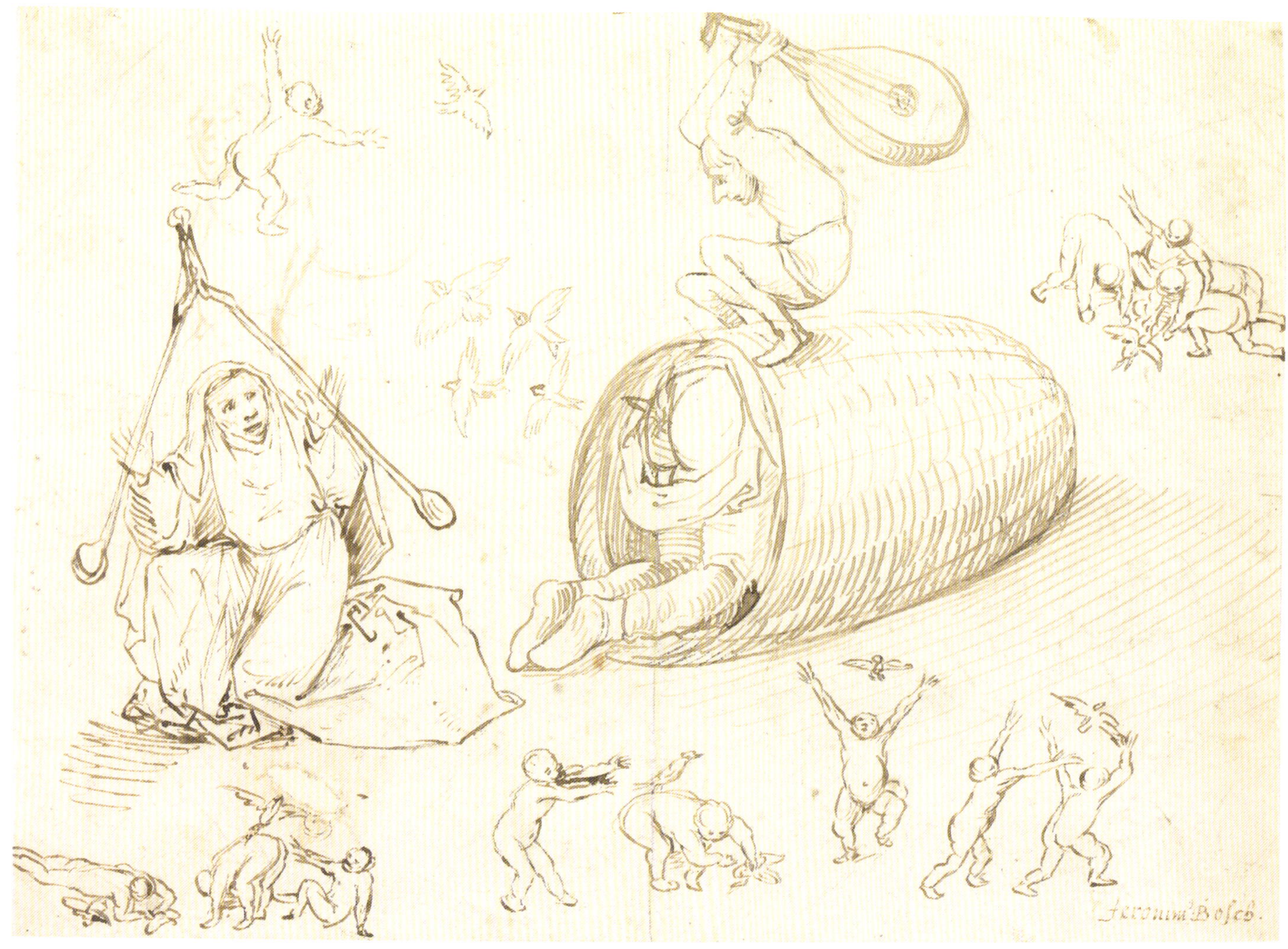

**Pen and brown and brown-grey ink
on paper, 192 × 270 mm
Vienna, ALBERTINA, 7797**

We find a painted version of the motif of the figure with a bare behind in a basket in the *Hermit Saints Triptych* (cat. 43). There an owl perches on the stick inserted into the figure's backside, drawing a mob of other birds as so often in Bosch.

The motif with birds, buttocks and basket is repeated on the other side of the sheet, now much more sketchily.

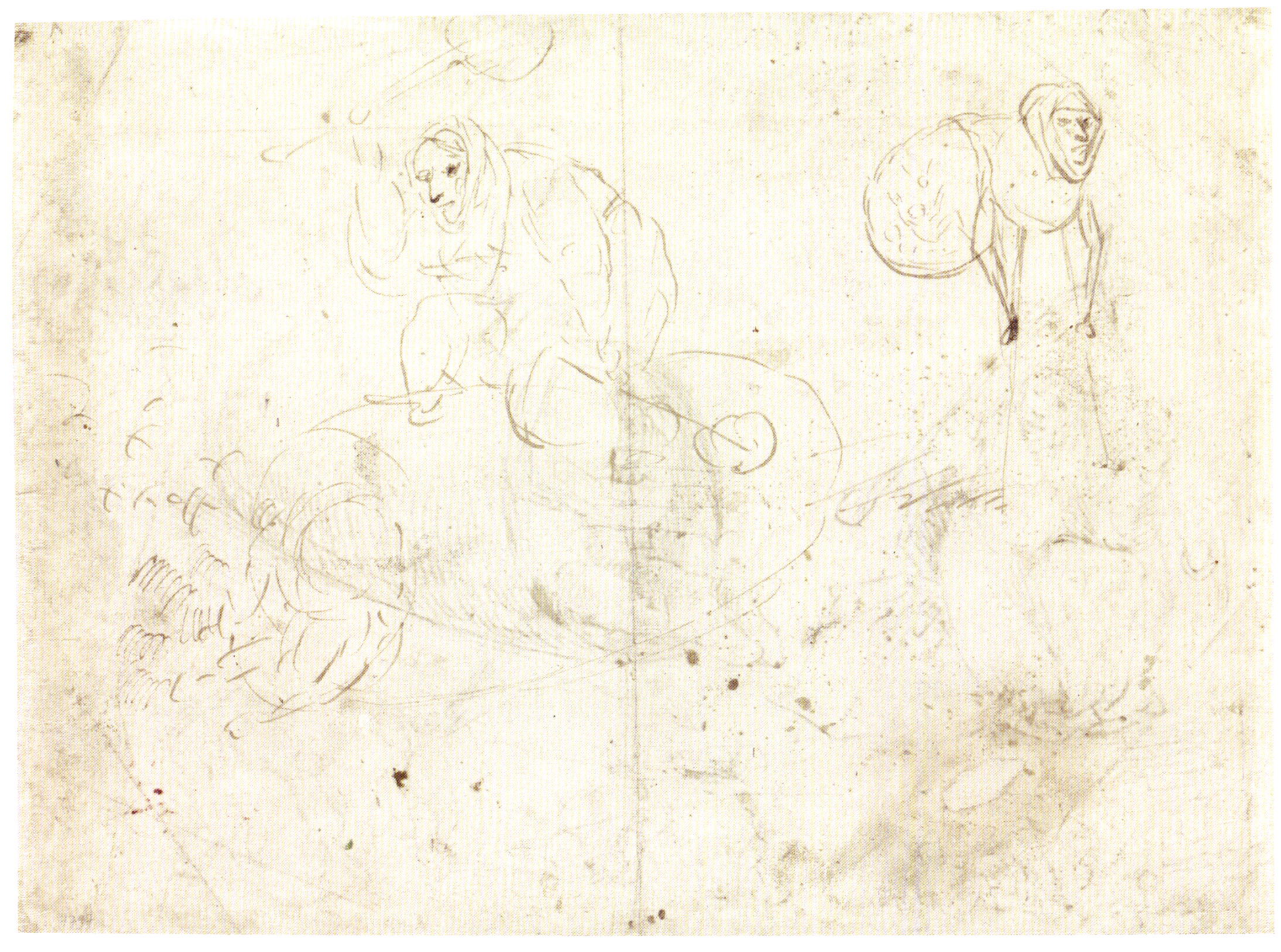

Hieronymus Bosch

23. The Conjurer

Pen and brown ink on paper,
276 × 203 mm
Paris, Musée du Louvre, Département
des Arts graphiques, 19197

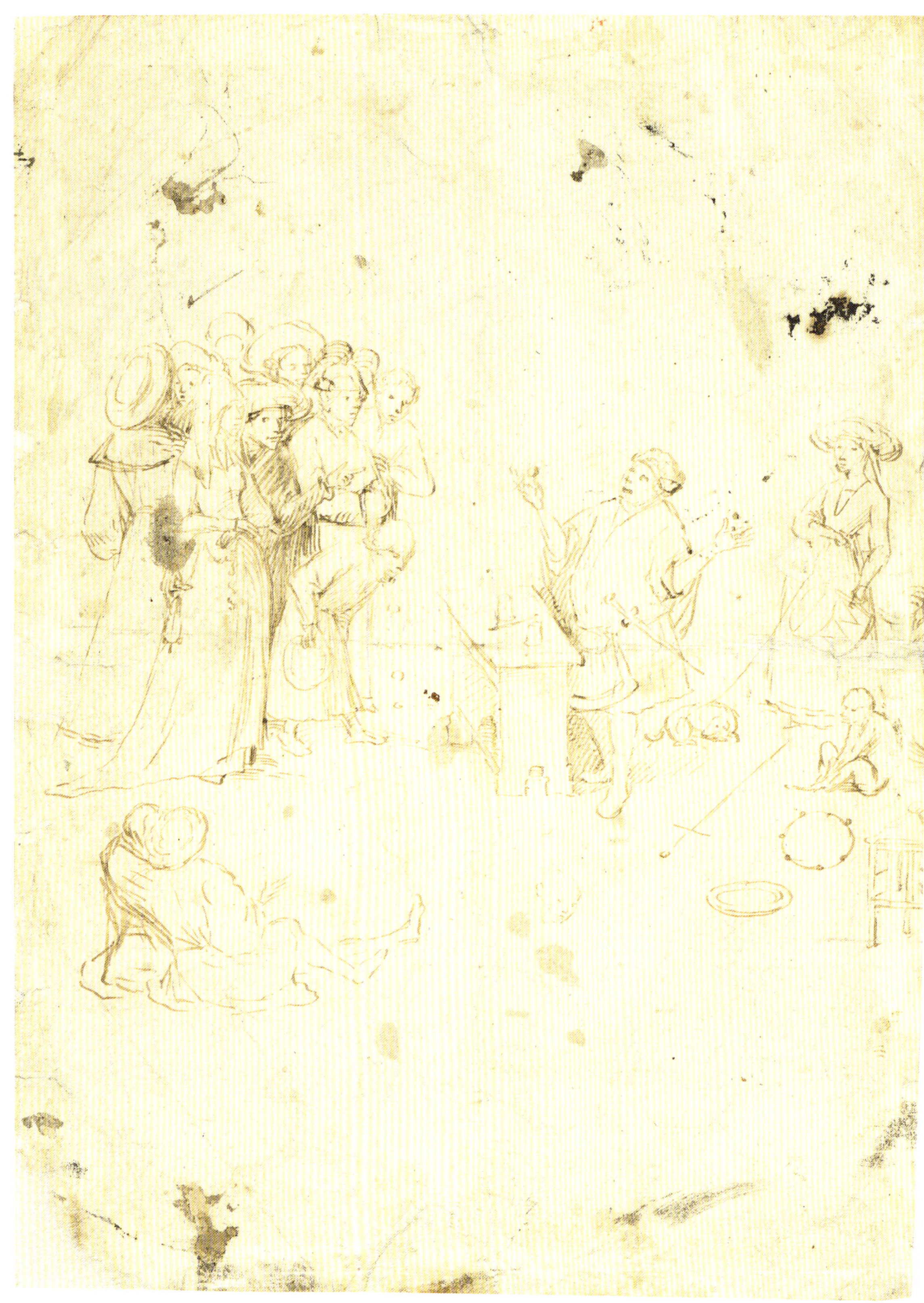

Hieronymus Bosch

24. The Conjurer

Pen and brown ink on paper,
208 × 283 mm
Liège, Musée des Beaux-Arts de Liège,
Album d'Arenberg, 534
(detail)

94   There are two autograph drawings of the *Conjurer*, several paintings by followers of Bosch, and a print dating from the middle of the sixteenth century. The drawing in the Louvre is the most interesting of these artistically (cat. 23). It is a rare example of a composition sketch in which an attempt has been made to visualize a figure group and the interaction between those figures. The speed of drawing contributes here to the energy of the spectacle, in which an adroit thief exploits the confusion to rob an unsuspecting woman of her purse. The situation has been set up by the fraud behind the table, who holds up a little ball. This is the conjurer; he is not working alone, but with the assistance of a band of Gypsies, identifiable from their turban-like headgear. The woman behind him builds the suspense with a drum roll, while other accomplices move among the audience to see what they can filch. The boy spitting balls out of his mouth must be part of the gang too. A couple of pals lounge in the foreground to watch the show; Bosch once again includes spectators to draw us into the scene: we follow their gaze as they observe an audience that watches but does not see, and whose attentive inattention allows it to be robbed of its possessions. It takes us a while to realize precisely what game is being played here; until we spot that one of the two figures in the left foreground is wearing the same sort of Gypsy cap as the other pickpockets; the friendly arm around his supposed mate's shoulder suddenly looks a lot more suspicious…

  A small, recently discovered drawing (cat. 24) has a very sketchy image of the conjurer holding up one ball, while the boy spits out several more. Bosch's method here of sketching the same composition several times, both slowly and more rapidly, matches what he did on the two sides of the sheet with the man in the basket.

The contrast between the drawings and the painting from Saint-Germain-en-Laye is fairly large; the latter is a colourful, jocular and clear composition. The conjurer stands on the right, holding up a little ball once again. The head of a barn owl sticks out of the wicker basket on his belt, warning us to be vigilant. A group of ten spectators stands on the other side of the table, one of whom pretends to be short-sighted, but is meanwhile cutting the purse of the man leaning over in front of him. Are there only two crooks here, or is the boy deliberately distracting the victim too? Or is the deceiver being deceived, and is the man spitting out frogs (!) the actual conjurer? And what about the shifty-looking man in green? Why is he holding his hand like that? Is he directing our attention to the frog crawling out of the bent-over figure's mouth, or is he reaching for the possessions of the man standing in front of him with his eyes closed? Or the man with one arm around the woman's shoulder and his other hand close to her bosom? Is he an innocent spectator or is he on the conjurer's team too? The man's gesture recalls the two lounging figures in the drawing, but it is hard to make out exactly who belongs with whom in the painting.

  There are several versions of this composition, of which this one seems the most closely related to Bosch. Analysis of the painting technique and the way the underdrawing was used to set up the composition shows that this is not an autograph work by Bosch himself but that of a follower. The two surviving autograph drawings suggest, however, that Bosch did once make a painting of a conjurer.

Follower of Hieronymus Bosch
The Conjurer, c. 1510–30
Oil on oak panel, 53.6 × 65.3 cm
Saint-Germain-en-Laye, Musée municipal
de Saint-Germain-en-Laye, 872.1.87

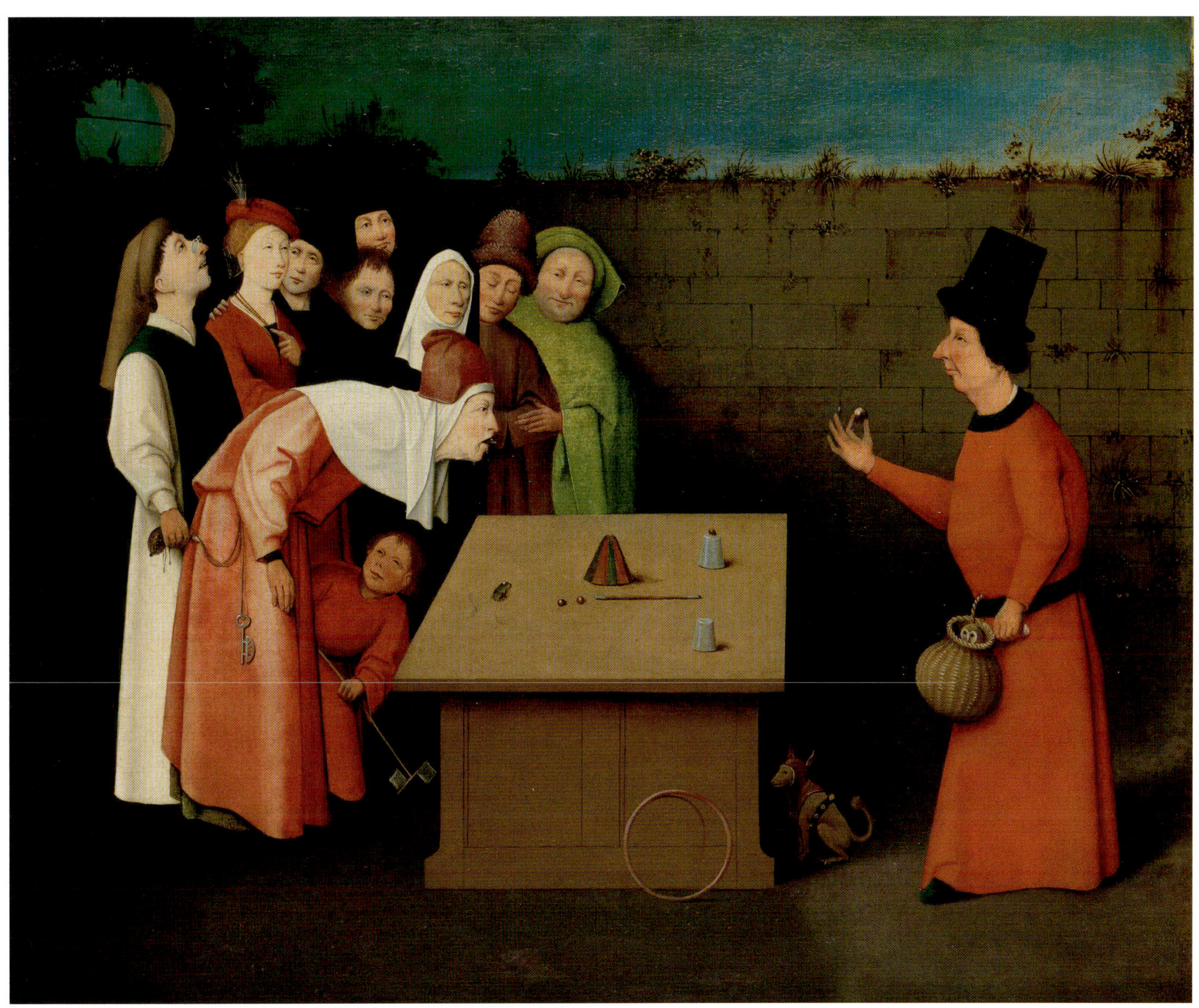

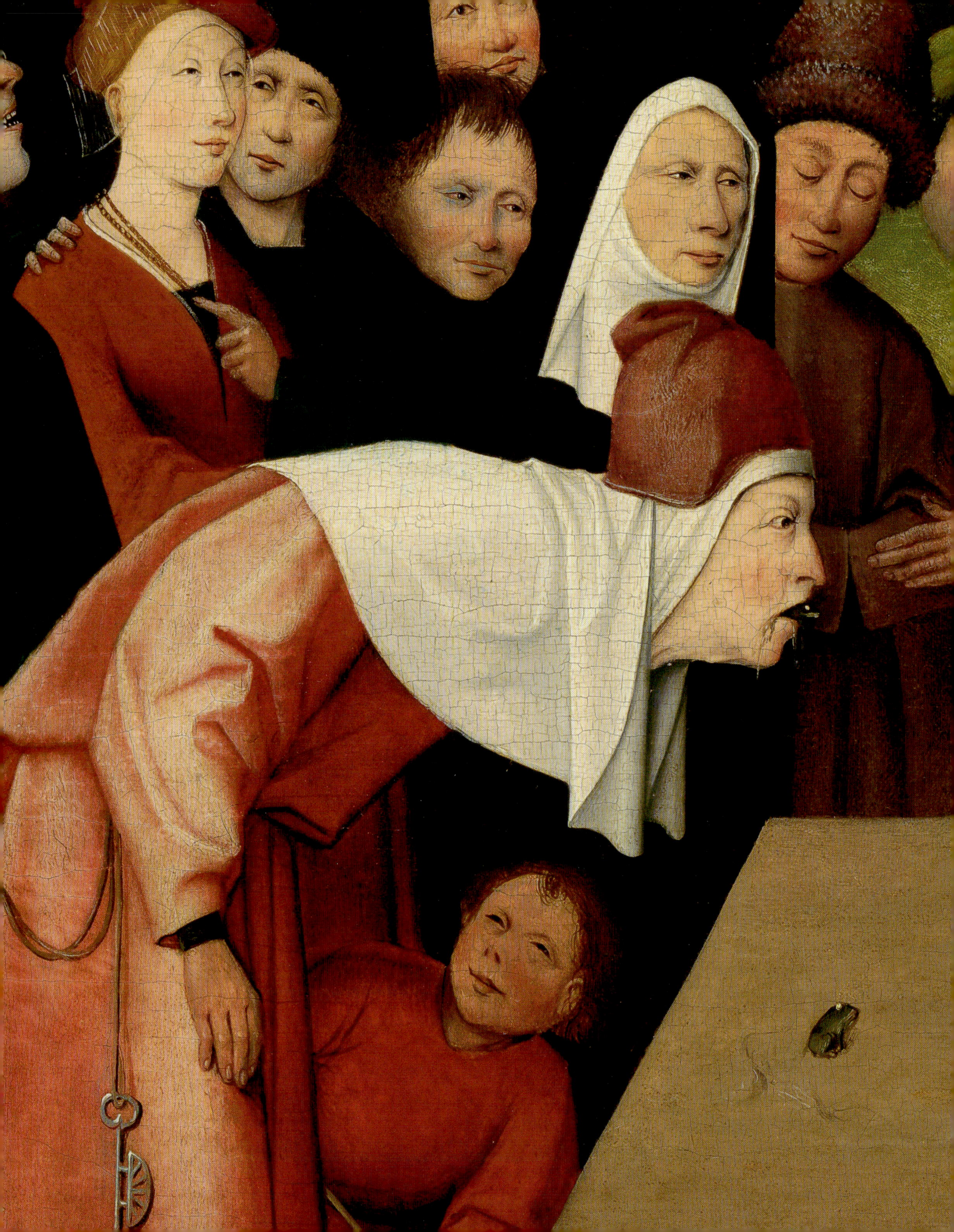

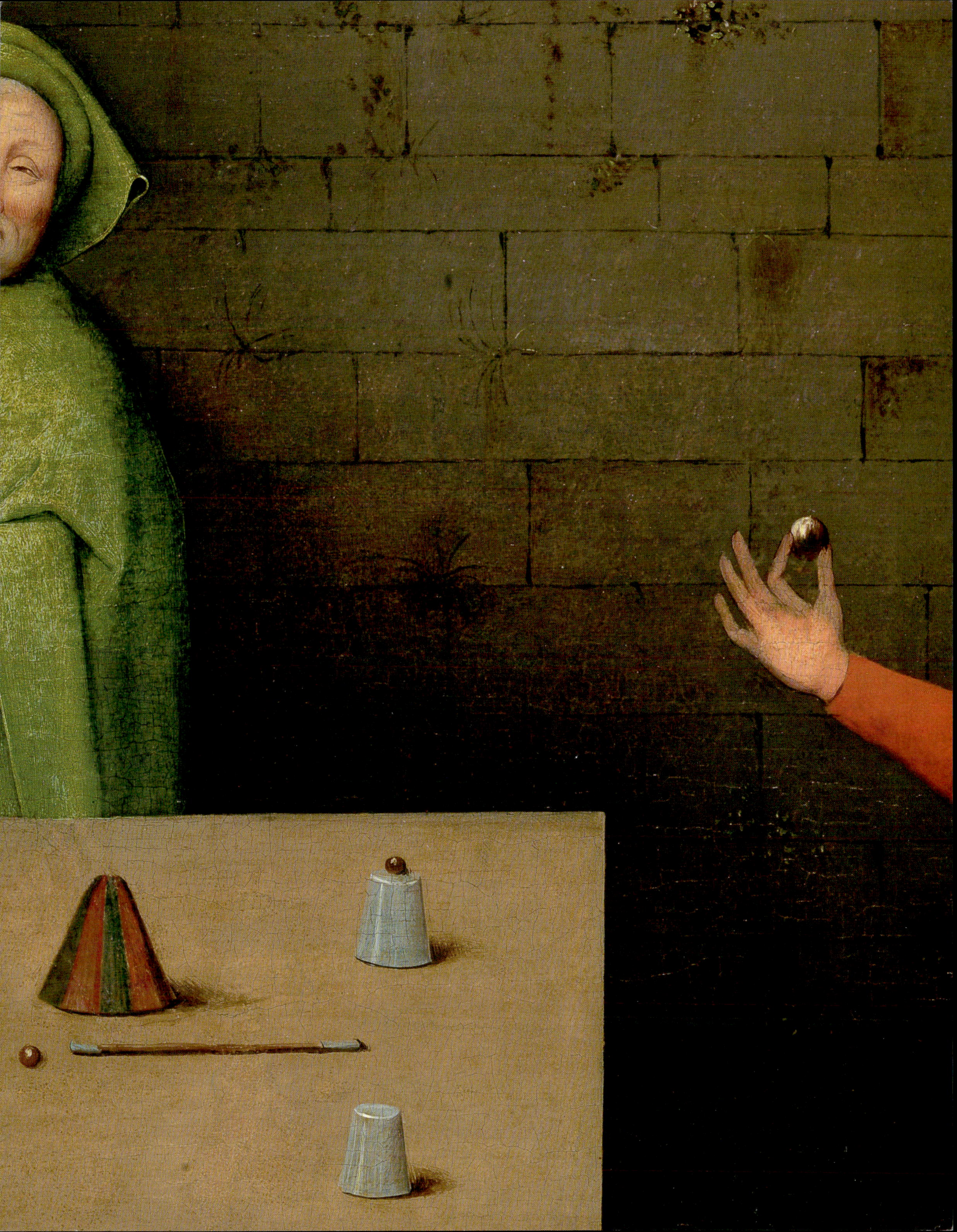

The drawing of ten men watching an event not shown in the sheet itself is very different in character from the *Conjurer* in Paris (cat. 23). It too is concerned with the interaction between people, but the overall effect is static. This partly reflects the subject matter, for what we see is probably a group of spectators of the kind that Bosch included in his *Ecce Homo* scenes (cat. 8, 14). The men appear to be looking at something unfolding before them, possibly at a higher level. They are dressed in an orientalizing style, making it likely that they were intended for a Passion scene.

The drawing style is a little tentative, which helps explain why for a long time this sheet was not included in the body of drawings attributed to Bosch. There are numerous affinities, however, with other drawings in the Bosch group. Nor is this a copy, as has sometimes been suggested: this is obvious from the head of the second man on the left, the continuous outline of which shows that he did not originally wear a cap.

The drawing was used as a quarry for a c. 1560 engraving of a *Christ Carrying the Cross*, which names Bosch as the inventor of the scene.

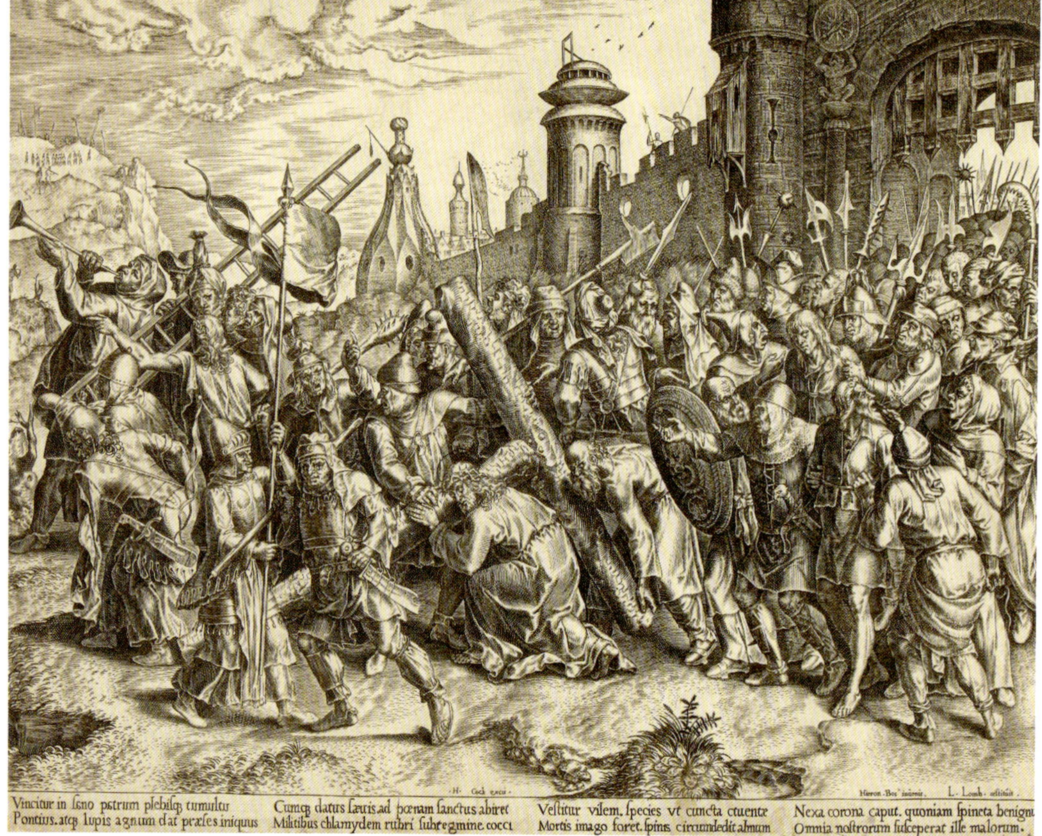

Cornelis Cort, after Lambert Lombard, *Christ Carrying the Cross*, c. 1560
Engraving, 32.3 × 40.4 cm

Pen and brown ink on paper,
124 × 126 mm
New York, The Morgan Library &
Museum, I, 112

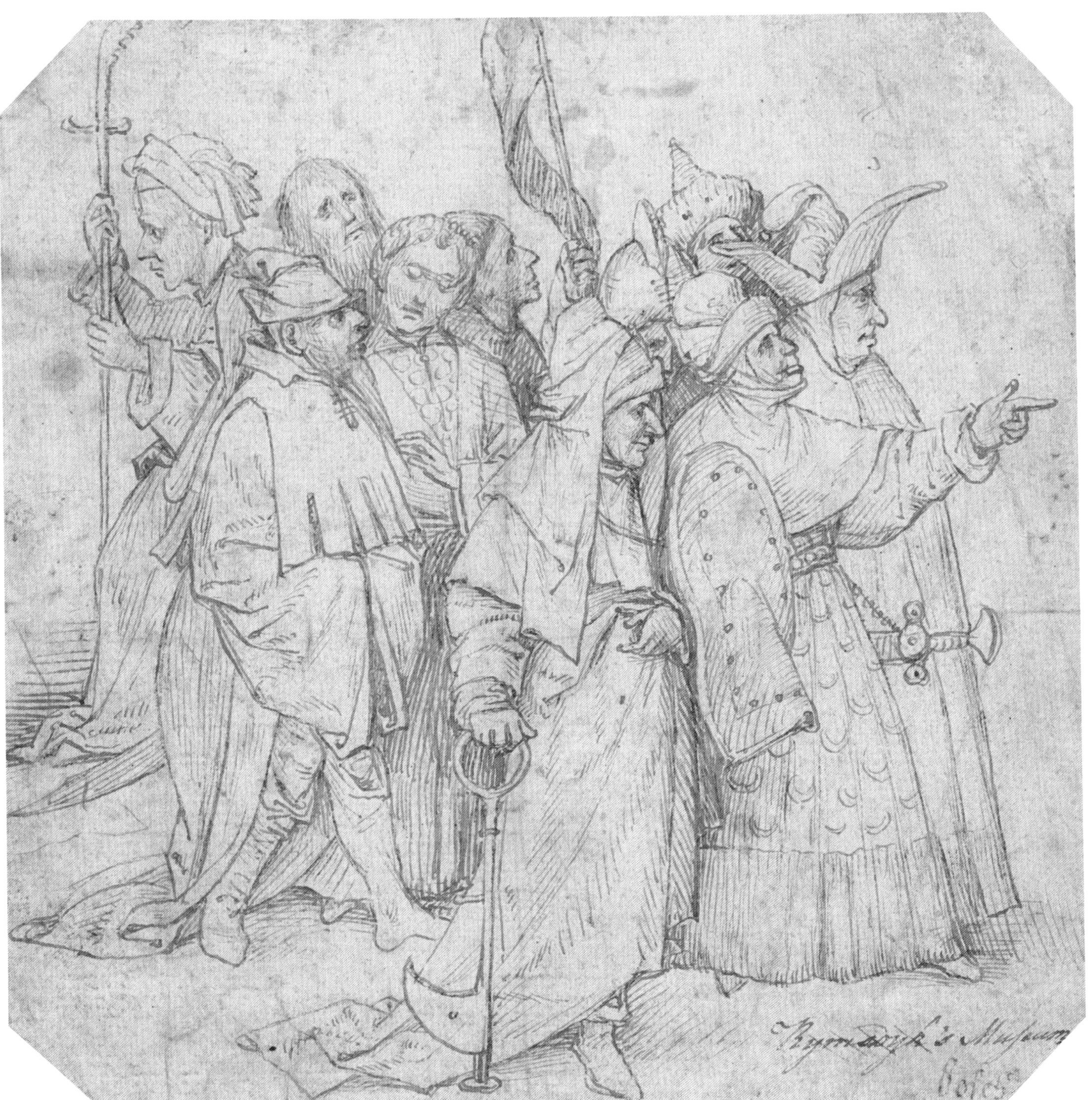

The Fall of Man, together with the Fall of the Rebel Angels, is the ultimate story of the origin of evil. The theme forms the point of departure for Bosch's large triptychs, the *Garden of Earthly Delights*, the *Last Judgement* and the *Haywain*. We currently know of only one drawn version by Bosch

– a rapid sketch and very small, but nevertheless done skilfully and convincingly. An elegant Eve stands on the left, seeming to hesitate about whether or not to accept the fruit she has been expressly prohibited from eating. Satan has tried to assume human form, but has not quite succeeded; his tail

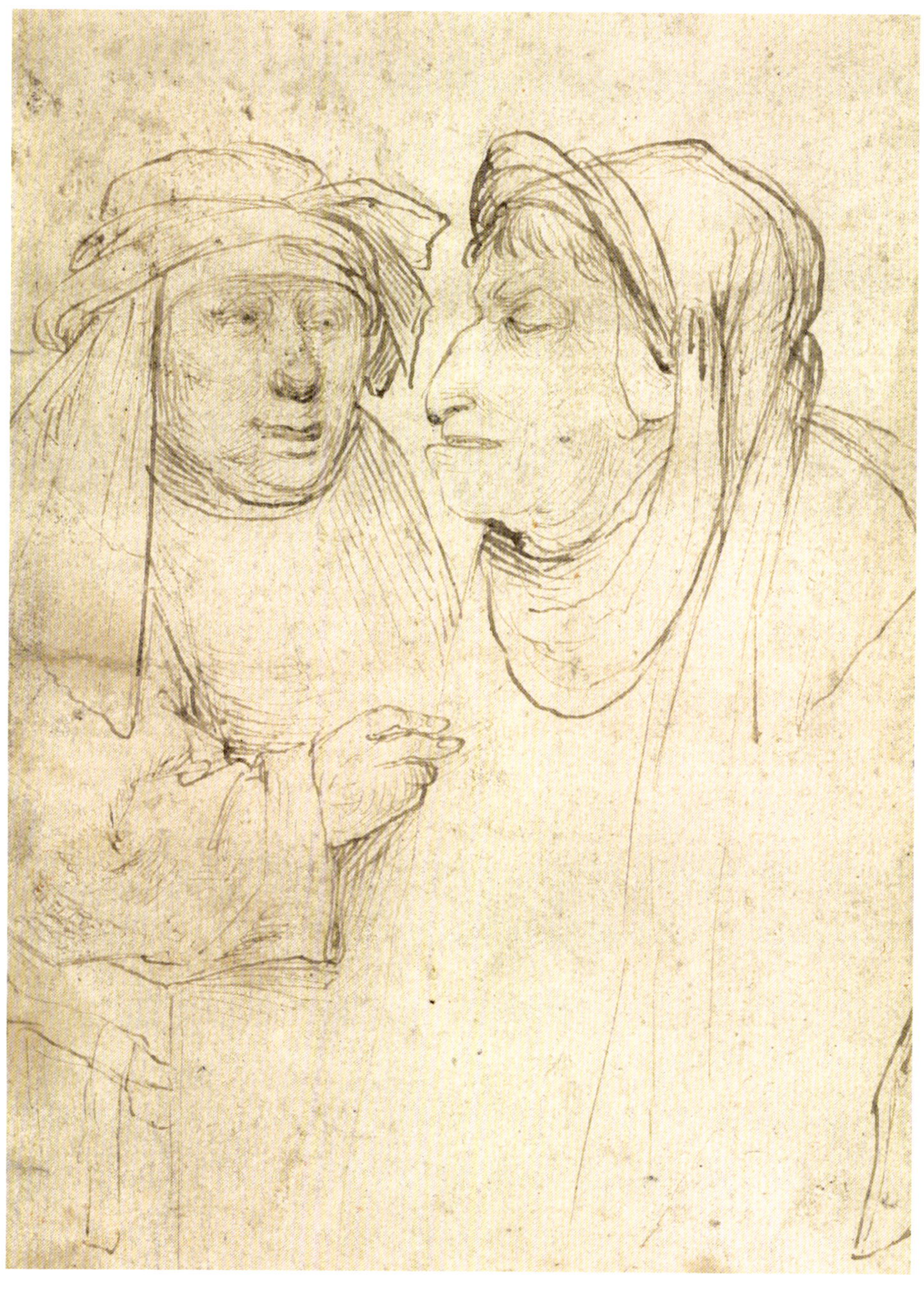

**Pen and grey-brown ink on paper,
137 × 103 mm
Private collection (Courtesy
The Metropolitan Museum of Art,
New York)**

hangs backwards in such a strange way that he has to hold on to the tree of the knowledge of good and evil to avoid falling over. All the same, we know he will succeed in foisting the apple on Eve.

Bosch drew two men's heads on the other side of the sheet. They are somewhat unsavoury-looking characters. The one on the right has a caricature-like face, of the kind we often find in Bosch for people from the fringes of society. The person within is expressed, as it were, on the outside.

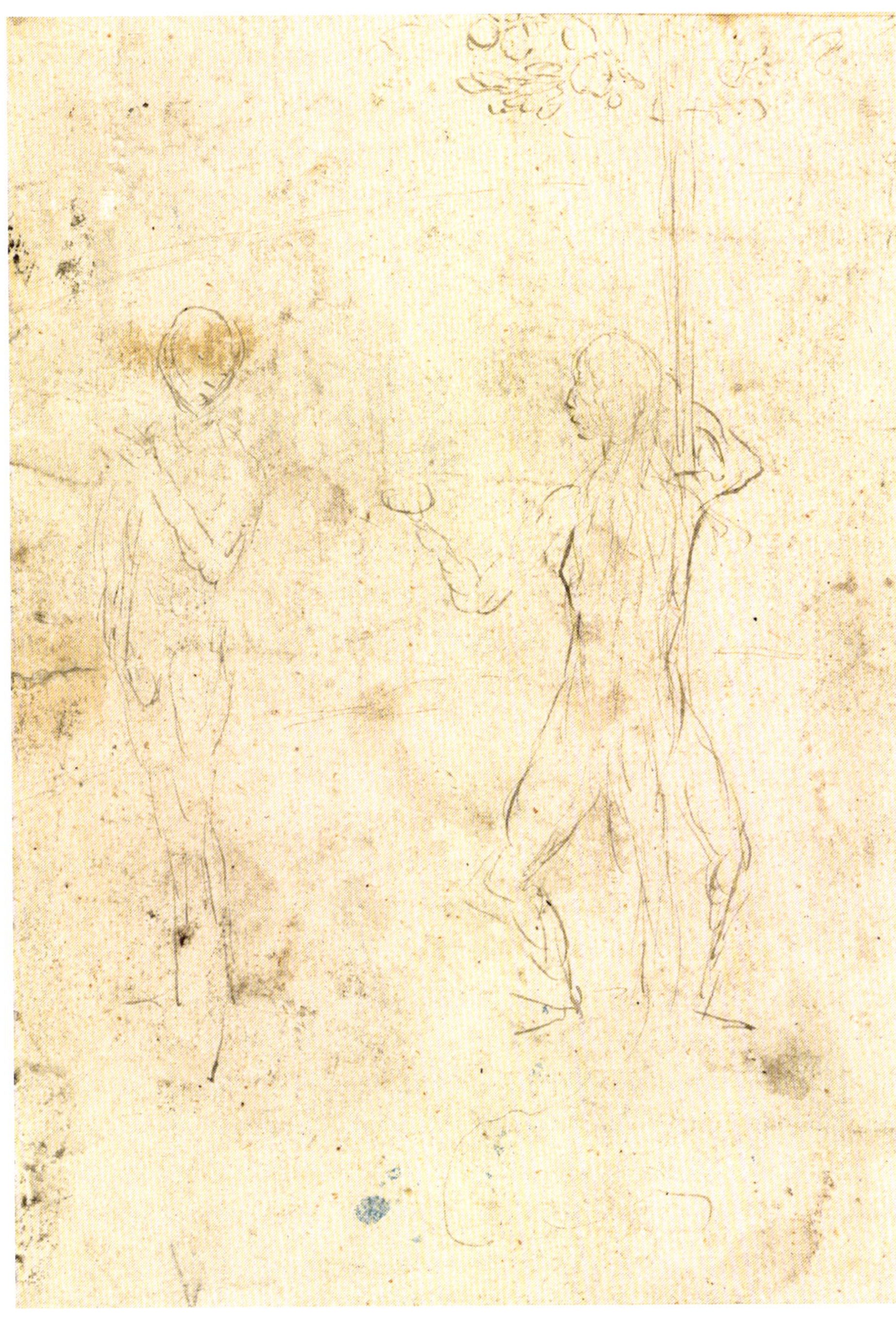

It is hard to say what types these two oriental men represent. They are neither crude nor ugly like the two men in the previous drawing. The figure on the right does look a bit mean, or is that a false impression? This drawing poses something of a challenge: it is worked out to a degree we do not find in other drawings by Bosch, including the use of white body colour to add highlights and create depth. It is executed so precisely and with such refinement that we doubt whether it can be attributed to Bosch, as has been done by so many authors. Not every fine drawing is by Bosch, of course, and despite certain affinities, it is hard to link this sheet with others belonging to the Bosch group.

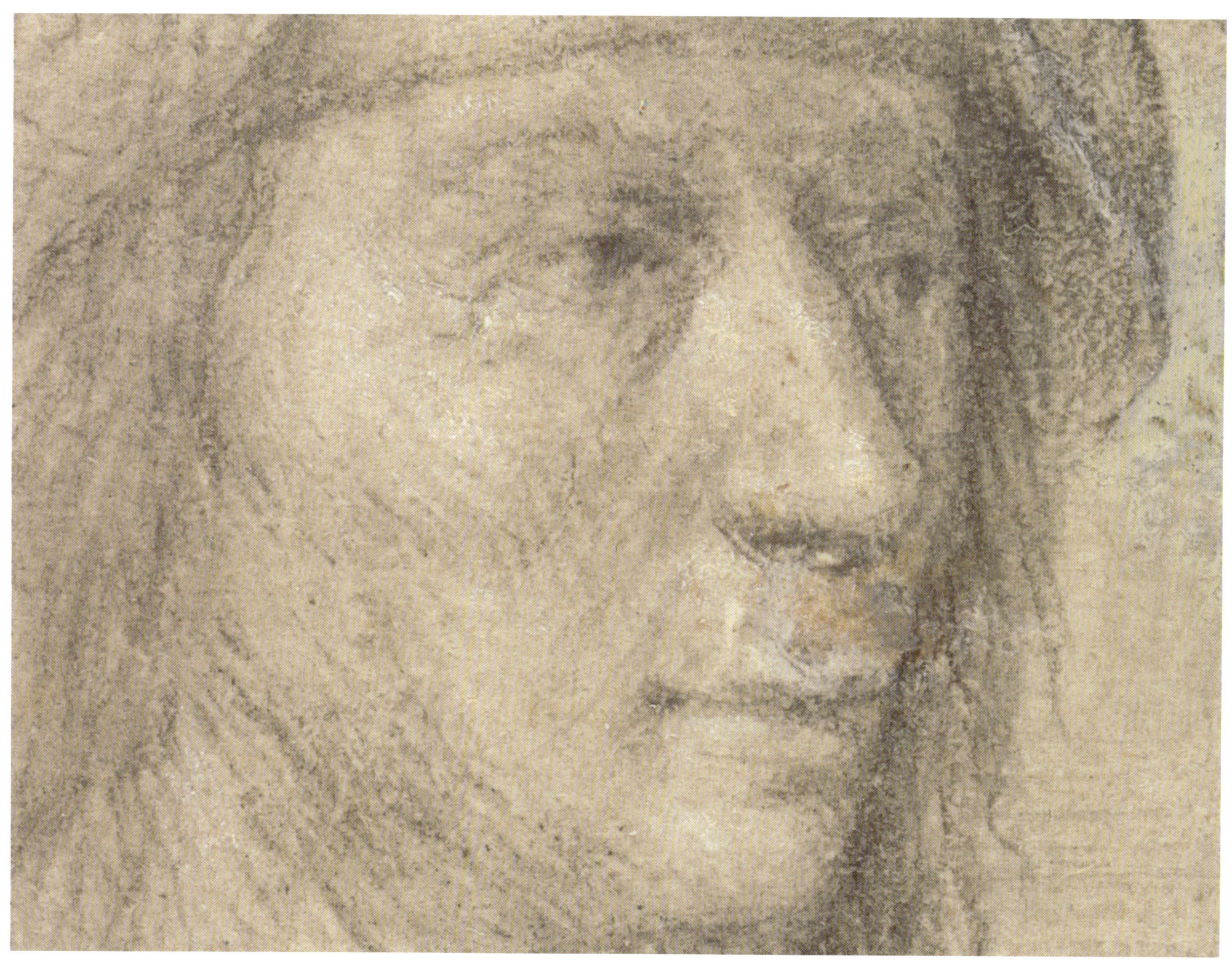

Pen and brush in grey-brown ink, black chalk,
white highlights, on paper, 138 × 108 mm
Berlin, Staatliche Museen zu Berlin,
Kupferstichkabinett, KdZ 5210

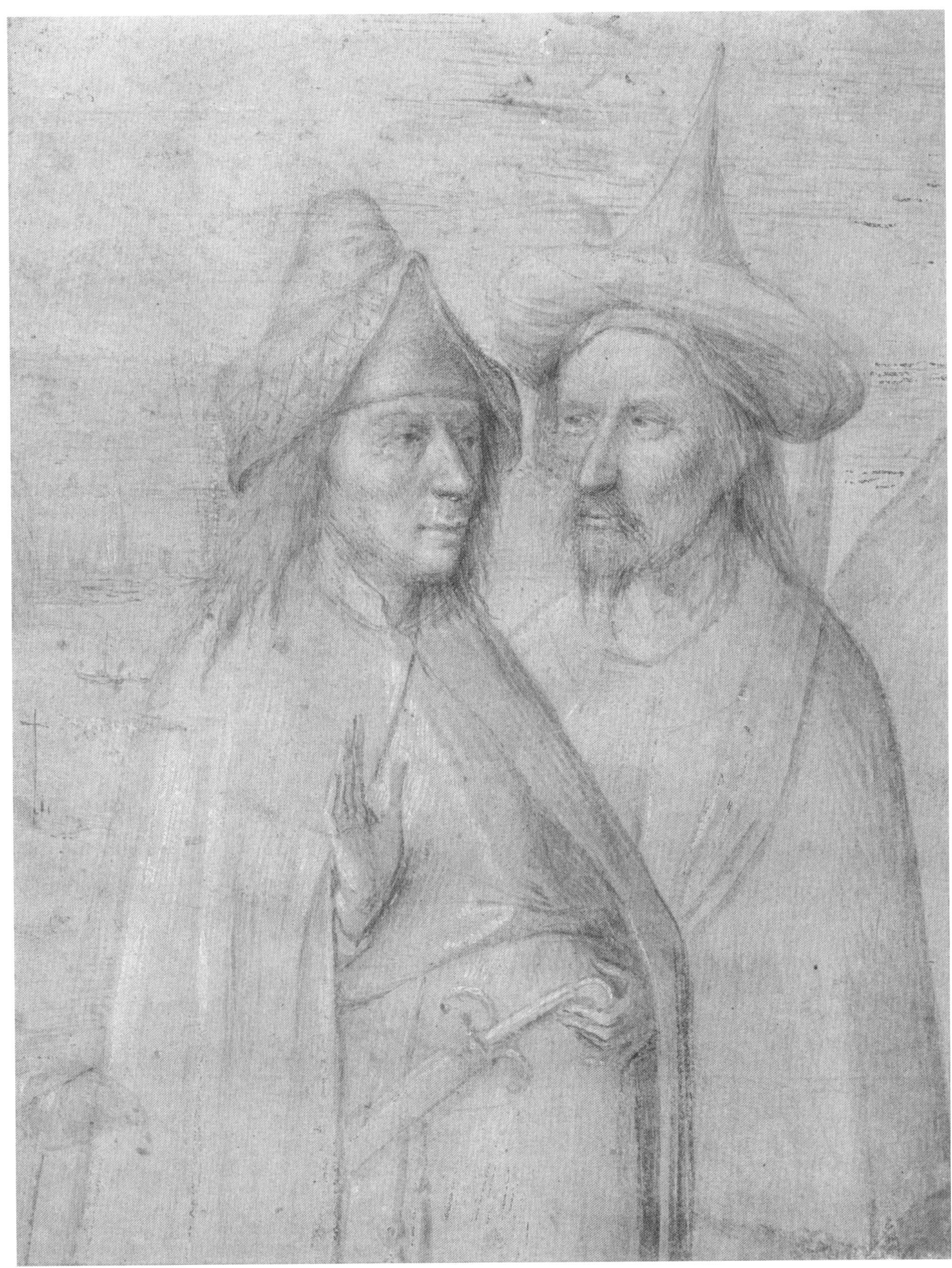

104

The *Entombment of Christ* is Bosch's most fully elaborated design drawing. It was done in different pens and inks and must have been produced at an advanced stage of the design for another work of art. We know from archive documents that Bosch created designs for stained glass, for instance, and for embroidery. He obviously prepared the images in his own paintings too, but his autograph work frequently shows evidence of him continuing to sketch, explore and adjust on the panel itself. This design will therefore have been intended for execution by others. It might well have been for a painting, but it is also possible that it is a preliminary drawing for a sculptural group. Whatever work was ultimately created from this drawing, it has not survived.

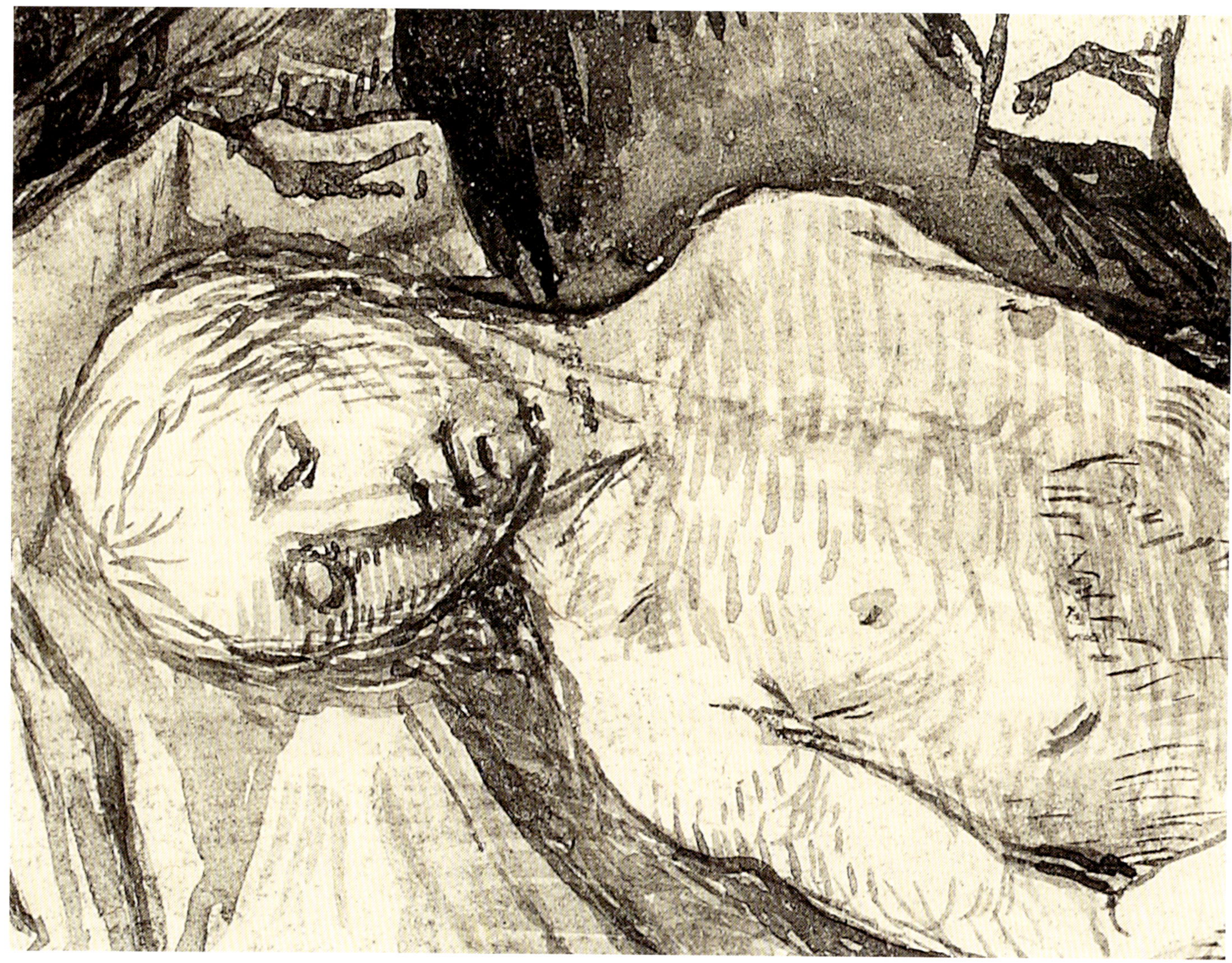

Pen and brush in grey and black ink over traces
of black chalk on paper, 252 × 304 mm
London, The British Museum, Department
of Prints & Drawings, 1952.0405.9

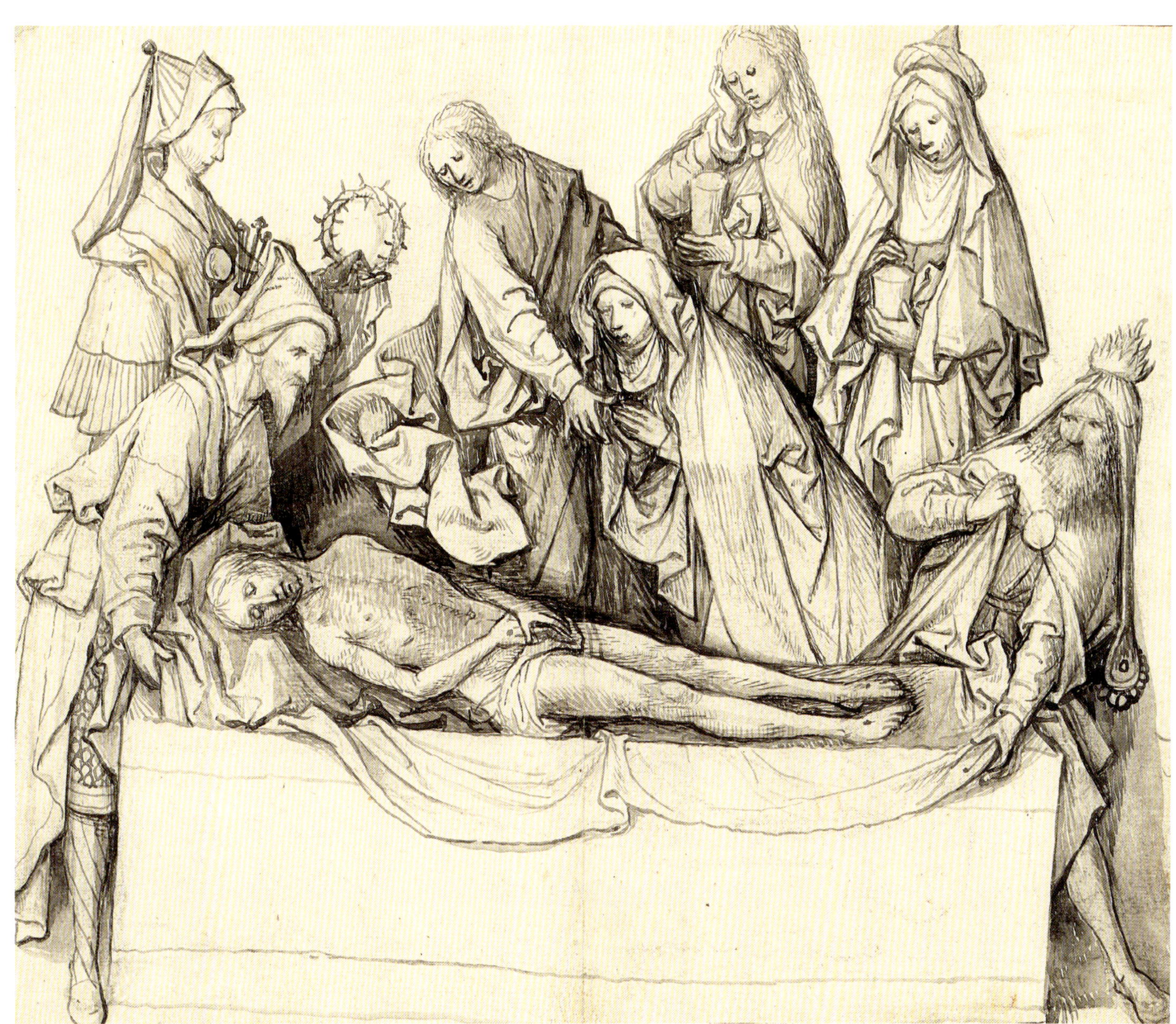

106

There are two drawings of crippled beggars that can be linked to Bosch – one in Vienna and one in Brussels. Each is a model sheet – a collection of separate motifs used as a stock of examples in the workshop. The Vienna drawing was used around 1570–80 for a print, which stated that Hieronymus Bosch was the 'inventor' of the image. Figures from both drawings had previously been used – some time before 1540 – in a tapestry design showing Saint Martin cutting his cloak panel in two to share with the poor. The tapestry was one in a series of five listed in an inventory of King Francis I of France's possessions in 1540 as having been made after designs by Bosch. These drawings are the work, therefore, of early followers of Bosch who might have been referring back to autograph work, as in the case of the Oxford model sheet (cat. 38).

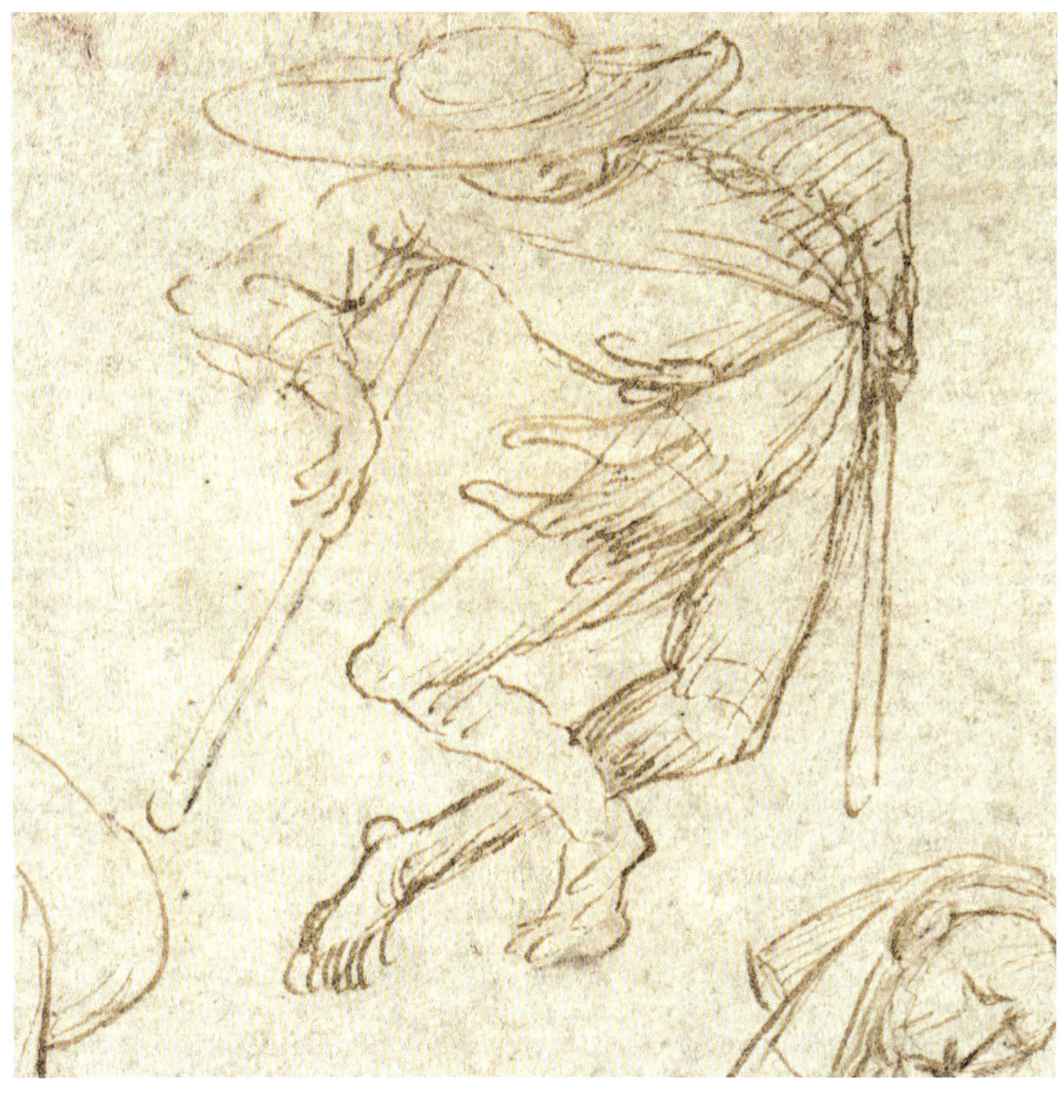

Pen and grey-brown ink on paper over
preparatory drawing in pen, 265 × 199 mm
Brussels, Bibliothèque royale de Belgique,
Cabinet des Estampes / Koninklijke
Bibliotheek van België, Prentenkabinet,
S.II 133708, folio C

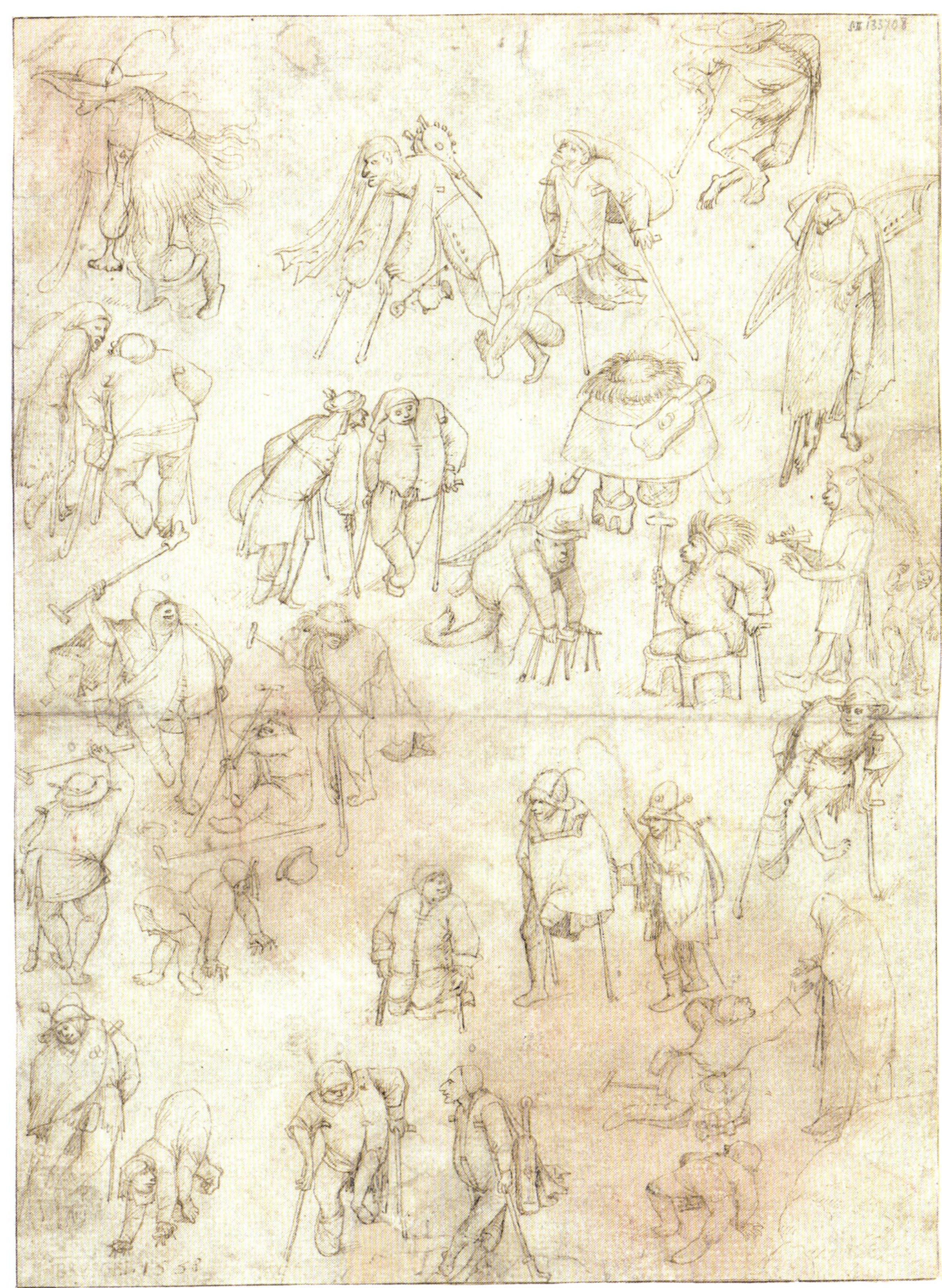

108 Macrophotography enables us to compare the two drawings (cat. 30 and cat. 31) in great detail. This reveals that the style in which the two drawings were done differs so much that we can only conclude that they were the work of two different artists.

Not only is the draughtsman's hand not the same, but the degree of precision and detail also differ. Four musical instruments in the Brussels sheet can be identified as attributes of the beggars, for instance, while the sheet in Vienna depicts twice as many and with greater accuracy.

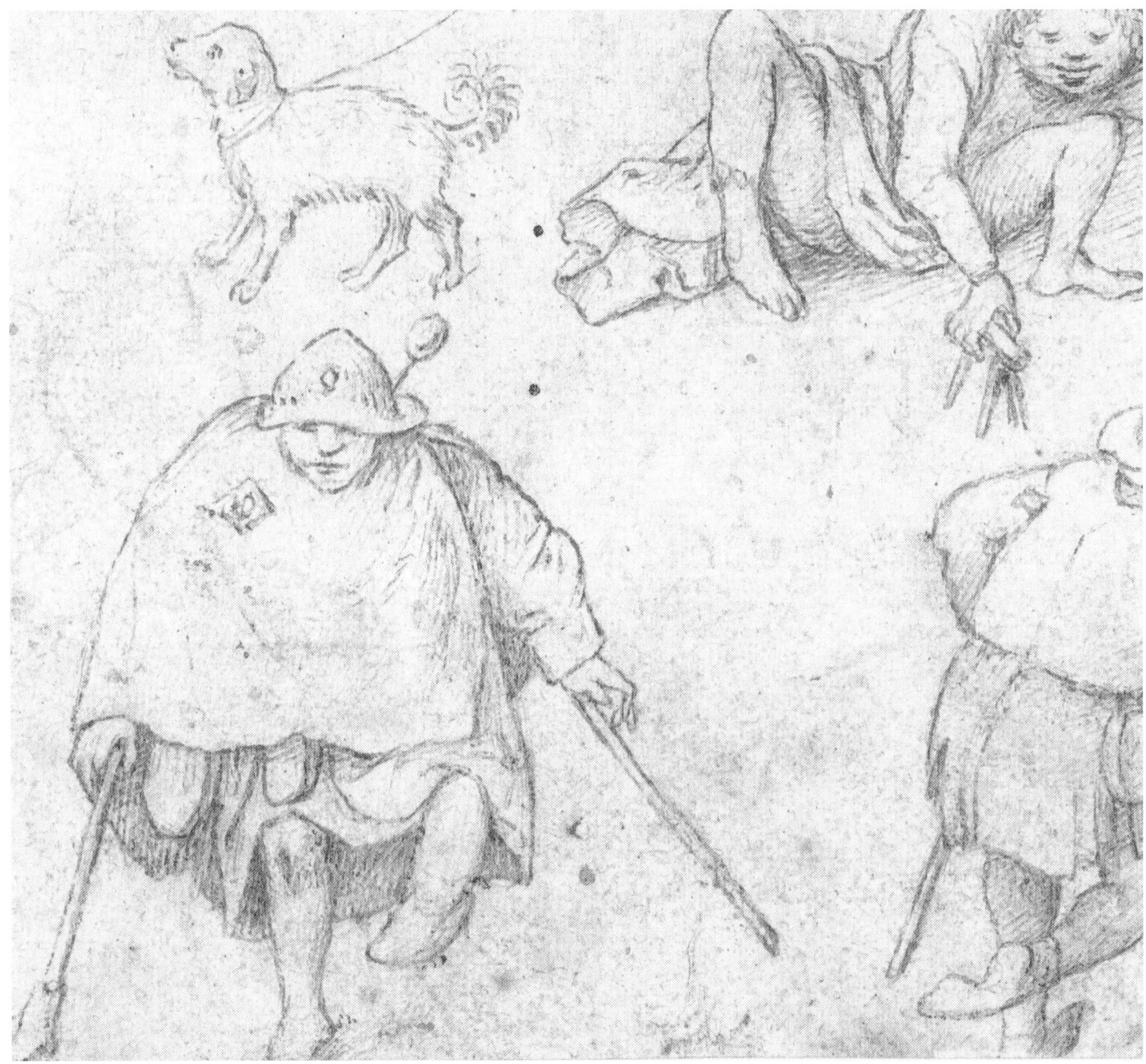

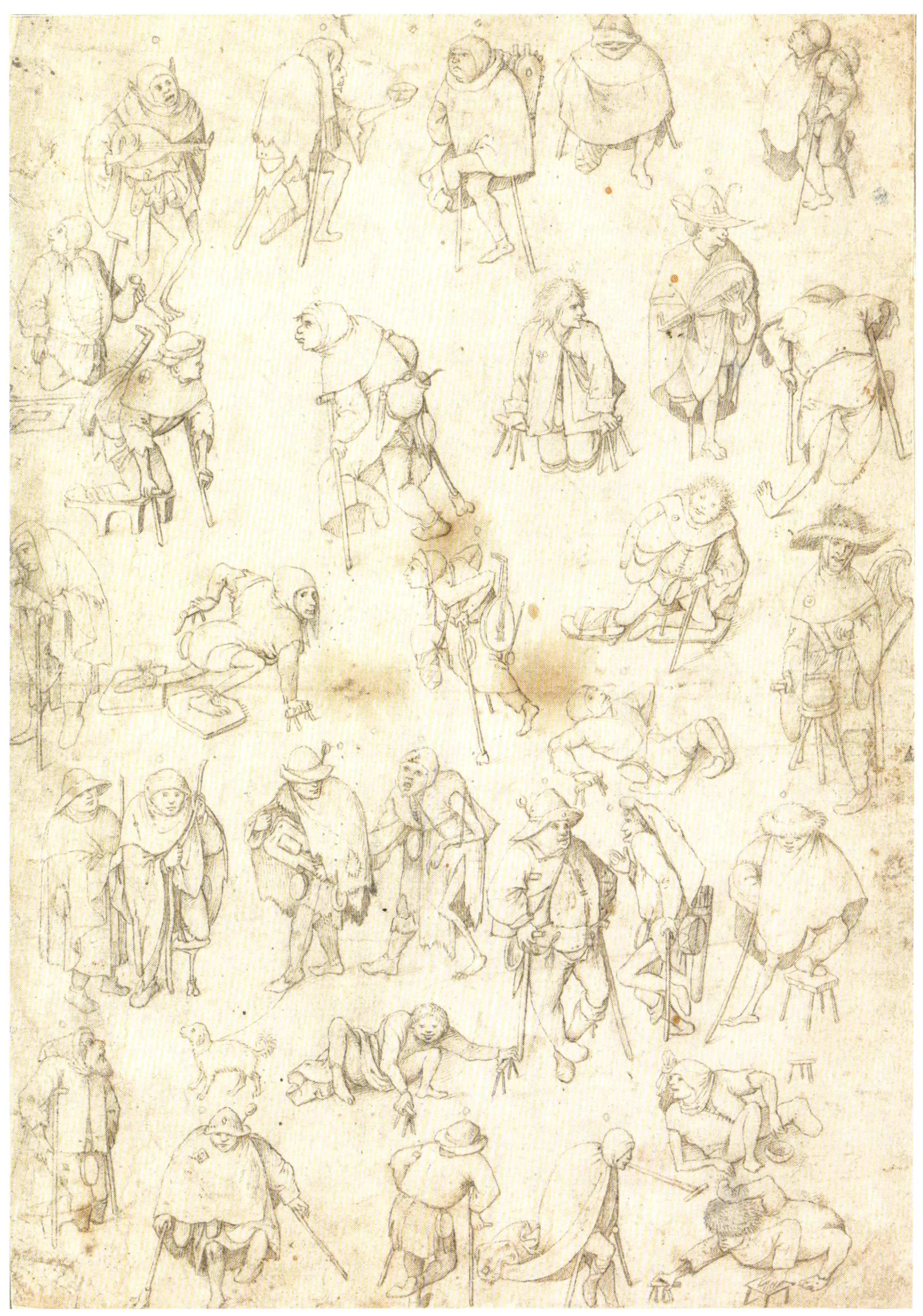

110 This little drawing with two monsters shows Bosch at his best. He has attached human hands to an animal's body, given it a swan's neck, and placed the whole thing on hindquarters that seem to come from yet another animal. Place its left leg in a sawn-off bone together with an arrow, give the monster another arrow to hold, and the result is a typical Bosch figure. The monster, like the growling creature beneath it, is wholly convincing in appearance, yet we cannot say what kind of beast it is.

There are two less impressive figures on the other side of the sheet. One is a salamander-like creature with a shell that merges into a horse's skull. The latter is a recurring motif in Bosch and also appears, for instance, in the exterior of the left wing of the *Haywain* (cat. 5).

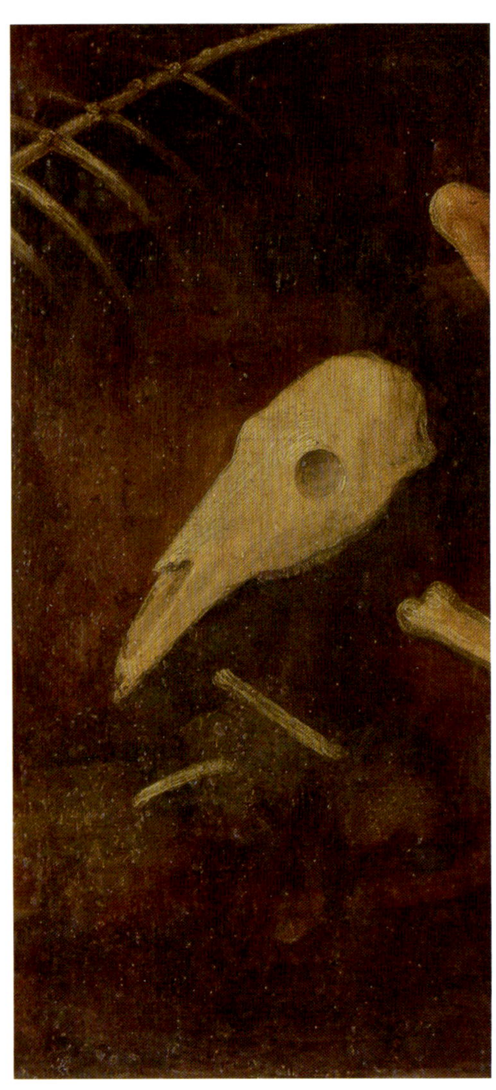

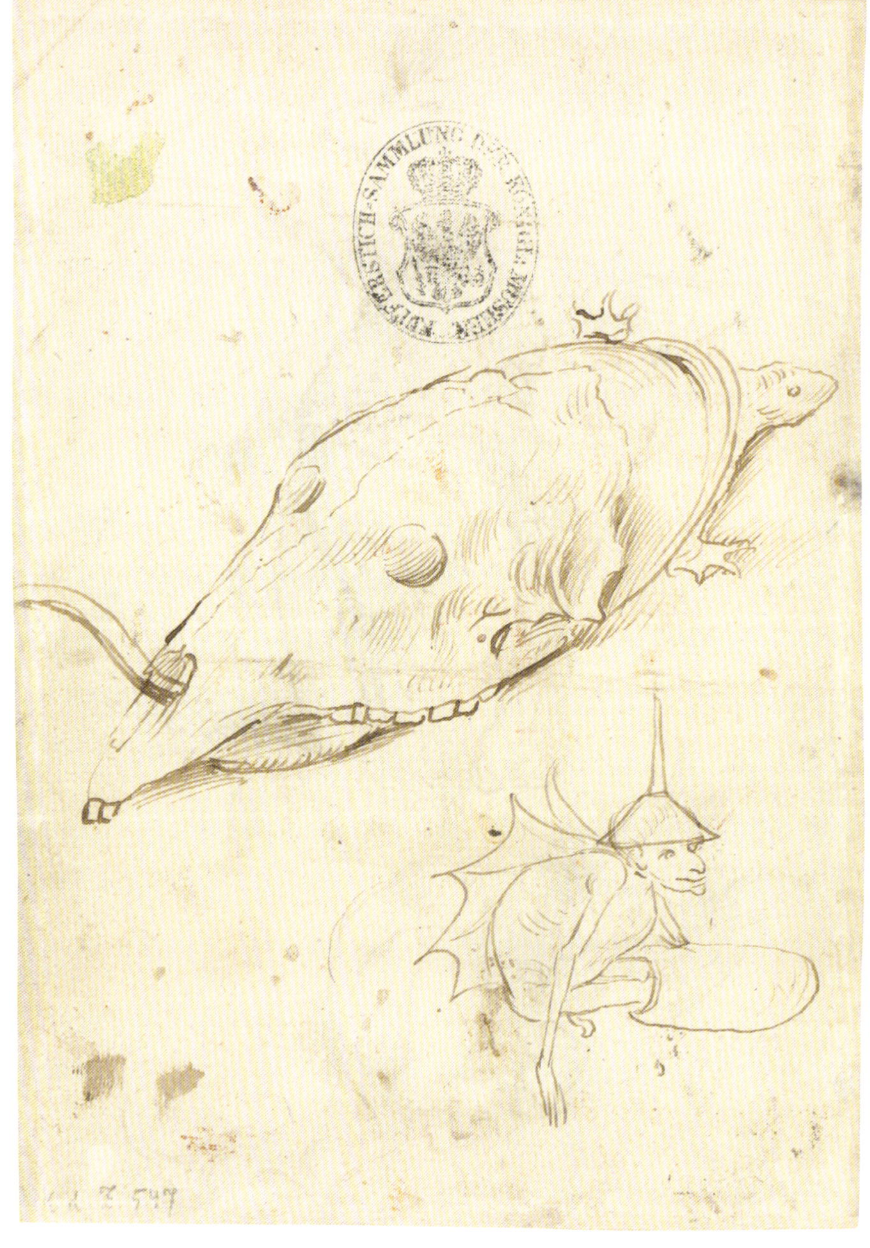

Pen and brown ink on paper,
163 × 116 mm
Berlin, Staatliche Museen zu Berlin,
Kupferstichkabinett, KdZ 547

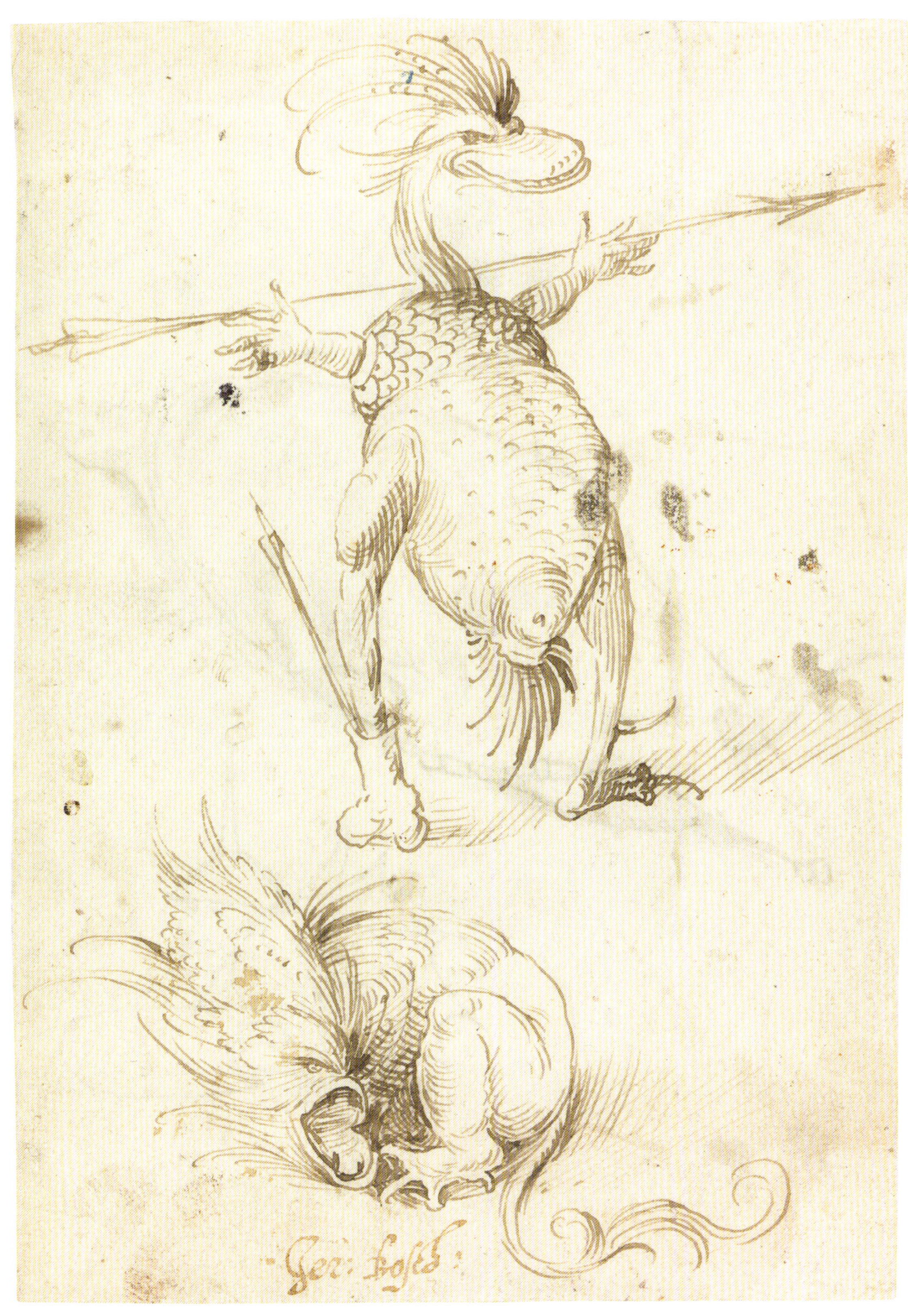

The drawings on this sheet are very appealing, but their quality is not among the highest in the Bosch group. Compared to the somewhat routine *Temptation*, *Singers in an Egg* on the verso is wittier, but its execution is nevertheless inferior to the figure drawings we know to be autograph drawings. It is therefore assumed that these drawings were produced by workshop assistants of Bosch. We nevertheless believe that they were produced in close proximity to the master, as two monstrous heads were also drawn in a different ink, now quite faded, on the side of the sheet where the singers in their egg were later added on top of them. These monsters do appear to be Bosch's own work.

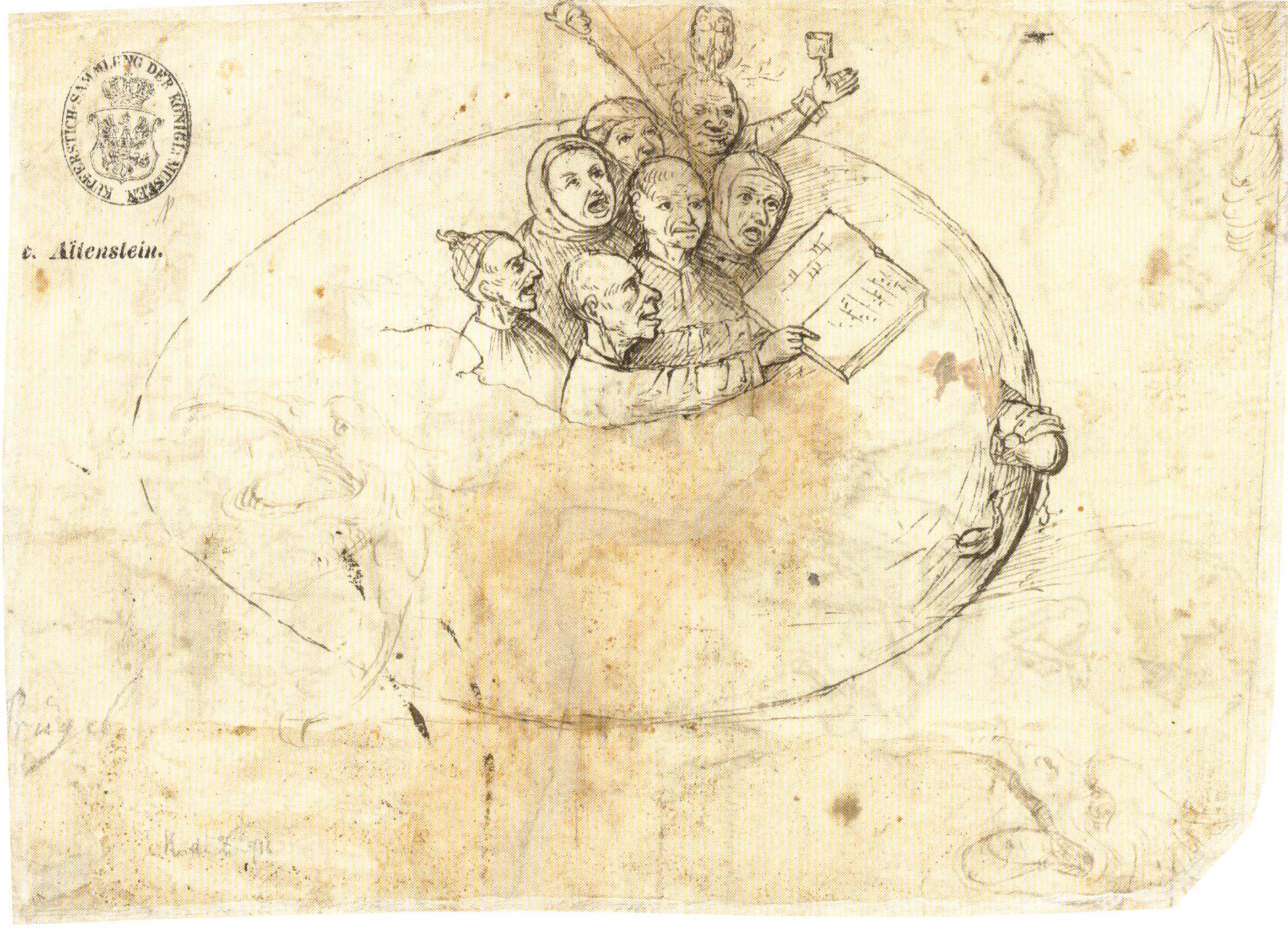

Pen and brown ink on paper,
179 × 258 mm
Berlin, Staatliche Museen zu Berlin,
Kupferstichkabinett, KdZ 711

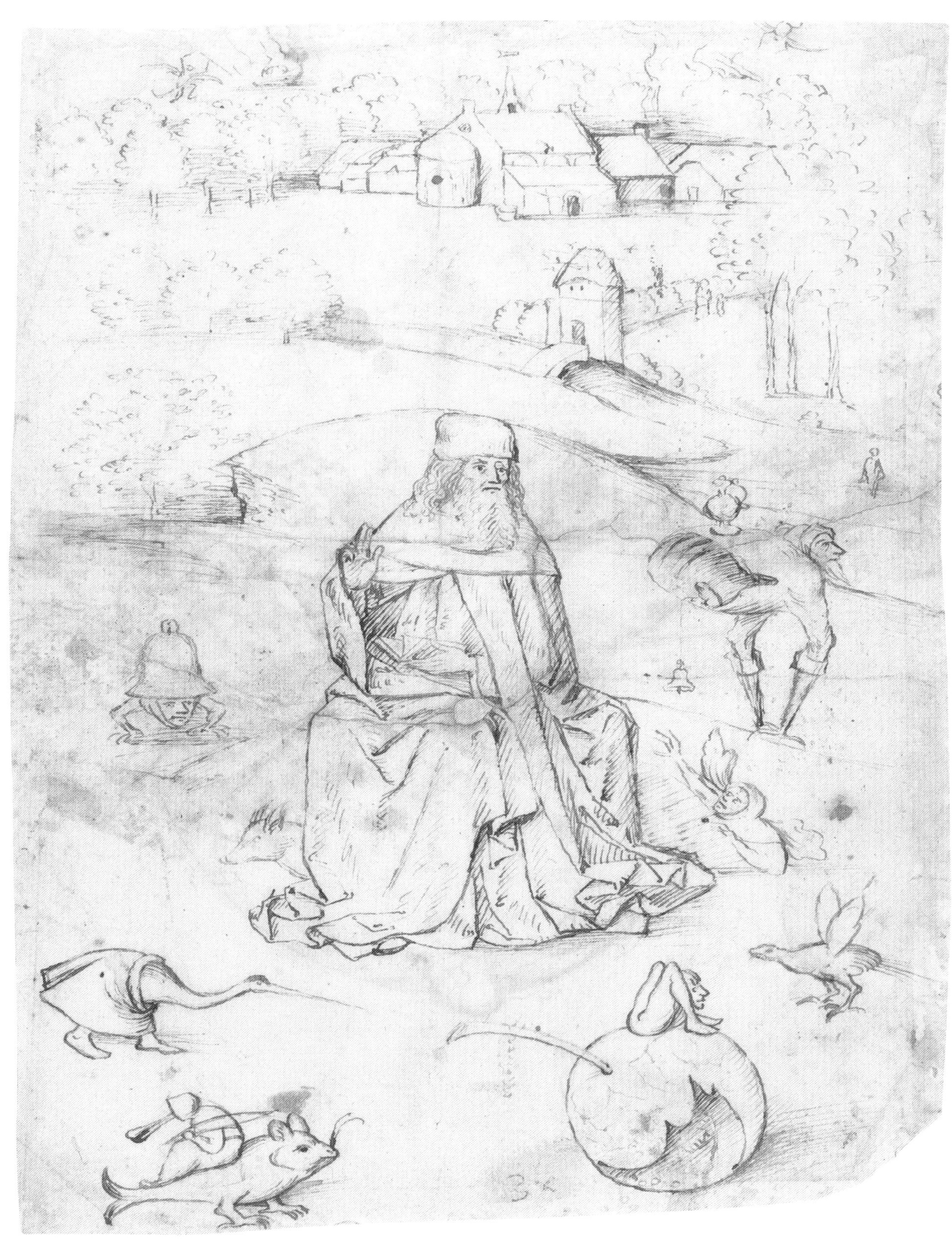

Pen and brown ink on paper,
259 × 197 mm
Private collection

114

This drawing of a scene from hell with fantastic monsters and freaks is presented here for the first time as an autograph work by Bosch. The size of the sheet and the richness of its content make it an extremely important addition to the body of drawings. The work is relatively unknown: it was auctioned in 2003, since when it has belonged to a private collection; it is shown here in public for the first time.

The scene is frenetic and chaotic, as we would expect of hell. At the centre of the composition, a net is used to fish for large numbers of lost souls, who are fed into the maw of a demonic monster via a giant paddlewheel. We also see human beings used as the clappers of a bell, a dragon vomiting out souls into a cauldron, people sitting on the blade of a knife, and a barrel on little legs. It is the kind of imagery we have come to describe as 'Boschian' and which we find in paintings incorporating scenes of hell, such as the *Garden of Earthly Delights* and the *Last Judgement* (both the Bruges (cat. 49) and Vienna versions).

Surprisingly, it is precisely the Boschian nature of the drawing that some have cited as an argument *against* attributing it to Bosch and for concluding instead that it is a pastiche, made by one of his workshop assistants. After careful study of the sheet and comparison with other drawings and paintings by Bosch, however, we believe that this is not the work of a follower or an apprentice but of the master himself. The quality of a detail like the helmeted creature sitting on a barrel on legs that contains another human figure is excellent. The drawing offers a fascinating insight into the associative and additive way in which Bosch composed his images. He worked here in precisely the same way that he built up the hell wing of the *Garden of Earthly Delights* – probably the most famous scene of the underworld in all Western art (fig. p. 57).

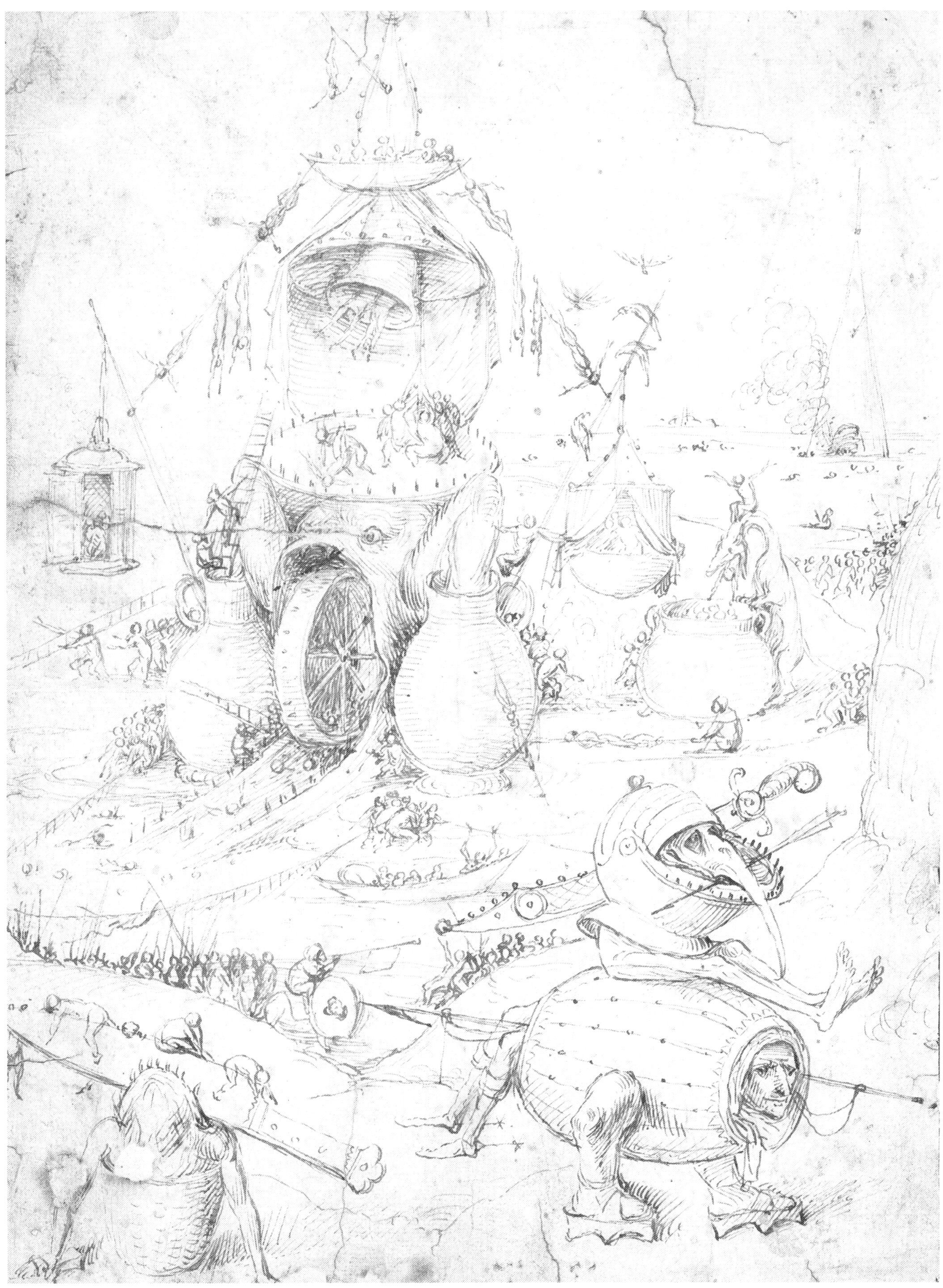

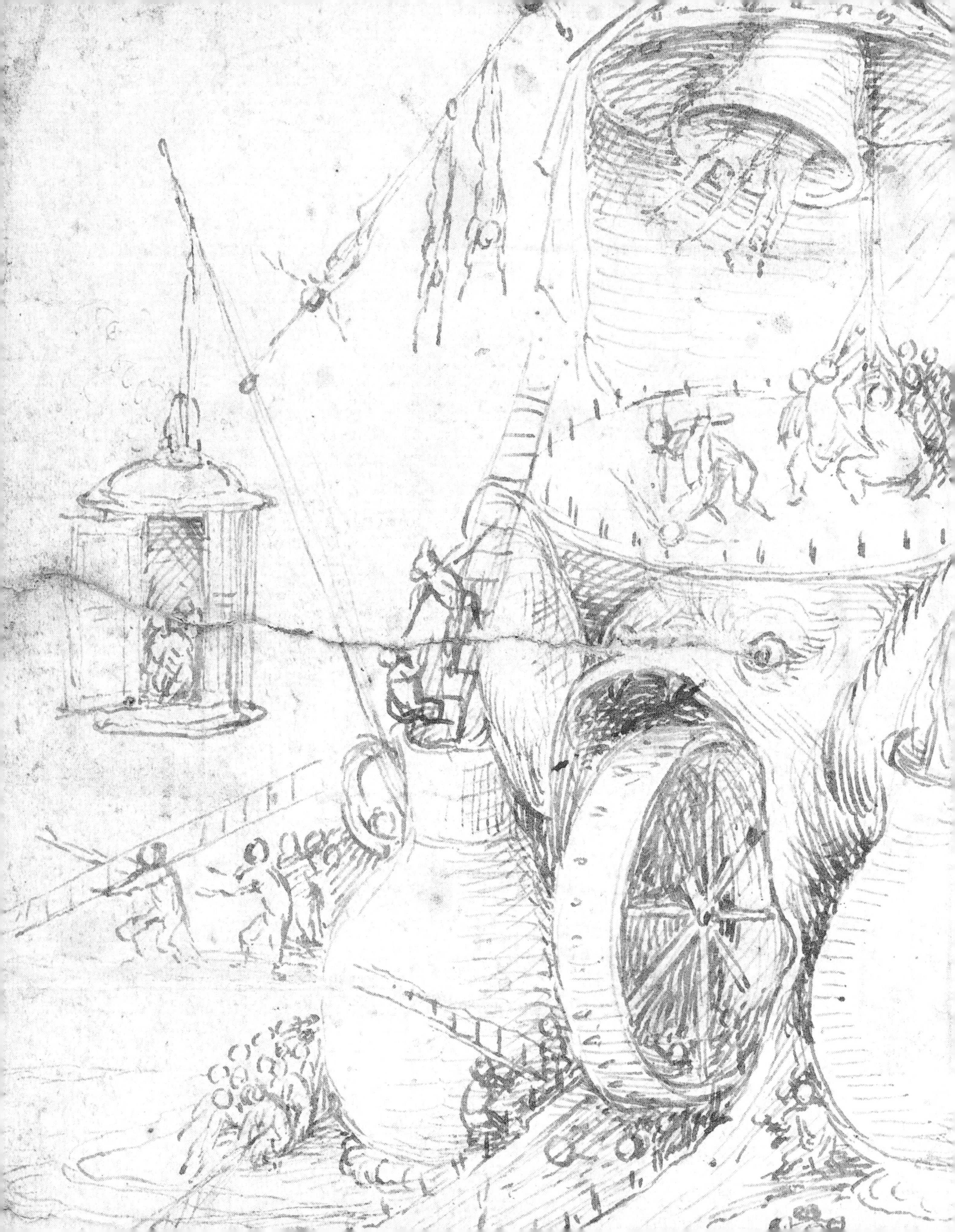

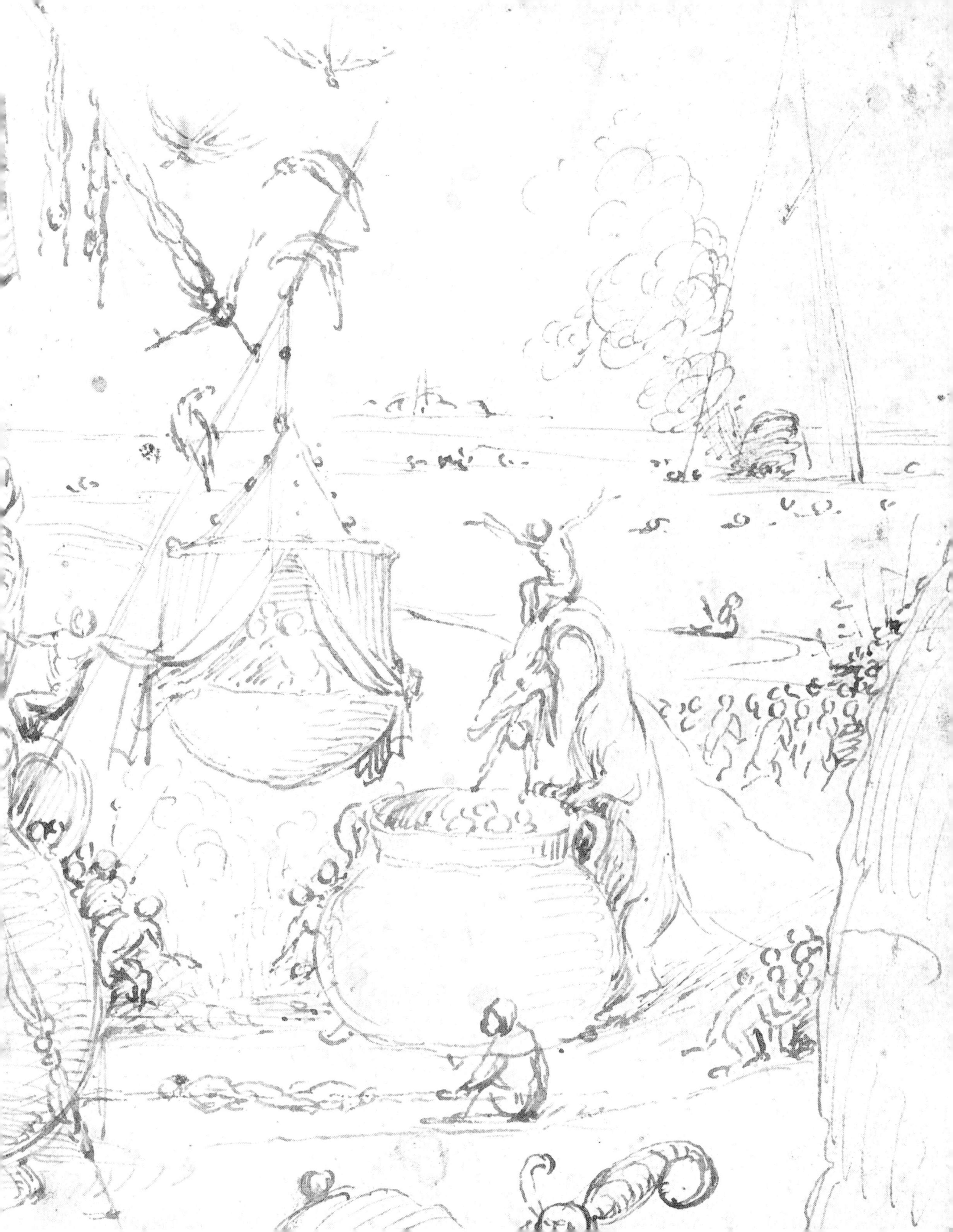

118

The *Burning Ship* from the Akademie der bildenden Künste in Vienna is much less ambitious than the *Infernal Landscape* (cat. 34), but is structured according to the same principles. It is a record of the kind of creative flash that Bosch must have had so often. If we look closely, we make out recurring elements, such as the figures who clamber among the masts and rigging (*Last Judgement*, Bruges, cat. 49) and the figure with a flock of birds flying out of its backside (see cat. 22).

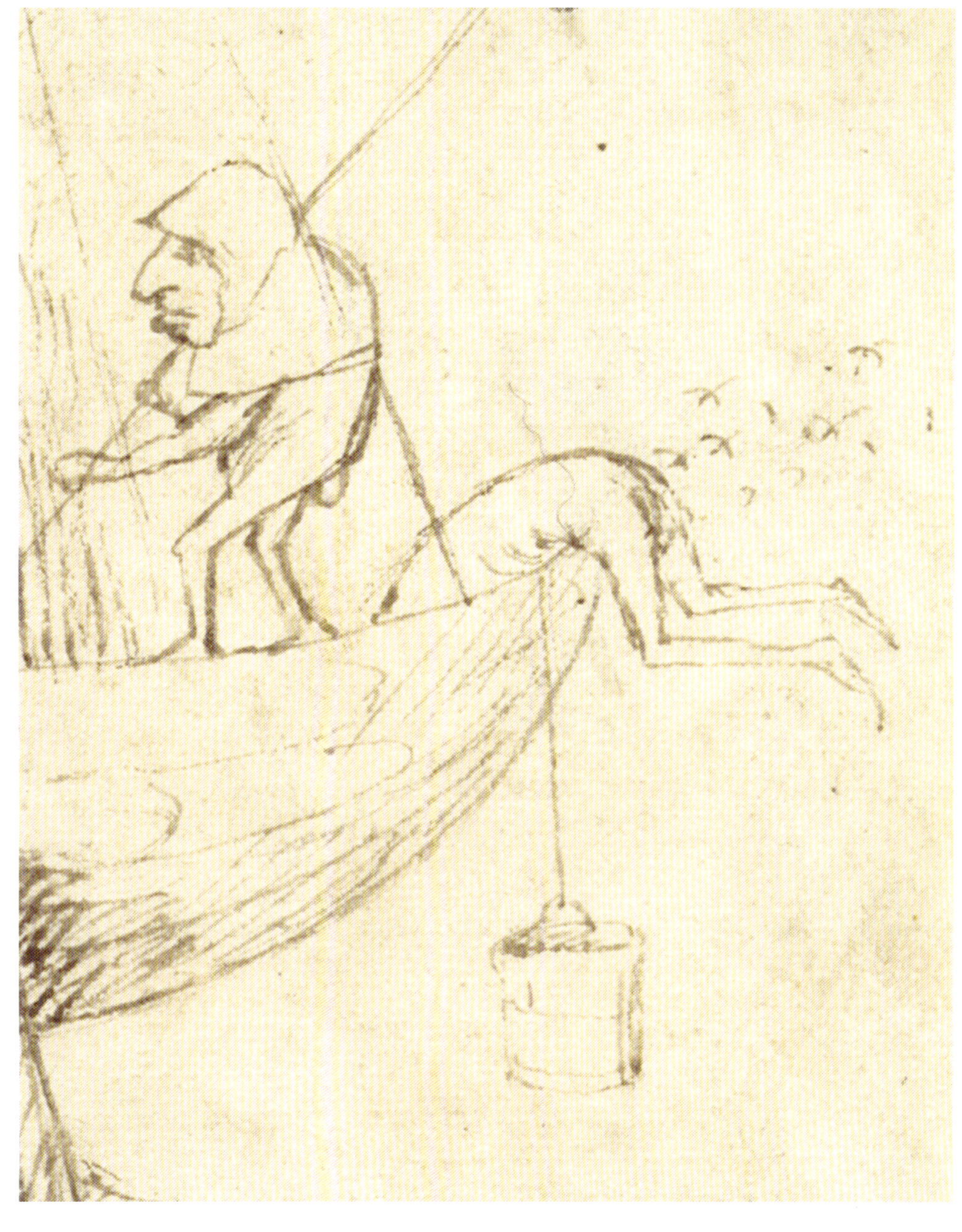

Brush and grey-brown ink on paper,
175 × 154 mm
Vienna, Akademie der bildenden
Künste, Kupferstichkabinett, 2554

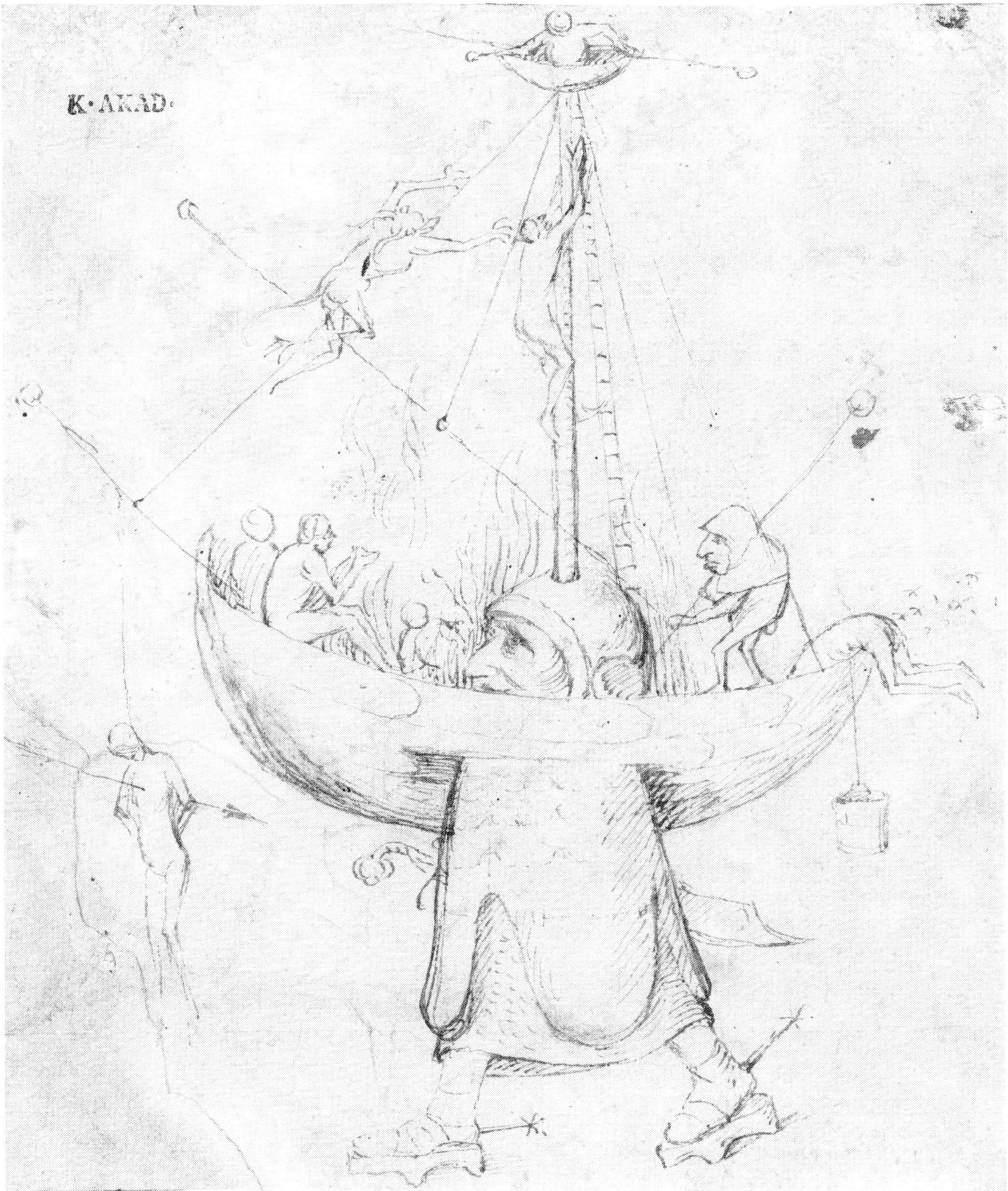

120   Bosch drew two fantastic creatures on the recto of this sheet, and a head-and-feet figure and another creature on the verso. This little drawing was almost certainly once larger, and will have contained more monsters than the two that remain. The paper was prepared before drawing with a layer of pigment, giving it its unusual pinkish-red colour. A workshop assistant used the crawling beast on the right of the recto in the so-called *Flood Panels* (cat. 48), in which it is inserted like some kind of decal. As far as we know, this is the only instance in which a drawing by Bosch is repeated in a painting from his workshop.

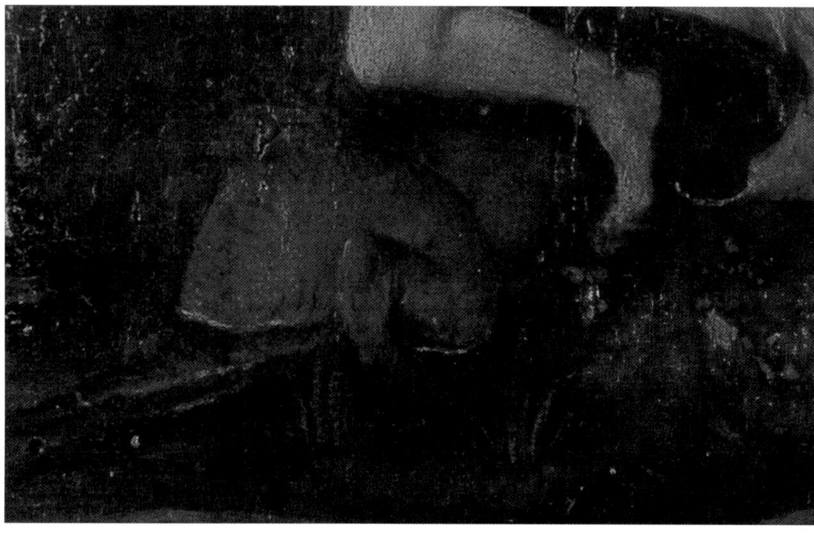

Detail of the *Flood Panels* (cat. 48a), reverse (fig. p. 162)

Pen and brown ink on red prepared
paper, 85 × 182 mm
Berlin, Staatliche Museen zu Berlin,
Kupferstichkabinett, KdZ 550

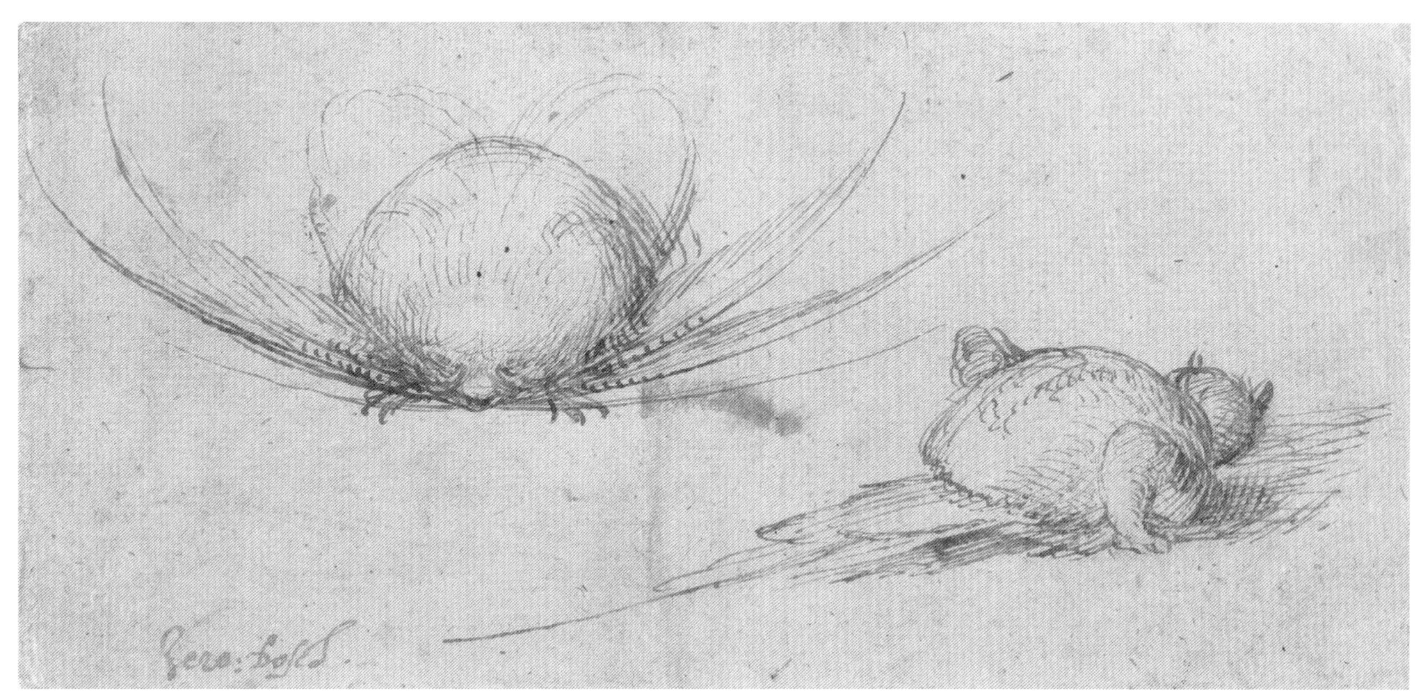

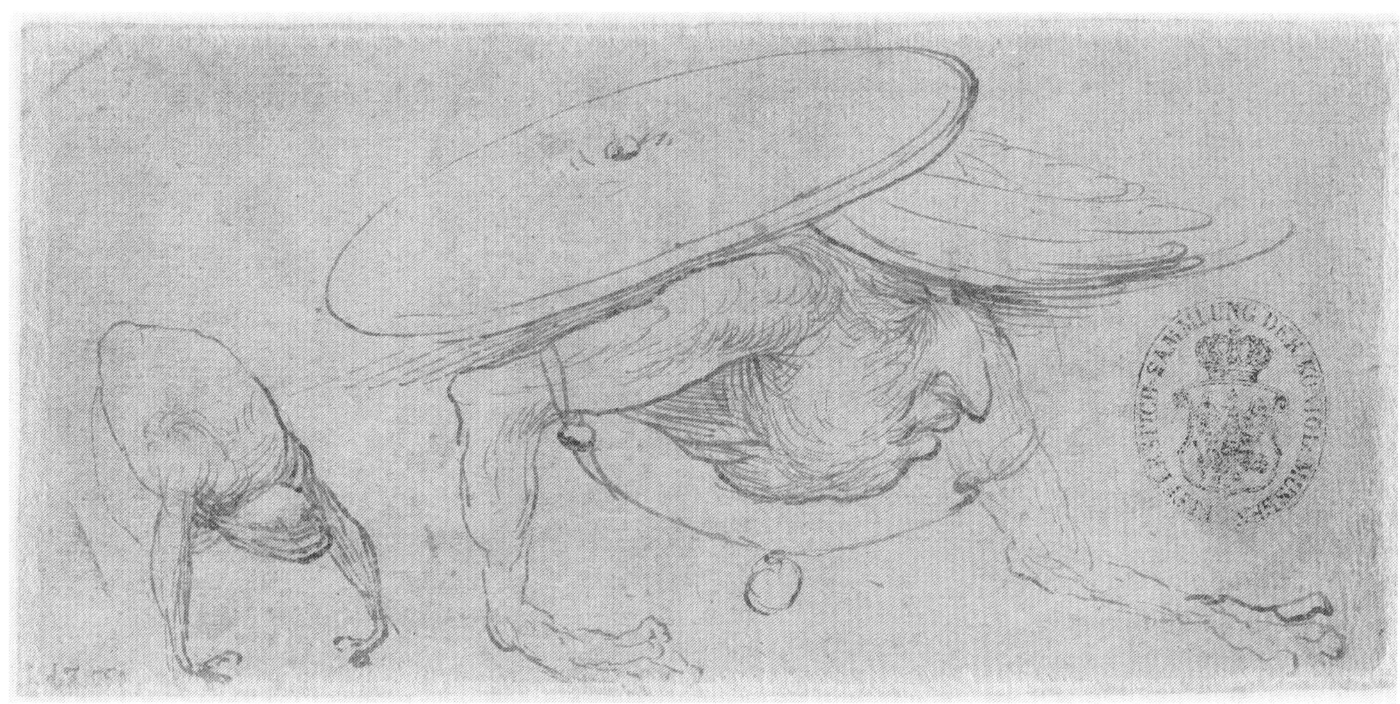

122   The monsters in this drawing were executed rapidly and are indicated very sketchily. Their appearance – head-and-feet figures and other weird hybrids – seems familiar. If we look more closely, however, we search in vain for them in Bosch's painted hell scenes, and we realize that each little figure has been invented afresh.

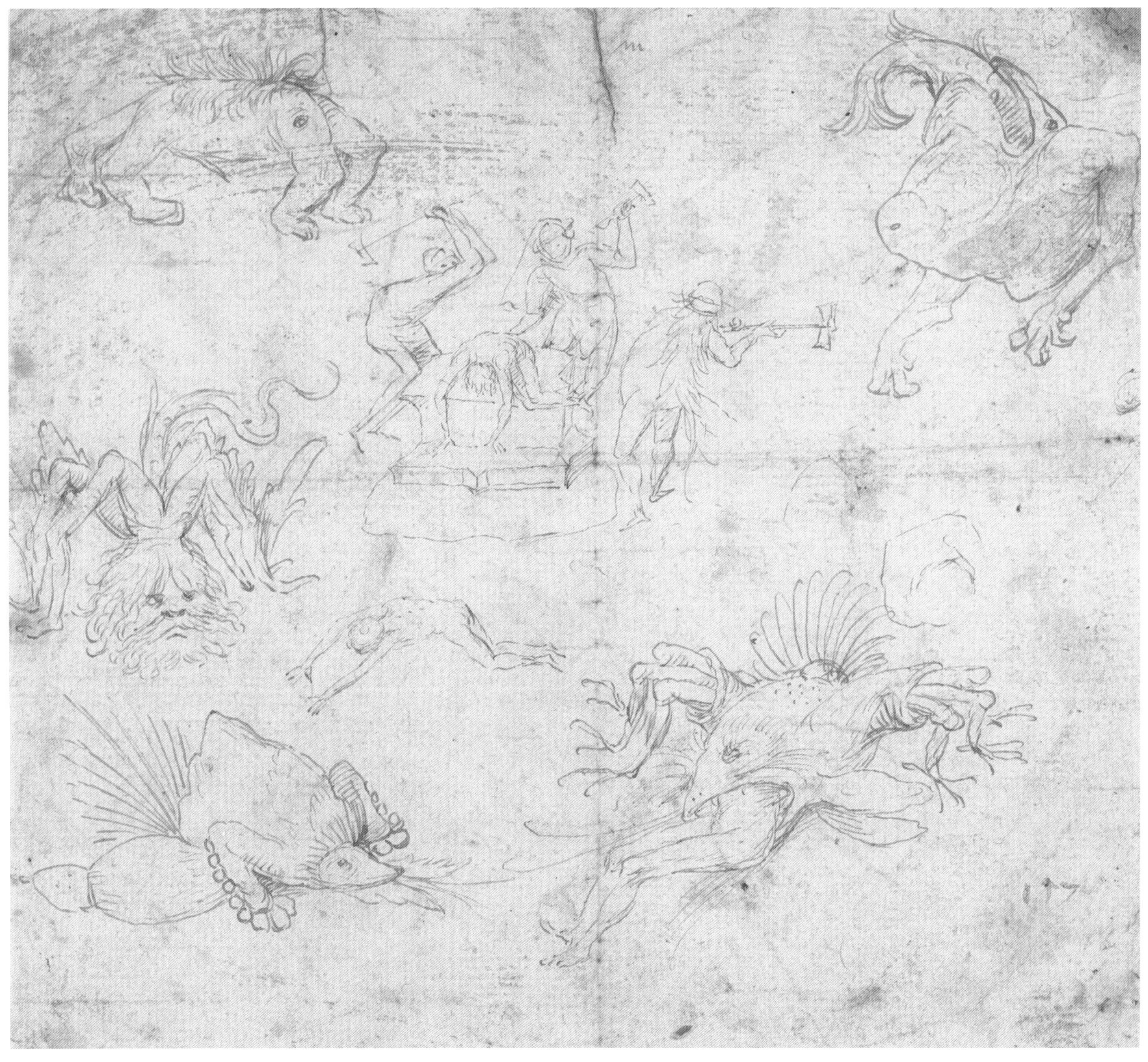

Pen and brown ink on paper,
156 × 170/176 mm
Berlin, Staatliche Museen zu Berlin,
Kupferstichkabinett, KdZ 548

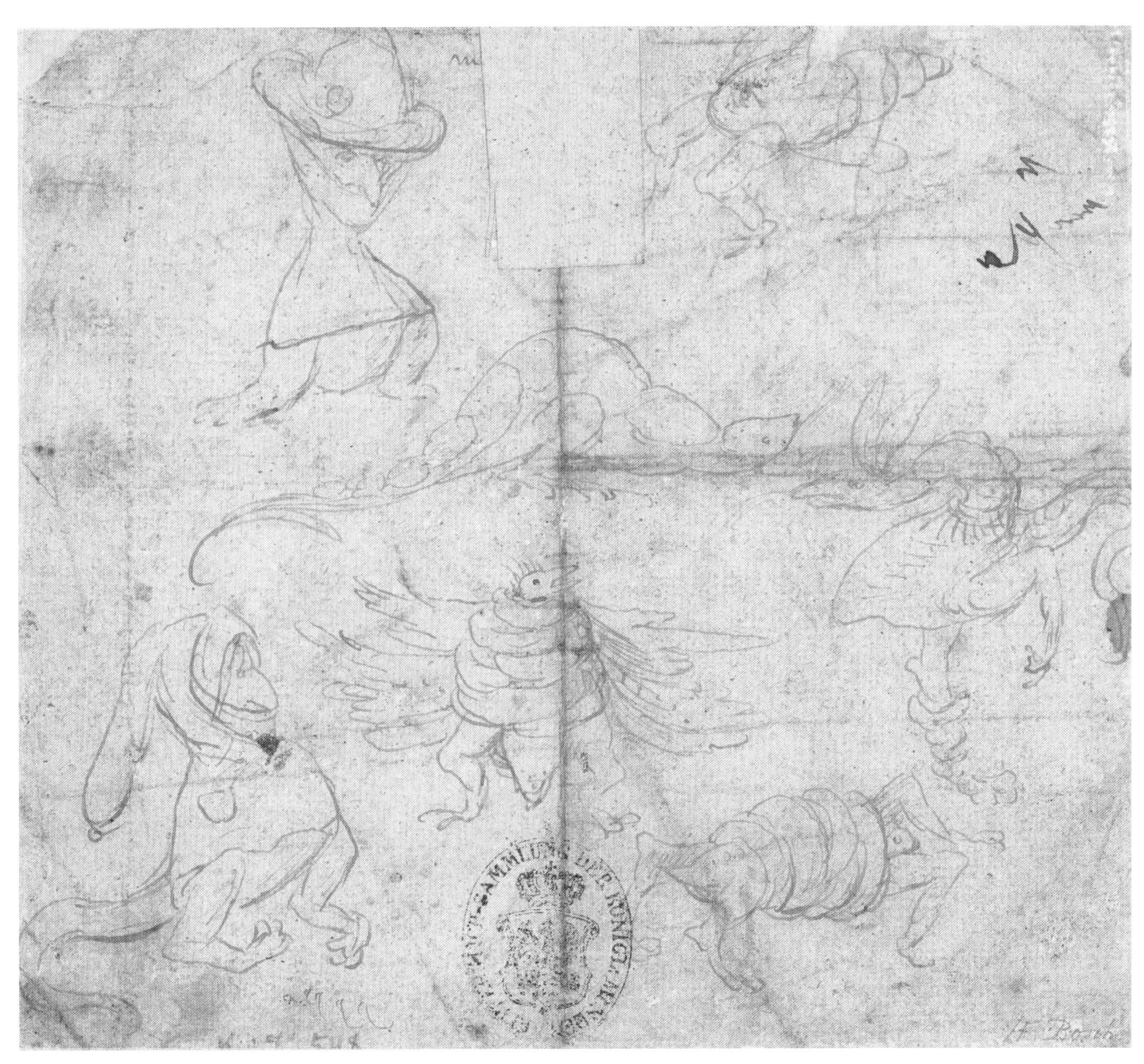

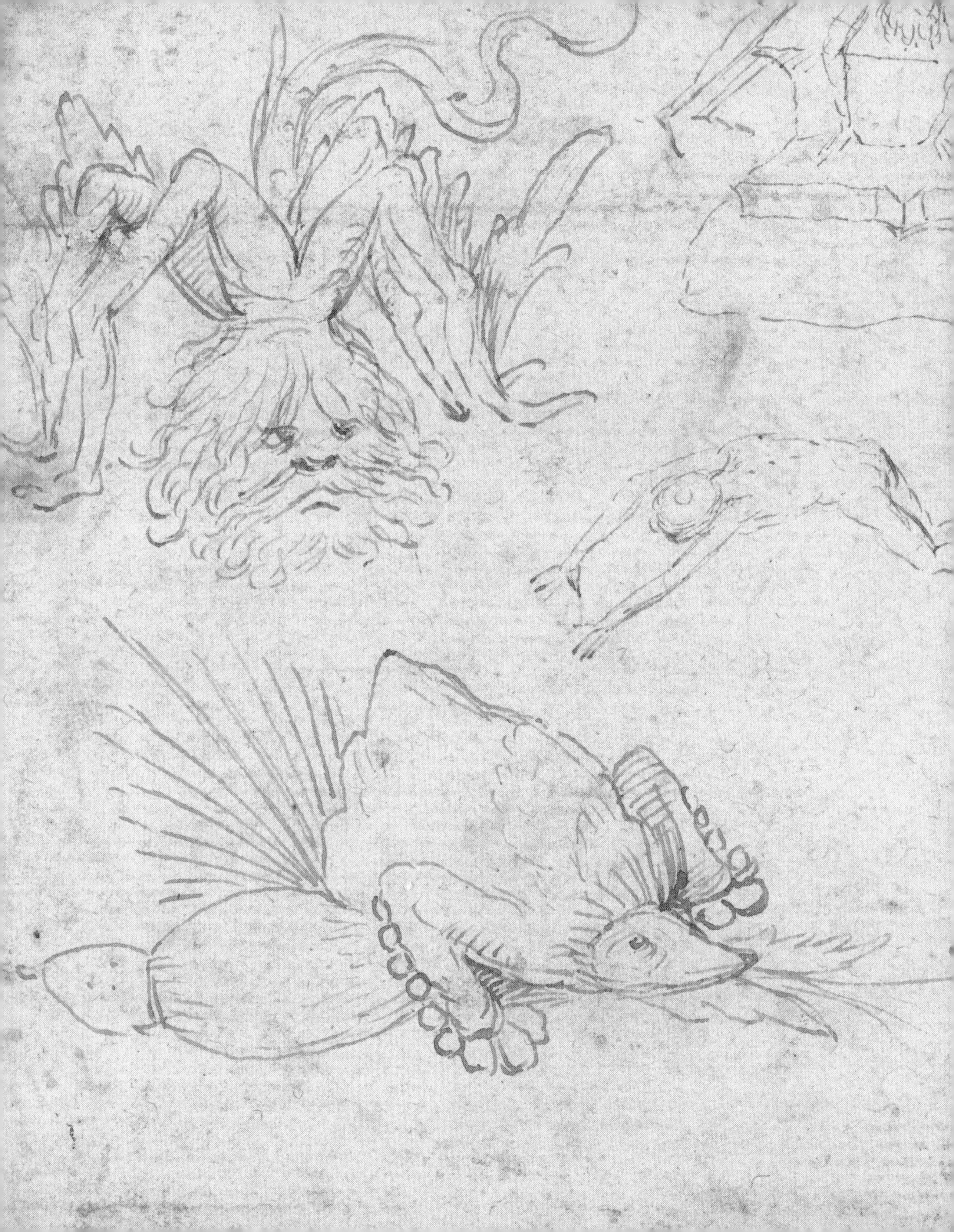

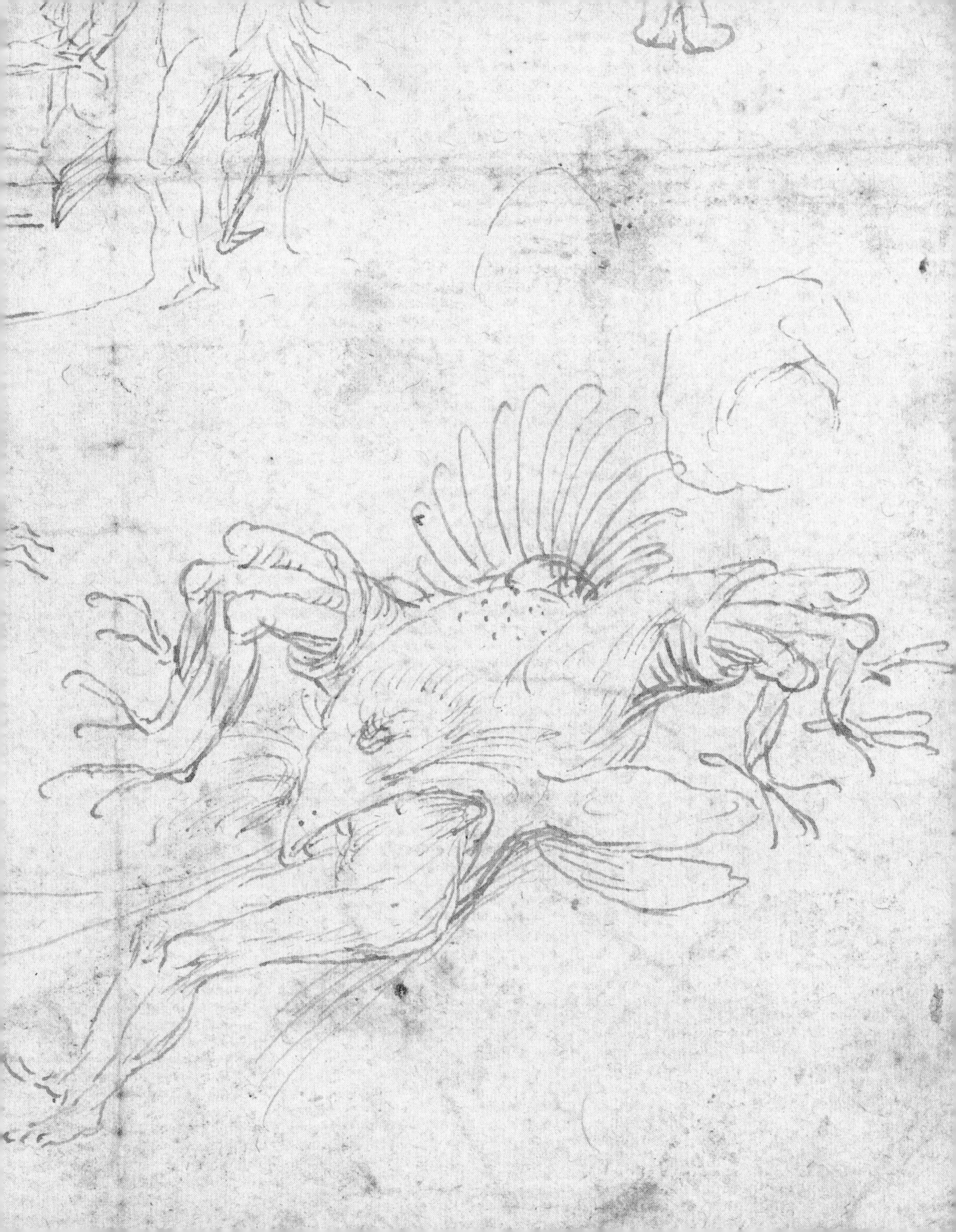

Pen and ochre-coloured ink on paper,
321 × 211 mm
Oxford, Ashmolean Museum, bequeathed
by Francis Douce, 1834, WA 1863.155

126 Bosch must have drawn considerably more than the twenty or so sheets that can still be attributed to him today. The model sheet from Oxford, containing a collection of wondrous creatures, is most likely evidence of this. The drawing differs in style from Bosch's autograph drawings, but it is interesting that parts of two figures in this sheet (one on the recto and one on the verso) also appear on the reverse of *The Wood Has Ears,* *The Field Has Eyes* (cat. 17; fig. p. 80). These little sketches are done in an uncertain hand, probably by an apprentice after an example by the master himself. The draughtsman of the Oxford sheet must have known and copied those inventions in their totality. There are grounds for supposing, therefore, that the figures in this drawing do indeed hark back to autograph sketches by Bosch.

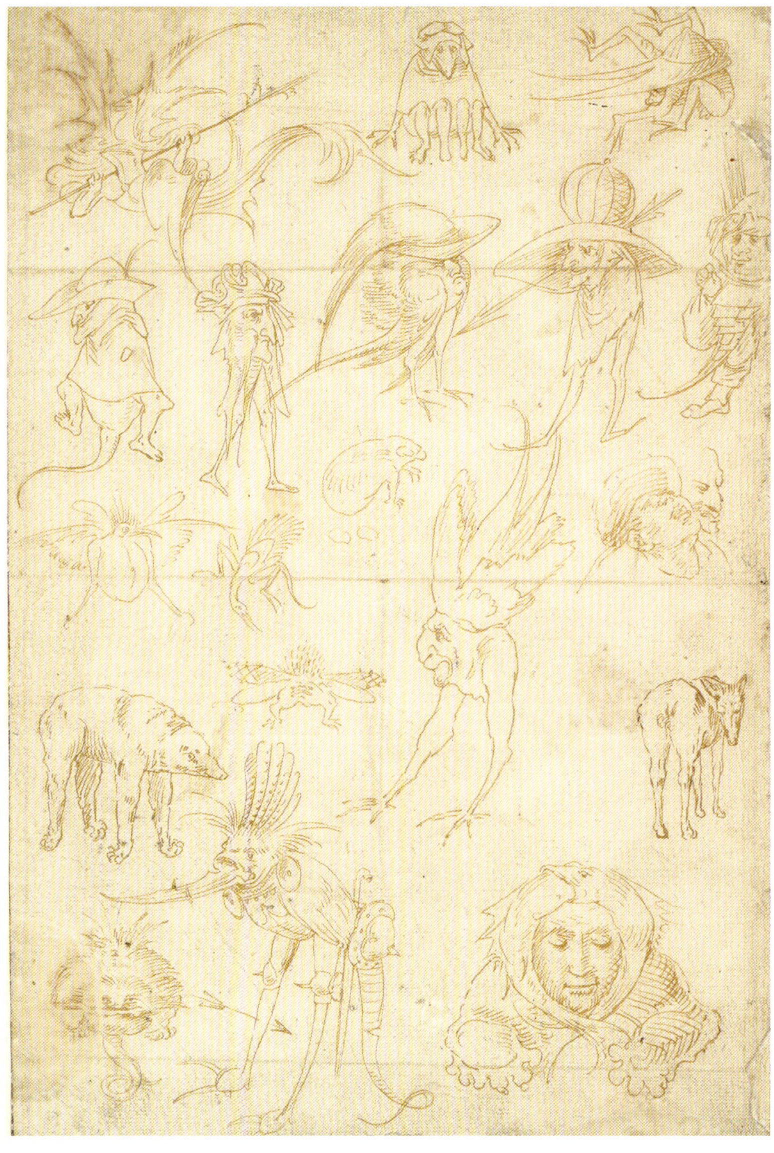

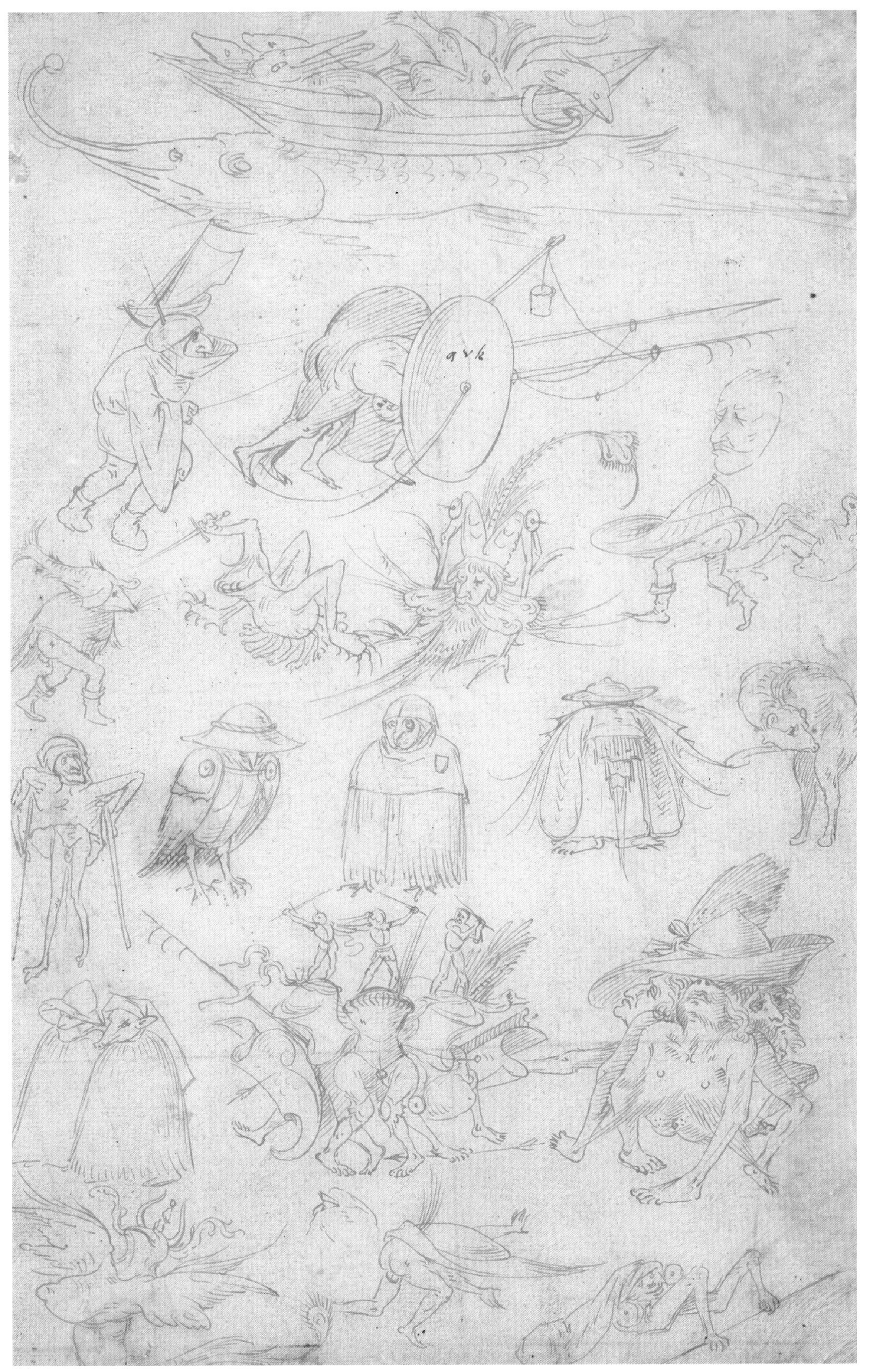

Pen and brown ink on paper,
311 × 212 mm
Providence, Rhode Island School
of Design Museum, 51.069

128   Fifteen monsters are included in this model sheet. Only one of them – the owl – has been observed from nature, although it too has been given a hood to wear. The two imaginary beasts shown upper left were borrowed directly from an autograph drawing by Bosch (cat. 32). A skull creature and a simian monster with a funnel on its head have been sketched on the back of that drawing. Both of them likewise feature in this model sheet, making it a particularly important document since the other figures in the drawing might also have been copied from Bosch.

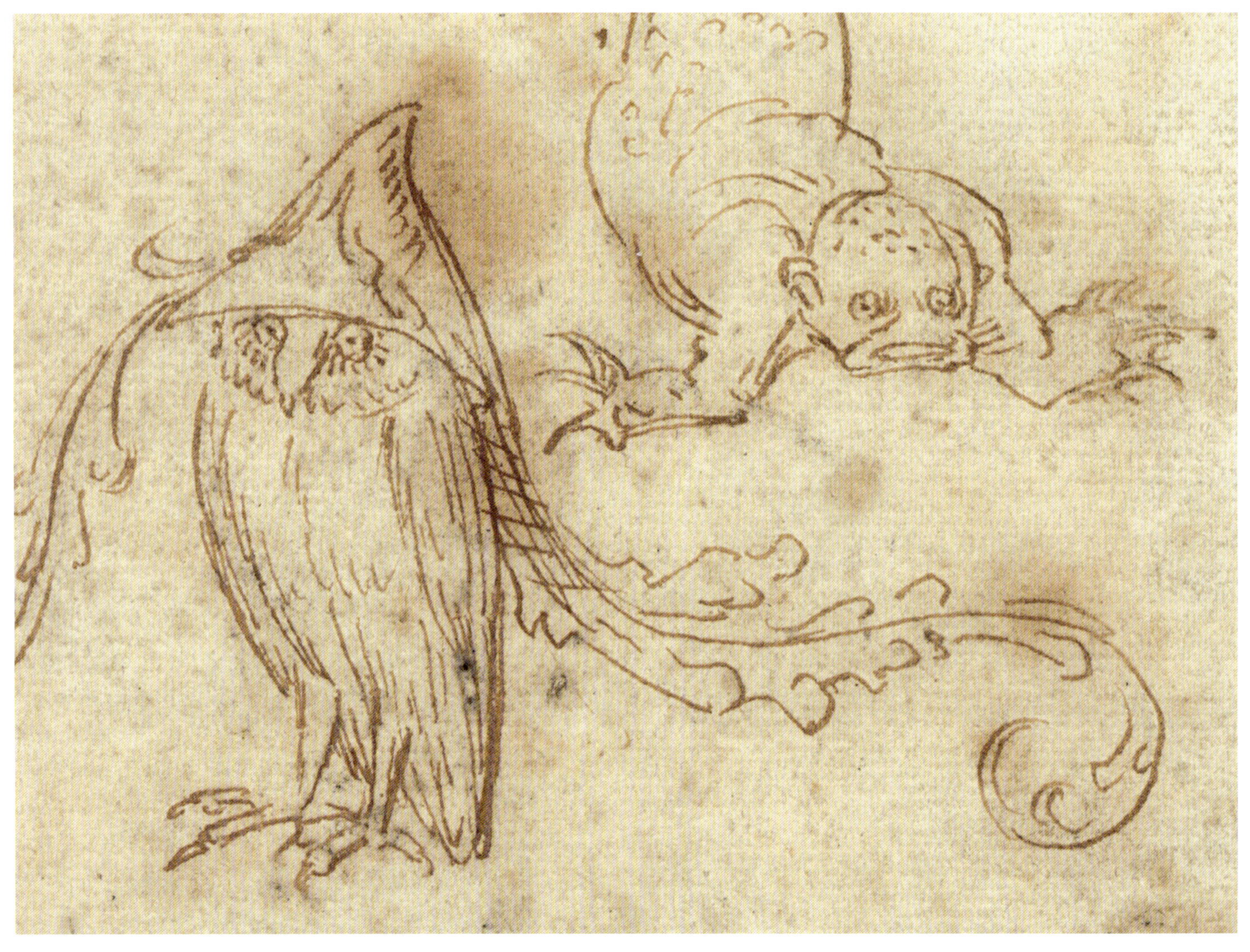

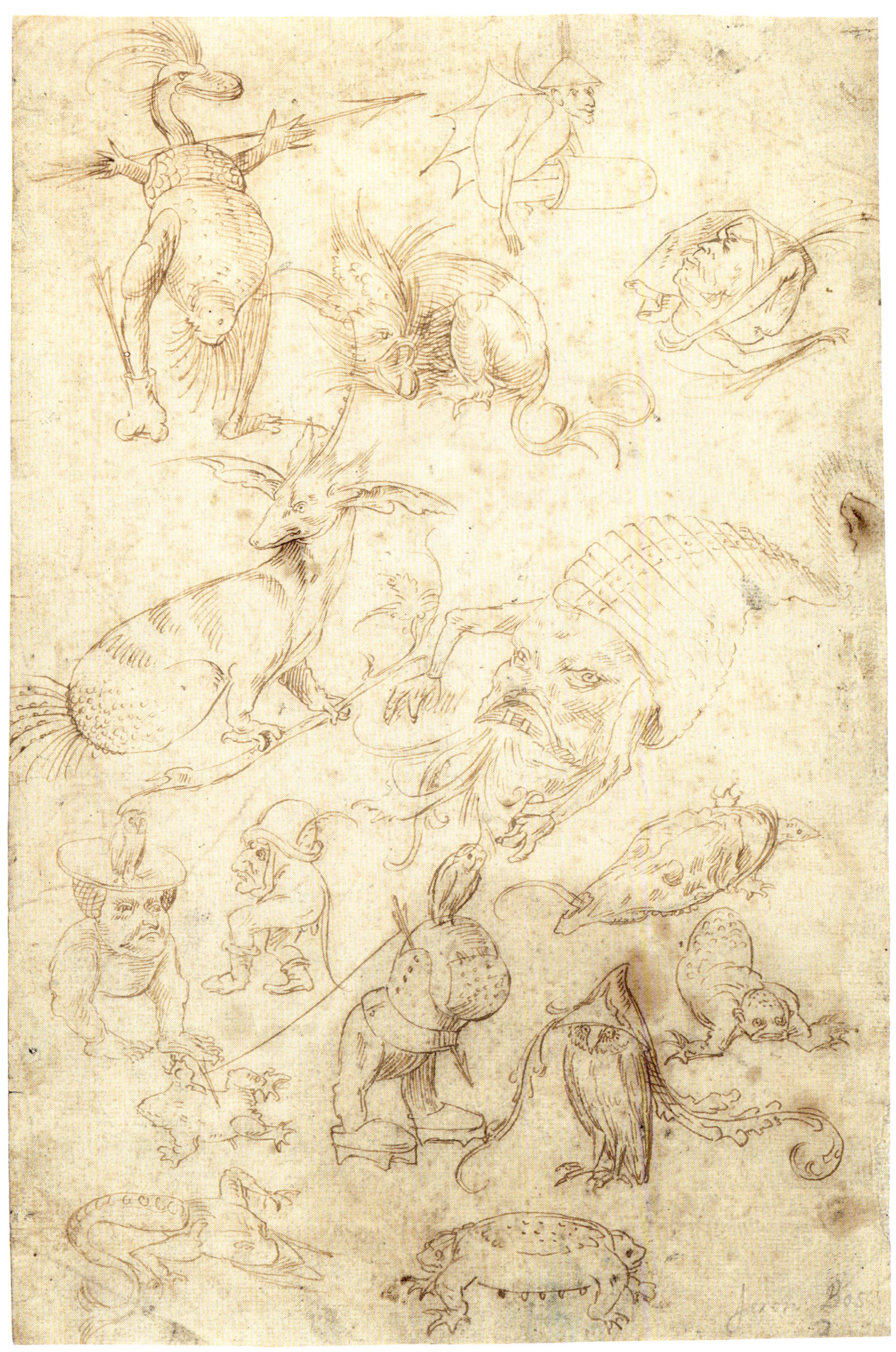

V

Saints

As far as we can tell from written sources and his surviving oeuvre, Hieronymus Bosch only painted a small number of different saints. This is surprising, given that veneration of these figures was particularly intense in the period in which he lived. St John's, for instance, the principal church in 's-Hertogenbosch, had some fifty altars devoted to saints as well as to Christ, the Virgin Mary and other biblical figures. One of them was dedicated in 1452 to the Church Father Saint Jerome, who was popular in the late Middle Ages as a learned cardinal, hermit and Bible translator. The third son of Antonius van Aken and Aleid van der Mynnen was named after Saint Jerome. Hieronymus, known in everyday life as 'Jeroen' or 'Joen', painted his patron saint on a number of occasions (cat. 42, 43) and also that of his father, Saint Anthony (cat. 43, 45). The relevant commissions were placed by others, however, showing that these particular saints enjoyed wide popularity in the fifteenth and sixteenth centuries. Even so, Bosch is bound to have felt a stronger connection than usual when painting them.

The other saints he is known to have depicted can be broken down into two groups – autonomous images and those included as patron saints accompanying the portraits of donors (although autonomous representations of saints can, of course, also refer to the person who commissioned the work or to the location for which it was made). While the Apostles and the Old Testament figure of Job do not, strictly speaking, belong to the category of 'saints', they were invoked and venerated in a similar way from the late Middle Ages onwards. We know of only ten different saints and biblical figures depicted by Bosch as the main subject of paintings or triptych panels: Anthony, Christopher, Giles, Jerome, Hippolytus, Gregory, James the Greater, John the Baptist, John the Evangelist and Wilgefortis (Uncumber). He also painted Peter and Agnes as name saints in the wings of the *Adoration of the Magi* (fig. p. 53). We know meanwhile that Saints Peter and Catherine were depicted as patron saints (cat. 8) in Bosch's workshop, and that Anthony, Jerome and the 'Holy Man Job' appeared in the panels of a triptych painted there (cat. 44).

Bosch continued to work within the existing tradition as far as the sources for these saints' images are concerned; he could hardly do otherwise, since his clients and contemporaries had to be able to recognize the represented saints if they were to be able to pray to them. Bosch based his designs on earlier images with which everyone was familiar, but then adapted the way he depicted them. In many cases, this will have occurred in consultation with the work's patron and possibly also with the assistance of learned advisers. In addition to visual sources, Bosch's compositions drew on texts and no doubt also on the knowledge he and those advisers had gained through their own study. Printed and written books, some of them illustrated, were accessible in monastic libraries, but were privately owned too. What is more, book printers and sellers were already active in 's-Hertogenbosch in Bosch's time. Books were copied by hand on parchment and paper at several monasteries, most notably the friary, in which scribes and illuminators produced written texts and miniatures; these were bound in leather bindings that were themselves frequently decorated with visual images.

We need to consider both this visual tradition and the written sources, therefore, if we are to identify the saints Bosch painted and to understand them correctly. The protagonist of the *Temptation of Saint Anthony* (fig. p. 150) appears no fewer than four times in the three panels that make up Bosch's painting. The holy hermit is immediately identifiable from his appearance and from the Tau cross of Saint Anthony on his cloak panel; however, if we are to analyse the four partially overlapping scenes, we need to consult the literature that was available to Bosch and his contemporaries. It then becomes apparent time and again that Bosch gave his own personal and creative interpretation to the existing tradition, and that this was precisely what drew his clients to this highly individual artist. This is what we find too in the discussion that follows of Bosch's images of saints. He succeeded, for instance, in presenting his patron saint (cat. 42) – a figure familiar to all his contemporaries from books and pictures – as a hermit within a characteristic and magnificent composition, which perfectly expresses the spirit of its maker, both as an ensemble and in its countless tiny details.

Hieronymus Bosch
Saint Christopher, c. 1490–1500
Oil on oak panel, 113.7 × 71.6 cm
Rotterdam, Museum Boijmans
Van Beuningen, St. 26

132 Bosch shows us a giant, viewed from a high vantage point. We follow the painter's eye beyond this immense figure into the distance, where the relatively narrow river flows into a larger body of water. The water through which the saint wades must be connected to it in one way or another, but it is not clear how. Whatever the case, the child wants to be carried on his shoulders to the other side. The giant, still called Reprobus at this point, had been put to work as a ferryman during his quest to find the mightiest lord on earth. He had served king and emperor, but every time he found that his master was afraid of one more powerful still. The emperor feared the devil and so, formidable though his sovereign was, the giant set out again to find the mightiest of all. When he met a group of hermits who had devoted their lives to one of whom even Satan was afraid, Christopher decided to join them. One day a child appeared and asked to be carried over the river. Bosch shows what happened when the giant was halfway across the water, which he ought to have been able to cross in five or six great strides. He sags under the toddler's weight, keeping his balance only with the aid of the tree trunk that serves as his traveller's staff. The ferryman cannot see the slender golden halo about the child's head, the crosier in his left hand or the gesture of blessing he makes with his right. This is the moment when the giant Reprobus becomes Christopher – Christophorus, 'bearer of Christ'. As he carries the Christ Child, he also bears the weight of the world on his shoulders: the child reveals himself to be the mightiest lord of all.

Bosch signed this painting in the lower left corner in his customary, carefully brushed Gothic letters. The scene itself also incorporates all sorts of details in which we recognize his hand and which lend added significance to the image. The most striking of these is the large dead fish hanging from the staff on which the giant relies to keep his footing. The wood of the staff is not dead but alive, as we see from the budding foliage. According to Christopher's biography, this was a sign intended to show the saint that it really was Christ whom he had carried over the river. The blood of the fish drips down the living wood, alluding to the fact that Christopher's true support is the Christian faith. The fish had been a symbol of Christ since the earliest days of the Church; the classical Greek *ichthus* ('fish') comprised the first letters of the words meaning 'Jesus Christ, Son of God, Saviour'.

The world around Saint Christopher – protector of travellers and shield against sudden death – is full of menace, evil and doom. A scary-looking flying fish is painted right behind him, while a little further off we see a hunter hanging a bear from a tree; he has just shot the animal in the heart with his crossbow. On the far side of the river, a naked man flees a monstrous dragon that looms up from the ruined castle, while more distant still, a fire rages in a village church surrounded by a forest. Christopher leaves it all behind him as he heads for the riverbank; one of the hermits – sitting in his jug-dwelling and dwarfed by the figure of the giant – holds up a lantern to serve as a beacon.

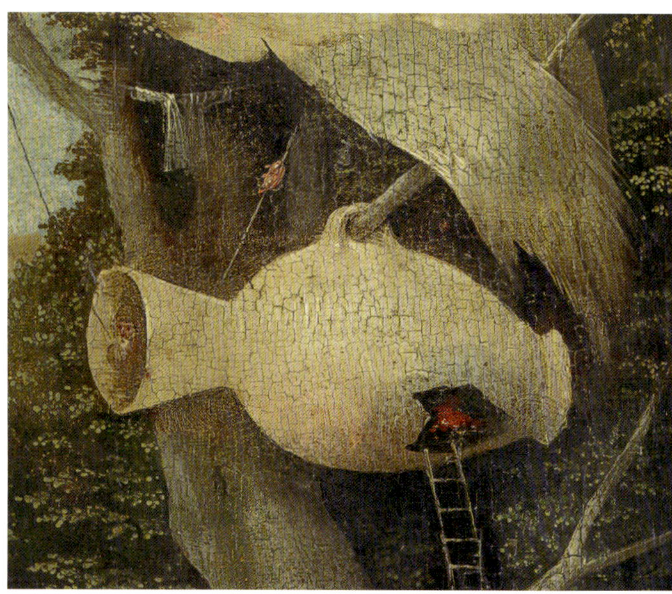

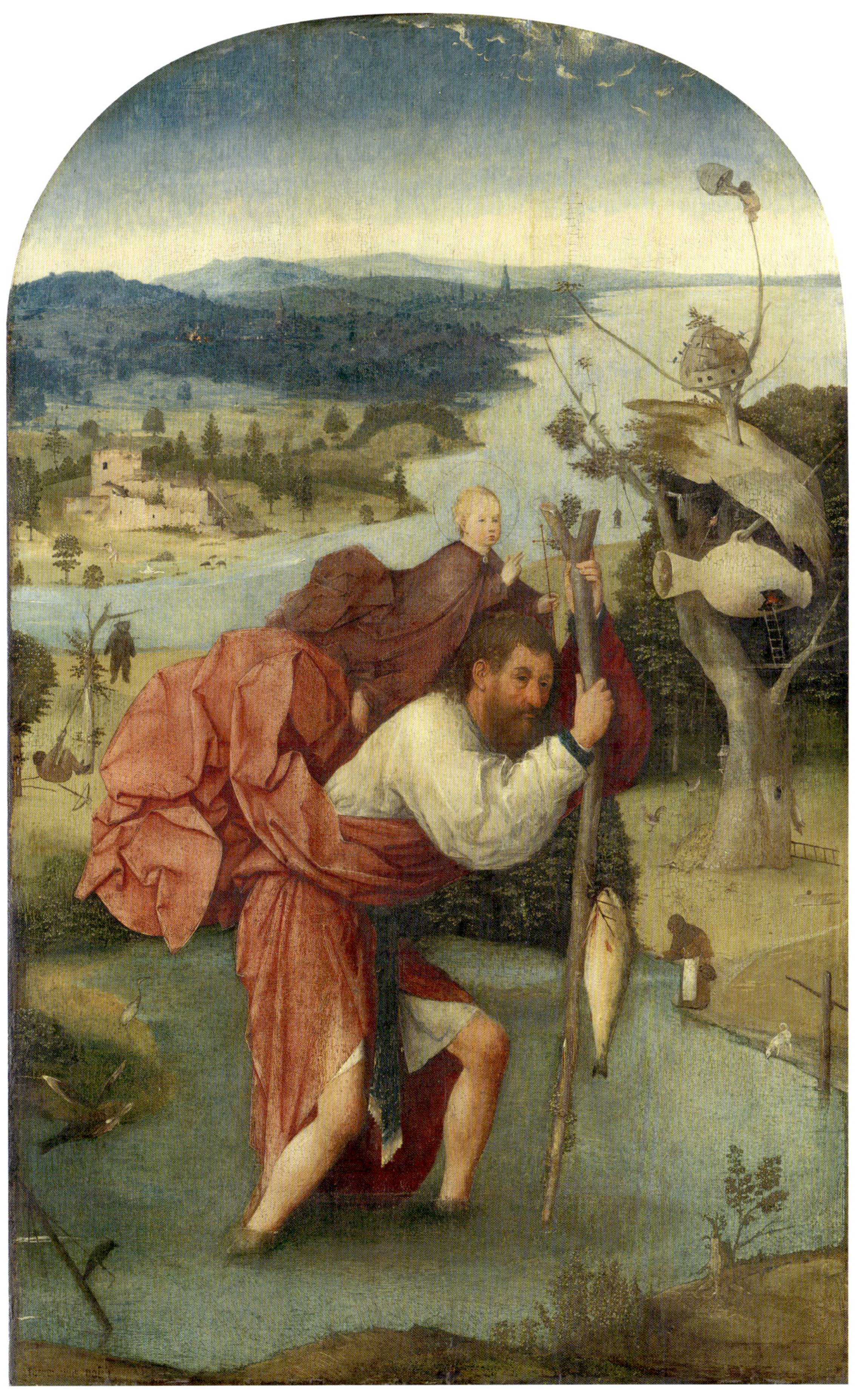

134 Saint Wilgefortis, tied to the cross where she will die a cruel martyr's death in imitation of Christ, towers above a large mass of people. The men standing beneath her left arm are evidently the ones responsible for her condemnation and have come to see their sentence carried out. The large and emotional group of men who press forward to her right are plainly devastated by the execution. Bosch has painted Wilgefortis herself in a pose that is more triumphant than agonized. Her martyrdom means that she will be wed to Christ, her lord, and that her prayer to be spared an earthly marriage with a heathen prince has been heard. According to the legend, her sudden and miraculous growth of a beard meant she was no longer acceptable as a bride, infuriating her father, who responded by sentencing her to the same death as Christ – the spiritual husband she refused to renounce. The man fainting at the foot of the T-shaped cross might be her intended. He has fallen from the other side of the cross to its right (from Wilgefortis's point of view) – in other words, from the negative to the positive side – where he is tended by two monks. His expensive clothes and gold cloak fastener suggest his high position. A little owl, sitting on a bare branch, is embroidered on his fashionable, tight parti-coloured hose. The bird is undoubtedly a symbol of evil, but the dramatic events have evidently led the man to repent.

The name 'Wilgefortis' has been read as *Virgo fortis* or 'valiant maid', which would be appropriate given the details of her fictitious *Vita*. Late-fifteenth-century Netherlandish manuscripts relate that when she was hanging on the cross a voice declared from the sky that she would be known henceforward as 'Uncumber', signifying that, as a saint, she would relieve ('disencumber') the suffering and anxiety of all those who invoked her. Her cult was widespread in Western Europe. In 's-Hertogenbosch too, at St John's Church, there was an altar dedicated to Saint Uncumber, on which, according to a local chronicle of around 1550, an *Oncummera barbata* (Uncumber with a beard) was displayed. This cannot, however, have been the triptych discussed here.

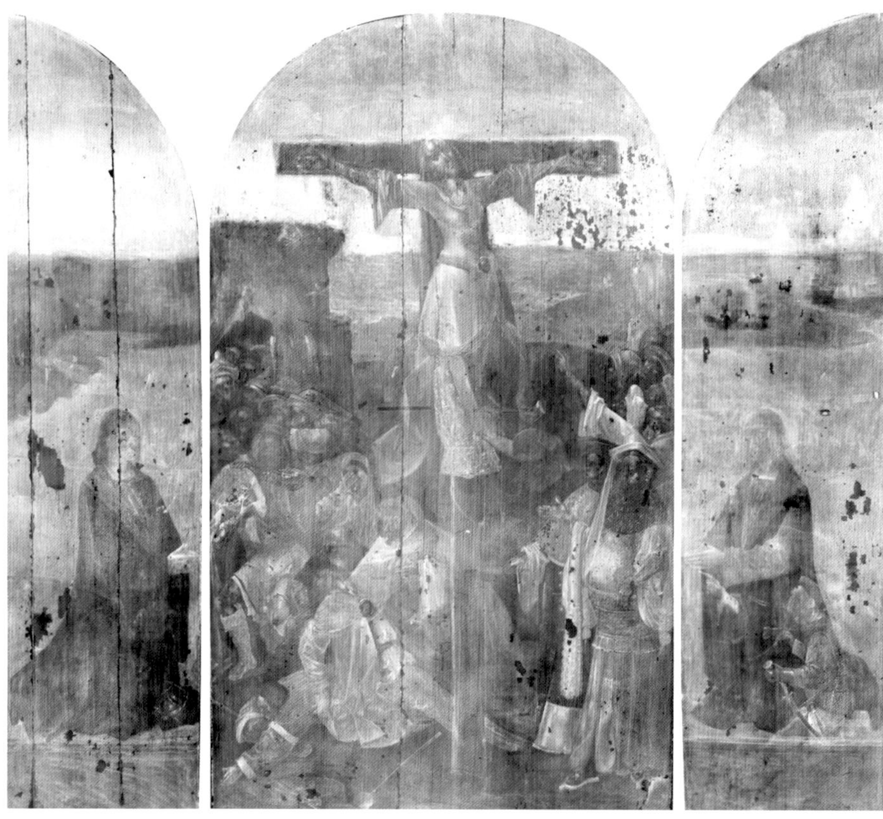

X-ray photograph

Hieronymus Bosch
Saint Wilgefortis Triptych, c. 1495–1505
Oil on oak panel, left wing 105.2 × 27.5 cm,
central panel 105.2 × 62.7 cm, right wing 104.7 × 27.9 cm
Venice, Gallerie dell'Accademia

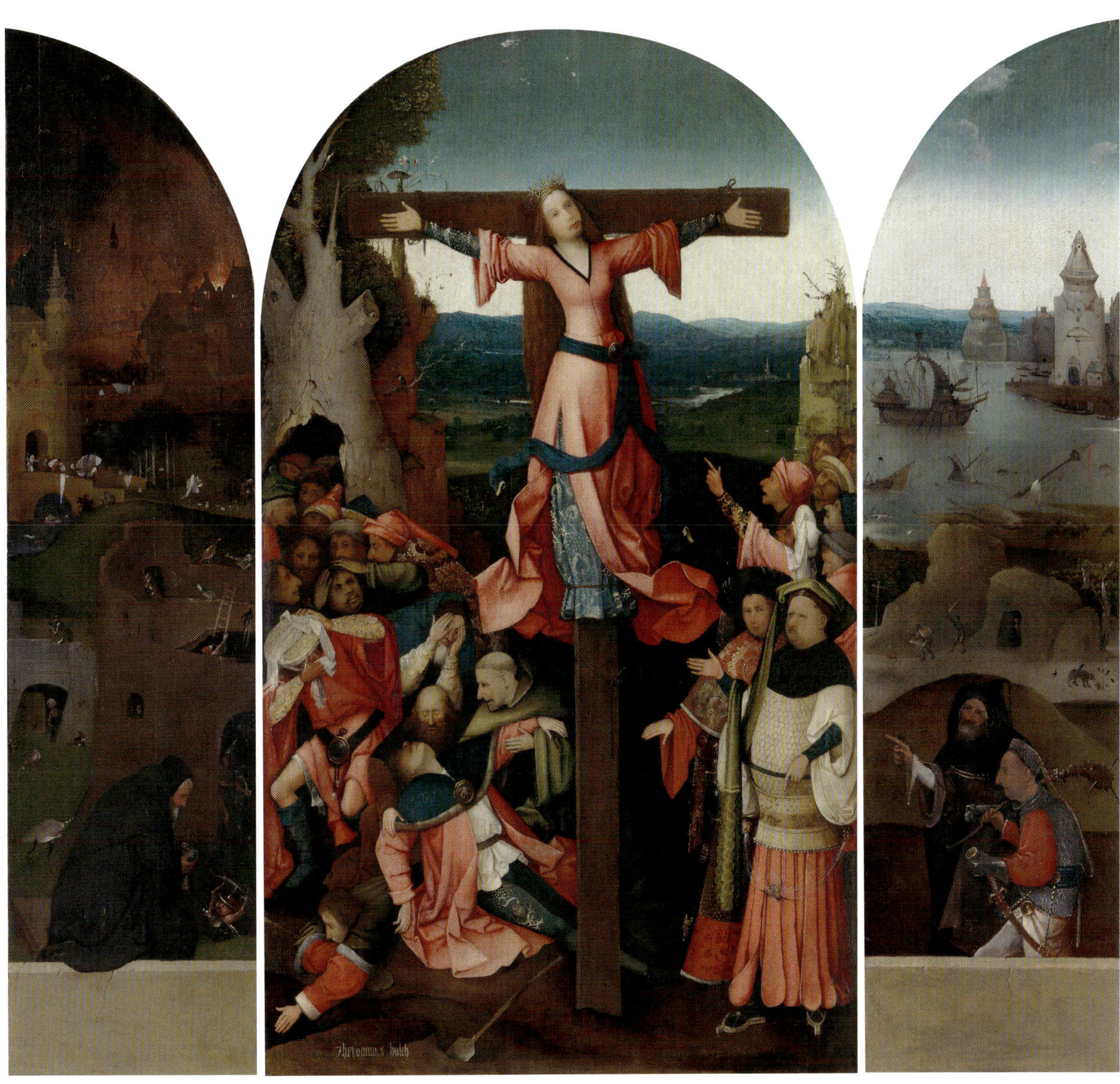

Hieronymus Bosch used an unusually large amount of red – the colour of martyrdom – in the central panel of this triptych. The tone is set by the costumes of the believers and the unbelievers running the full width of the scene beneath the cross, above whom the saint then rises up in her bright-red robe. As a result, the altarpiece is not only gripping when viewed in all its detail from closeby, but is also extremely dramatic and compelling from a significant distance.

The earliest description of the triptych with the crucified female martyr dates from 1664, when it was already in Venice. An eighteenth-century guidebook notes that there was some doubt as to whether this was a female or a male saint. The same debate persisted until the recent restoration of 2013–15, which demonstrated that a wispy beard was indeed painted on the martyr's face in a dark colour. Hieronymus Bosch rendered the crucified martyr's beard very subtly, as had Hans Memling, for instance, in the Wilgefortis who features in his 1480 *Triptych of Adriaan Reins* in St John's Hospital, Bruges. Wilgefortis was, after all, supposed to have been an attractive young princess.

The crucifixion scene was originally flanked by two kneeling donors. Both men, dressed in rather opulently coloured clothes, clasp their hands together and gaze devoutly at the central scene. They were painted out at an early stage, still in Bosch's workshop. The circumstances of the commission had evidently altered significantly, possibly because of their sudden death. The figure of Saint Anthony as a hermit was painted over the donor in the left wing, while two figures were added in the right wing, where they are probably intended as a continuation of the group of men standing on the right of the central panel. Whatever painting there was on the exterior wings was lost centuries ago.

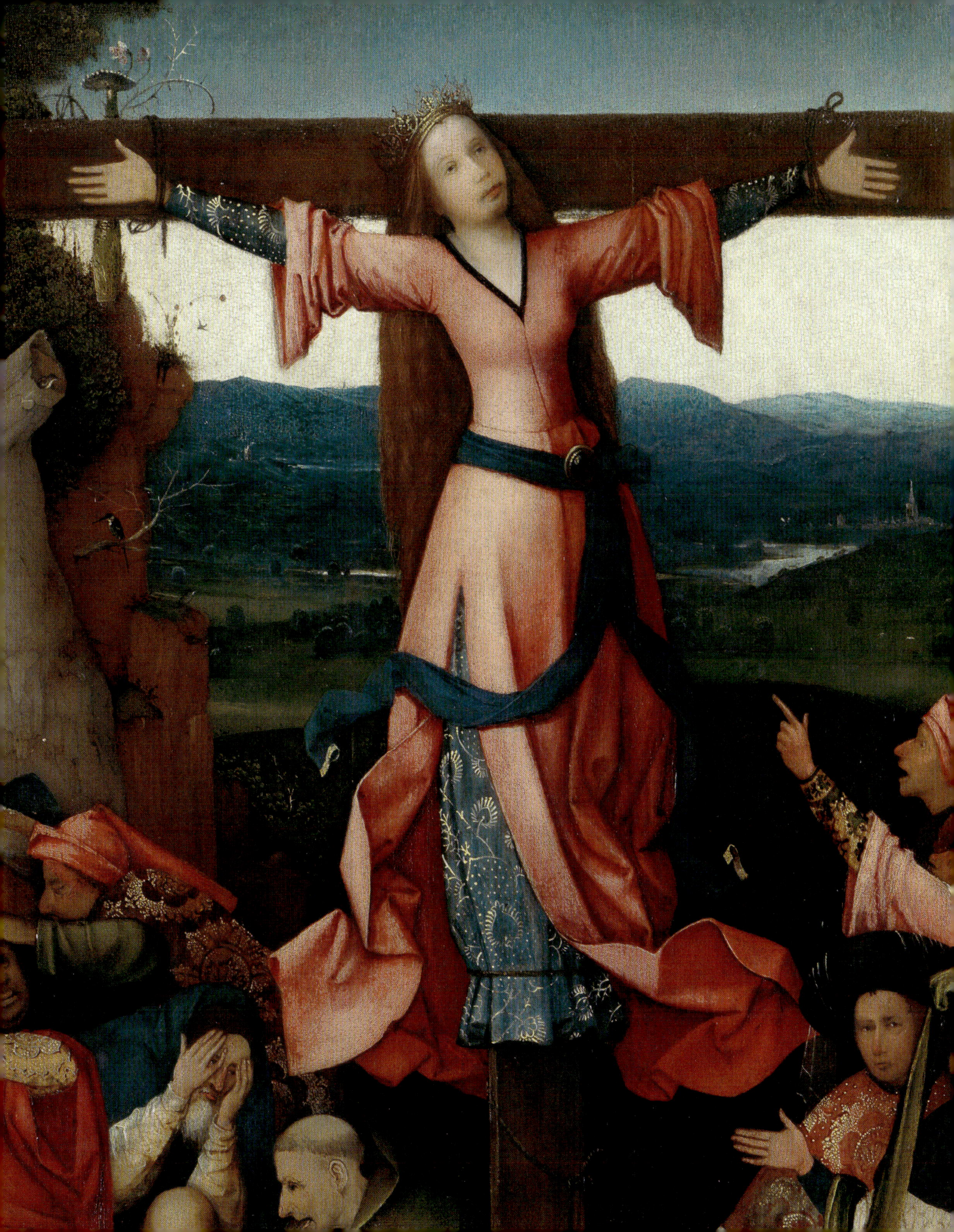

Hieronymus Bosch
Saint Jerome at Prayer, c. 1485–95
Oil on oak panel, 80 × 60.7 cm
Ghent, Museum voor Schone Kunsten,
1908-H

Saint Jerome, whose name was interpreted in the Middle Ages as meaning 'sacred grove' or 'holy wood' (*heilig bosch*), must have had a special significance for his namesake, Hieronymus Bosch, who painted him on a number of occasions, and even made Jerome the protagonist of his *Hermit Saints Triptych* (cat. 43). The learned saint's uncompromising moralism and his personal religious commitment made him a worthy model for Bosch (and for anyone looking at his paintings), whose work depicts immoral behaviour while simultaneously expressing profound religious devotion.

Jerome is the main subject of the panel in Ghent, which is one of Bosch's greatest achievements. The saint stretches out on the ground in an ominous landscape, praying with utter absorption to Christ. He embraces the crucifix with both arms, his hands clasped together and his eyes closed. The rock with which he has just chastised himself lies nearby. Jerome meditates on the physical torments suffered by Christ, while wrestling with his own earthly desires. The Church Father and Bible translator withdrew into solitude for three years, partly to do penance. A closed book lies between his cassock and his cardinal's hat, alluding to his scholarship and the years he spent working on the Vulgate. On the left of the painting we see the lion, which was tamed when Jerome extracted a thorn from his paw, following which the beast became his faithful companion.

The lion, cardinal's hat, book, rock and crucifix are all standard attributes in images of the penitent Saint Jerome praying in the wilderness. Pictures of this type, in which the saint is almost always shown kneeling, with his eyes fixed on the crucified Christ and beating himself on the chest with a rock, were immensely popular in the fifteenth century. A woodcut in a late-fifteenth-century edition of the *Passionael* (the Middle Dutch translation of the *Legenda aurea*, the most important collection of saints' lives in the Middle Ages) shows Jerome in his dual role as scholar and penitent.

Bosch deviates from this visual tradition in his Saint Jerome panel: here the moment of physical mortification has passed, and the focus has shifted from the external to the internal. Purified of sinful thoughts, the saint now has the space for meditation and submission. The idea of purification is alluded to in a detail in the background, where a woman washes her clothes in the river; they are the same immaculate white as Jerome's robe and Christ's loincloth. The way Bosch poses Jerome in the Ghent panel, embracing the crucifix, is also rare in images of this saint: it is more reminiscent of the iconography associated with Mary Magdalene, the remorseful sinner, for whom a similarly intimate position was reserved in Crucifixion scenes. Jerome's intimacy with Christ is an important element of the Ghent painting, which is part of what distinguishes it from other images of the penitent saint.

The wildness of Jerome's surroundings is emphasized by the contrast with the brightly lit and cultivated landscape, complete with bleaching fields, in the background. Jerome has not picked the most peaceful of spots in which to calm his mind: the strange rock formation with its thorny plants where he has sought shelter radiates a certain hostility, and the tombstone above his head is not terribly reassuring either. Other elements too in the scene have a sinister and admonitory character, such as the mauled remains lower left of a cockerel, which evidently got a little too close to the innocent-looking fox sleeping nearby; or the large dead tree trunk with an owl on one of its branches, gazing steadily at the viewer (a second little owl was discovered during the recent restoration of this painting, keeping an eye on its fellow on the branch). These visual elements are found in a different context, but to similar effect, in the drawing *The Wood Has Ears, The Field Has Eyes* (cat. 17). Bosch's nature is unreliable – an ordeal that has to be endured vigilantly. The image of Saint Jerome exhorts the beholder to observe carefully, and then to close his or her eyes to all worldly distractions.

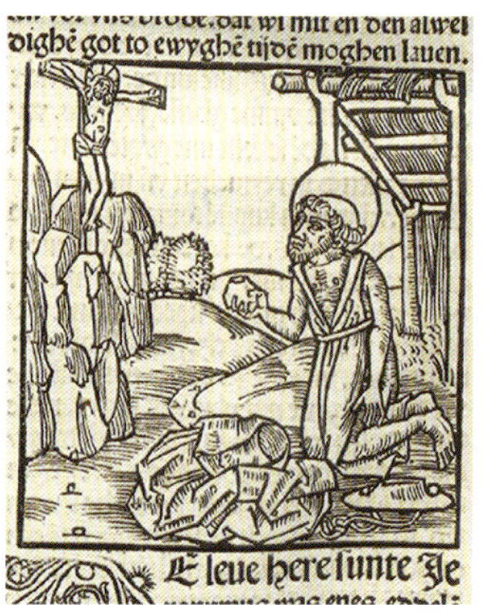

Jacobus de Voragine, *Passionael efte dat Levent der hyllighen*, Lübeck (Steffen Arndes), 1507, fol. 497 (detail): Jerome as a hermit and cardinal
Munich, Bayerische Staatsbibliothek, Rar. 2222

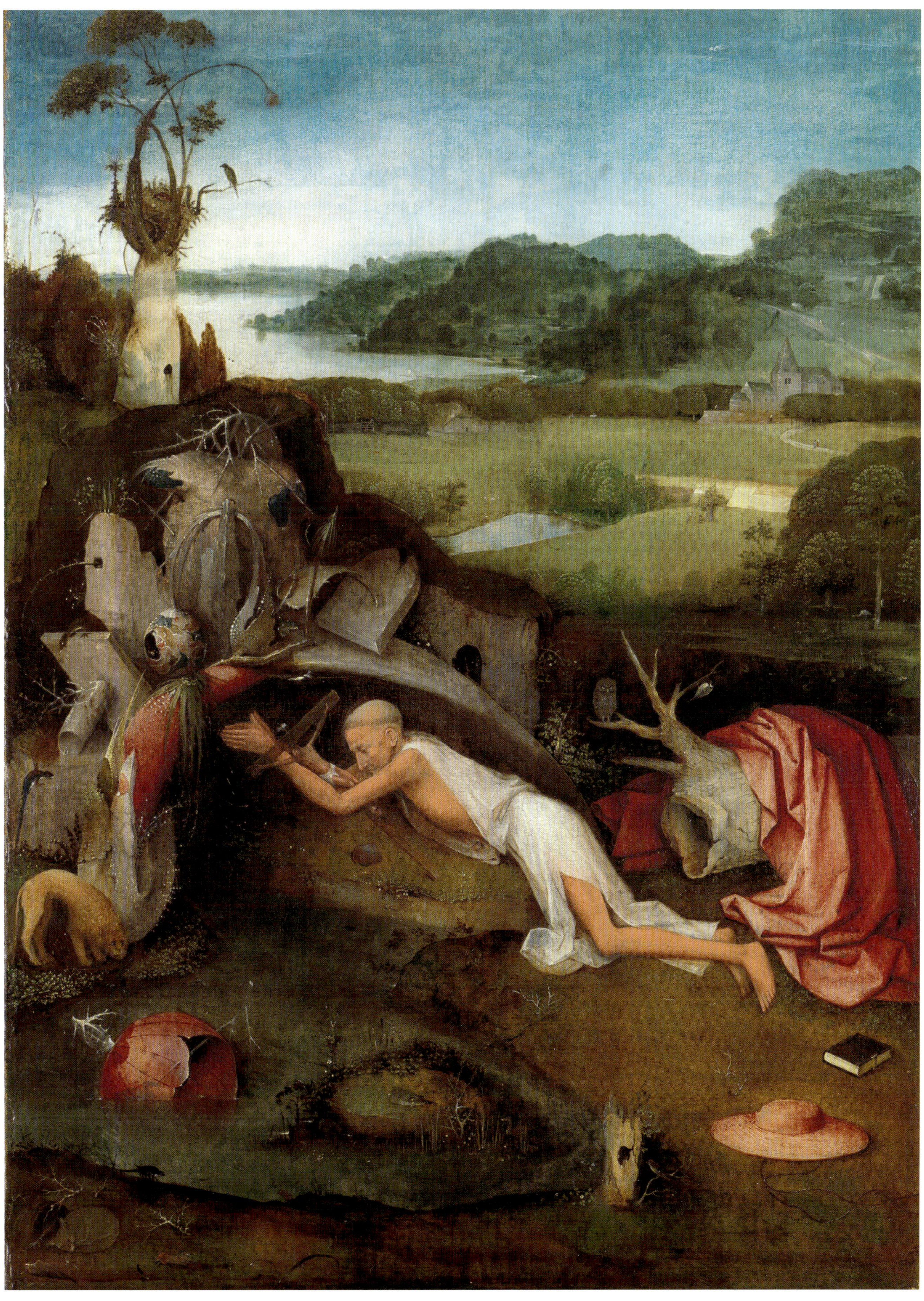

*140*The early Christian saints Anthony, Jerome and Giles withdrew into the desert as hermits to devote their lives entirely to God and to free themselves of earthly desires. Bosch shows them in the *Hermit Saints Triptych* in pious reflection, far from the world of people. The rectangular triptych was originally semi-circular at the top, with the same format as the *Saint Wilgefortis Triptych* (cat. 41), which, like this painting, spent several centuries in Venice. When the *Hermit Saints Triptych* was transferred temporarily to Vienna in the nineteenth century, the tops of the panels were sawn off, and the wings were cropped slightly at the bottom.

As a Church Father and Bible translator, Jerome was exceedingly popular throughout the Middle Ages. The saint can be identified in the central panel from his red robe and cardinal's hat. He is shown kneeling in the ruin of what was once probably a palace, surrounded by traces of a pagan culture. The figure of an idol, for instance, topples from a pillar just behind him, on which a praying man is painted, more or less a mirror image of Jerome himself, beneath a sky with sun, moon and stars. Jerome kneels before a crucifix placed on a throne-like structure. In his right hand, he holds the rock with which, according to tradition, he beat himself as a form of penance.

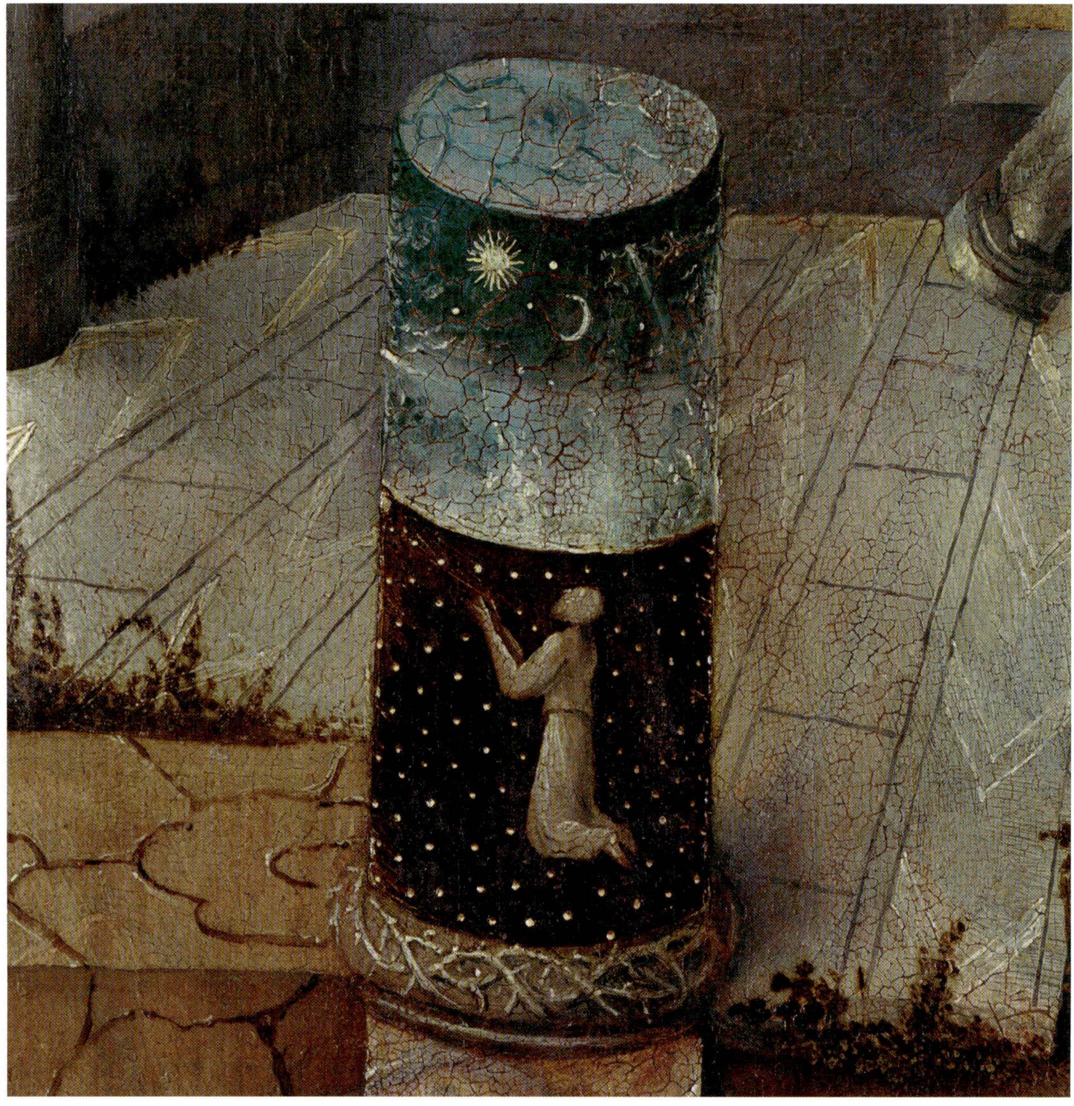

Hieronymus Bosch
Hermit Saints Triptych, c. 1495–1505
Oil on oak panel, left wing 85.4 × 29.2 cm,
central panel 85.7 × 60 cm,
right wing 85.7 × 28.9 cm
Venice, Gallerie dell'Accademia

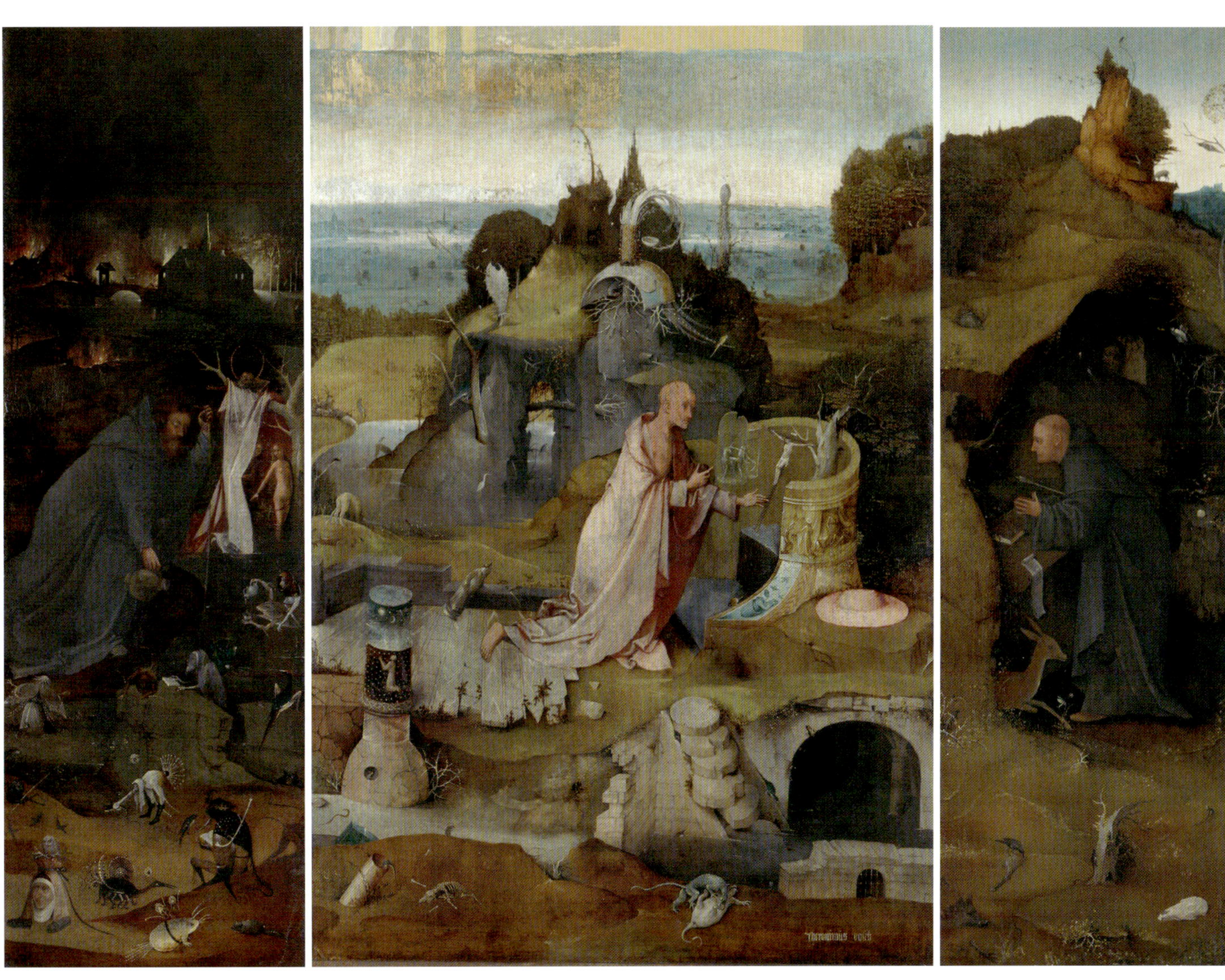

The throne before which Jerome is positioned is decorated with scenes painted in monochrome, not all of which are readily identifiable. At the bottom, we make out a scene with a small figure that has crawled into a basket up to its waist. A stick protrudes from its backside, on which perches what is probably the tiniest of all Bosch's owls, being mobbed by other birds. The relief on the left shows a man who is about to mount an all but untameable unicorn, while on the outside of the throne we see a depiction of the story of Judith and Holofernes. The Old Testament general's decapitated body lies on a camp bed in a tent, with a guard still sleeping on the ground in front of him. Judith emerges from the tent holding the severed head of Holofernes, which she will place in the basket brought by her maidservant. The two latter scenes with Judith, the biblical heroine who saved her city while preserving her honour, and the unicorn, which, according to legend, could only be captured by a virgin, undoubtedly allude to Jerome's inner struggle to conquer his sinful thoughts.

A lion is painted in the far left background, standing at the water's edge. The animal is barely noticeable, but can still be clearly identified from his tail. It became Jerome's companion after the saint removed a thorn from its paw, and is a fixed attribute in images of the saint. The equivalent for Saint Giles, shown in the right wing in a landscape that seems to run continuously from the central panel, is a hind, which God sent to him to provide occasional milk. The hermit is shown at a table on which lie a book and a scroll. He has been shot through the heart with an arrow aimed by a hunter at the deer lying uninjured at his feet. A figure peers through an opening into the dark cave to which Giles has withdrawn; he is probably meant to represent the king who, according to the saint's legend, discovered the wounded hermit as he followed his hunters. The king offered Giles medical assistance, but the saint refused, going so far as to ask God never to heal his wounds, as he believed that intense suffering was a means of perfecting virtue.

During his isolation in the desert, Saint Anthony was visited by all manner of demons, who sought to tempt him off the path of righteousness. The left wing shows the saint leaning on his staff and drawing water from a river. In the background we see a burning city, while the foreground is peopled by a variety of little monsters. The devil tries to tempt Anthony by revealing a young woman bathing behind a curtain. The extensive recent restoration of the triptych (2013–15) has given the woman back much of her original allure. All the same, Anthony keeps a cool head and does not allow himself to be distracted.

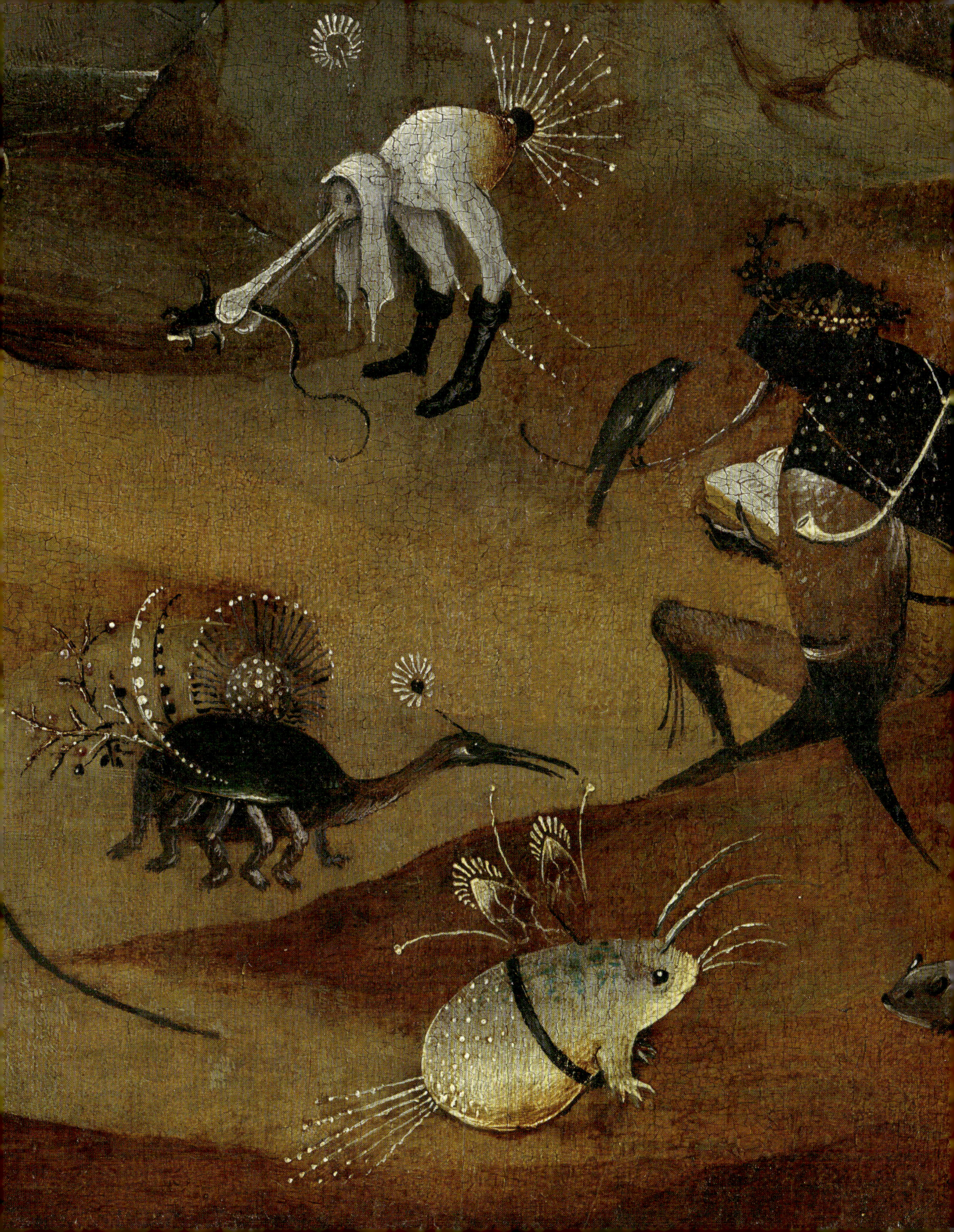

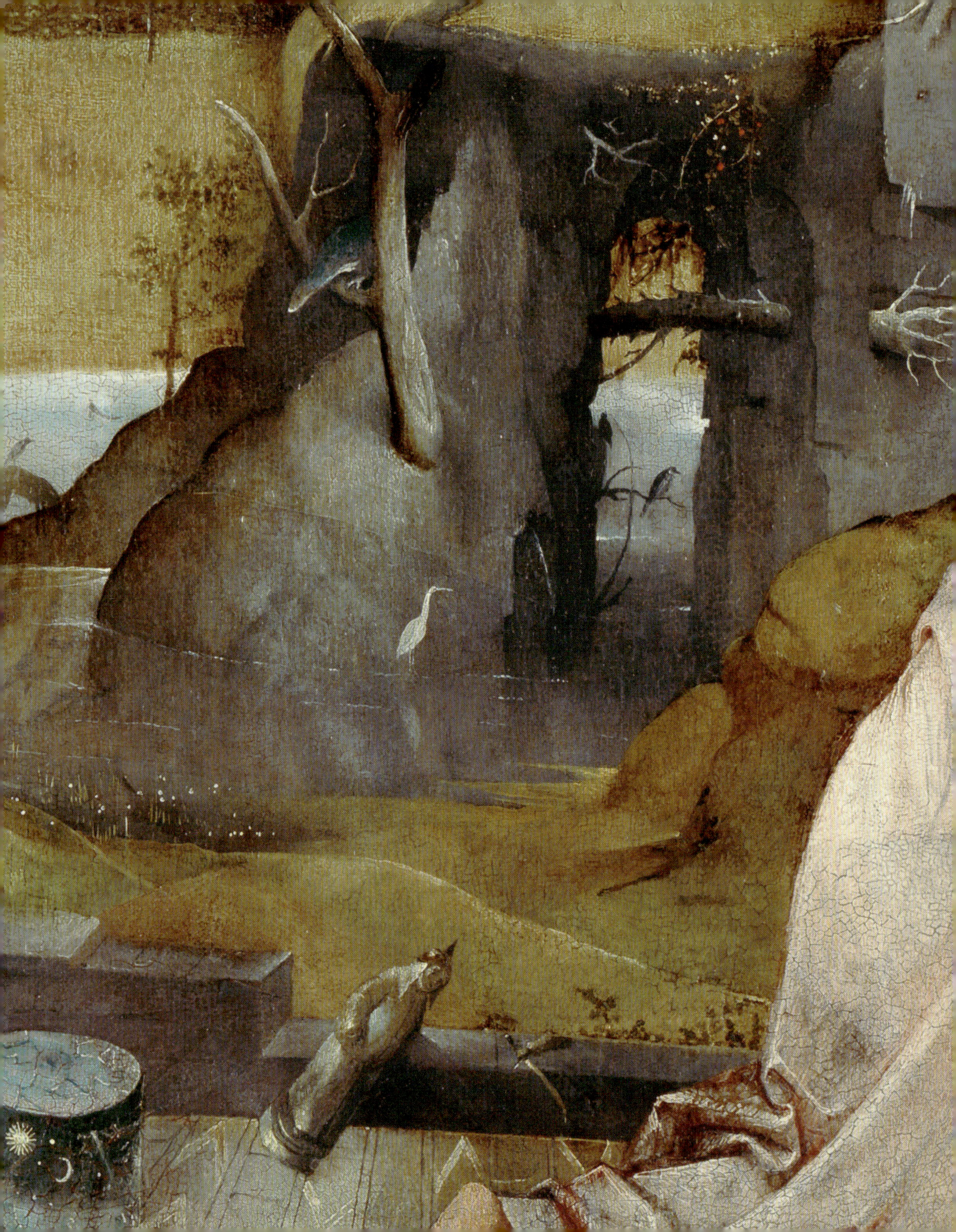

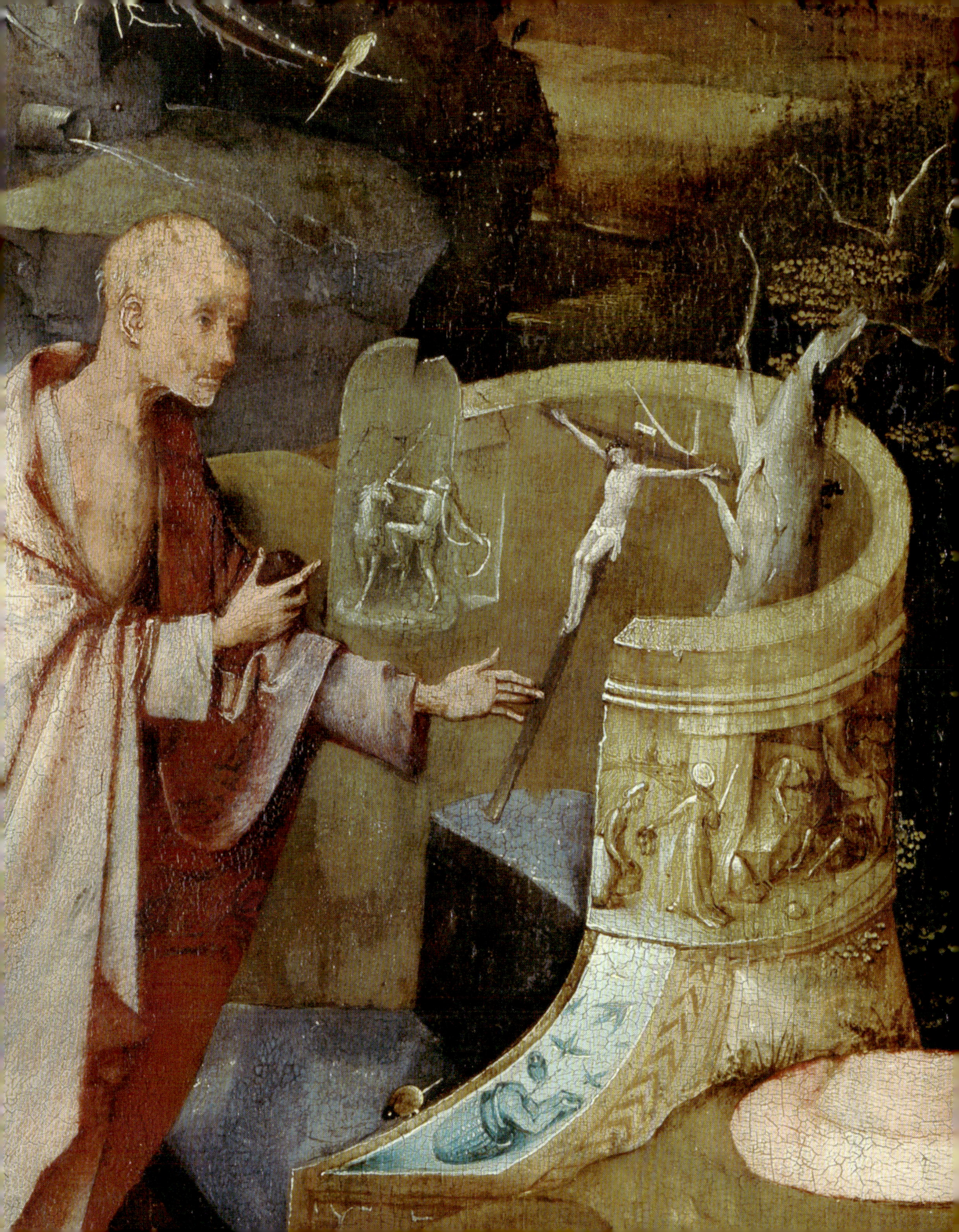

Job, who was once so wealthy, sits under the awning of his ruined house. Semi-naked and his body covered in sores, he has lost everything: his children, his possessions and his health. According to the Old Testament, this was God's way of testing Job's faith.

Job is accompanied by a group of six musicians with weird instruments, such as the horse's skull which, although not strung, is nonetheless played with a fiddle bow. The scene refers to the miracle tale in which musicians offer Job solace and distraction in his misery – a legend that had become popular in the late fifteenth century. According to this account, Job paid the musicians with scabs picked off his wounds, which then turned into gold coins. This ironic (?) consolation is interrupted in the painting by the arrival of a demon with a fox's head. Job turns round to look at the creature, which, dressed in a monk's habit, appears from inside the ruined building behind him. Perhaps this is a last attempt to provoke him. According to the Bible, God gave Satan free rein to drive Job to the limit, but the man never abandoned his trust in the Lord.

The same goes for Saint Anthony, whom we see in the left wing surrounded by demons who torment him incessantly. The saint is deep in prayer in the cave to which he has withdrawn in isolation. He holds a long string of prayer beads in this hands and faces a simple cross made of two slender branches on the other side of the improvised altar. There is a small monster standing by this altar, which Anthony has evidently tamed, as its armoured hands are bound behind its back.

The right wing shows Saint Jerome kneeling before the crucifix he has installed on a chair or throne. He touches the cross with his left hand, while in his right he holds a rock with which to chastise himself. Snakes and other ominous creatures crawl about among the plants and stones just above his head. Jerome's faithful companion, the lion, devours a deer in the distant background.

The way the two hermits in the wings are turned away from the central panel emphasizes both their own isolation and that of the 'Holy Man Job'. All three succeeded in withstanding their earthly trials and persisted in their faith in God.

The exterior wings were probably painted in Antwerp around 1520 with imitation stone and four coats of arms. The latter belong to the couples Pieter van der Voirt and Maria Smaechs on the one hand, and Diego de Haro and Johanna Pijnappel on the other. All four belonged to the same Antwerp mercantile elite as the commissioners of the *Adoration of the Magi* in the Prado. The inclusion of the coats of arms made the *Job Triptych* a memorial for the two couples, who were linked with one another by the marriage of their son Jacob van Voirt and (step)daughter Christina van Driel respectively. The pictured saints were intended to intercede on behalf of the people memorialized by the painting. The triptych was probably commissioned by Johanna Pijnappel on the death of Diego de Haro. The couple owned houses and other properties in 's-Hertogenbosch, the native city of Johanna's family.

The artistic quality of the *Job Triptych* is significantly inferior to that of the paintings that form the core group of Hieronymus Bosch's oeuvre. Notwithstanding this, a striking number of elements in this triptych correspond closely with details from other works by Bosch. Details from *Saint Jerome* in Ghent (cat. 42) and the *Hermit Saints Triptych* in Venice (cat. 43) are also found in the image of Jerome in the right wing of the *Job Triptych*: the vault beneath which the hermit kneels and the skull-shaped outcrop of rock with plants and fruit above it are almost identical to the location in which the Ghent Jerome has withdrawn in prayer; the throne-like structure, meanwhile, in front of which the saint kneels can be found – worked out in greater detail – in the central panel of the Venice triptych. The *Job Triptych* is likely, therefore, to have been produced in Bosch's workshop, where drawn and painted models and *ricordi* were available for reference. This probably occurred in the second decade of the sixteenth century.

Workshop of Hieronymus Bosch
Job Triptych, c. 1510–20
Oil on oak panel, left wing 98.1 × 30.5 cm,
central panel 98.3 × 72.1 cm, right wing 97.8 × 30.2 cm
Bruges, Stad Brugge, Groeningemuseum, 0000.GRO.0209
(extended loan from Sint-Jacob-de-Meerderekerk in Hoeke, Damme)

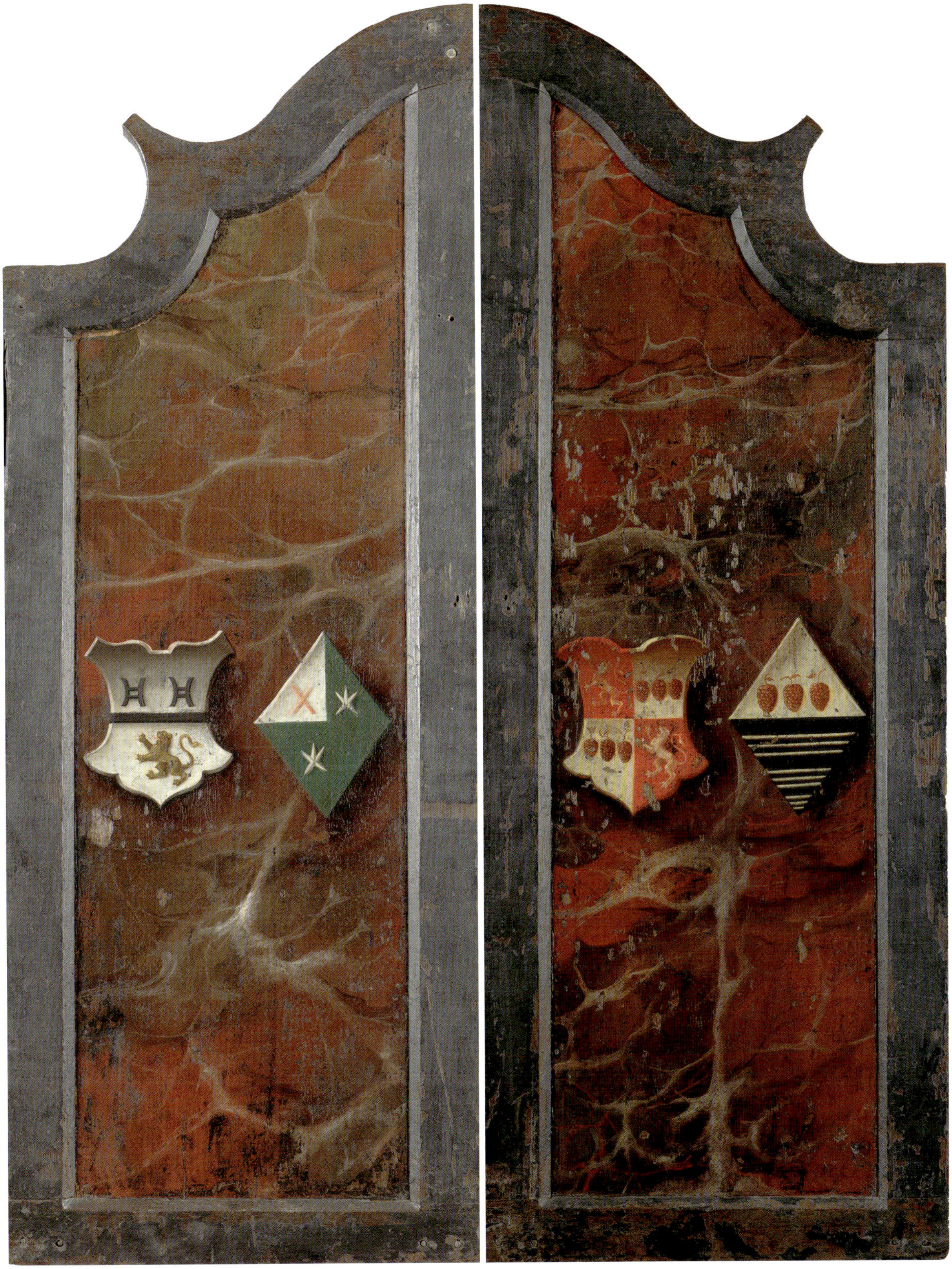

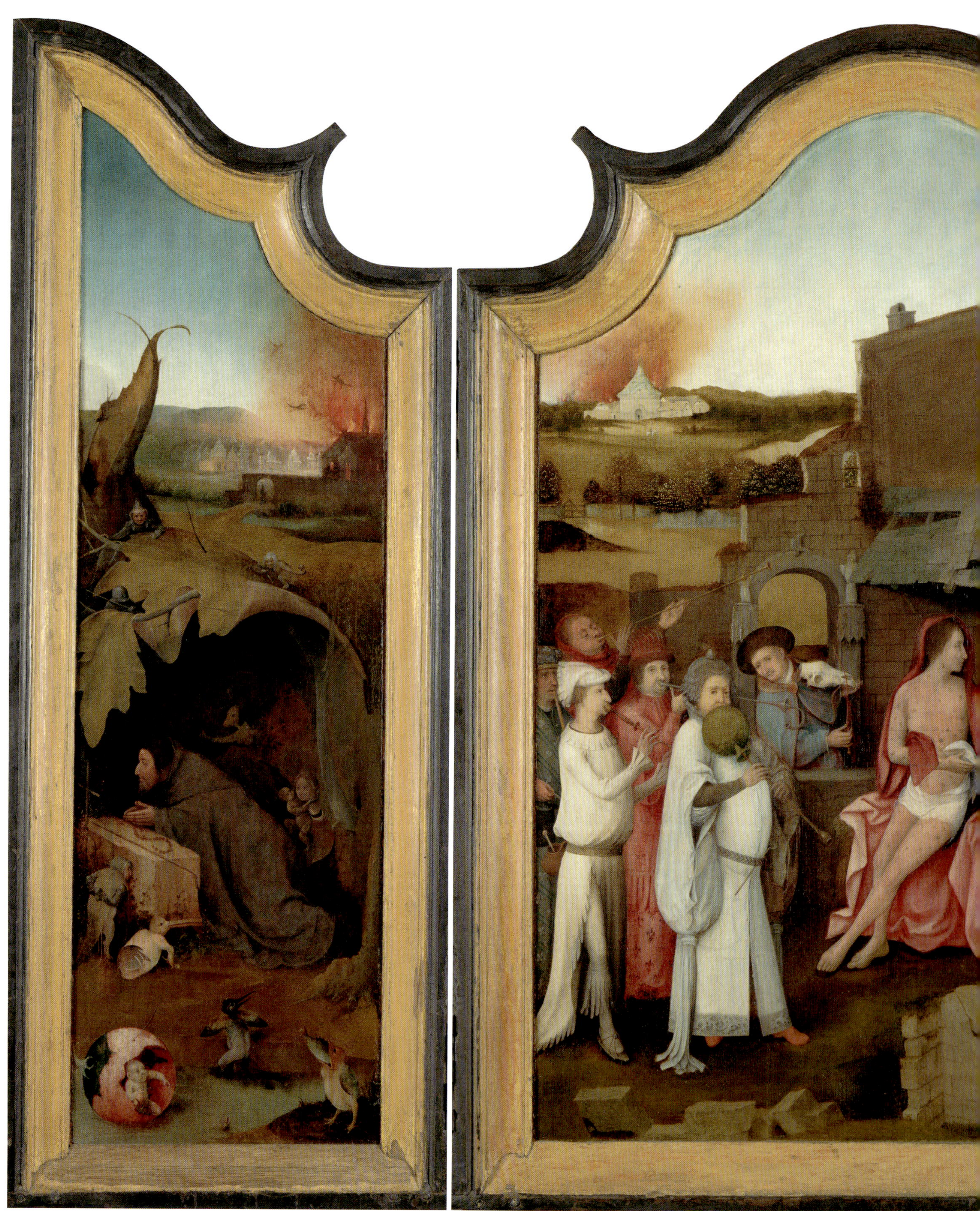

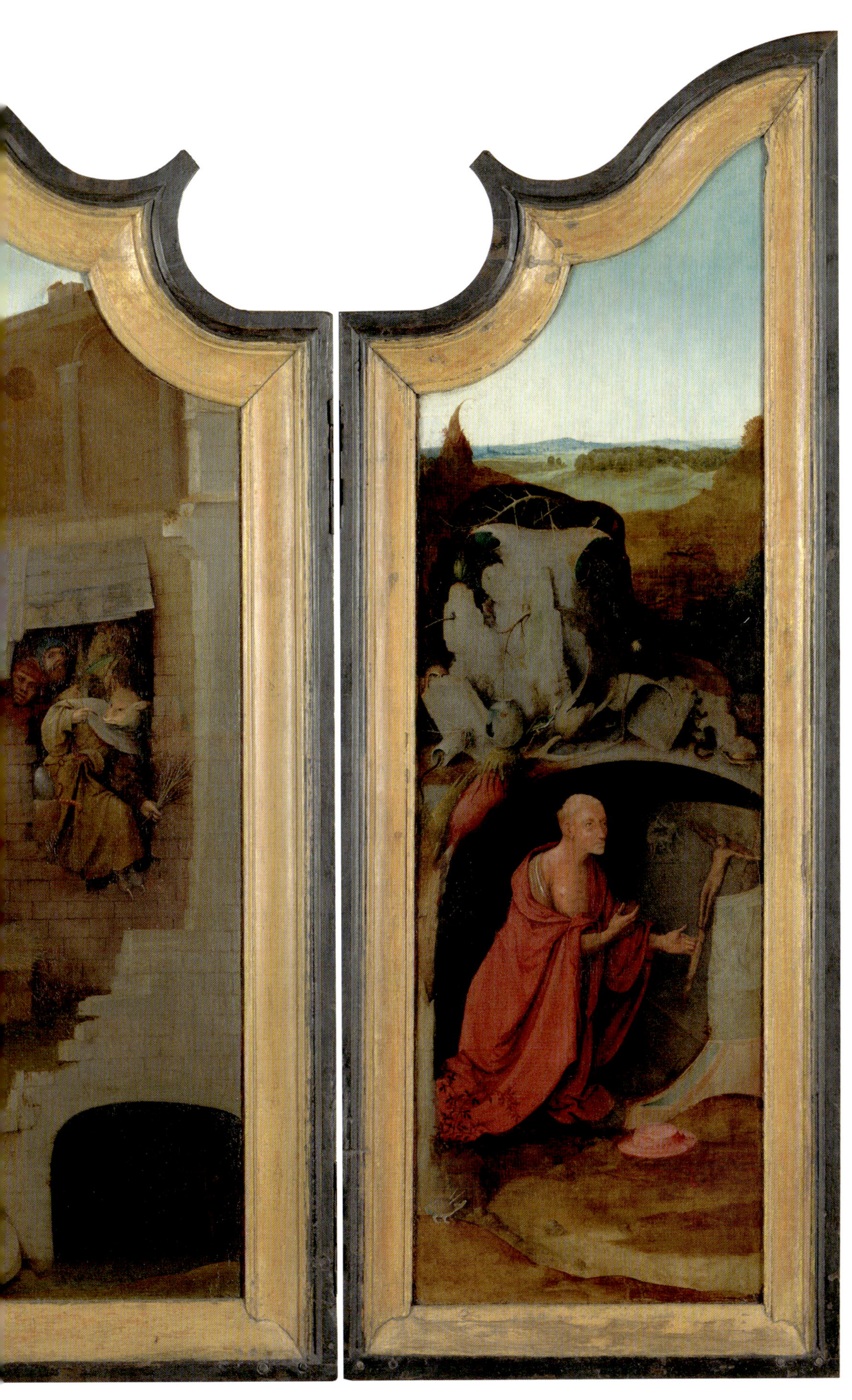

Hieronymus Bosch
The Temptation of Saint Anthony (fragment), c. 1500–10
Oil on oak panel, 38.6 × 25.1 cm
Kansas City, Missouri, The Nelson-Atkins Museum of Art,
purchase William Rockhill Nelson Trust, 35–22

150 Analysis by the Bosch Research and Conservation Project indicates that this small fragment with Saint Anthony, which has been in the Nelson-Atkins Museum since 1935, ought definitively to be included in the autograph oeuvre of Hieronymus Bosch. Although the image was heavily retouched and overpainted in the third quarter of the twentieth century, Bosch's hand is still clearly recognizable in the original brushwork. Our view is particularly hindered by the repainting of the saint's long, slightly wavy hair and extended beard, and the opaque overall finish. When we look through all this, however, it becomes clear how closely the image of Saint Anthony corresponds in particular with the left wing of the *Hermit Saints Triptych* (cat. 43), the *Saint Anthony Triptych* in Lisbon and the Bruges *Last Judgement* (cat. 49).

The underdrawings revealed by infrared photography (ill. p. 153) and reflectography are also a perfect match for what has been found in other panels from Hieronymus Bosch's core oeuvre. A fairly thick brush and a watery medium were used in a general and exploratory way to set down how the image would appear on the panel. This preparatory sketch is particularly legible beneath the face of the saint and the right hand with the earthenware jug. It is clear from the detail of the hand with the jug how the artist searched for the right shapes and position while drawing, how he reduced the size of the jug and how he settled on the final form while actually painting. We recognize the same exploratory approach that we find in virtually all the other works attributed to Bosch.

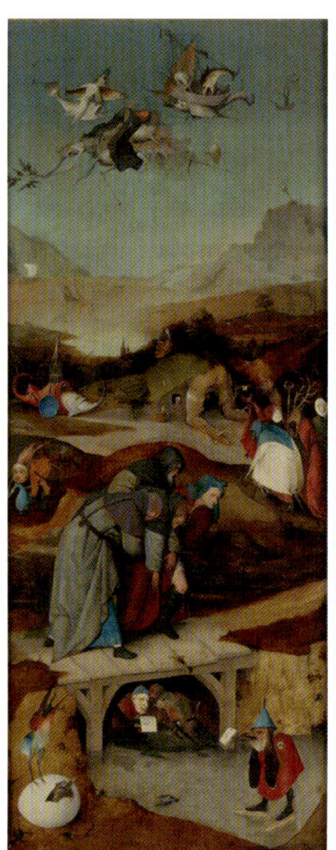
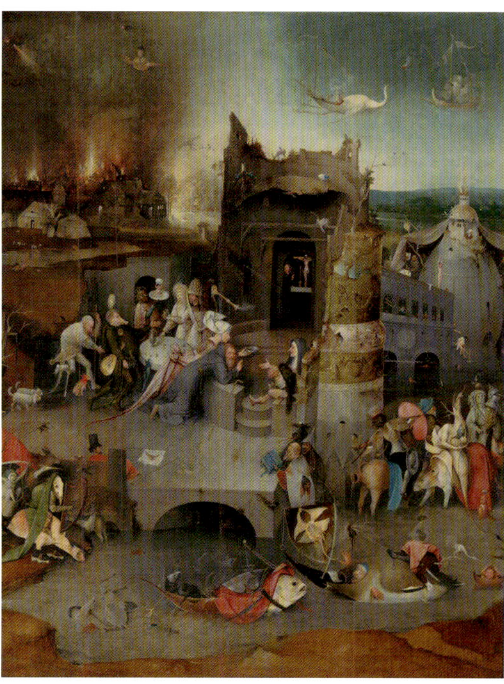
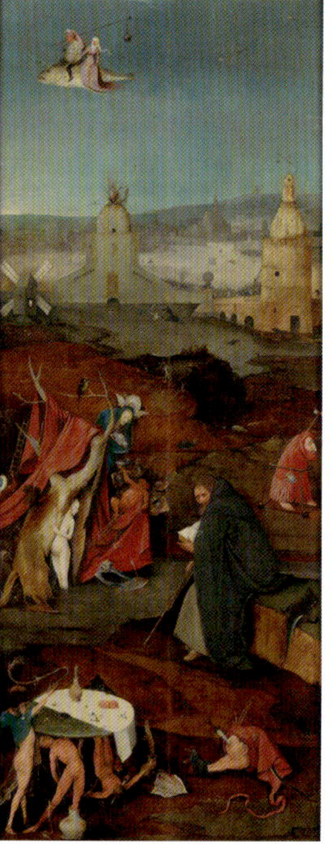

Hieronymus Bosch
Saint Anthony Triptych, c. 1500–10
Oil on oak panel,
left wing 144.8 × 66.5 cm;
central panel 145.1 × 132.8 cm;
right wing 144.8 × 66.7 cm
Lisbon, Museu Nacional de Arte Antiga,
1498

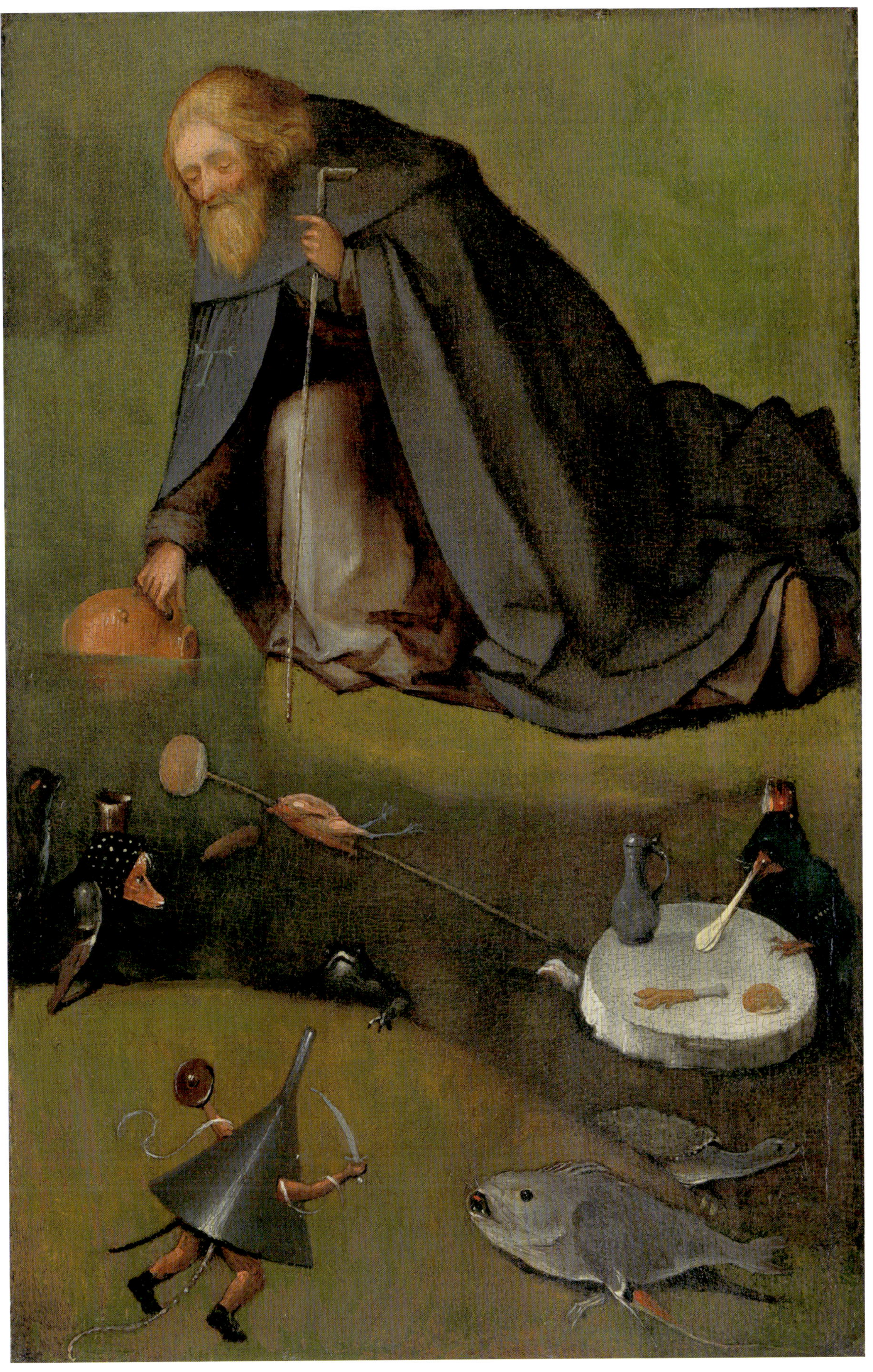

Every detail of the image of Saint Anthony kneeling and scooping up water in a setting filled with bizarre creatures fits seamlessly into Bosch's wider oeuvre. The figure of the saint closely matches that of Anthony in the left wing of the *Hermit Saints Triptych* (cat. 43) and is also related to the water-scooping female monster in the central panel of the *Last Judgement* in Bruges (cat. 49). Here and in the right wing, moreover, we find two creatures, hiding under a funnel, which resemble the one in the fragment in Kansas City. The monster with the fox's head on the left is very similar, meanwhile, to the equivalent figure in the right wing of the *Saint Anthony Triptych* in Lisbon. The little figure with the spoonbill's beak on the right is likewise found in the left wing of the *Hermit Saints Triptych*. The pig's trotter lying on the floating tabletop also appears in the *Wayfarer* in Rotterdam (cat. 1), the fragment in New Haven (cat. 3) and the right wing of the *Saint Anthony Triptych*. The tortoise-like animal in the right foreground is familiar from the drawing in Berlin (cat. 37 verso) and the back of a sketch sheet with studies of Saint Anthony in Paris. There are further details too that are found in other paintings by Bosch, such as the floating sausage, the little cup on the head of the fox-monster, the tabletop and the pewter jug on it, and the toad clambering out of the water. While all these motifs are directly comparable, the evidence of Bosch's characteristic painting style is more important still. Take the way the artist has set down the staff on which the saint supports himself: a thin greyish stripe, outlined in brown-black on one side and heightened on the other with very finely and irregularly applied lead white. The greyish stripe is not visible about Anthony's leg, where Bosch used his gown as mid-tone. The T-shaped cross on the cloak and the legs of the skewered bird in the same bright blue colour are both drawn more than they are painted. Bosch often worked with different colours in still wet paint, for instance in the head and wing of the stranded flying fish. It is reminiscent of the fish in *Saint Christopher* (cat. 40) and the *Saint Anthony Triptych* (Lisbon). The fish and the funnel creature in the Kansas City panel are more impastoed and less transparent, but that is due to the fact that they have not been left in reserve from the background.

The little panel in Kansas City has been cropped on all sides. The board is approximately four millimetres thick and the back is bare oak. This all indicates that it is a fragment of an originally much larger painting, probably the wing of a dismantled triptych. The saint will have been painted in a much more extensive hostile environment, such as we find in the left wing of the *Hermit Saints Triptych* (cat. 43).

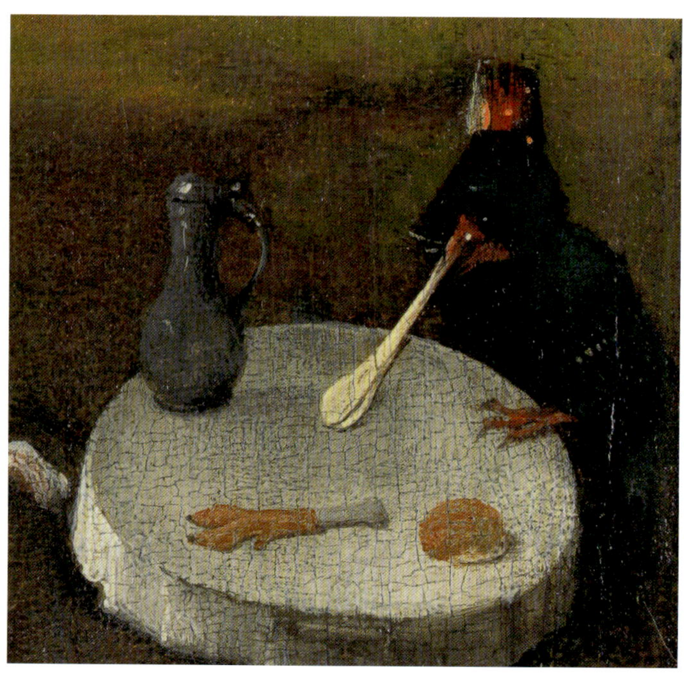

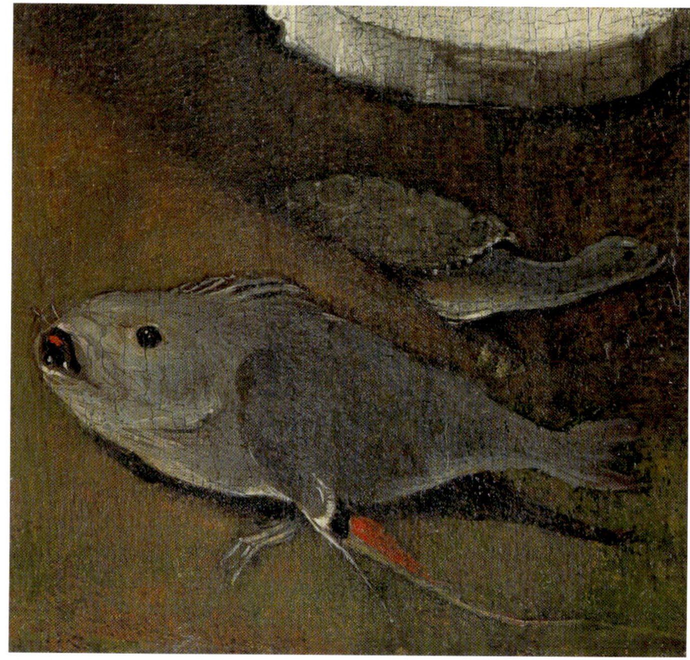

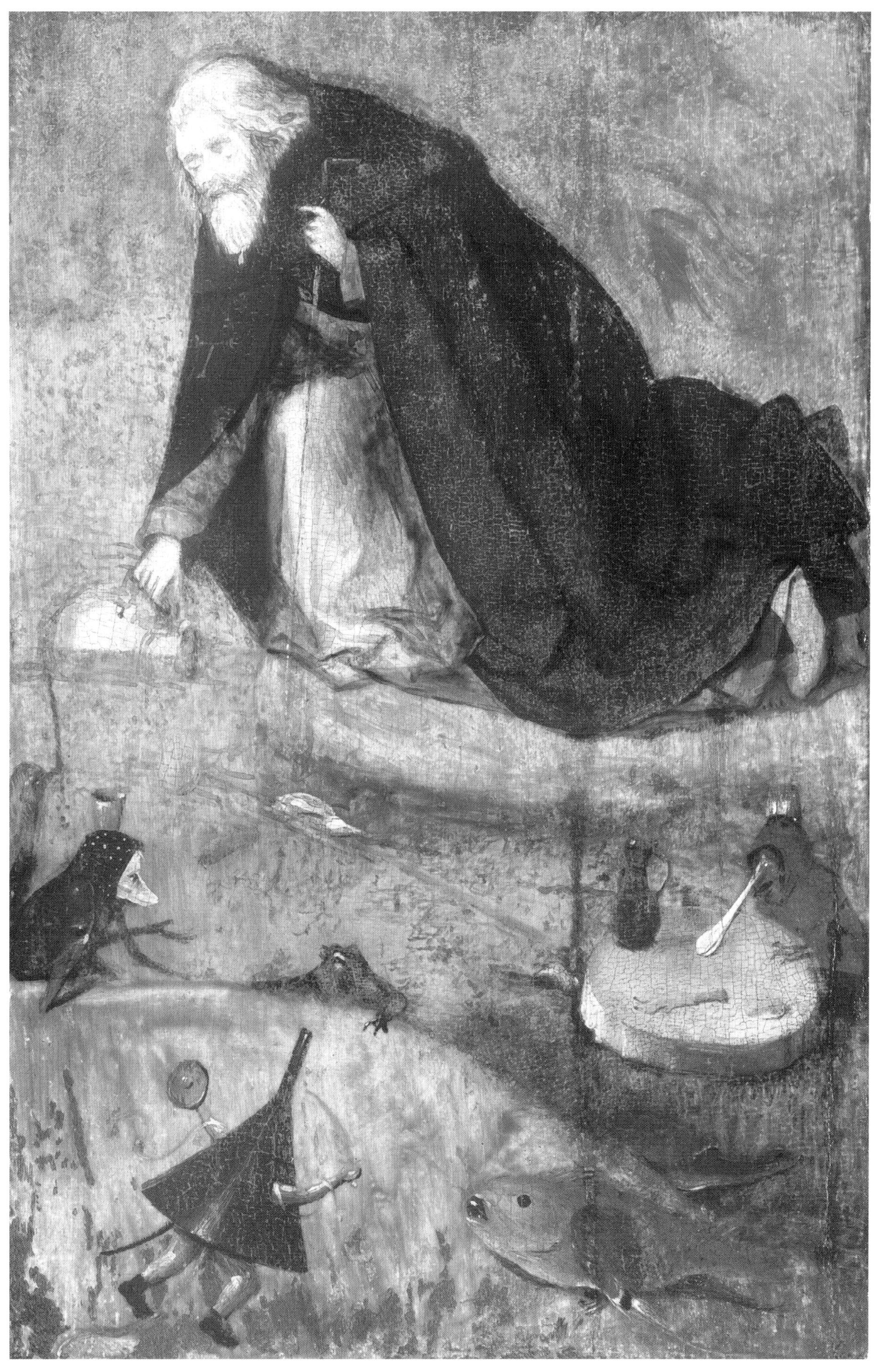

Saint Anthony sits on the bank of a stream, deep in thought. The grey habit he wears identifies the pious elderly man as a monk and hermit. The pig – his customary attribute since the late Middle Ages – lies next to him. The bell in the animal's right ear tells us that this is a Saint Anthony's pig, of the kind that rooted around in late-medieval cities. Neither seems concerned by the monsters that approach them from every side. The somewhat exotic building in the middleground behind the saint is not only the shelter to which he withdrew, but also recognizable as an Antonine monastery from the distinctive T-shaped cross above its entrance. The monastery too is under attack, and we even make out the first signs of arson.

   As the great example for all later monks – above all the Antonines – the saint himself wears a habit on which a T-shaped cross (also known as a Tau or Saint Anthony's cross) has been embroidered. His clasped hands signify that he is absorbed in prayer, and a prayerbook hangs from the leather belt around his waist. This 'girdle book' is bound in leather in a typical late-medieval style, with long flaps used to protect it. A precious crystal ball is attached to the belt to stop it slipping away. The saint, who sits beneath a makeshift straw shelter, is chiefly recognizable as a late-medieval monk; the overall context clearly shows, however, that this is the Desert Father from whom every monastery and convent in the Christian world ultimately derived.

This painting with its image of Anthony Abbot is recorded from an early date in Spanish inventories, probably beginning with one drawn up for the Escorial in 1574. The unsigned *Temptation of Saint Anthony* was already attributed at that point to Hieronymus Bosch, along with eight other paintings that King Philip II had transferred to the palace-monastery in that period. The panel was exhibited as an authentic Bosch without qualification at the anniversary exhibition in 's-Hertogenbosch in 1967. Since then, however, it has been almost universally accepted that the panel was painted by a follower of Bosch. This happened in two phases. Technical examination demonstrated that the panel originally had a semi-circular top and that it was later extended to make it rectangular; the painting was also retouched. Such drastic intervention is likely to have been prompted by serious damage – a hypothesis supported by the substantial overpainting of the figure of Saint Anthony. All this must have occurred after 1574, because the painting was still recorded at that time as having a curved top.

   Although the damage and overpainting make it difficult to determine the original appearance of the work, it is clear that the painting is a free imitation after the 's-Hertogenbosch master. The panel's atmosphere and subject matter were inspired by Bosch, yet it deviates from his oeuvre in almost every respect – composition, depth effects, style and technique. The monsters depicted here are amusing cartoons that do not frighten the viewer any more than they do the saint; not at all what we are accustomed to with Bosch himself. A 2001 study of all Hieronymus Bosch's paintings in the Prado concluded that he might well have painted the original panel – smaller and with a semi-circular top – which was enlarged and overpainted to form the work we see today.

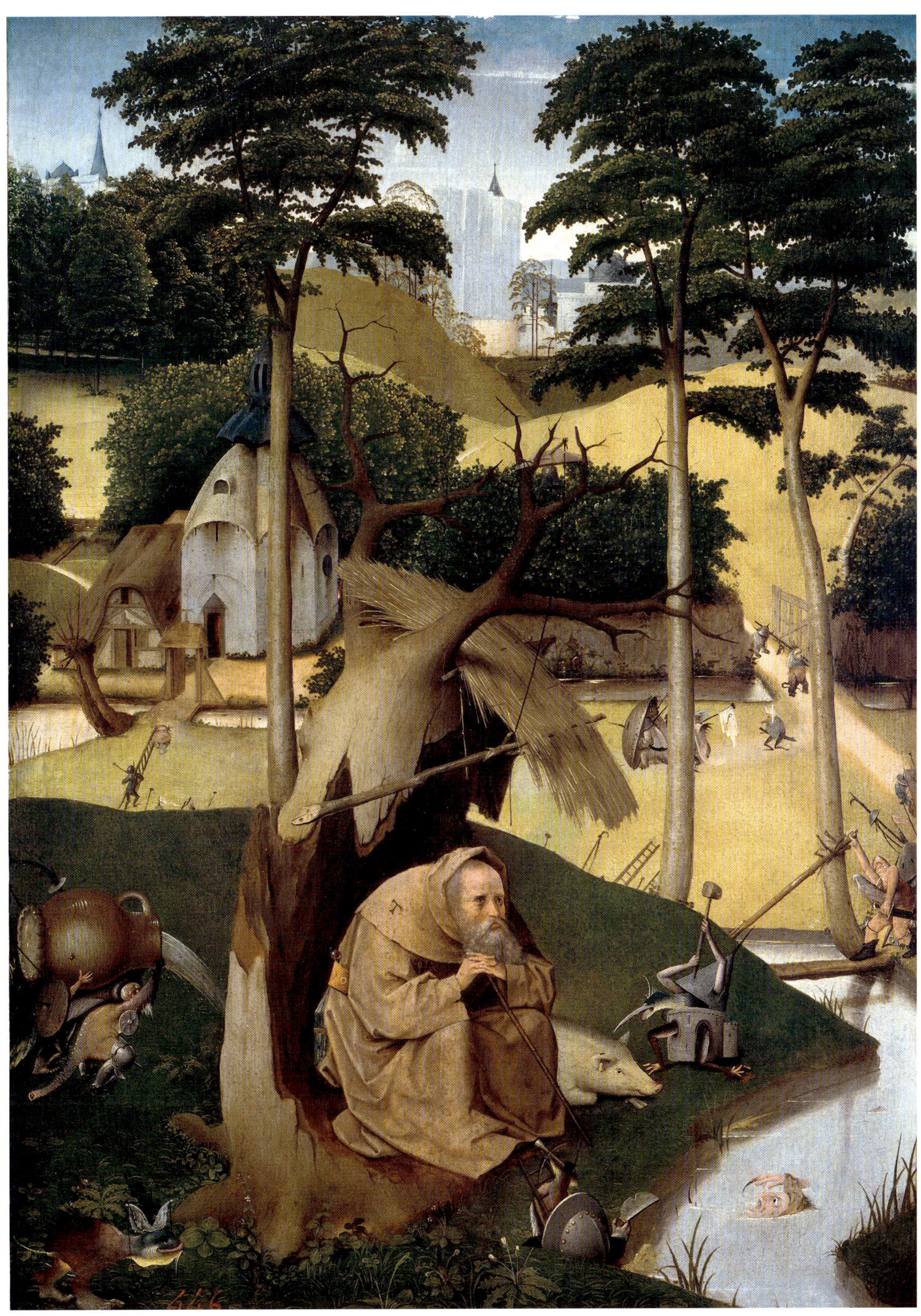

Follower of Hieronymus Bosch
The Temptation of Saint Anthony,
c. 1530–40 and after 1574
Oil on oak panel, 73 × 52.5 cm
Madrid, Museo Nacional del Prado, P2049

For centuries, 's-Hertogenbosch had to make do with Hieronymus Bosch's memory and a body of largely forgotten archives: not a single work by the local master remained in the city. A bronze statue of the painter was unveiled in 1930 on the Markt, close to the houses where Bosch lived as a child and following his marriage to Aleid van de Meervenne. The commemorative sculpture was installed on the initiative of the city's then mayor, F. J. van Lanschot, and was made by the sculptor August Falise. The figure was inspired by an apocryphal portrait of Bosch, and was billed as bringing the 'Painter of Devils' ('le faizeur de Dyables') back to his native city. Thirty-five years later, another member of the Van Lanschot family of bankers purchased a Saint Anthony panel attributed to Hieronymus Bosch, which remains in the family's collection in 's-Hertogenbosch to this day. Sadly, the acquisition of an original work by Bosch for the city once again proved elusive. Although Max J. Friedländer, the great connoisseur of early Netherlandish painting, attributed the panel to Bosch in 1927, doubt was cast on this identification almost immediately. The work was linked at the same time to the similar *Last Judgement* fragment in Munich (cat. 50), which was considered to be an autograph painting by Bosch for some considerable time. The two panels were exhibited in 1967 at the high-profile Bosch exhibition in 's-Hertogenbosch, since when both have been viewed as imitations of the great master. Opinions also differ as to its date. Some believe it was painted under Bosch's influence around 1515 and that it is thus contemporary with him. In our view, both panels were painted later and form part of the wave of Bosch imitations that were produced in the mid-sixteenth century in the Southern Netherlands, particularly in Antwerp.

Even though the *Temptation of Saint Anthony* cannot be viewed as an original work by Bosch, it remains a highly intriguing painting. Anthony is depicted as a hunched abbot and hermit, surrounded by twenty or so monsters and freaks that hark back to creatures imagined by Bosch. The saint, who appears unperturbed, can be identified from his T-shaped staff, the bell he holds in his hand and the rosary with a small Saint Anthony's cross, which hangs from his belt together with a girdle book. The panel itself is surprisingly old, with dendrochronological analysis showing that it could have been painted as early as 1461 and more likely from 1463. Examination under infrared light confirmed what could already be made out to some extent with the naked eye: the *Temptation of Saint Anthony* was painted on top of another work. Two earlier phases can be identified, in fact. The scene that we see was painted over a fairly linear underdrawing done on a memorial panel, the existing picture of which was partially removed. A group of small donors' portraits is located in the foreground. Four veiled women kneel on the right, while on the left there are at least three and possibly four or five men. They are positioned in front of a standing figure of Christ as the Man of Sorrows, Mary baring her right breast, and God the Father blessing his son with his right hand. The group is an example of a 'Stairway of Salvation' or *Intercessio* image, highlighting the way prayers directed to God will be heard through the intercession of the Virgin Mary and of her son, who sacrificed himself on behalf of humanity. This devotional image was itself painted over an earlier picture still – most likely a slightly different 'Stairway of Salvation' composition. The memorial scene with donors can be dated stylistically to the final quarter of the fifteenth century. It was overpainted with the *Temptation of Saint Anthony* just under half a century later.

Follower of Hieronymus Bosch
The Temptation of Saint Anthony,
c. 1530–40
Oil on oak panel, 60.1 × 52.1 cm
's-Hertogenbosch, Art Collection
Van Lanschot

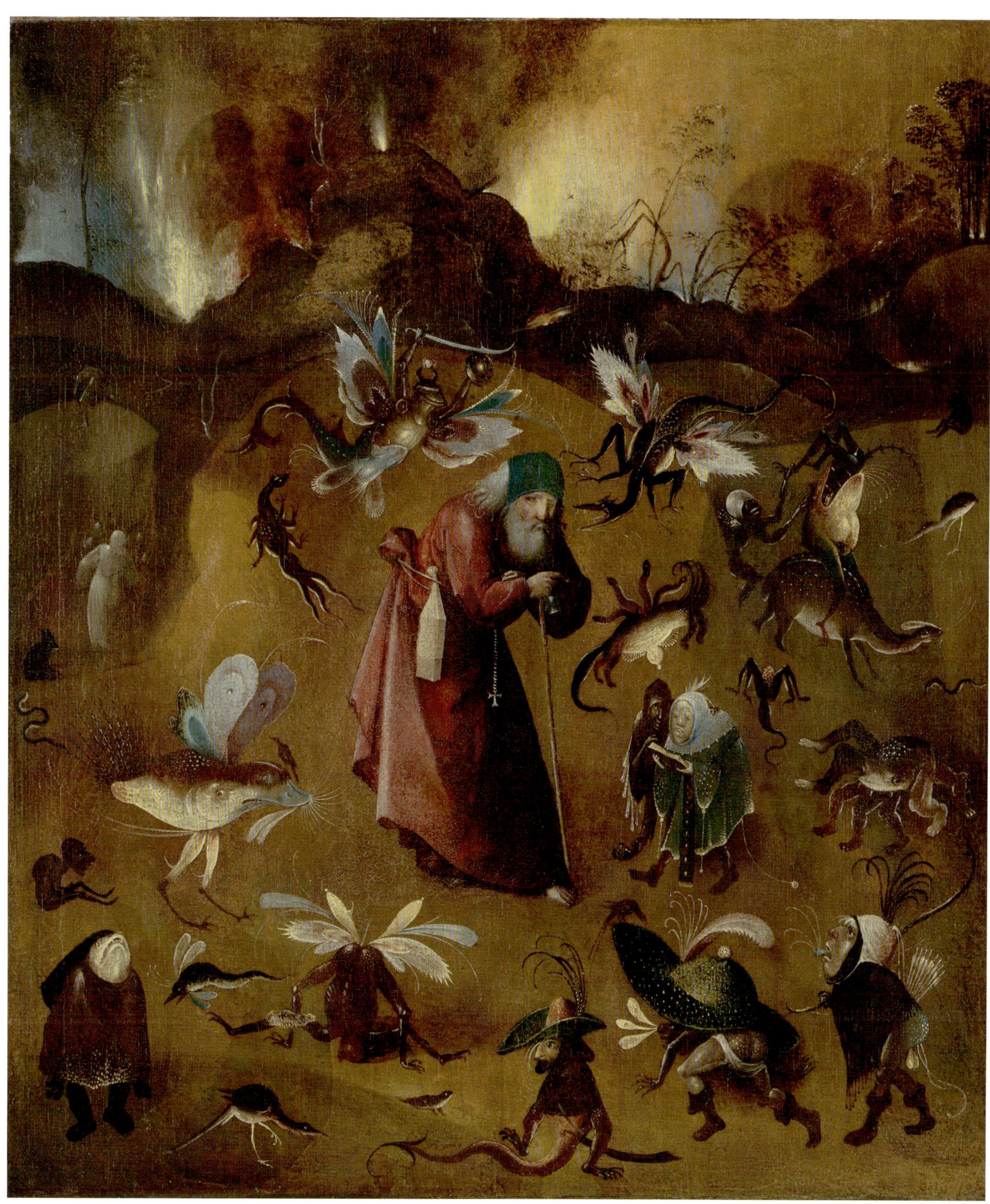

VI

The End of Days

Hieronymus Bosch's most prestigious client was undoubtedly Duke Philip the Fair of Burgundy, who was in 's-Hertogenbosch more or less continuously between 9 September 1504 and the end of May 1505. The duke cannot have wasted any time in commissioning the celebrated local artist to paint a large panel showing the Last Judgement with heaven and hell. The work was probably never delivered, however, as there is no further mention of it in the ducal accounts following the record of the down-payment. This is nonetheless an important piece of information, as it shows that the duke, who was very knowledgeable about Southern Netherlandish art, was sufficiently intrigued by the idiosyncratic work of Hieronymus Bosch to commission a painting from him. Hippolyte de Berthoz, born in Burgundy and a senior treasury official from Philip's entourage, had previously ordered a work from Bosch and his workshop, most likely the *Last Judgement Triptych* now in Vienna. The central panel of the triptych shows the End of Days and the Last Judgement, with the Garden of Eden and Adam and Eve in the left wing and hell in the right. Bosch applied the same formula in the *Garden of Earthly Delights* (see cat. 10) and the *Haywain* (cat. 5), in which he also links the beginning and the end of history in the wings of a triptych, in the form of a Garden of Eden and a hell scene. It is made clear in all three paradise scenes that evil was present in the world from the very beginning of creation: rebel angels, transformed into demons, are cast down to earth, while bloodthirsty beasts devour other creatures in the Garden of Eden. In this way, Bosch is able to connect his vision of the beginning of creation with that of hell.

The End of Days, the destruction of creation and God's judgement on all of humanity are represented in Bosch's surviving oeuvre in four works and in four different ways. Two triptych wings were painted in his workshop in the 1510s, showing the dramatic consequences of God's destruction of his own creation: the world *After the Flood* and the world *After the Last Judgement* (cat. 48a–b). The Flood made it clear just how terrible that destruction was, and God promised not to repeat it until the end of time. As far as we can tell, this double representation of total destruction is unique: no other artist was ever tempted to present such gruesome visions.

In the Bruges triptych showing the *Last Judgement* (cat. 49), Bosch presents his visionary account of Judgement Day across the three panels, in which the world is destroyed and the dead rise from their graves. The left wing shows a sunny Garden of Eden, where the blessed souls on God's right hand are helped on their way to heaven. In the right wing, by contrast, the souls of the damned are driven from a scorched earth into hell. The fragment of a large *Last Judgement* by a follower of Bosch (cat. 50) paints a realistic picture of the resurrection of the dead from their graves and the punishment meted out to sinners. Hieronymus Bosch himself used an unusual painting technique with light colours on a evenly black background to show what awaits every human being, both good and bad, after the Last Judgement: *The Way to Heaven* (cat. 51a–b) and *The Way to Hell* (cat. 51c–d). In four spectacular visions of the future, he set the terrifying *Fall of the Damned* and *The River to Hell* against the hopeful *Garden of Eden* and *Ascent of the Blessed*. Bosch's ultimate message, that there is salvation and hope, is expressed by a hallucinatory tunnel, at the end of which angels receive the souls of the righteous into the eternal light.

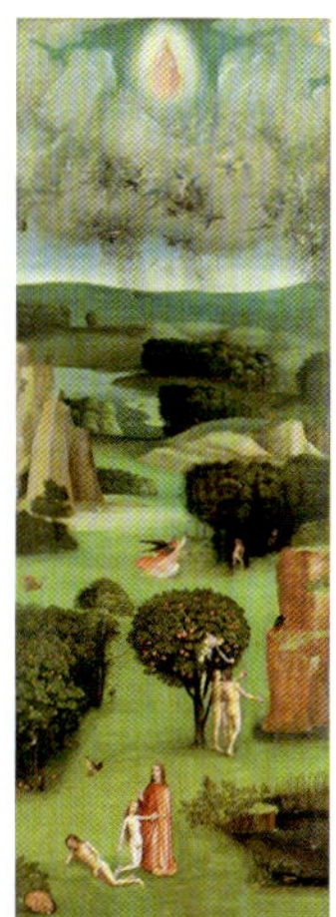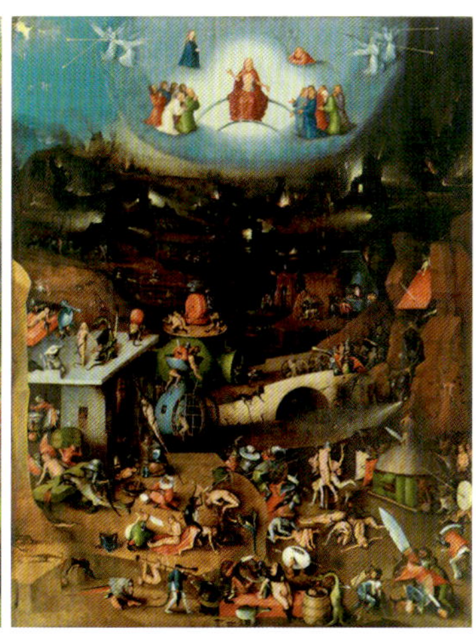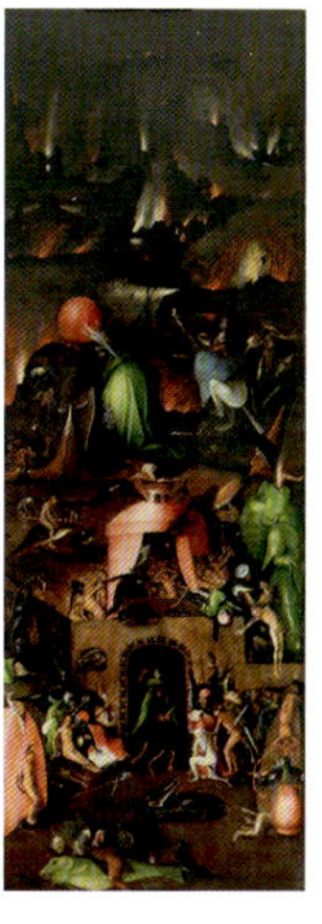

Hieronymus Bosch and Workshop
The Last Judgement, c. 1500–05
Oil on oak panel, central panel 163 × 127 cm; wings c. 167 × 60 cm
Vienna, Gemäldegalerie der Akademie der bildenden Künste, GG-579-GG-581

160

The two double-sided paintings known as the *Flood Panels* were originally the wings of a relatively small triptych, the missing central panel of which must have been about a metre wide. They were discovered in Spain in the 1920s, following which they were acquired by Dutch collectors. In 1941 D. G. van Beuningen donated the two little panels, heavily overpainted at the time, to the Rotterdam museum that bears his name. They were restored in the 1980s in line with the prevailing practice of the time: the overpainting was removed down to the bare oak panel and very little retouching was allowed, so as to ensure the greatest possible degree of honesty. Both the front and the back of the panels received this 'archaeological' treatment.

The closed triptych displayed two pairs of tondi, one above the other. Each of these four scenes shows an example of the demonic forces with which humanity is threatened, and which can only be overcome with God's help. The latter is shown in the first scene on the lower left, where God the Father or Christ blesses a kneeling man who has been saved from drowning; his ship can be seen foundering in the background. In the scene above, a man is attacked by three demons. In the upper right tondo of the other wing, a woman flees a burning house towards a man in the foreground. A demon in the gateway next to the house beats a child who is also trying to escape. The fourth and final tondo shows another demon waylaying a farmer who was sowing seed and harrowing his field on horseback. Although the overall theme is the vulnerability of human beings and their dependence on God's grace, it has not been possible to advance a more precise and convincing iconographical explanation.

When the shutters were opened, the now unknown central panel was displayed, with the *Flood Panels* on either side. The meaning of these scenes has been debated ever since the paintings were discovered. Only the one with Noah's Ark, which has come to rest on Mount Ararat as the Flood recedes, can be clearly identified. This panel, which we believe to have been positioned on the left, shows Noah and his family looking out from the Ark at the newly dry land and the animals disembarking from the vessel. This is the world *After the Flood*. God's decision to eradicate all the evil that had come into the world has been carried out; he then promised Noah and his descendants, along with all other living creatures, that he would never again destroy the earth (Genesis 9).

The other panel depicts an equally desolate world, from which all life has once again disappeared. Demons and monsters have taken possession of the scorched earth, while the fires continue to burn on the horizon. A female demon produces a surviving cripple from a cave, and a few other people might also still be sheltering beneath the vault in the foreground. What we see is the aftermath of Judgement Day as prophesied by Christ himself (Luke 17:24–27). This is the End of Days: the world *After the Last Judgement*. As pendants, these bleak scenes depict the destruction of the world: creation is wiped out by God's judgement, drowned beneath the waters in one instance and consumed by fire in the other. The central panel is likely to have depicted a Last Judgement, probably in colour.

Both wings were carefully prepared with drawings on the ground layer, which can still be seen clearly with the help of infrared light, despite the extensive damage. The final painting of the scene with Noah's Ark was altered fundamentally compared to the underdrawing and initial painting, thoroughly altering the import of the scene in the process. In the preliminary version, the Flood was still at its height; the Ark was afloat, and the artist drew the figures of people swimming, while others sought to flee the rising waters. During a second phase, the floodwaters were replaced by an already dry Mount Ararat, on which the Ark is beached. The Flood is over and the waters have receded: the animals, originally placed in a smaller Ark, now disembark from the larger, repainted version of the same vessel. The difference is crucial, as the painting now no longer focuses upon the destruction of God's creation but, on the contrary, on the salvation of all life.

Workshop of Hieronymus Bosch
48a. *After the Flood* (interior),
c. 1510–20
Oil on oak panel, 70 × 39.2 cm
Rotterdam, Museum Boijmans
Van Beuningen, St. 28

Workshop of Hieronymus Bosch
48b. *After the Last Judgement* (interior),
c. 1510–20
Oil on oak panel, 70.5 × 37.4 cm
Rotterdam, Museum Boijmans
Van Beuningen, St. 27

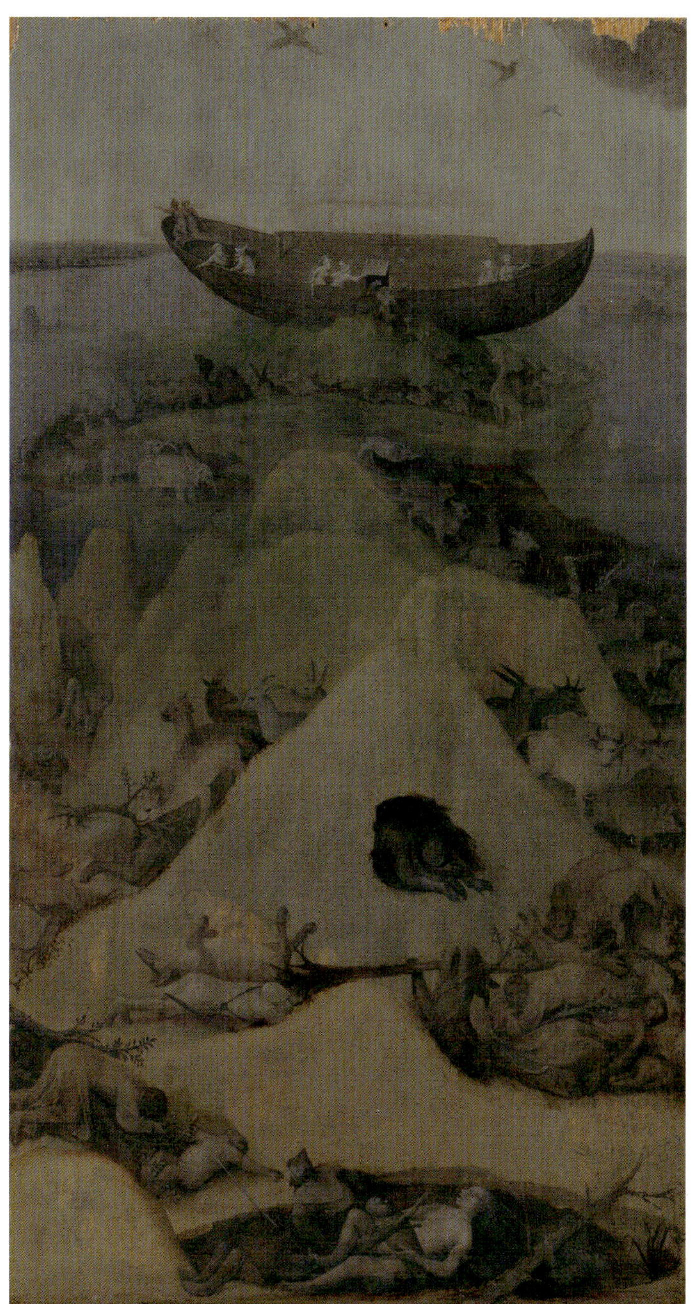

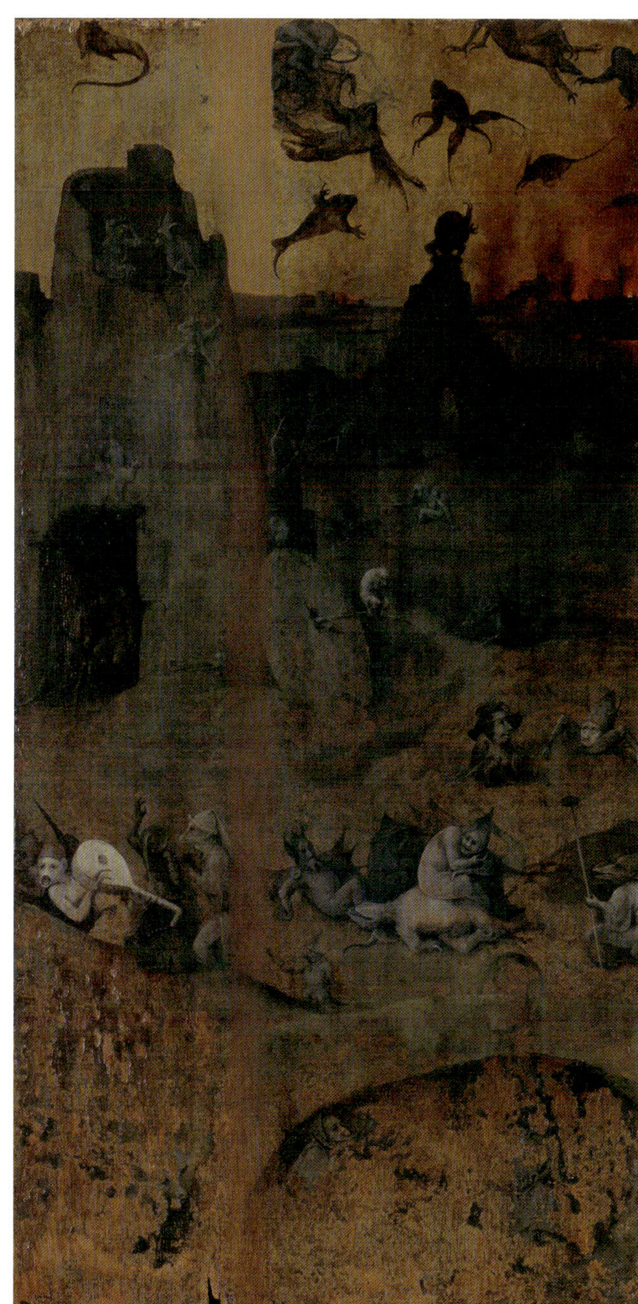

Workshop of Hieronymus Bosch
Two Tondi (exterior), c. 1510–20
Oil on oak panel, 70 × 39.2 cm
Rotterdam, Museum Boijmans
Van Beuningen, St. 28

Workshop of Hieronymus Bosch
Two Tondi (exterior), c. 1510–20
Oil on oak panel, 70.5 × 37.4 cm
Rotterdam, Museum Boijmans
Van Beuningen, St. 27

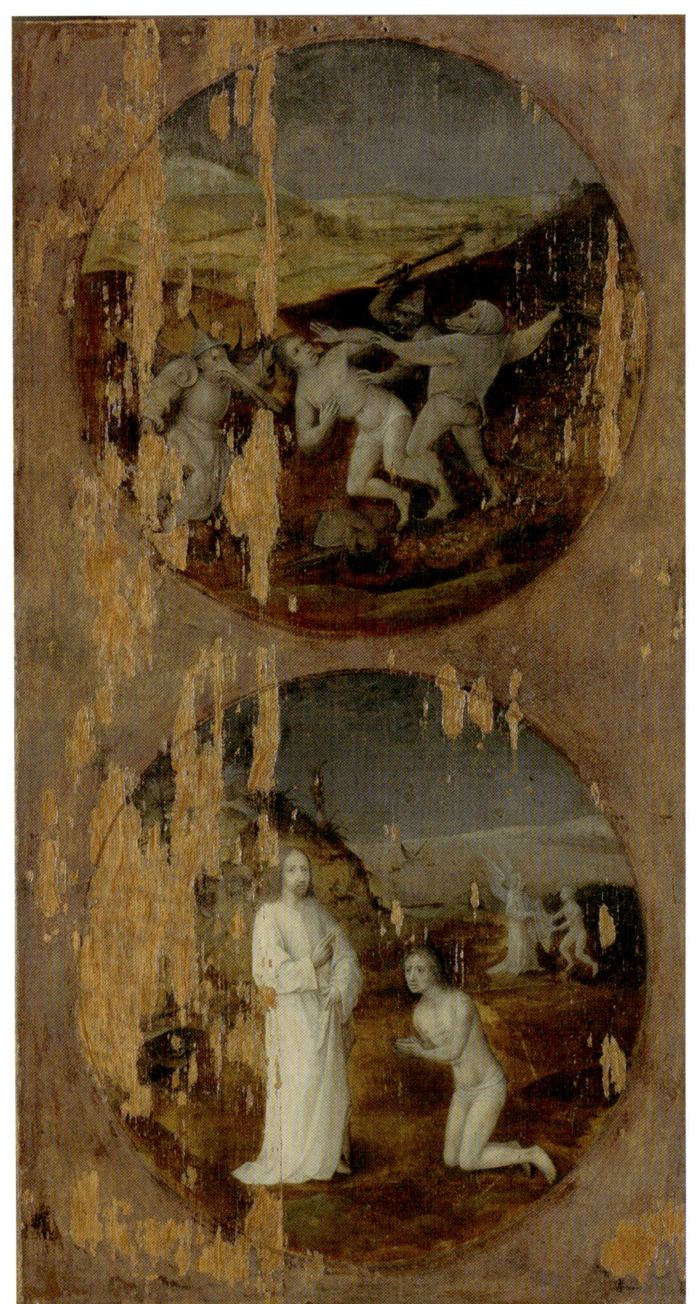

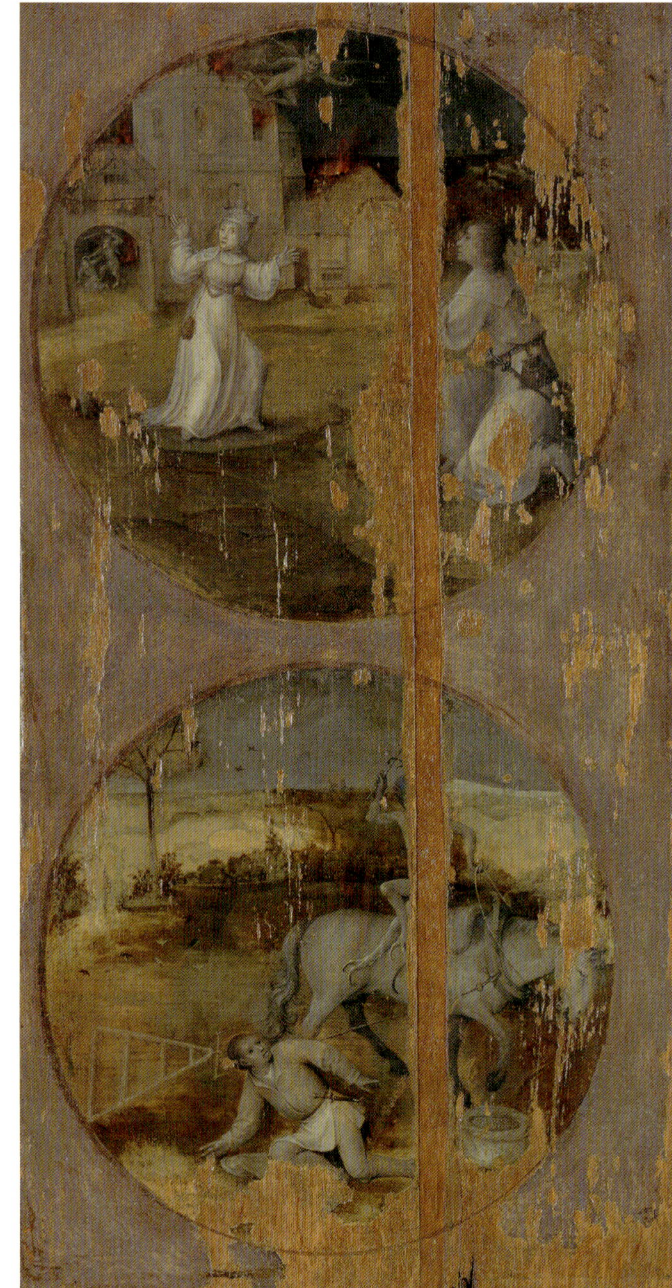

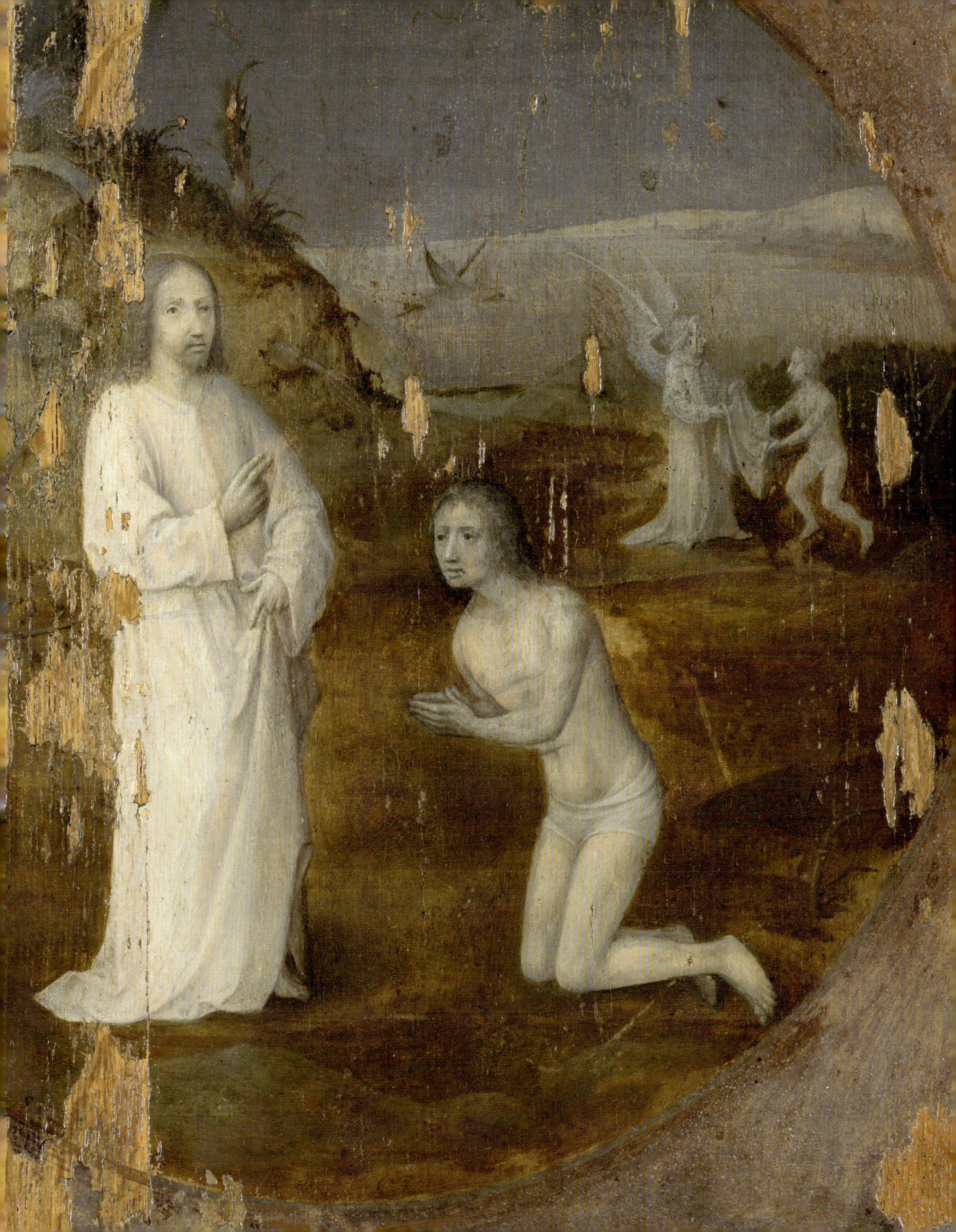

Hieronymus Bosch
The Last Judgement, c. 1495–1505
Oil on oak panel, left wing 99.5 × 28.8 cm,
central panel 99.2 × 60.5 cm, right wing 99.5 × 28.6 cm
Bruges, Stad Brugge, Groeningemuseum, 0000.GRO.0208.I

The Bruges *Last Judgement* has an interesting pedigree. The painting was probably already in the possession of Cardinal Domenico Grimani (1461–1523) in Venice by the early sixteenth century, together with the Hermit Saints and Wilgefortis triptychs. It did not return to the Low Countries – by way of the collection of the Spanish Cardinal Antonio Despuig y Dameto (1745–1813) – until the beginning of the twentieth century. The two other works remained in Venice. The triptych was dismantled in the first half of the nineteenth century and the wings combined and framed. The three panels were then reunited in 1906. Even then, however, the grisaille painting on the outside of the wings was totally ignored: the open triptych could only be displayed against the wall, and the shutters could not be closed. This was not remedied until the 2014–15 restoration, when the panels were placed in a new frame. Justice has once more been done, moreover, to the grisaille painting, which is essential to the ensemble as a whole.

When closed, the triptych displays a grisaille of *Christ Crowned with Thorns*. Christ is shown sitting, surrounded by six guards. A balding man on the left places the crown of thorns, held in an armoured glove, on Jesus's head. The theme is not only a depiction of how Christ – mockingly described by Pilate as 'King of the Jews' – is 'crowned' by the Jewish people, but also illustrates his willingness to sacrifice himself. The exterior wings form a prelude to the open triptych, in which we see Christ again, now in his role of humanity's judge. He is pictured in a circle of bright blue sky and forms the absolute focus of the image as a whole. Where the closed triptych shows a dark grisaille painting with large figures, the open ensemble – twice as large – consists of a brightly coloured scene populated with small figures and glowing with the flames of hell and damnation, yet also with a luminous paradise wing at Christ's right hand.

The structure of the Bruges *Last Judgement* differs from that of other triptychs painted by Bosch, such as the *Haywain*, the *Garden of Earthly Delights* and the Vienna *Last Judgement*, all of which are conceived as narrative sequences: the Garden of Eden in the left wing and Hell in the right, with a central image linking the two in a variety of ways. A narrative structure of this kind was also intended in the first instance for the Bruges triptych. The underdrawing revealed in infrared photographs shows that the expanse of cloud in the left wing conceals a figure of God the Father, traces of which can be made out with the naked eye. It seems as though a Garden of Eden scene was originally planned here, referring to the first days of creation.

During restoration

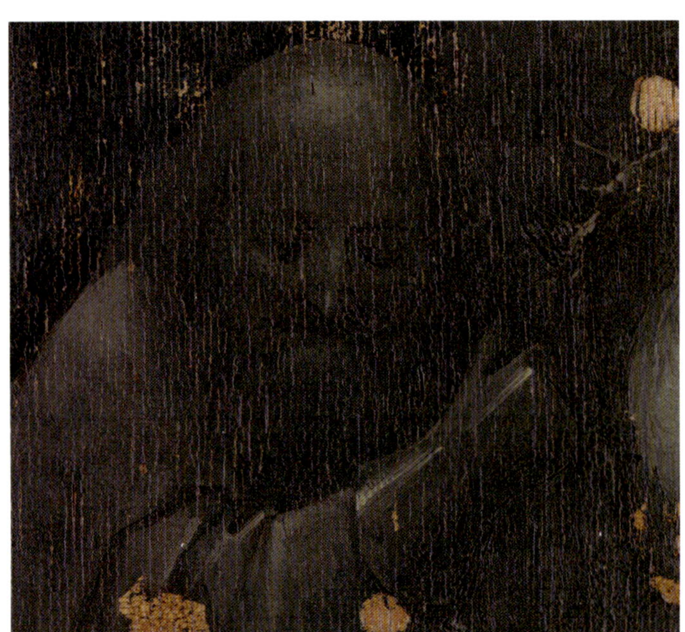

During restoration

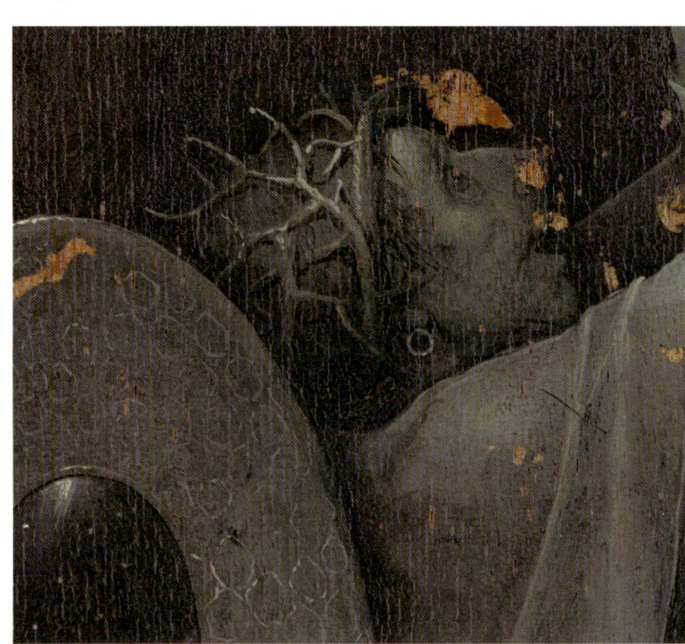

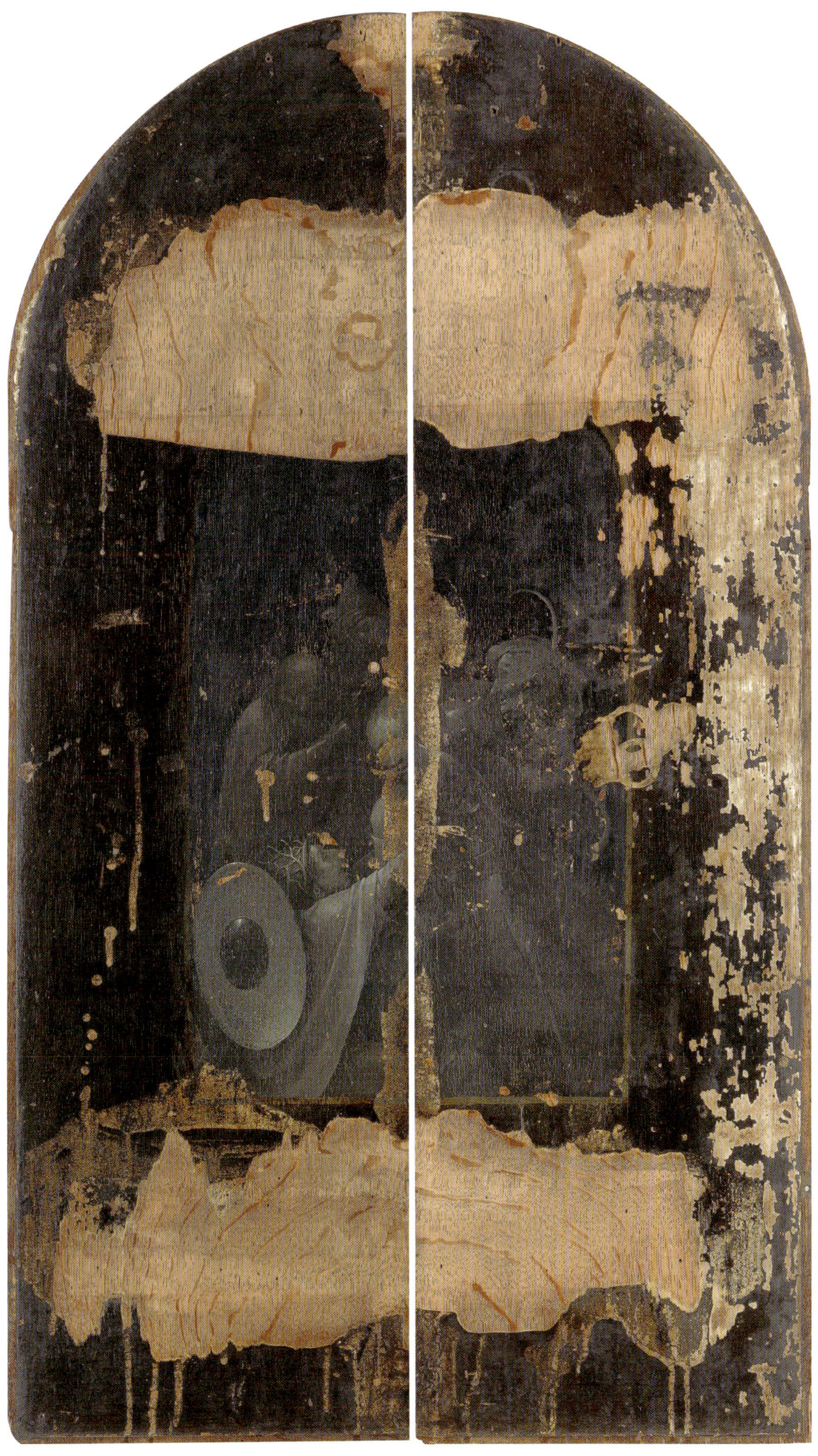

The paradise scene as it appears now can be read as a kind of gateway to heaven, through which the souls of the blessed have to pass on their way into God's kingdom. The right wing shows its pendant, hell. The two images of the afterlife flank the scene showing the End of Days in the central panel. Chaos reigns here: demons take over the earth, while Christ sits in judgement over humankind. His eyes are directed towards the viewer to remind us that it is to him that we will have to give account on Judgement Day. Unlike the Vienna *Last Judgement*, there are no angels or devils here to lead the people away. It is plain, nonetheless, that the damned souls will be dragged from the central panel to hell, while the souls of the blessed can count on a place in heaven, reached via the earthly paradise in the left wing.

Although the attribution of the painting has regularly been contested, the triptych as a whole matches the workshop practice of Hieronymus Bosch in terms of conception, imagery, technique and the way in which compositional and iconographic adjustments were made. Several details are also found in other works by Bosch. On the basis of the new documentation of both the underdrawings and the painting process, and our improved understanding of the triptych thanks to its conservation and restoration in 2014–15, we conclude that the work has to be attributed to Hieronymus Bosch himself, as the authentic signature likewise insists. The shift in conception, whereby the open triptych became a large Judgement Day scene rather than the characteristic narrative sequence over the three panels, makes it likely that the triptych is a relatively late work.

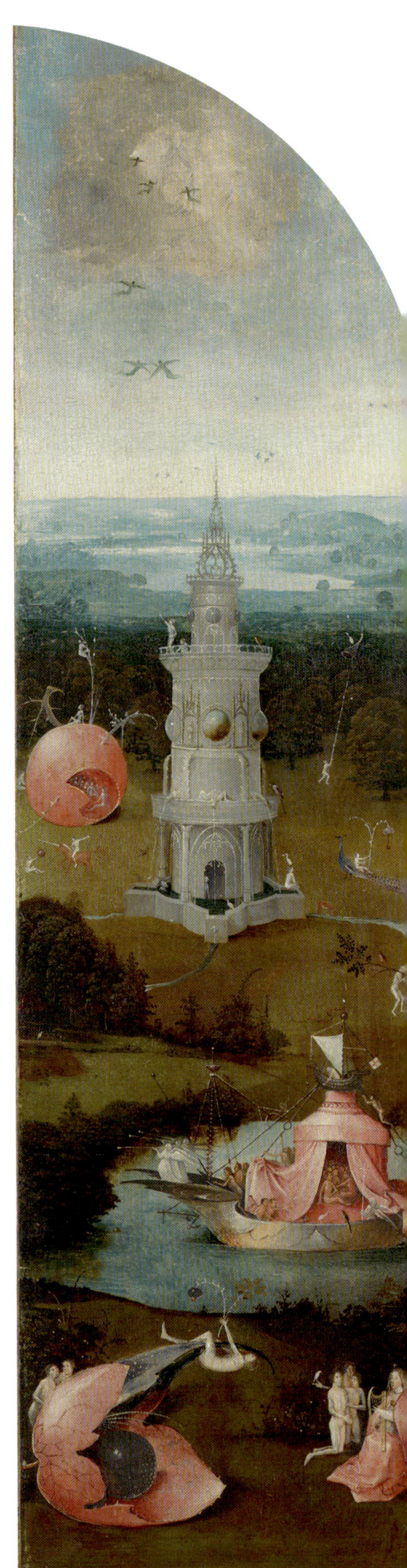

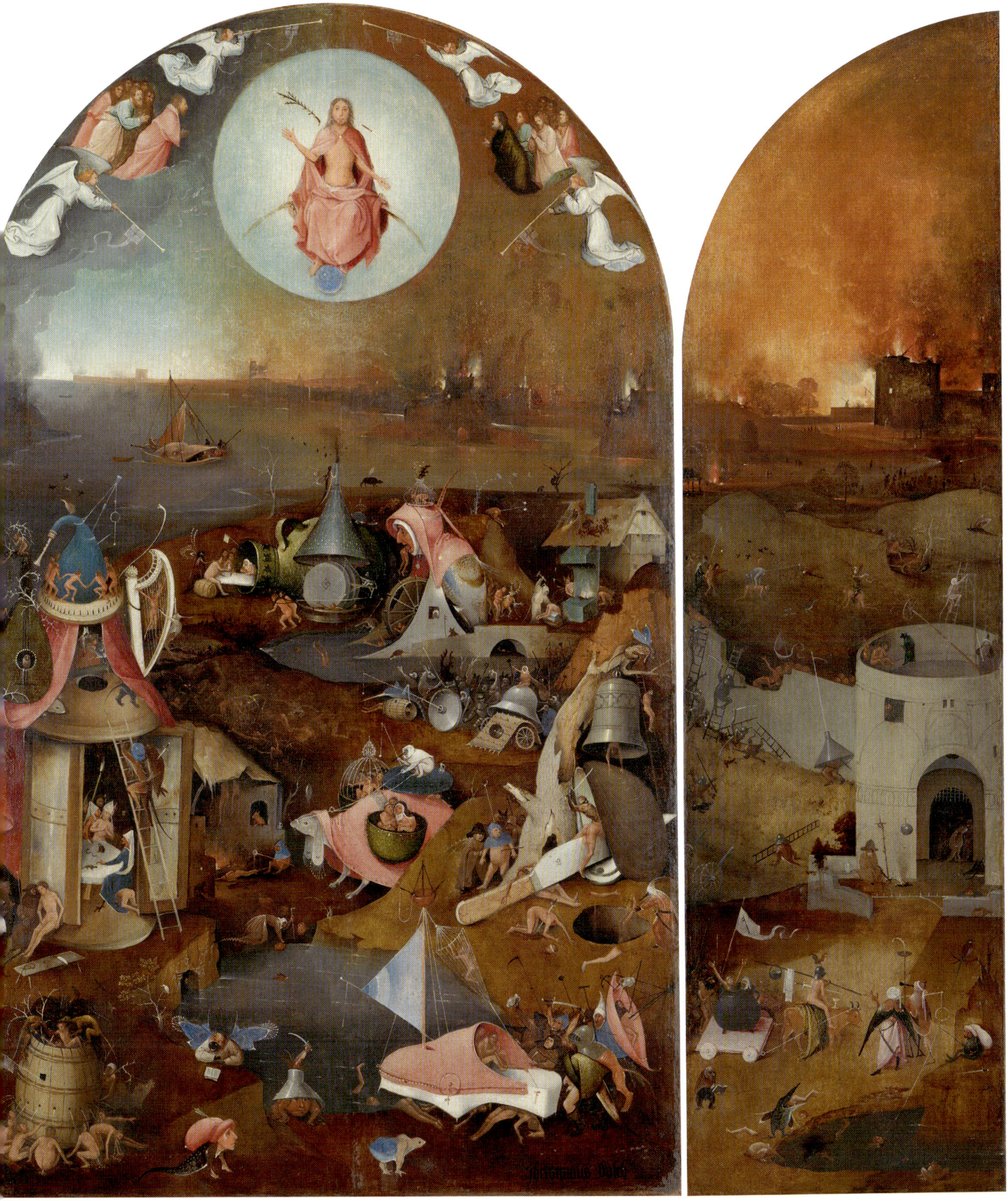

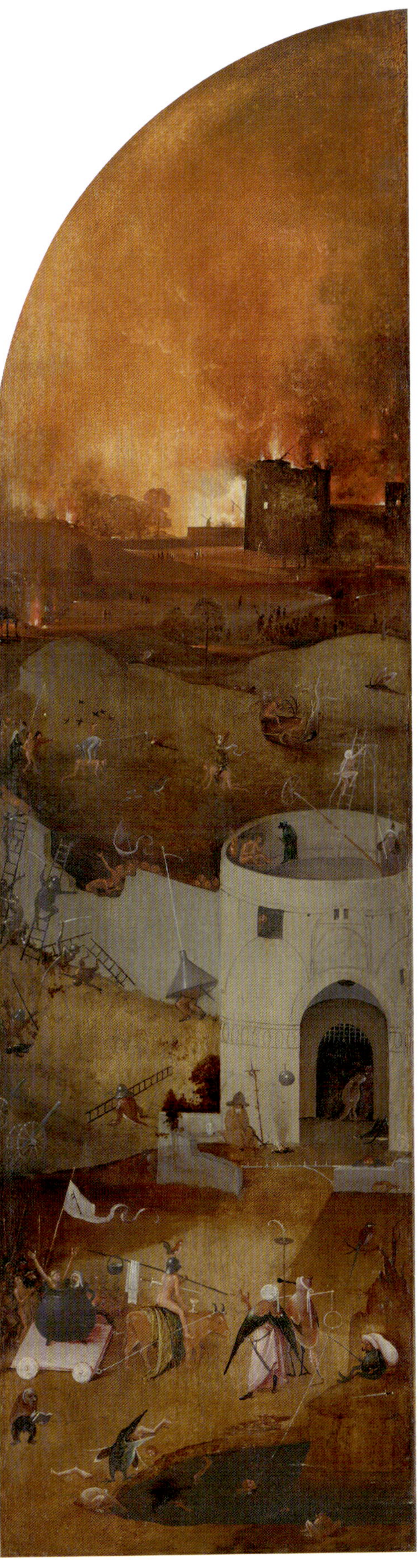

Jheronimus bosch

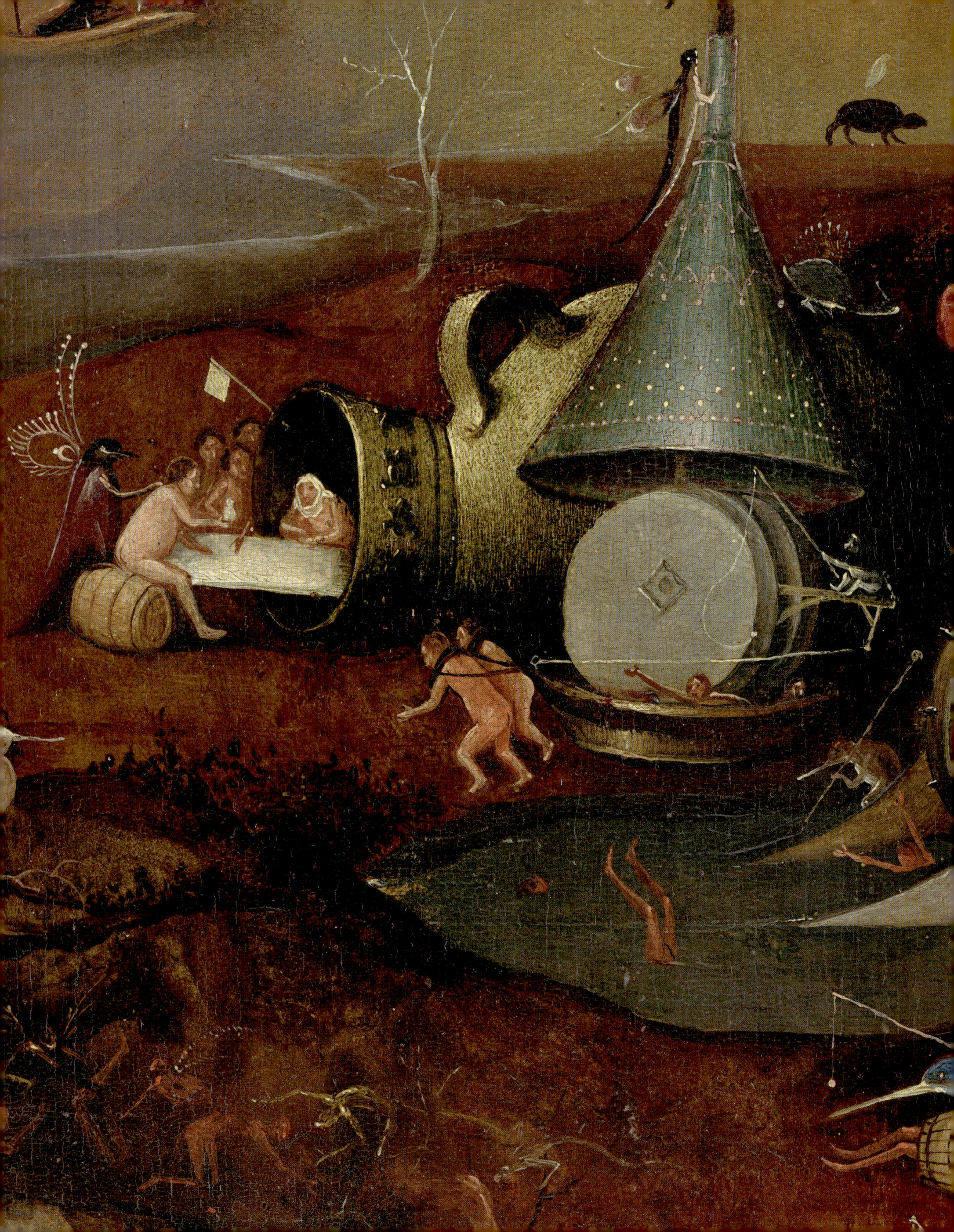

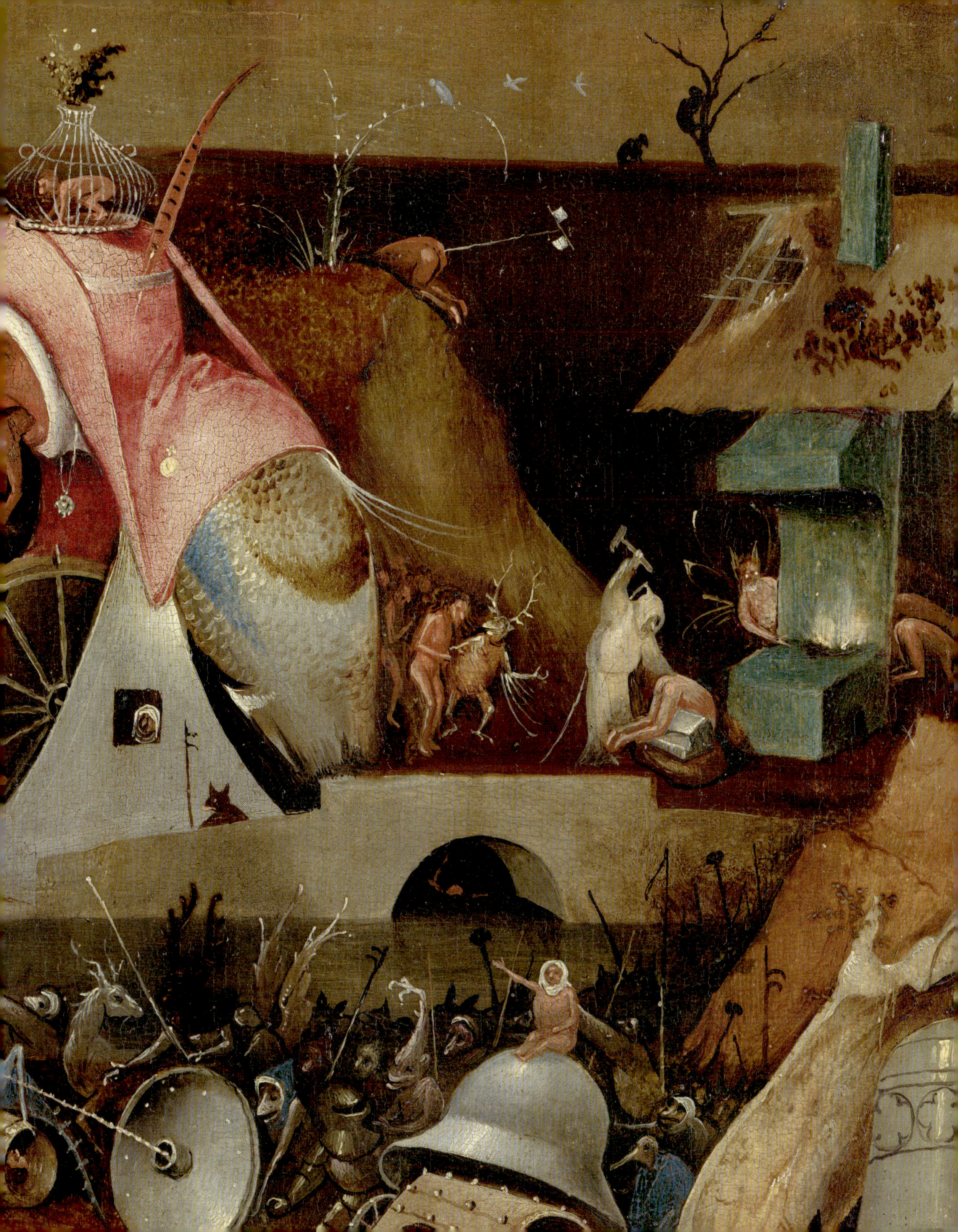

This fragment of a Last Judgement was attributed to Hieronymus Bosch towards the end of the nineteenth century, having previously been ascribed to various artists including Pieter Brueghel the Younger (1564/65–1638) – the 'Hell Brueghel'. A degree of doubt persisted, however, until the panel was restored in the 1930s and was published as an autograph work by the 's-Hertogenbosch master. The celebrated Bosch expert Charles de Tolnay went so far in his 1937 monograph as to state that it was a fragment of the *Last Judgement* that Duke Philip the Fair had commissioned from Bosch in 1504. This hypothesis was still being advanced in 1967 at the time of the major anniversary exhibition, the catalogue of which even declared 'that the authenticity of the painting is not in any doubt. We do not find the technique that Bosch uses here, of a non-spatial base layer combined with markedly plastic bodies, in any other work by him…' It was stressed at that time, in other words, that the painting differs significantly from Bosch's other works. The critical debate sparked by the exhibition in 's-Hertogenbosch settled the issue; the consensus since then has been that the Munich fragment is not by Bosch, nor is it a faithful copy of a Bosch original. All the same, it is a fascinating painting that draws on Hieronymus Bosch's imagery and testifies to the artist's immense popularity in the sixteenth century.

The panel is a fragment of a much larger whole; only the right-hand side is original: it has been cropped on all the other sides, where the painting continued. The left half of the surviving fragment shows the resurrection of the dead on the Day of Judgement. Naked men and women emerge from fifteen or so open graves; they include a king, an emperor, a bishop and a cardinal, each identifiable by his headgear. In the right half, demons take charge of the dead, who are evidently being led off to hell. A piece of blue fabric remains in the lower left corner of the fragment, which must originally have belonged to the robes of a large figure. It was concluded from this that the panel was the right half of a very large Last Judgement scene, with the standing figure of the Archangel Michael – the weigher of souls, robed in blue – as its central focus. Similarities were therefore imagined with the large *Last Judgements* of Rogier van der Weyden in Beaune and Hans Memling in Gdańsk. In the case of the *Last Judgement* to which the Munich fragment belonged, this would imply a panel painting measuring almost three metres across – a gigantic work, given that the central panel of the *Garden of Earthly Delights* is 195 cm wide (fig. p. 57) and that of the Vienna *Last Judgement* 127 cm (fig. p. 159). Moreover, Van der Weyden's and Memling's *Last Judgements* are not painted on one panel, but on seven and three joined panels respectively. The central panel of Bosch's Vienna *Last Judgement*, however, provides us with an intriguing alternative point of reference. The underdrawing of its left foreground includes a kneeling donor who, for some unknown reason, was never actually painted. His wide cloak panel is spread out on the ground in front of and around him. It is possible, therefore, that the drapery in the Munich fragment might also be the front part of a kneeling donor's cloak panel. If so, to continue the parallel with the Vienna composition, there might have been a brightly lit entrance to heaven high above him, at the right hand of Christ enthroned in the centre. The darkness of hell is then likely to have been shown at Christ's left hand – in the upper right from the beholder's point of view.

The Munich fragment occupies a place of its own among the large group of Bosch imitations painted in the Southern Netherlands from the second quarter of the sixteenth century. Only one known painting displays a marked affinity with this panel (cat. 47); both works include demons and monsters of the same type, which can be linked in turn to several drawings by early-sixteenth-century followers of Bosch.

Detail: Four-footed
human-bird monster

Follower of Hieronymus Bosch
The Last Judgement (fragment), c. 1530–40
Oil on oak panel, 59.4 × 112.9 cm
Munich, Bayerische Staatsgemäldesammlungen,
Alte Pinakothek, 5752

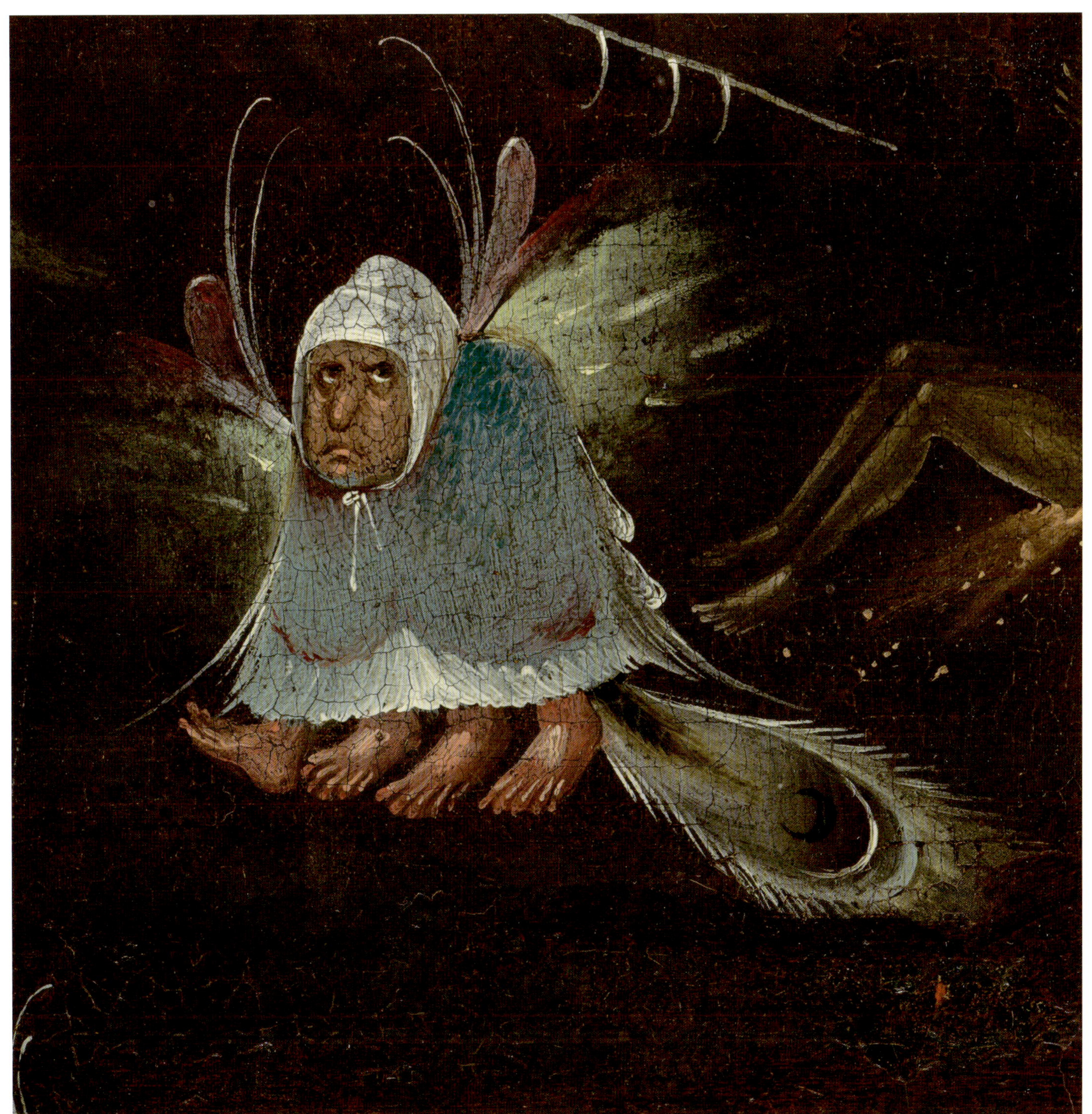

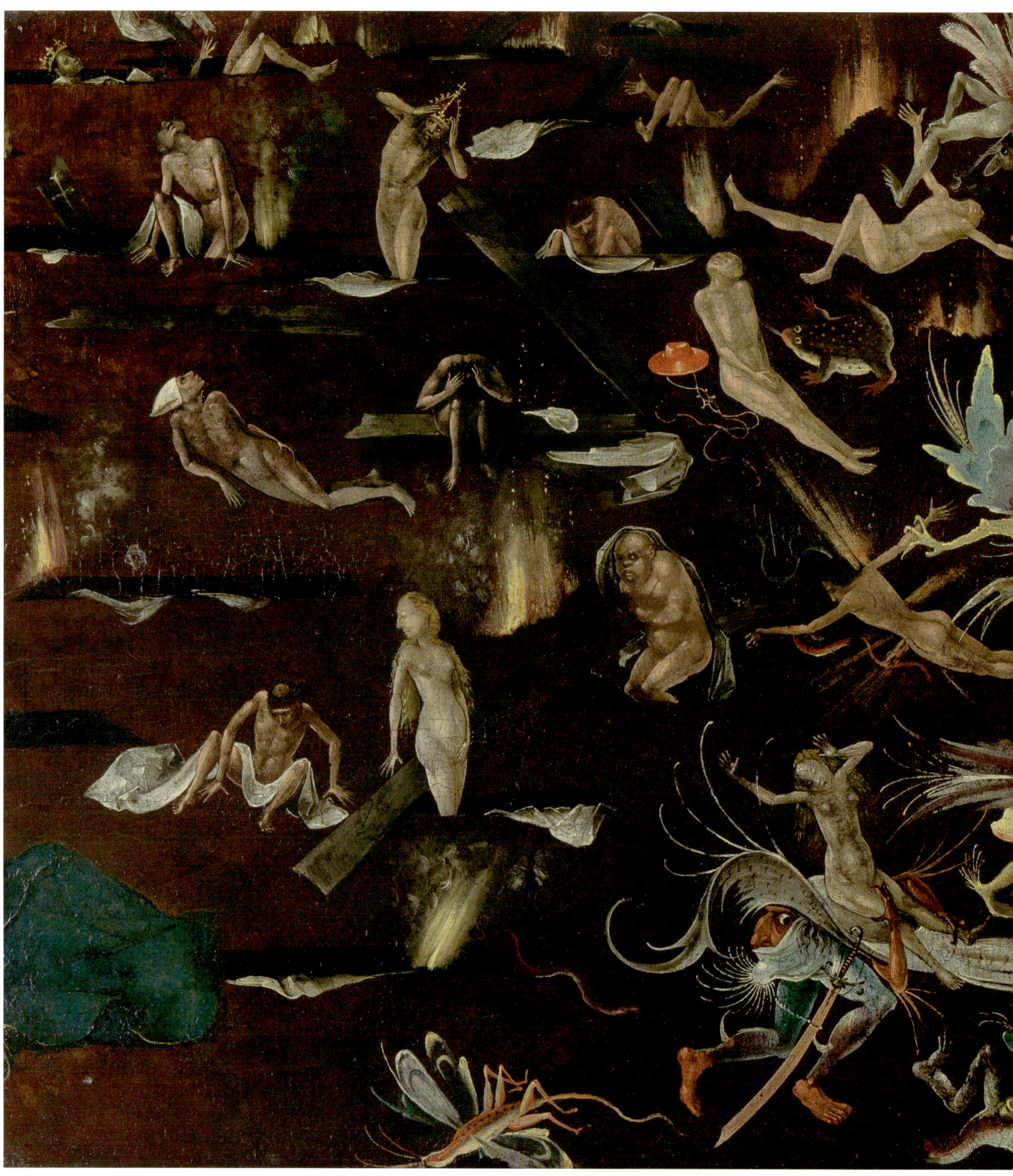

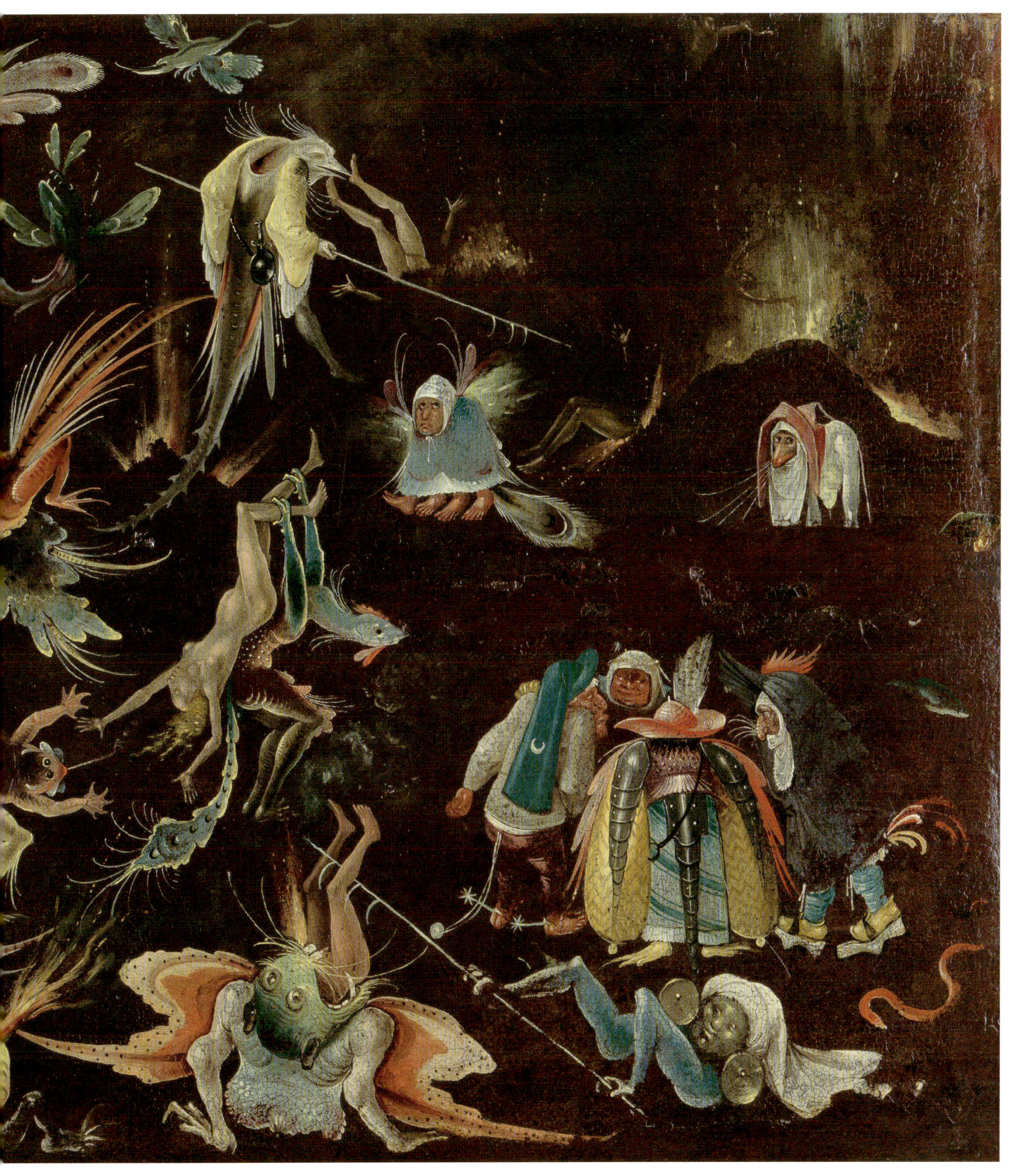

174 The four Hereafter panels were probably in the possession of Cardinal Domenico Grimani in Venice as early as about 1520. They are known to have been displayed in the Doge's Palace there shortly after the middle of the seventeenth century. The panels were originally in separate frames, and must have functioned as the wings on either side of a composition referring to the End of Days and the Last Judgement. Two of the panels show the souls of the blessed, who have been judged and found worthy, on their way to heaven, while the two other wings show the fate of the damned, disappearing into hell. Heaven and hell themselves are not depicted. Angels lead the blessed upwards from the Garden of Eden. They ascend through the clouds to a tunnel leading to the eternal light, where they are received by another angel, rendered all but invisible by the intense backlighting. Bosch painted him very subtly wet-in-wet in the near-white impasto. The most logical arrangement of the four panels is not side-by-side in pairs, but one above the other, which would place the glimpse of heaven in the upper left. The panels with the damned would then be viewed in the opposite direction. Terrifying demons are shown in a setting of near-total darkness, storm clouds and lightning bolts, casting down the souls of sinners denied forgiveness. They land in a river that flows away at an angle to carry them deeper into hell. A fierce fire glows in the background, suggesting that the water of the infernal river is boiling hot.

When the shutters were closed, the backs of the panels were displayed. They are painted in a surprisingly abstract, almost modern way, which was probably intended to imitate red porphyry and green serpentine marble – costly types of stone used since classical antiquity to pay tribute to the highest power. According to the presumed order of the panels, with the *Garden of Eden* lower left and the *River to Hell* lower right, the colours on the exterior wings would alternate between red and green at the bottom and green and red at the top.

Hieronymus Bosch employed a special technique for these panels, which speak strongly to the imagination and which the literature frequently describes as 'visionary'. The ground layer on the reverses was laid down in uniform red and uniform green respectively; paint was then spattered and dripped onto this, before being finished with a layer of translucent colour.

The other side was prepared with a uniform layer of black paint, onto which Bosch painted the respective scenes. He must, therefore, have approached the panels in an entirely different way from normal. The lighter parts were laid down using a relatively large amount of thicker paint over a minimal (if any) bluish-grey underdrawing applied with a brush; the darker passages, by contrast, make use of the black base layer, which they allow to show through. Pigments containing lead white have grown more transparent with age, reducing the legibility of the images – an effect exacerbated by the wear suffered by the paint surface. The contrast between the heaven and hell sides will, therefore, originally have been stronger. The painter displays extraordinary skill in these panels, which might have belonged to an exceptionally prestigious commission comparable with a small group of extremely precious black illuminated parchment manuscripts that were made for the Burgundian court in the third quarter of the fifteenth century.

Bosch must have referred here to models and *ricordi* from his workshop, as there are many details that display strong affinities with figures in his other paintings. The artfully rendered figure lying on its back as a demon cuts its throat is also found, for instance, in the *Saint Anthony Triptych* in Lisbon (fig. p. 150), the *Haywain Triptych* (cat. 5) and the *Garden of Earthly Delights* (fig. p. 57), where we also find the same demons. Several of the 'souls' and angels correspond with figures from the panel with *Death and the Miser* (cat. 4) and the three aforementioned triptychs. The angel in the left foreground of the Garden of Eden panel is similar to the one in *Saint John on Patmos* (fig. p. 37).

The unusual technique and the many links with other works by Hieronymus Bosch lead us to conclude that he probably painted the *Visions of the Hereafter* quite late. According to dendrochronological dating, they could have been done any time from around 1485 onwards; nevertheless, a date in the period 1505–15 is more likely.

Hieronymus Bosch
51b. *The Ascent of the Blessed*;
51a. *The Garden of Eden*, c. 1505–15
Oil on oak panel, 88.5 × 39.8 cm and
88.8 × 39.9 cm
Venice, Museo di Palazzo Grimani, 184

Hieronymus Bosch
51c. *The Fall of the Damned*;
51d. *The River to Hell*,
c. 1505–15
Oil on oak panel, both panels 88.8 × 39.6 cm
Venice, Museo di Palazzo Grimani, 184

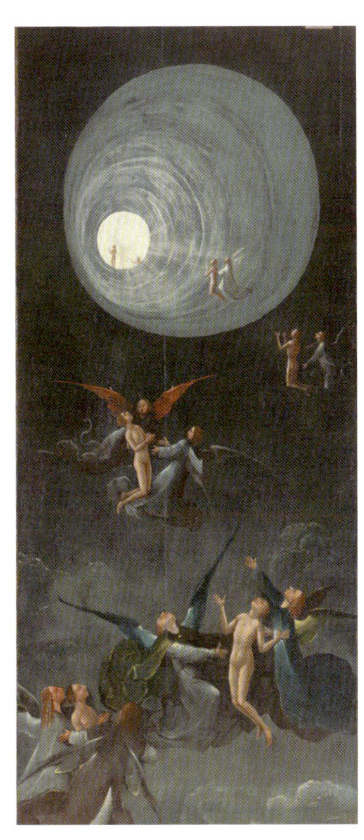

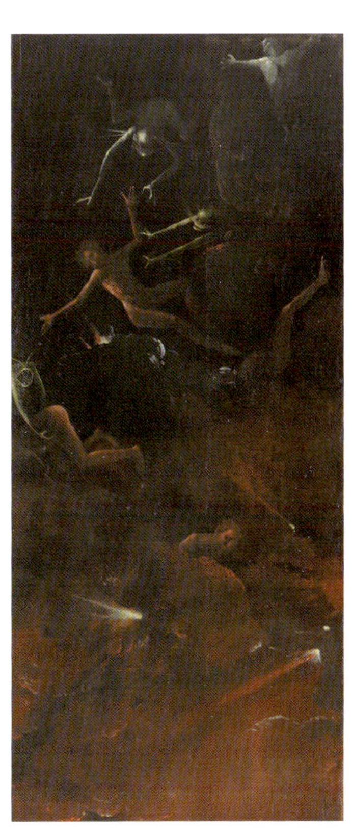

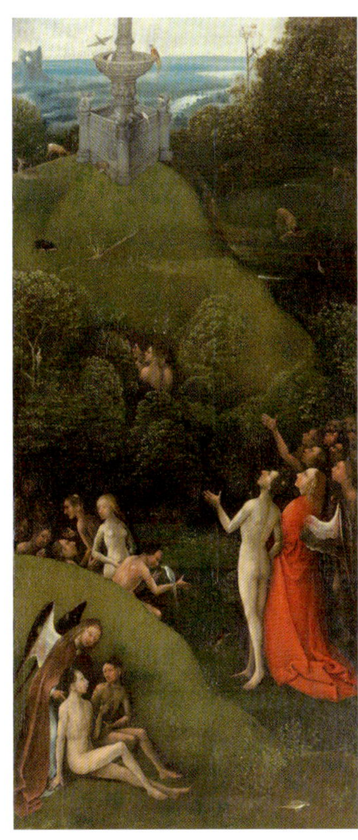

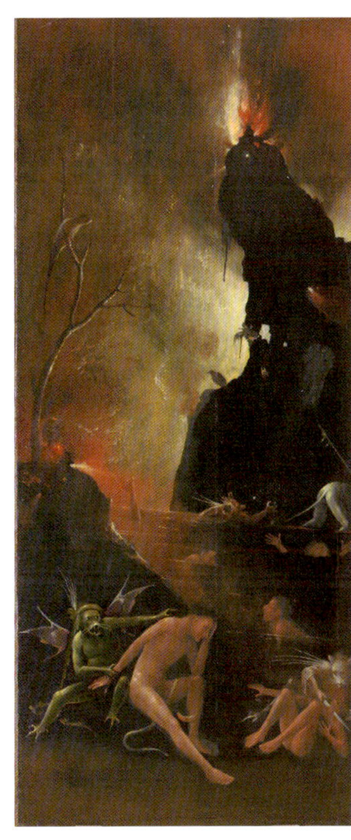

The Ascent of the Blessed and
The Garden of Eden (reverse)

The Fall of the Damned and
The River to Hell (reverse)

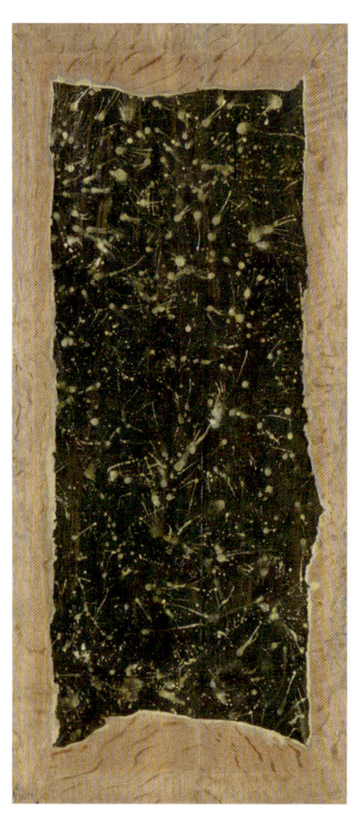

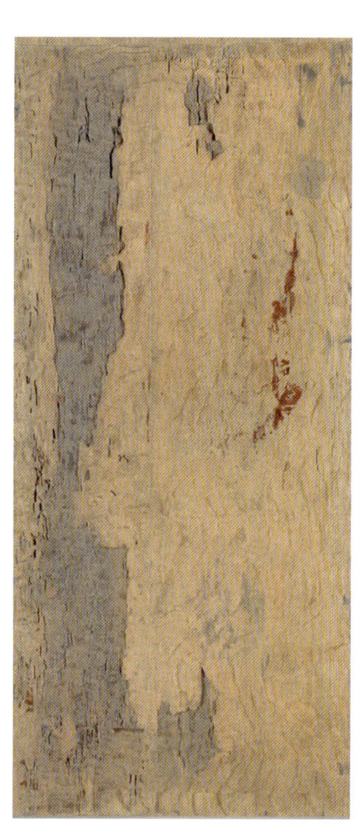

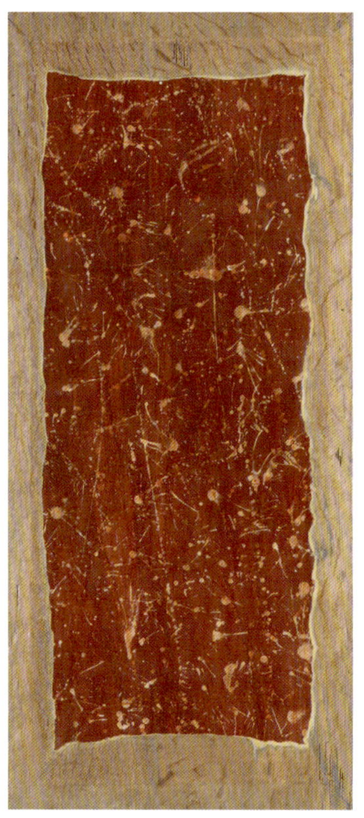

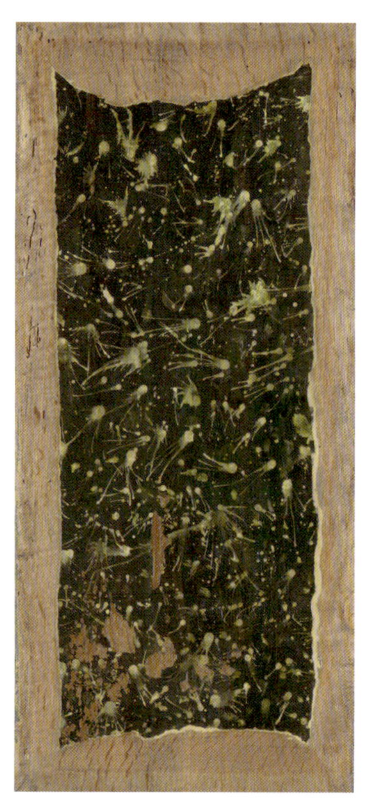

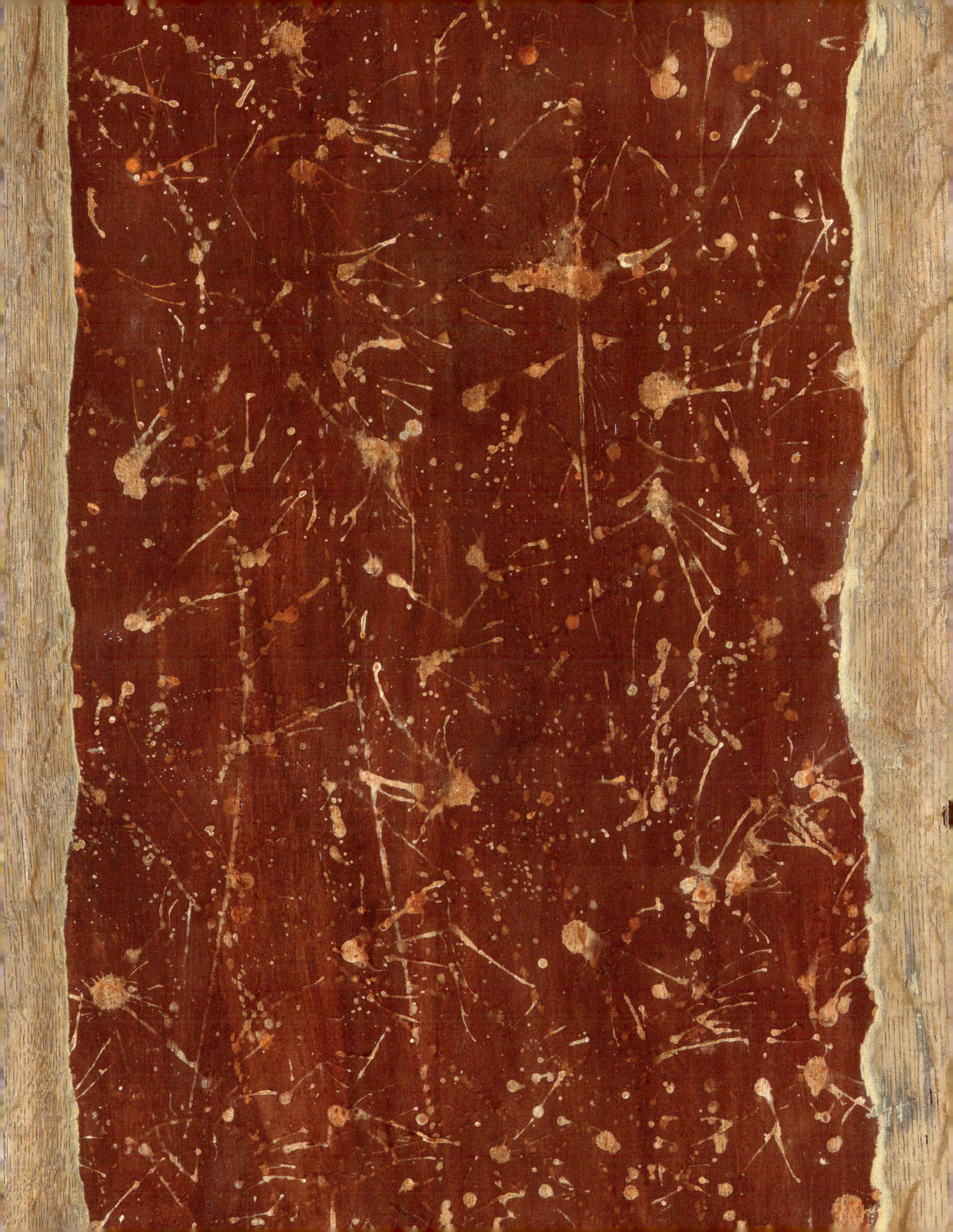

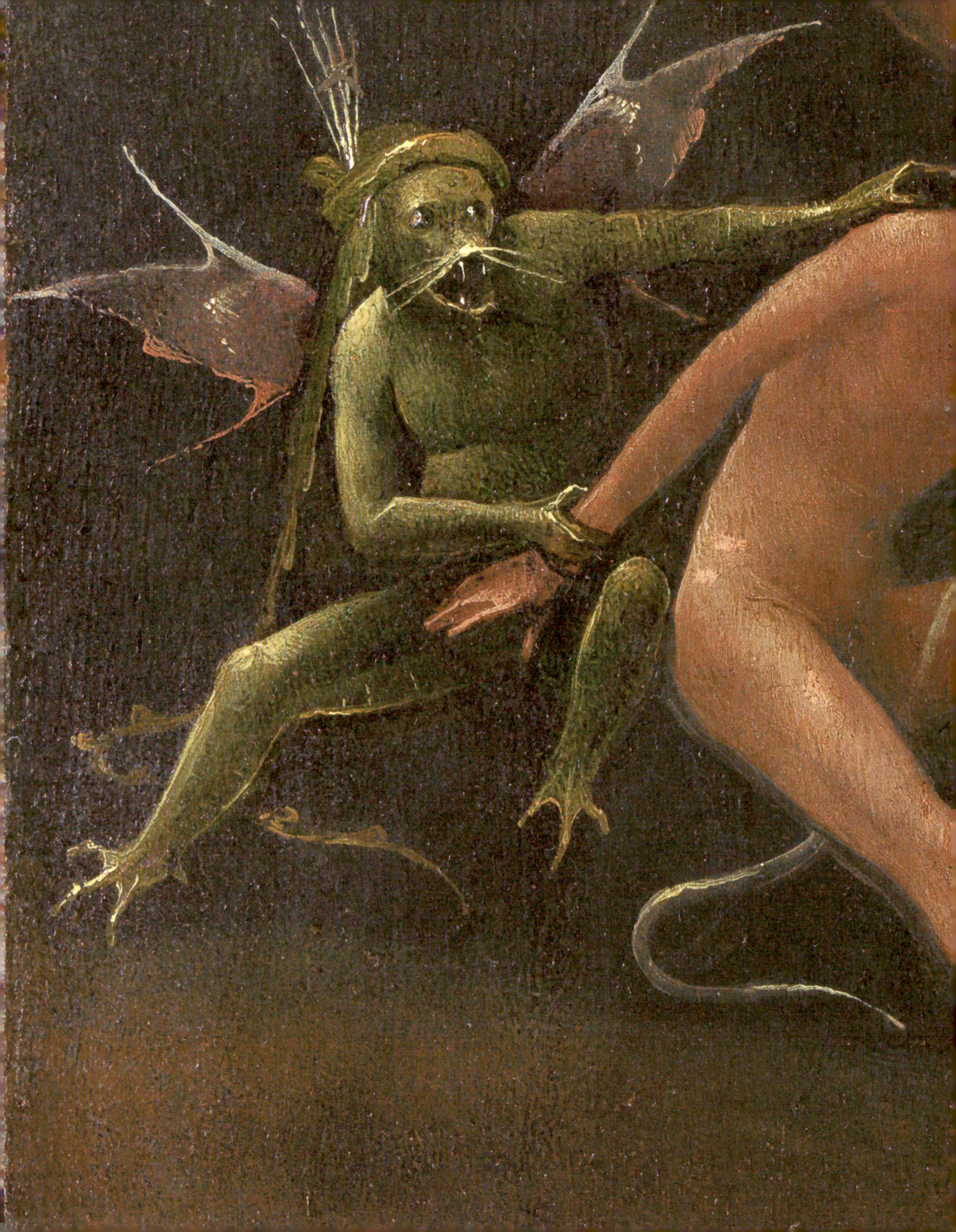

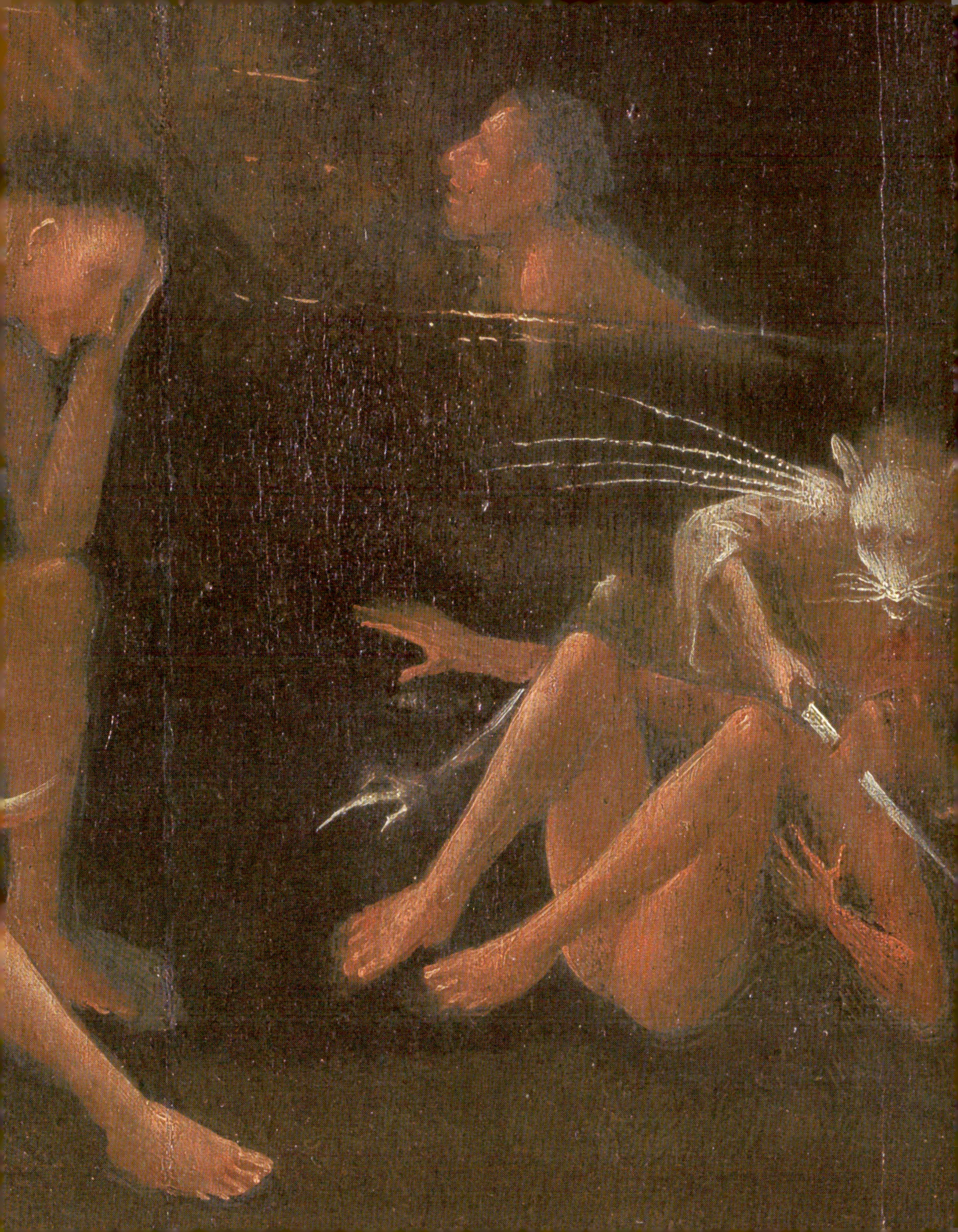

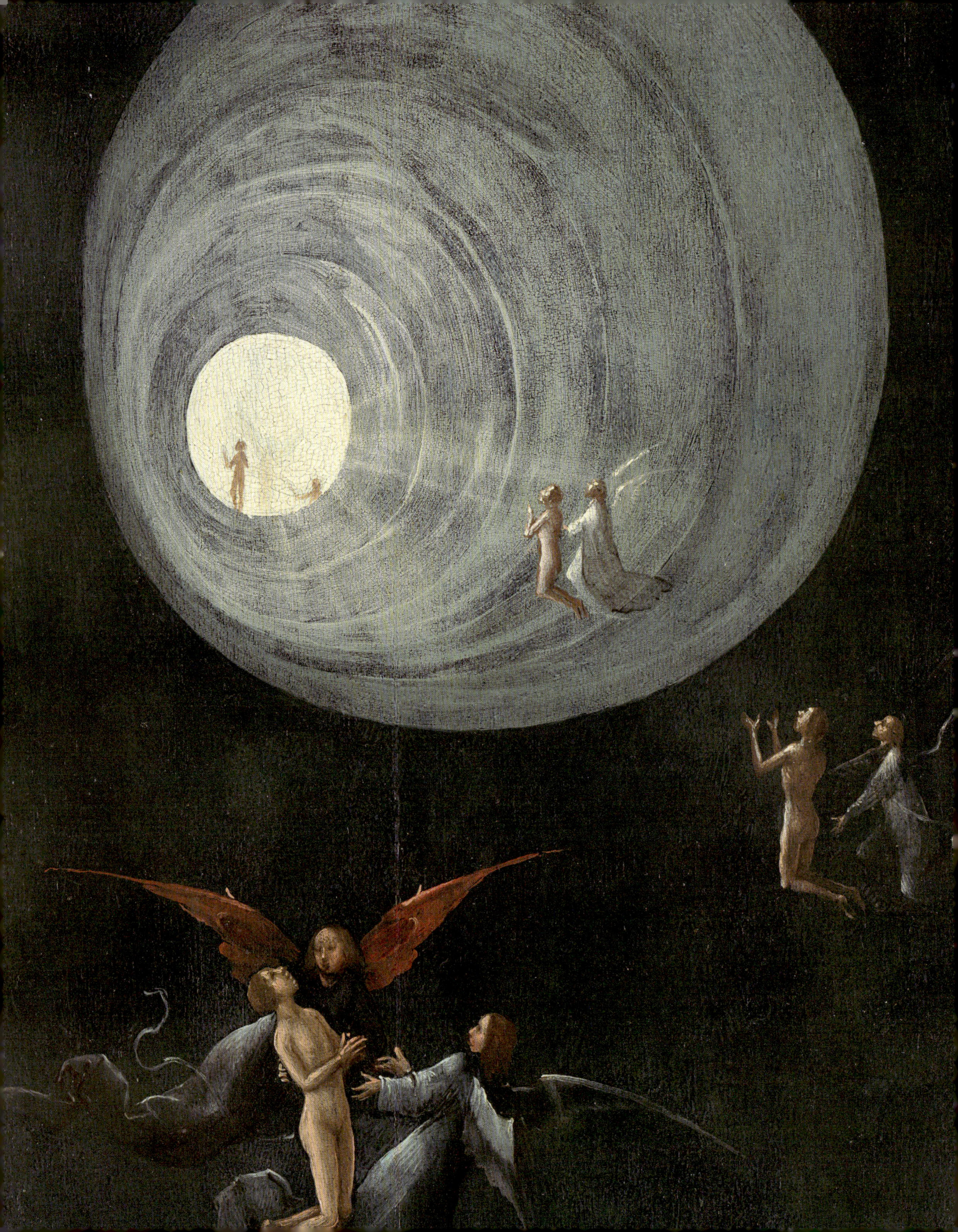

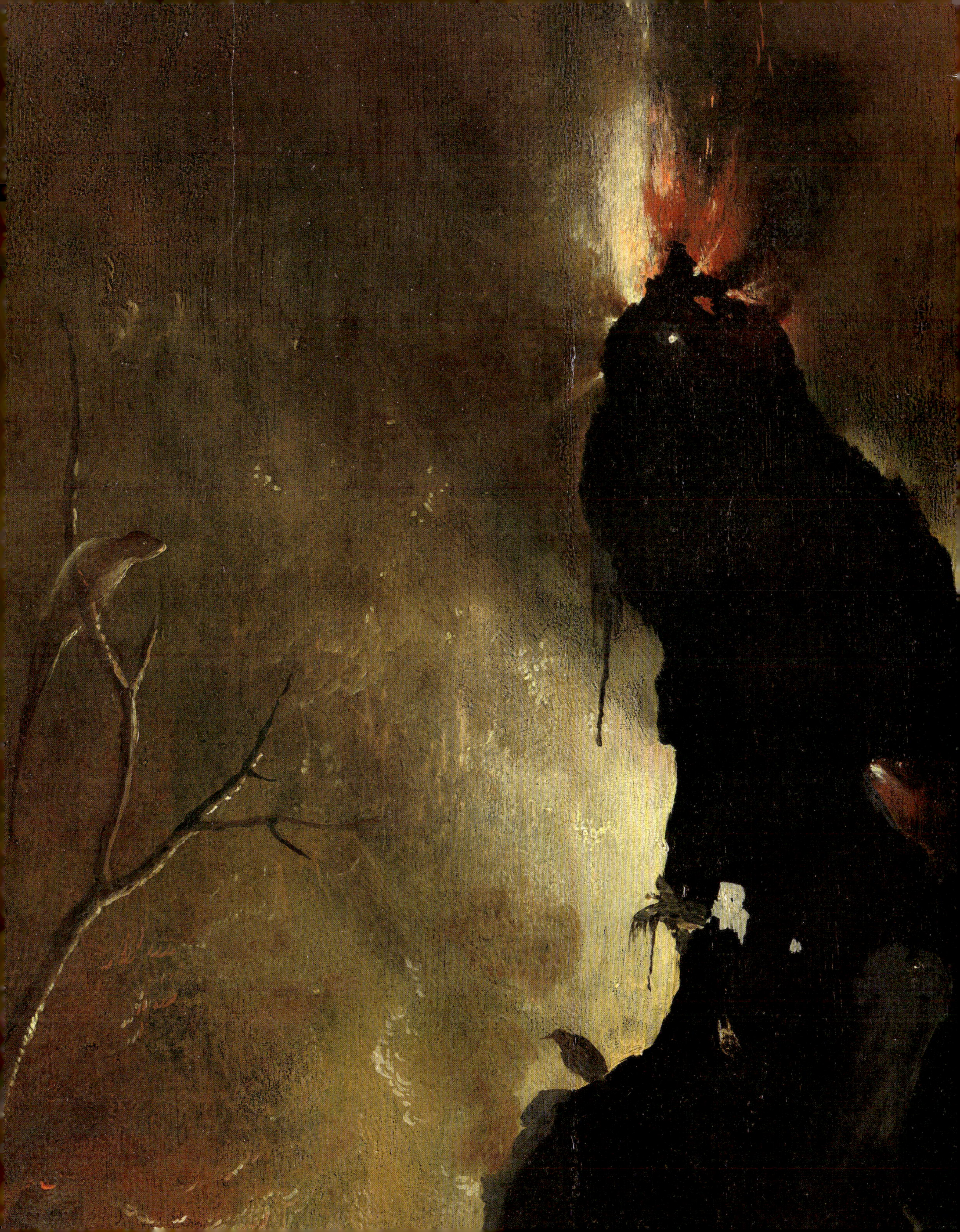

List of works exhibited

I. Life's Pilgrimage

1.
Hours of Joanna of Castile
Bruges, 1496–1506
Parchment, 11 × 8 cm
London, The British Library, Add Ms 18852, fol. 5v (detail)

2.
Sebastian Brant
Ship of Fools
Paris (Guy Marchant), 1500
Letterpress, 4to
Paris, Bibliothèque nationale de France, Bibliothèque François Mitterrand,
RES–YH–64

3.
Hieronymus Bosch
The Ship of Fools, c. 1500–10
Oil on oak panel, 58.1 × 32.8 cm
Paris, Musée du Louvre, Département des Peintures, RF 2218
see cat. 2

4.
Hieronymus Bosch
Gluttony and Lust (fragment of Ship of Fools), c. 1500–10
Oil on oak panel, 34.9 × 30.6 cm
New Haven, Yale University Art Gallery, 1959.15.22,
Gift of Hannah D. and Louis M. Rabinowitz
see cat. 3

5.
Der Spiegel der Vernunft
Germany, c. 1488
Woodcut, 40.4 × 29.1 cm
Munich, Staatliche Graphische Sammlung, 118319 D, Schr. 1861

6.
Thomas à Kempis
The Imitation of Christ
'Dit is een schoen boecken ende is gheheeten Qui sequitur me'
Antwerp (Alder naest den Grooten Mortier), 1505
Letterpress, 13.5 × 10.5 cm
Utrecht, Museum Catharijneconvent, BMH PI30

7.
Den spieghel der salicheit van Elckerlijc
Antwerp (Govaert Back), 1501
Letterpress, 13.2 × 8.8 cm
The Hague, Koninklijke Bibliotheek, KW 231 G 51

8.
Hieronymus Bosch
The Wayfarer, c. 1500–10
Oil on oak panel, 71.3 × 70.7 cm
Rotterdam, Museum Boijmans Van Beuningen, 1079
see cat. 1

9.
Ars Moriendi, 'The Art of Dying'
'Quamvis secundum philosophum tertio Ethicorum …'
'Dat sterf boeck'
Delft (Christiaen Snellaert), 1488
Woodcut, 4to
The Hague, Koninklijke Bibliotheek, KW 169 G 84

10.
Ars Moriendi, 'The Art of Dying'
'Quamvis secundum philosophum tertio Ethicorum …'
Cologne (Nicolaus Götz), c. 1475
Letterpress, 28 × 20 cm
Sint Agatha, Erfgoedcentrum Nederlands Kloosterleven, I–0042

11.
Ars Moriendi, 'The Art of Dying'
'Quamvis secundum philosophum tertio Ethicorum …'
Zwolle (Peter van Os), 1491
Letterpress, fo.
The Hague, Koninklijke Bibliotheek, KW 171 E 29

12.
Hieronymus Bosch
Death and the Miser, c. 1500–10
Oil on oak panel, 94.3 × 32.4 cm
Washington, National Gallery of Art, Samuel H. Kress Collection, 1952.5.33
see cat. 4

13.
Hieronymus Bosch
The Haywain Triptych, 1510–16
Oil on oak panel, left wing 136.1 × 47.7 cm, central panel 133 × 100 cm,
right wing 136.1 × 47.6 cm
Signed on central panel, bottom right: *Jheronimus bosch*
Madrid, Museo Nacional del Prado, P2052
see cat. 5

14.
Bible
Bible, mit horen boecken, vol. 2
Delft (Jacob Jacobszoon van der Meer and Mauricius Yemantszoon), 1477
Letterpress, 27.5 × 22 cm
The Hague, Koninklijke Bibliotheek, KW 169 E 55 [–56]

II. Hieronymus Bosch in 's-Hertogenbosch

15.
Anonymous
The Cloth Market, 's-Hertogenbosch
's-Hertogenbosch, c. 1530
Oil on panel, 134 × 76.5 cm
's-Hertogenbosch, Het Noordbrabants Museum, 01596

16.
Aert van Tricht (Maastricht, active 1492–1501)
Figures from the baptismal font of St John's Church
Maastricht, 1492
Brass, height c. 80 cm
's-Hertogenbosch, Parochie Heilige Johannes Evangelist

17.
Peter Danielssoen van Dordrecht
Book of Hours
Made in the scriptorium of the Koudewater Brigittines monastery
's-Hertogenbosch (Rosmalen), 1457
Paper and parchment, 13.3 × 10 cm
Uden, Museum voor Religieuze Kunst, 7738

18.
Jacobus van Gruitrode
Meditatiën, vol. 2
From the convent of Sint-Elisabeth-Bloemkamp, 's-Hertogenbosch
panelled binding with image of Christ as the Man of Sorrows
's-Hertogenbosch, c. 1500
Calf, 13.9 × 9.8 cm
Tilburg, Universiteit van Tilburg, Brabantcollectie, PG HS. 637

19.
Dionysius the Carthusian
Tractaet vanden loflijken maeghdelijken leven
's-Hertogenbosch (Laurens Hayen), 1510
Letterpress, 8vo
Utrecht, Universiteitsbibliotheek Uithof, THO: RAR 2–91 oct dl. 1–3

20.
Gerardus Zerbolt de Zutphiana
**Een devoet ende suverlyck boexken ende is ghenoemt: den boem
des levens des ghecruysten jesu ...**
's-Hertogenbosch (Laurens Hayen), c. 1514
Letterpress, 8vo
The Hague, Koninklijke Bibliotheek, KW 227 G 27 [1]

21.
Master with the Crescent Moon
Ciborium
's-Hertogenbosch, 1512/13
Silver, height 35 cm, diameter 16 cm
Uden, Museum voor Religieuze Kunst, 220
(extended loan from Parochie Heilige Nicolaas, Helvoirt)

22.
Master with the Orb
Chalice
From the Clares convent, 's-Hertogenbosch
's-Hertogenbosch, 1493
Silver gilt, height 22 cm, diameter c. 15 cm
Mechelen, Aartsbisdom Mechelen-Brussel

23.
Master with the Winged Devil
Retable monstrance
's-Hertogenbosch, 1514/15
Silver and silver gilt, height 75 cm, width 22 cm
's-Hertogenbosch, Het Noordbrabants Museum, 99.194
(extended loan from Parochie Heilige Willibrord, Loon op Zand)

24.
Master with the Winged Devil
Pyx
's-Hertogenbosch, 1514/15
Silver and silver gilt, height 3.1 cm, diameter 9.3 cm
's-Hertogenbosch, Het Noordbrabants Museum, 99.195
(extended loan from Parochie Heilige Willibrord, Loon op Zand)

25.
Eusebius Hieronymus
Vitae sanctorum patrum
From the library of the Baseldonk Wilhelmite convent, 's-Hertogenbosch
Nuremberg (Anton Koberger), 1478
with initials made in the Wilhelmite scriptorium
Paper, fo.
Amsterdam, Universiteitsbibliotheek Vrije Universiteit,
Bijzondere Collecties, XC05240

26.
Friar Georgius van Balen
Antifonarium
Music manuscript made in the Baseldonk Wilhelmite scriptorium, 's-Hertogenbosch
's-Hertogenbosch, 1516
Pen and gold leaf on parchment, 51.5 × 36 cm
Amsterdam, Universiteitsbibliotheek Vrije Universiteit, HS. XV.05006

27.
Missal with Crucifixion miniature
Made in the scriptorium of the Crutched Friars, 's-Hertogenbosch
's-Hertogenbosch, 1475–1500
Parchment in brown leather binding over wooden boards, with brass fittings,
36.5 × 25 cm
Sint Agatha, Erfgoedcentrum Nederlands Kloosterleven, Hs–101

28.
Alart Duhameel (c. 1450 – Antwerp c. 1506)
Saint Christopher
's-Hertogenbosch, c. 1490
Engraving, 19.9 × 33.4 cm
Amsterdam, Rijksmuseum, RP-P-OB-1098

29.
Accounts 1495–1501 of the Brotherhood of Our Lady
's-Hertogenbosch, 1498/99
record of the banquet at the home of Hieronymus 'the painter':
'... doemen den swaen att ... daer Jheronimus van Aken scilder dat laken lede ...'
Paper, 33 × 25 cm
's-Hertogenbosch, Museum Het Zwanenbroedershuis,
BHIC, AILVB, 123, fol. 198v–199r

30.
Accounts 1507–1513 of the Brotherhood of Our Lady
's-Hertogenbosch, 1509/10
Record of the banquet at the home of 'Jheronimus van Aken, who styles himself
Bosch': '... in de huise Jheronimi van Aeken scilder die hem scrift Bosch ...'
Paper, 33 × 25 cm
's-Hertogenbosch, Museum Het Zwanenbroedershuis,
BHIC, AILVB, 125, fol. 186v–187r

31.
Accounts 1513–1519 of the Brotherhood of Our Lady
's-Hertogenbosch, 1516/17
Record of the funeral of 'Jheronimus van Aken, painter', 9 August 1516:
'... Ter ierster exequie van Jeronimus van aken maelder ix' augusti ...'
Paper, 33 × 25 cm
's-Hertogenbosch, Museum Het Zwanenbroedershuis,
BHIC, AILVB, 126, fol. 166v

32.
Follower of Hieronymus Bosch
Ecce Homo
's-Hertogenbosch (?), c. 1530
From the Koudewater Brigittines convent
Oil on panel, 73 × 54.5 cm
Uden, Museum voor Religieuze Kunst, 33
(extended loan from Rijksmuseum Amsterdam, SK-A-4252)

33.
Pierre Coustain (Pieter Coustens, died 1487?)
Blazon of Edward IV of England (1443–1483), painted for
the Chapter of the Golden Fleece in St John's Church, 's-Hertogenbosch, 1481
Oil on panel, 120.5 × 72 cm
's-Hertogenbosch, Het Noordbrabants Museum, 12064
(extended loan from Rijksmuseum Amsterdam, SK-A-4641)

34.
Pierre Coustain (Pieter Coustens, died 1487?)
Blazon of James I of Luxemburg, Lord of Fiennes, painted for
the Chapter of the Golden Fleece in St John's Church, 's-Hertogenbosch, 1481
Oil on panel, 101 × 67.5 cm
's-Hertogenbosch, Het Noordbrabants Museum, 15802
(extended loan from Rijksmuseum Amsterdam, SK-A-4642)

35.
Workshop or follower of Hieronymus Bosch
The Cure of Folly, c. 1510–20
Oil on oak panel, 48.8 × 34.6 cm
Inscription: *Meester snijt die keye ras / Myne name Is lubbert das*
Madrid, Museo Nacional del Prado, P2056
see cat. 9

36.
Israhel van Meckenem (c. 1440/45 – Bocholt 1503)
Pelican
Bocholt, 1475–1500
Engraving, 90 × 65 mm
Vienna, ALBERTINA, DG1926/1287

37.
Hieronymus Bosch
Saint John on Patmos – Passion Scenes, c. 1490–95
Oil on oak panel, 63 × 43.2 cm
Signed bottom right: *Jheronimus bosch* (damaged)
Berlin, Staatliche Museen zu Berlin, Gemäldegalerie, 1647
see cat. 6

38.
Adriaen van Wesel (Utrecht c. 1415 – c. 1490)
The Vision of John: Saint John on Patmos
Wing from the Altarpiece of the Brotherhood of Our Lady
Utrecht, 1475–77
Oak with traces of the original polychromy, 86.5 × 61.6 × 32 cm
(image 48.2 × 34.5 × 17 cm)
's-Hertogenbosch, Museum Het Zwanenbroedershuis, B7

39.
Adriaen van Wesel (Utrecht c. 1415 – c. 1490)
The Vision of Emperor Augustus: Augustus and the Tiburtine Sibyl
Wing from the Altarpiece of the Brotherhood of Our Lady
Utrecht, 1475–77
Oak with traces of the original polychromy, 86.7 × 61.5 × 32 cm
(image 48.2 × 34.5 × 17 cm)
's-Hertogenbosch, Museum Het Zwanenbroedershuis, B8

40.
Hieronymus Bosch
Saint John the Baptist, c. 1490–95
Oil on oak panel, 48.5 × 40.5 cm
Madrid, Museo Fundación Lázaro Galdiano, 8155
see cat. 7

41.
Saint John on Patmos
Indulgence booklet of the Brotherhood of Our Lady
's-Hertogenbosch (Laurens Hayen), 1518–19
Woodcut and letterpress, 13 × 10 cm
Brussels, Bibliothèque royale de Belgique / Koninklijke Bibliotheek van België,
II 29.403A

42.
Workshop of Hieronymus Bosch
Ecce Homo Triptych, c. 1495–1500/1500/1503
c. 1495–1500 (Ecce Homo), c. 1500 (interior wings and predella),
mid-1503 (exterior wings)
Oil on oak panel, left wing 69.3 × 26 cm, central panel 73.4 × 58.4 cm,
right wing 69.2 × 26 cm, predella 15.5 × 68.4 cm
Boston, Museum of Fine Arts, William K. Richardson Fund;
William Francis Warden Fund; Juliana Cheney Edwards Collection, 53.2027;
and Gift of Arthur Kauffmann, 56.171
see cat. 8

43.
Marius van Beugen ('s-Hertogenbosch, active 1835–54)
Insignia of the Brotherhood of Our Lady
's-Hertogenbosch, 1835–54
Silver, 5.5 × 3.2 cm
's-Hertogenbosch, Het Noordbrabants Museum, 05295

44.
Saint Catherine badge
Excavation find 's-Hertogenbosch, 15th century
Silver, 3.8 × 2.4 cm
's-Hertogenbosch, Het Noordbrabants Museum/Gemeente 's-Hertogenbosch,
Afdeling Erfgoed, BAM I 7137

45.
Saint Catherine badge
Excavation find 's-Hertogenbosch, 15th century
Tin-lead, 3.8 × 3.2 cm
Langbroek, Van Beuningen family collection

III. The Life of Christ

46.
Bible
Bible, mit horen boecken, vol. 2
from the Crutched Friars convent, 's-Hertogenbosch
Delft (Jacob Jacobszoon van der Meer and Mauricius Yemantszoon), 1477
Letterpress, 27.5 × 22 cm
Sint Agatha, Erfgoedcentrum Nederlands Kloosterleven, I-0055

47.
Follower of Hieronymus Bosch
Left wing of the Garden of Earthly Delights, c. 1520–30
The Creation of the World (exterior) and The Garden of Eden (interior)
Oil on oak panel, 186 × 77 cm
El Escorial, Patrimonio Nacional, Real Monasterio de San Lorenzo de El Escorial.
Extended loan from the Museo Nacional del Prado, P2053
see cat. 10

48.
Hartmann Schedel
Weltchronik
Nuremberg (Anton Koberger), 1493
Letterpress, 45 × 33 cm
Sint Agatha, Erfgoedcentrum Nederlands Kloosterleven, Inc. 1

49.
Follower of Hieronymus Bosch
Central panel of the Garden of Earthly Delights, c. 1530–60
Oil on canvas, 182 × 168 cm
Private collection

50.
Hieronymus Bosch
Christ Carrying the Cross – Christ Child, c. 1490–1510
Oil on oak panel, 59.7 × 32 cm
Vienna, Kunsthistorisches Museum, Gemäldegalerie, GG-6429
see cat. 15

51.
Hieronymus Bosch
The Adoration of the Magi, c. 1470–80
Oil on oak panel, 71.1 × 56.7 cm
New York, The Metropolitan Museum of Art, John Stewart Kennedy
Fund, 1913, 13.26
see cat. 11

52.
Workshop of Hieronymus Bosch
The Adoration of the Magi, c. 1495–1520
Oil on oak panel, 77.5 × 55.9 cm
Philadelphia, Philadelphia Museum of Art, John G. Johnson Collection, 1917, 1321
see cat. 12

53.
Hieronymus Bosch
Ecce Homo, c. 1475–85
Oil on oak panel, 71.4 × 61 cm
Inscription, top left: *ecce homo*; centre: *Crucifige eu[m]*;
bottom left: *Salva nos Xp[ist]e r[e]de[m]ptor*
Frankfurt am Main, Städel Museum, Eigentum des Städelschen Museums-Vereins
e.V., 1577
see cat. 14

54.
Follower of Hieronymus Bosch
The Arrest, Crowning with Thorns and Flagellation of Christ
Antwerp, c. 1530–40 (central panel) and 1540–50 (wings)
Oil on oak panel, left wing 152.2 × 85.6 cm, central panel 139.7 × 170.2 cm,
right wing 152.4 × 84.5 cm
Signed: *Jheronimus – bosch*
On the foremost tormentor's sleeve: *spqr*; on the frame of the central panel: *o bone
iesv per corona[m] hanc spinea. que tvvm mvltis pvnctvris/ verticem divvlneravit. perqve
tam tvrgidam ev…[?]/ percvssionibvs facie. lacrimis et plagis lividam. ac effvso/ sangvine
spvtisqve fedatam. serva nos ineternvm.*
Valencia, Museo de Bellas Artes de Valencia, 264–266
see cat. 13

55.
Workshop of Hieronymus Bosch
After the Flood – Two Tondi, c. 1510–20
Oil on oak panel, 70 × 39.2 cm
Rotterdam, Museum Boijmans Van Beuningen, St. 28
see cat. 48a

56.
Workshop of Hieronymus Bosch
After the Last Judgement – Two Tondi, c. 1510–20
Oil on oak panel, 70.5 × 37.4 cm
Rotterdam, Museum Boijmans Van Beuningen, St. 27
see cat. 48b

IV. Bosch as Draughtsman

57.
Follower of Hieronymus Bosch
Beggars
Pen and ochre-coloured ink on paper, 285 × 208 mm
Vienna, ALBERTINA, 7798
see cat. 31

58.
Follower of Hieronymus Bosch
Beggars
Pen and ochre-coloured ink on paper, 265 × 199 mm
Brussels, Bibliothèque royale de Belgique, Cabinet des Estampes / Koninklijke
Bibliotheek van België, Prentenkabinet S.II.133.708, folio c
see cat. 30

59.
Hieronymus Bosch?
Two Oriental Men
Pen and brush in grey-brown ink, black chalk, white highlights, on paper,
138 × 108 mm
Berlin, Staatliche Museen zu Berlin, Kupferstichkabinett, KdZ 5210
see cat. 28

60.
Hieronymus Bosch
Infernal scene with anvil and monsters (recto, not on display)
Monsters (verso)
Pen and brown ink on paper, 156 × 170/176 mm
Berlin, Staatliche Museen zu Berlin, Kupferstichkabinett, KdZ 548
see cat. 37

61.
Hieronymus Bosch
Burning Ship
Brush and grey-brown ink on paper, 175 × 154 mm
Vienna, Akademie der bildenden Künste, Kupferstichkabinett, 2554
see cat. 35

62.
Hieronymus Bosch
Infernal Landscape
Pen and brown ink on paper; red ink in the helmeted monster's right eye,
259 × 197 mm
Private collection
see cat. 34

List of works exhibited

63.
Hieronymus Bosch
The Entombment of Christ
Pen and brush in grey and black ink over traces of black chalk on paper,
252 × 304 mm
London, The British Museum, Department of Prints & Drawings, 1952.0405.9
see cat. 29

64.
Hieronymus Bosch
Ten Spectators
Pen and brown ink on paper, 124 × 126 mm
New York, The Morgan Library & Museum, I, 112
see cat. 26

65.
Follower of Hieronymus Bosch
Model sheet with monsters and a donkey (recto)
Model sheet with monsters and a fish (verso)
Pen and ochre-coloured ink on paper, 321 × 211 mm
Oxford, Ashmolean Museum, bequeathed by Francis Douce, 1834, WA 1863.155
see cat. 38

66.
Hieronymus Bosch
Two monsters (recto, not on display)
Two monsters (verso)
Pen and brown ink on paper, 163 × 116 mm
Berlin, Staatliche Museen zu Berlin, Kupferstichkabinett, KdZ 547
see cat. 32

67.
Follower of Hieronymus Bosch
Monsters
Pen and brown ink on paper, 311 × 212 mm
Providence, Rhode Island School of Design Museum, 51.069
see cat. 39

68.
Hieronymus Bosch
Two monsters (recto)
A head-and-feet figure and a monster (verso, not on display)
Pen and brown ink on red prepared paper, 85 × 182 mm
Berlin, Staatliche Museen zu Berlin, Kupferstichkabinett, KdZ 550
see cat. 36

69.
Hieronymus Bosch
Two old women (recto)
Fox and cockerel (verso)
Pen and brown and brown-grey ink on paper, 120 × 85 mm
Rotterdam, Museum Boijmans Van Beuningen, N 190
see cat. 21

70.
Hieronymus Bosch
Two men (recto)
The Temptation of Eve (verso)
Pen and grey-brown ink on paper, 137 × 103 mm
Private collection (Courtesy The Metropolitan Museum of Art, New York)
see cat. 27

71.
Hieronymus Bosch
Man in a basket, old woman with tongs and children (recto)
Sketch of a man in a basket and a head-and-feet figure (verso)
Pen and brown and brown-grey ink on paper, 192 × 270 mm
Vienna, ALBERTINA, 7797
see cat. 22

72.
Hieronymus Bosch
The Wood Has Ears, The Field Has Eyes (recto)
Study of a beggar and workshop sketches (verso, not on display)
Pen and brown ink on paper, 205 × 130/127 mm
Berlin, Staatliche Museen zu Berlin, Kupferstichkabinett, KdZ 549
see cat. 17

73.
Two city seals of 's-Hertogenbosch
's-Hertogenbosch, date unknown
Green and brown wax, diameter 7.5 cm
's-Hertogenbosch, Gemeente 's-Hertogenbosch,
Afdeling Erfgoed, Stadsarchief, Collectie Originele Zegels Stad, and
Middelburg, Zeeuws Archief, Archief 195.4–49

74.
Albertus Brixiensis
Van die konste van spreken ende van swighen
's-Hertogenbosch (Gerard Leempt), 1484–88
Letterpress, 4to
The Hague, Koninklijke Bibliotheek, KW 150 C 30

75.
Pseudo-Boethius with commentary by Pseudo-Thomas Aquinas
De disciplina scholarium
Deventer (Jacobus de Breda), 1500
Letterpress, 4to
The Hague, Koninklijke Bibliotheek, KW 172 C 25

76.
Hieronymus Bosch
Model sheet with 'witches'
Pen and brown ink over black chalk on paper, 204 × 264 mm
Paris, Musée du Louvre, Département des Arts graphiques, 19721
see cat. 18

77.
Hieronymus Bosch and Workshop
The Temptation of Saint Anthony (recto, not on display)
Singers in an Egg and two sketches of monsters (verso)
Pen and brown ink on paper, 179 × 258 mm
Berlin, Staatliche Museen zu Berlin, Kupferstichkabinett, KdZ 711
see cat. 33

78.
Hieronymus Bosch
The Owl's Nest
Pen and brown ink on paper, 140 × 196 mm
Rotterdam, Museum Boijmans Van Beuningen, N 175
see cat. 16

79.
Bartholomeus Anglicus
De proprietatibus rerum
'Van den proprieteyten der dinghen'
Haarlem (Jacob Bellaert van Ziericzee), 1485
Letterpress, fo.
The Hague, Koninklijke Bibliotheek, KW 168 E 8

80.
Die historien ende fabulen van Esopus die leerlic wonderlick ende seer ghenoechlick syn
Delft (Hendrik Eckert van Homberch), 1498
Letterpress, fo.
Ghent, Universiteitsbibliotheek, RUG01:001698665

81.
Nicolaus Pergamenus
Dialogus creaturarum moralisatus
'Een genoechlick boeck gheheten dyalogus der creaturen'
Delft (Christiaen Snellaert), 1488
Letterpress, fo.
The Hague, Koninklijke Bibliotheek, KW 170 E 9

82.
Hieronymus Bosch
Gathering of the Birds
Pen and brown ink on paper, 195 × 284 mm
Berlin, Staatliche Museen zu Berlin, Kupferstichkabinett, KdZ 13136
see cat. 19

83.
Hieronymus Bosch
Battle of the Birds and Mammals
Pen and brown ink on paper, 203 × 290 mm
Berlin, Staatliche Museen zu Berlin, Kupferstichkabinett, KdZ 14715
see cat. 20

84.
Hieronymus Bosch (verso) **and Follower** (recto)
The Conjurer (verso)
Christ Carrying the Cross and beggars (recto, not on display)
Pen and brown ink on paper, 283 × 208 mm
Liège, Musée des Beaux-Arts de Liège, Album d'Arenberg, 534
see cat. 24

85.
Hieronymus Bosch (recto) **and Follower** (verso)
The Conjurer (recto)
Comical Concert and studies of helmets, three heads and a plough
(verso, not on display)
Pen and brown ink on paper, 276/279 × 203/207 mm
Paris, Musée du Louvre, Département des Arts graphiques, 19197
see cat. 23

86.
Follower of Hieronymus Bosch
The Conjurer, c. 1510–30
Oil on oak panel, 53.6 × 65.3 cm
Saint-Germain-en-Laye, Musée municipal de Saint-Germain-en-Laye, 872.1.87
see cat. 25

V. Saints

87.
Hieronymus Bosch
The Temptation of Saint Anthony (fragment), c. 1500–10
Oil on oak panel, 38.6 × 25.1 cm
Kansas City, Missouri, The Nelson-Atkins Museum of Art,
purchase William Rockhill Nelson Trust, 35–22
see cat. 45

88.
Follower of Hieronymus Bosch
The Temptation of Saint Anthony, c. 1530–40 and after 1574
Oil on oak panel, 73 × 52.5 cm
Madrid, Museo Nacional del Prado, P2049
see cat. 46

89.
Follower of Hieronymus Bosch
The Temptation of Saint Anthony, c. 1530–40
Oil on oak panel, 60.1 × 52.1 cm
's-Hertogenbosch, Art Collection Van Lanschot
see cat. 47

90.
Follower of Hieronymus Bosch
The Last Judgement (fragment), c. 1530–40
Oil on oak panel, 59.4 × 112.9 cm
Munich, Bayerische Staatsgemäldesammlungen, Alte Pinakothek, 5752
see cat. 50

91.
Hieronymus Bosch
Saint Wilgefortis Triptych, c. 1495–1505
Oil on oak panel, left wing 105.2 × 27.5 cm, central panel 105.2 × 62.7 cm,
right wing 104.7 × 27.9 cm
Venice, Gallerie dell'Accademia
see cat. 41

92.
Hieronymus Bosch
Saint Christopher, c. 1490–1500
Oil on oak panel, 113.7 × 71.6 cm
Signed bottom left: *Jheronimus bosch*
Rotterdam, Museum Boijmans Van Beuningen, St. 26
see cat. 40

93.
Albrecht Dürer (1471 Nuremberg–1528 Nuremberg)
Saint Jerome in the Desert
Nuremberg, 1494–98
Engraving, 31.6 × 22.5 cm
Amsterdam, Rijksmuseum, RP-P-OB-1225

94.
Sebastian Brant after Jacobus de Voragine
Passionael efte dat levent der hylligen to düde
Basel (Adam Petri) 1511
Letterpress, fo.
Cologne, Universitäts- und Stadtbibliothek, GBIV2314

List of works exhibited

95.
Panelled binding with image of Saint Jerome, patron saint of the Brethren of the Common Life of 's-Hertogenbosch
's-Hertogenbosch, Friars House, 1516
Leather over wooden boards, 12 × 9 cm
Nijmegen, Universiteitsbibliotheek, MS 10 (I A 1)

96.
Hieronymus Bosch
Saint Jerome at Prayer, c. 1485–95
Oil on oak panel, 80 × 60.7 cm
Ghent, Museum voor Schone Kunsten, 1908–H
see cat. 42

97.
Hieronymus Bosch
Hermit Saints Triptych, c. 1495–1505
The hermit saints Anthony, Jerome and Giles
Oil on oak panel, left wing 85.4 × 29.2 cm, central panel 85.7 × 60 cm,
right wing 85.7 × 28.9 cm
Signed central panel: *Jheronimüs bosch*
Venice, Gallerie dell'Accademia
see cat. 43

98.
Workshop of Hieronymus Bosch
Job Triptych, c. 1510–20
Oil on oak panel, left wing 98.1 × 30.5 cm, central panel 98.3 × 72.1 cm,
right wing 97.8 × 30.2 cm
Bruges, Stad Brugge, Groeningemuseum, 0000.GRO.0209
(extended loan from Sint-Jacob-de-Meerderekerk in Hoeke, Damme)
see cat. 44

VI. The End of Days

99.
Hieronymus Bosch
The Last Judgement, c. 1495–1505
Oil on oak panel, left wing 99.5 × 28.8 cm, central panel 99.2 × 60.5 cm,
right wing 99.5 × 28.6 cm
Signed central panel, bottom right: *Jheronimus bosch*
Bruges, Stad Brugge, Groeningemuseum, 0000.GRO.0208.I
see cat. 49

100.
Hieronymus Bosch
Visions of the Hereafter, c. 1505–15
The Way to Heaven: The Garden of Eden, c. 1505–15
Oil on oak panel, 88.5 × 39.8 cm
Venice, Museo di Palazzo Grimani, 184
see cat. 51a

101.
Hieronymus Bosch
Visions of the Hereafter, c. 1505–15
The Way to Heaven: The Ascent of the Blessed, c. 1505–15
Oil on oak panel, 88.8 × 39.9 cm
Venice, Museo di Palazzo Grimani, 184
see cat. 51b

102.
Hieronymus Bosch
Visions of the Hereafter, c. 1505–15
The Way to Hell: The Fall of the Damned, c. 1505–15
Oil on oak panel, 88.8 × 39.6 cm
Venice, Museo di Palazzo Grimani, 184
see cat. 51c

103.
Hieronymus Bosch
Visions of the Hereafter, c. 1505–15
The Way to Hell: The River to Hell, c. 1505–15
Oil on oak panel, 88.8 × 39.6 cm
Venice, Museo di Palazzo Grimani, 184
see cat. 51d

Text credits and literature

As the texts in this book and the exhibition of the same name at the Noordbrabants Museum, 's-Hertogenbosch, are primarily based on the results of the Bosch Research and Conservation Project (BRCP), 2010–16, the reader is referred in the first place to the brcp publications and websites :

Matthijs Ilsink, Jos Koldeweij, Ron Spronk, Luuk Hoogstede, Robert G. Erdmann, Rik Klein Gotink, Hanneke Nap, Daan Veldhuizen, *Jheronimus Bosch, Painter and Draughtsman. Catalogue Raisonné*, Brussels: Mercatorfonds, 2016.

Luuk Hoogstede, Ron Spronk, Jos Koldeweij, Matthijs Ilsink, Robert G. Erdmann, Rik Klein Gotink, Hanneke Nap, Daan Veldhuizen, *Hieronymus Bosch, Painter and Draughtsman. Technical Studies*, Brussels: Fonds Mercator, 2016.

Bosch on Line (web application with documentation of all paintings), *BoschDoc* (all historical documents on Bosch and his work until 1800), Boschproject.org

Major studies on Hieronymus Bosch since 2000, all with earlier bibliography:

Stefan Fischer, *Hieronymus Bosch. Complete Works*, Cologne: Taschen, 2014.

Fritz Koreny, Gabriele Bartz, Erwin Pokorny, *Hieronymus Bosch: die Zeichnungen: Werkstatt und Nachfolge bis zum Ende des 16. Jahrhunderts: catalogue raisonné*, Turnhout: Brepols, 2012.

Marc Rudolf de Vrij, *Jheronimus Bosch. An Exercise in Common Sense*, Amsterdam: MRV, 2012.

Reindert Falkenburg, *The Land of Unlikeness. Hieronymus Bosch, The Garden of Earthly Delights*, [Zwolle]: WBOOKS, 2011.

Matthijs Ilsink, *Bosch en Bruegel als Bosch: kunst over kunst bij Pieter Bruegel (c. 1528–1569) en Jheronimus Bosch (c. 1450–1516)* (Nijmeegse Kunsthistorische Studies 17), Edam: Orange House, 2009.

Jeanne van Waadenoijen, *De 'geheimtaal' van Jheronimus Bosch: een interpretatie van zijn werk*, Hilversum: Verloren, 2007.

Roger H. Marijnissen, with Peter Ruyffelaere, *Hieronymus Bosch. The Complete Works* (1987), Brussels: Fonds Mercator, revised edition, 2007.

Larry Silver, *Hieronymus Bosch*, New York [etc.]: Abbeville Press, 2006.

Frédéric Elsig, *Jheronimus Bosch: la question de la chronologie*, Geneva: Droz, 2004.

Paul Vandenbroeck, *Jheronimus Bosch: de verlossing van de wereld*, Ghent and Amsterdam: Ludion, 2002.

Jos Koldeweij, Paul Vandenbroeck and Bernard Vermet, *Hieronymus Bosch. The Complete Paintings and Drawings*, Rotterdam: NAi Publishers/Ghent: Ludion, 2001.

Jos Koldeweij, Bernard Vermet and Barbera van Kooij, *Hieronymus Bosch: New Insights into his Life and Work*, Rotterdam: NAi Publishers / Ghent: Ludion, 2001.

Jan van Oudheusden, Aart Vos, R.A.H.M. Glaudemans et al., *The World of Bosch*, 's-Hertogenbosch: Heinen / ABC, Stichting Archeologie, Bouwhistorie en Cultuur / Stadsarchief, 2001.

Esther Vink, *Jeroen Bosch in Den Bosch: de schilder tegen de achtergrond van zijn stad* (Nijmeegse Kunsthistorische Cahiers 7), Nijmegen: Nijmegen University Press, 2001.

Eric De Bruyn, *De vergeten beeldentaal van Jheronimus Bosch: de symboliek van de Hooiwagen-triptiek en de Rotterdamse Marskramer-tondo verklaard vanuit Middelnederlandse teksten*, 's-Hertogenbosch: Adr. Heinen / ABC, Stichting Archeologie, Bouwhistorie en Cultuur, 2001.

G.C.M. van Dijck, *Op zoek naar Jheronimus van Aken alias Bosch: de feiten: familie, vrienden en opdrachtgevers ca. 1400–ca. 1635*, Zaltbommel: Europese Bibliotheek, 2001.

Carmen Garrido and Roger Van Schoute, *Bosch at the Museo del Prado [technical study]*, Madrid: Museo del Prado: Aldeasa, 2001.

Pilar Silva Maroto (ed.), *El jardín de las delicias de El Bosco: copias, estudio técnico y restauración*, Madrid: Museo del Prado, 2000.

The Bosch Research and Conservation Project (BRCP) was realized by:
Rob G. Erdmann (digital infrastructure), Luuk Hoogstede (paintings conservator, art historian), Matthijs Ilsink (project coordinator, art historian), Rik Klein Gotink (photography), Jos Koldeweij (chairman, art historian), Hanneke Nap (research assistant, art historian), Travis Sawyer (digital infrastructure assistant), Ron Spronk (technical art historian) and Daan Veldhuizen (research assistant, art historian).

Photograph credits

Lenders to the exhibition

Austria
Vienna, Akademie der bildenden Künste, Kupferstichkabinett
Vienna, ALBERTINA
Vienna, Kunsthistorisches Museum, Gemäldegalerie

Belgium
Bruges, Stad Brugge, Groeningemuseum
Brussels, Bibliothèque royale de Belgique / Koninklijke Bibliotheek van België
Brussels, Bibliothèque royale de Belgique, Cabinet des Estampes / Koninklijke Bibliotheek van België, Prentenkabinet
Ghent, Museum voor Schone Kunsten
Ghent, Universiteitsbibliotheek
Liège, Musée des Beaux-Arts de Liège
Mechelen, Aartsbisdom Mechelen-Brussel

France
Paris, Bibliothèque nationale de France, Bibliothèque François Mitterrand
Paris, Musée du Louvre, Département des Arts graphiques
Paris, Musée du Louvre, Département des Peintures
Saint-Germain-en-Laye, Musée municipal de Saint-Germain-en-Laye

Germany
Berlin, Staatliche Museen zu Berlin, Gemäldegalerie
Berlin, Staatliche Museen zu Berlin, Kupferstichkabinett
Cologne, Universitäts- und Stadtbibliothek
Frankfurt, Städel Museum
Munich, Bayerische Staatsgemäldesammlungen, Alte Pinakothek
Munich, Staatliche Graphische Sammlung

Italy
Venice, Gallerie dell'Accademia
Venice, Museo di Palazzo Grimani

The Netherlands
Amsterdam, Rijksmuseum
Amsterdam, Universiteitsbibliotheek Vrije Universiteit
The Hague, Koninklijke Bibliotheek
's-Hertogenbosch, Brabants Historisch Informatie Centrum
's-Hertogenbosch, Gemeente 's-Hertogenbosch, Afdeling Erfgoed
's-Hertogenbosch, Het Noordbrabants Museum
's-Hertogenbosch, Kunstcollectie Van Lanschot
's-Hertogenbosch, Museum Het Zwanenbroedershuis
's-Hertogenbosch, Parochie Heilige Johannes Evangelist
Langbroek, Collectie familie Van Beuningen
Loon op Zand, Parochie Heilige Willibrord
Middelburg, Zeeuws Archief
Nijmegen, Universiteitsbibliotheek
Rotterdam, Museum Boijmans Van Beuningen
Sint Agatha, Erfgoedcentrum Nederlands Kloosterleven
Tilburg, Universiteit van Tilburg, Brabantcollectie
Uden, Museum voor Religieuze Kunst
Utrecht, Museum Catharijneconvent
Utrecht, Universiteitsbibliotheek Uithof

Spain
El Escorial, Patrimonio Nacional, Real Monasterio de San Lorenzo de El Escorial
Madrid, Museo Fundación Lázaro Galdiano
Madrid, Museo Nacional del Prado
Valencia, Museo de Bellas Artes de Valencia

United Kingdom
London, British Museum, Department of Prints & Drawings
London, The British Library
Oxford, Ashmolean Museum

United States
Boston, Museum of Fine Arts
Kansas City, Missouri, The Nelson-Atkins Museum of Art
New Haven, Yale University Art Gallery
New York, The Metropolitan Museum of Art
New York, The Morgan Library & Museum
Philadelphia, Philadelphia Museum of Art
Providence, Rhode Island School of Design Museum
Washington, National Gallery of Art

and those lenders who wish to remain anonymous

Colophon

Hieronymus Bosch – Visions of Genius is published on the occasion of the exhibition of the same name in Het Noordbrabants Museum, 's-Hertogenbosch, 13 February to 8 May 2016.

Publishers
Mercatorfonds, Brussels (director Bernard Steyaert)
Het Noordbrabants Museum, 's-Hertogenbosch

Authors
Matthijs Ilsink
Jos Koldeweij
Charles de Mooij (Foreword and List of exhibited works)

Coordination
Ann Mestdag, Mercatorfonds, Brussels; Marianne Thys

Translation
Ted Alkins, Helen Simpson (Foreword)

Edited by
Paul Van Calster, Anagram, Ghent

Graphic design
Studio frederik de wal, Schelluinen

Picture research
Alice d'Ursel, Mercatorfonds, Brussels

Technical assistance
Tijdsbeeld & Pièce Montée, Ghent
Ronny Gobyn and Rik Jacques (directors)

Reprographic advice
Sebastiaan Hanekroot, Colour & books

Separations, printing and binding by
Die Keure, Bruges

Typeset in Arnhem, printed on Magno satin 150 g

Copyright © 2016 Het Noordbrabants Museum, 's-Hertogenbosch; Mercatorfonds, Brussels; the authors

All rights reserved. No part of this publication may be reproduced, stored in a retrieval system or transmitted in any form or by any means, electronic, mechanical, photocopying, recording or otherwise, without prior permission of the publisher.

Distributed in Belgium, the Netherlands and Luxembourg
by Mercatorfonds, Brussels
ISBN 978-94-6230-118-4
D/2016/703/8

Distributed outside Belgium, the Netherlands and Luxembourg
by Yale University Press, New Haven and London
www.yalebooks.com/art – www.yalebooks.co.uk
ISBN 978-0-300-22013-1
Library of Congress Control Number: 2016930233

www.mercatorfonds.be
www.hetnoordbrabantsmuseum.nl
www.bosch500.com

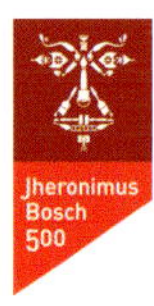

The exhibition 'Hieronymus Bosch – Visions of Genius' is part of the Jheronimus Bosch 500 event and is made possible by

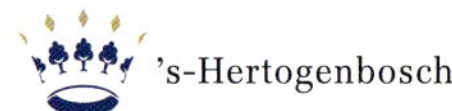
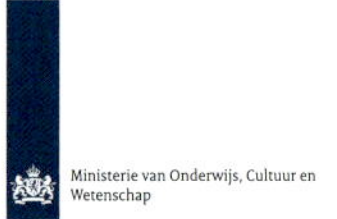
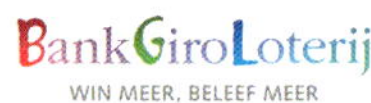
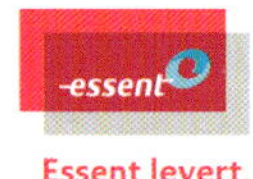
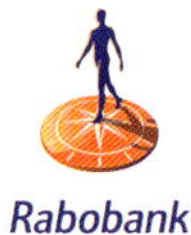
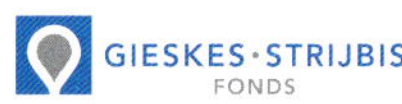
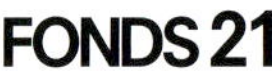
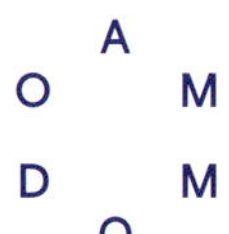
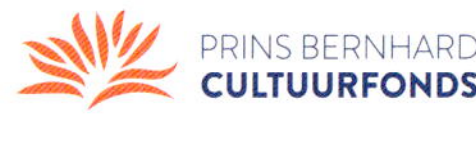
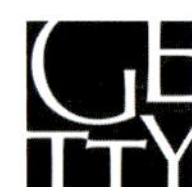
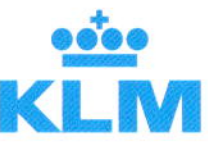

The exhibition is facilitated by the Dutch government. It is indemnified by the Cultural Heritage Agency of the Netherlands on behalf of the Minister of Education, Culture and Science and the Minister of Finance.